Connected Learning

American Society of Missiology Monograph Series

Series Editor, James R. Krabill

The ASM Monograph Series provides a forum for publishing quality dissertations and studies in the field of missiology. Collaborating with Pickwick Publications—a division of Wipf and Stock Publishers of Eugene, Oregon—the American Society of Missiology selects high quality dissertations and other monographic studies that offer research materials in mission studies for scholars, mission and church leaders, and the academic community at large. The ASM seeks scholarly work for publication in the series that throws light on issues confronting Christian world mission in its cultural, social, historical, biblical, and theological dimensions.

Missiology is an academic field that brings together scholars whose professional training ranges from doctoral-level preparation in areas such as Scripture, history and sociology of religions, anthropology, theology, international relations, interreligious interchange, mission history, inculturation, and church law. The American Society of Missiology, which sponsors this series, is an ecumenical body drawing members from Independent and Ecumenical Protestant, Catholic, Orthodox, and other traditions. Members of the ASM are united by their commitment to reflect on and do scholarly work relating to both mission history and the present-day mission of the church. The ASM Monograph Series aims to publish works of exceptional merit on specialized topics, with particular attention given to work by younger scholars, the dissemination and publication of which is difficult under the economic pressures of standard publishing models.

Persons seeking information about the ASM or the guidelines for having their dissertations considered for publication in the ASM Monograph Series should consult the Society's website—www.asmweb.org.

Members of the ASM Monograph Committe who approved this book are:

Michael A. Rynkiewich, Professor of Anthropology (retired), Asbury Theological Seminary

William P. Gregory, Associate Professor of Religious Studies, Clarke University

RECENTLY PUBLISHED IN THE ASM MONOGRAPH SERIES

Craig Hendrickson, *Charismatic Leadership and Missional Change: Mission-Actional Ministry in a Multiethnic Church*

Matthew Aaron Bennett, *Narratives in Conflict: Atonement in Hebrews and the Qur'an*

Connected Learning
How Adults with Limited Formal Education Learn

L. Lynn Thigpen

FOREWORD BY
Tom Steffen

American Society of Missiology
Monograph Series vol. 44

☙PICKWICK *Publications* · Eugene, Oregon

CONNECTED LEARNING
How Adults with Limited Formal Education Learn

American Society of Missiology Monograph Series 44

Copyright © 2020 L. Lynn Thigpen. All rights reserved. Except for brief quotations in critical publications or reviews, no part of this book may be reproduced in any manner without prior written permission from the publisher. Write: Permissions, Wipf and Stock Publishers, 199 W. 8th Ave., Suite 3, Eugene, OR 97401.

Pickwick Publications
An Imprint of Wipf and Stock Publishers
199 W. 8th Ave., Suite 3
Eugene, OR 97401

www.wipfandstock.com

PAPERBACK ISBN: 978-1-5326-7937-7
HARDCOVER ISBN: 978-1-5326-7938-4
EBOOK ISBN: 978-1-5326-7939-1

Cataloguing-in-Publication data:

Names: Thigpen, L. Lynn, author. | Steffen, Tom, foreword.

Title: Connected learning : how adults with limited formal education learn / by L. Lynn Thigpen; foreword by Tom Steffen.

Description: Eugene, OR: Pickwick Publications, 2020. | American Society of Missiology Monograph Series 44 | Includes bibliographical references and index.

Identifiers: ISBN 978-1-5326-7937-7 (paperback) | ISBN 978-1-5326-7938-4 (hardcover) | ISBN 978-1-5326-7939-1 (ebook)

Subjects: LCSH: Adult learning. | Non-formal education. | Adult education. | Education—Cambodia.

Classification: LC45.3 T55 2020 (print) | LC45.3 (ebook)

Scripture quotations marked NASB are taken from the *New American Standard Bible* © 1960, 1962, 1971, 1972, 1973, 1975, 1977, 1995 by The Lockman Foundation. Used by permission.

Scripture quotations marked TM are taken from *The Message* © 1993, 1994, 1995, 1996, 2000, 2001, 2002. Used by permission of NavPress Publishing Group.

Manufactured in the U.S.A.   04/16/20

To Woody and Bethany Thigpen,
Louise and Jane Morrison,
and all my ALFE friends.

"To fail to engage the alterity of orality with sensitive attunement is an act of continued imperialism, which is morally unacceptable, epistemologically naive, and ecologically suicidal in cognitive and natural terms."

—JILL A. WATSON, *INTERPRETING ACROSS THE ABYSS*

"When a European has been living for two or three years among savages,[1] he is sure to be fully convinced that he knows all about them; when he has been ten years or so amongst them, if he be an observant man, he finds that he knows very little about them, and so begins to learn."

—LORIMER FISON IN *THE MELANESIANS* BY ROBERT H. CODRINGTON, 1891

"Knowledge exists in two forms—lifeless, stored in books, and alive in the consciousness of men. The second form of existence is after all the essential one; the first, indispensable as it may be, occupies only an inferior position."

—ALBERT EINSTEIN

---

1. Unfortunate terminology which I definitely do not endorse.

"Being a consummate literate-preference learner, I used to struggle to grasp the importance of understanding orality and oral teaching methods. People like Dr. L. Lynn Thigpen are a huge help to people like me. She opens our eyes to the world of oral learners and shows us how to facilitate their acquisition of new knowledge, values, and skills. Dr. Thigpen's book is a significant contribution to a growing body of literature on orality and oral learners."

—**Richard L. Starcher**, Professor of Intercultural Education and Missiology, Biola University; Editor-in-Chief of *Missiology: An International Review*

"Jesus has commanded us to make disciples of all nations—not just those who prefer a Western style of formal education. And if we are going to teach everyone, we are going to need to take the time to explore how they best learn. Lynn has made an excellent contribution to that conversation."

—**Brad Roderick**, Chairman of Missions, Mid-America Baptist Theological Seminary

"Lynn, and her husband Woody, have exemplified commitment to the gospel and a passion to communicate it effectively for over twenty years. Lynn's research reflects that passionate commitment and fills an important gap of understanding about communicating to the large portion of our world who do not primarily learn through reading. I recommend this book to anyone who shares truth with the majority of the world, who learn best through informal, traditional, 'connected' learning methods."

—**Don Dent**, Director, Kim School of Global Missions, Gateway Seminary

"As one who lived in Cambodia for sixteen years, I am thankful for Lynn Thigpen's gleanings via entering the world of Cambodian adult learners. I am convinced that her research plays an important role in helping foreigners put the cross-cultural work back on their own shoulders, rather than unknowingly crushing the dignity of the local people by converting them to one's own seemingly sacred learning models."

—**Jean Johnson**, Director, Five Stones Global; author of *We Are Not the Hero*

"Dr. Lynn Thigpen has written a deeply-researched and moving account of her journey to understand how adults with limited formal education learn—and the heart-breaking reasons why they often flounder. Her findings challenge conventional education and they point to promising alternatives. Along the way she gives a deserved critique to simplistic and mistaken descriptions of orality. I learned a lot from this book, it moved me, and I intend to make changes because of it."

—**Grant Lovejoy**, Director of Orality Strategies, International Mission Board of the Southern Baptist Convention

"As an educator of the next generation of missionaries and ministers, I am profoundly grateful for Lynn's research. Her decades of experience in one of the most difficult demographics adds a credibility to this project. Lynn's research findings are indispensable for her immediate context and will provide a new paradigm that could have much broader global implications."

—**Brett Golson**, Chair of the Department of Intercultural Studies and Christian Ministries, Associate Professor of Religion, William Carey University

"Those who want to transform the lives of oral learners should follow this study: understand the shame, isolation, and hopelessness oral learners face and then build relationships with them of trust, respect, and empathy. The result? An incarnational wisdom that non-readers have as much to teach as those who can read."

—**Daniel B. Lancaster**, The Follow Jesus Project

"In this ground-breaking study, Thigpen explores the learning strategies of ALFE (Adults with Limited Formal Education) in Cambodia. Combining thoughtful scholarship with richly descriptive narrative, Thigpen's research challenges traditional educational dichotomies through her compelling account of 'connected learning' along with its implications for more inclusive learner-centered educational models. An important contribution to the theory and practice of adult education, especially within today's pluralistic contexts. Highly recommended!"

—**Rhonda M. McEwen**, Associate Professor of Education and Culture, Regent College; Director of Regent Exchange: Churches for the Common Good

Contents

List of Tables and Figures | x
Foreword by Tom Steffen | xiii
Preface | xvii

1. Research Purpose and Questions: The Setting | 1
   Problem Statement | 8
   Purpose Statement | 9
   Research Questions | 9
   Definitions | 9
   Scope | 11
   Limitations | 11
   Significance Statement | 12

2. Introductory Literature Review: The Context and Construct | 15
   The Context: Cambodia | 17
   The Complex Construct: Orality and ALFE Learning | 29
   Chapter Summary | 58

3. Research Method and Design: The Quest | 59
   Overall Research Approach | 59
   Ethical Considerations | 71
   Validation Strategies | 74
   Chapter Summary | 76

4. Data Analysis: Mining for Knowledge | 78
   Chapter Overview and Background | 78
   Research Setting and Background of Participants | 80
   Research Question Findings and Descriptive Vignettes | 83
   Chapter Summary | 97

5. Interpretation and Synthesis: The Central Understanding | 99
   Central Understanding and Inclusive Themes | 100
   Connected Learning: Learning that Resembles Socialization | 101
   Chapter Summary | 127

6. Interpretation and Synthesis: The Inclusive Themes | 130
   Connected Learning Incorporated the Self | 130
   Connected Learning Incorporated Faith or Spirituality | 140
   Connected Learning Incorporated Context | 141
   Connected Learning Involved Special Packaging | 144
   Chapter Summary | 146

7. Conclusions: The Practical Wisdom | 149
   Empathetic *Verstehen* (Understanding): An Unexpected By-Product | 150
   Phronesis (Practical Wisdom): A Sought-After Prime Product | 152
   Wisdom Applied: Phronetic Conclusions | 153
   Chapter Reflections | 173

8. Recommendations: The Practical Wisdom Concluded | 175
   Wisdom Applied: Recommendations | 175
   Final Reflections | 195

Appendix A: Khmer Terms Used | 199
Appendix B: Conversing with Orality: My Experience as a Non-Reader | 202
   Meeting Orality | 203
   Why Autoethnography? | 204
   Who Is Conversing with Orality? | 204
   Reflections: My Side of the Conversation | 205
   Conclusions | 210

Appendix C: Participant Demographics | 211
Appendix D: Demographics of Additional Informants | 213
Appendix E: Interview Guide | 214
Appendix F: Intermediate Level Codes Visualized | 215
Appendix G: Verbal Informed Consent Form | 216
Appendix H: Alternate Connected Learning Schematic | 218

Bibliography | 219
Author Index | 263
Subject Index | 265
Scripture Index | 269

Tables and Figures

Table 1: General fields of orality divided into specializations, with sample contributors for each | 32

Table A1: Khmer Terms Used | 199

Table D1: Participant Demographics | 211

Table E1: Demographics of Additional Informants | 213

Figure 1: Dissertation focus at the intersection of contexts, construct, and varied content | 16

Figure 2: Conceptual framework for exploring literature on orality and ALFE learning | 34

Figure 3: Influences on the work of Ong (1982) | 36

Figure 4: Conceptual framework for researching oral/ALFE ways of learning | 55

Figure 5: Schematic of grounded theory method to be followed in addressing the research problem and research questions in this study | 68

Figure 6: Integration of conceptual model for data analysis with modes of grounded theory (Artinian, 2009) and levels of abstraction in coding (Birks and Mills, 2011) | 70

Figure 7: Conceptual model integrating grounded theory with Rowley's (2007) modified DIKW hierarchy | 74

Figure 8: Groups of ALFE in Cambodia | 81

Figure 9: Connected Learning Schematic | 101

Figure 10: Components of connected learning | 103
Figure 11: Learning Quadrants | 111
Figure F1: Intermediate level codes visualized | 216
Figure H1: Alternate Connected Learning Schematic | 219

Foreword

I FIRST MET THE author at a Biola extension doctoral course held at McGilvary College of Divinity (Payap University) in Chiang Mai, Thailand. As students introduced themselves, the next to speak was a stately veteran IMB missionary who, along with her husband, Woody, had invested decades of service in Cambodia. Her story fascinated me. As the class listened, parallel images ran through my mind of my own years of ministry among the Antipolo-Amduntug Ifugao of the Philippines—animists moving swiftly from a predominant oral society to a more literate one, with implications for those left behind and those who moved ahead in literacy. It was evident she knew her audience not just linguistically but culturally as well. It was also evident she had a strong background in teaching and education and knew how these could and should impact adult learners. I immediately connected with her story.

As is custom in my graduate classes—and I believe constitutes a great share of its success or failure—students are not just encouraged but are also expected to add their life experiences to the discussion. I give extra credit *on the spot* (public honor) for the best questions asked and/or comments made.

Speaking from years of not just service, but *scrutinized service*, scholar Thigpen did not disappoint; she made significant contributions to her classmates in every class I was privileged to have her. And a number of her contributions have found their way into my PowerPoints and publications.

Connected Learning does not just focus on western education—it looks at it through *cross-cultural eyes*. *Connected Learning* does not just repeat what is known about adult learners with limited formal education—it *adds* to the discussion and literature. *Connected Learning* does not just address the needs of Cambodian adult learners with limited formal education—its findings have *global implications and applications* for a growing population around the globe.

To discover how adults with limited formal education acquire new information, values, and so forth, the researcher conducted a three-stage study: (1) *no reading* for five days (try that sometime), (2) a concurrent observation stage, and (3) interviews with 30 groups of Cambodian adults with six or less years of formal schooling. Using grounded theory, the research revealed these adults prefer to learn through *people rather than print*. But not just through *any* person; they preferred to learn through people they *trusted*. But there is more—something often missed in the secular west—they also learned best when listening to *trusted sacred messages*. Learning for these adults transpired best through trusted relationships and religion; they preferred *wisdom and age* over *academic expertise*—not a little disconcerting to a formally educated teacher there to make an impact on the community!

The literate outsider is often quick to wonder—but do not they understand: "I have a number of degrees from prestigious institutions and taught in various schools of higher learning. Don't they realize I have not just read numerous textbooks but outlined, analyzed, and taught them? Don't they realize I have published in peer reviewed journals? "

Behind these questions lie a number of assumptions. A major assumption related to this benchmark study is learning originates formally from print. That hurts when the audience is not impressed with the outsider's lifework. But many of the communities coming from shame-based cultures know how to answer politely and soothe the expatriate's wounded spirit. To save face, including their own, the audience seemingly agrees with the educated one, but in their heart of hearts they are asking, *"Can we trust this person as a friend?"*

This question is what the first Dean of the Cook School of Intercultural Studies at Biola, Marvin Mayers, repeatedly referred to in his classes as the *"prior question of trust"* (PQT). For the Cambodian audience, safe and secure connections on human and spiritual levels laid the groundwork for lifelong learning.

Here is one of many diamonds the reader will discover in this classic contribution to missiology. The researcher notes that Walter Ong focused strongly on *communication* but gave little attention to the *communicator* who actually drove the process. This naturally set up the "Great Divide" between orality and literacy, which meant for Ong that literates were on one side of the spectrum and those not proficient in reading were on the other.

If Ong had given more attention to the communicator, argues the author, he may have discovered that these adults did not see the "Great Divide" between the spoken and the written as the issue at all. Rather, their issue was not between orality and literacy but between people and print. These adults appreciated apprenticeships more than lectures; they wanted observation and interaction; they wanted trusted relationships.

A central issue faced by adult learners with limited formal education is shame. For we literates coming from a strongly guilt-innocence driven society where right and wrong, black and white, truth and justice prevail, this may not seem to be a big deal. Not so for those coming from a shamed-based culture where shame and honor drive everything they do.

Shame does not just address the self; it extends to the family, the community, the nation. Its impact and devastation have widespread implications for adults. All this is because *shame is relational;* it separates from the family; it disconnects and isolates from the community and nation. And all this in a community where groupness and collectivism are considered norm. There is nothing worse to fear or experience for insiders in shame-based cultures than social separation and social isolation.

Lest those from the West believe this to be something that happens *over there*, certainly not here on the home front, think again. Former editor of *Christianity Today*, Andy Crouch, concludes the Americas are changing fast to a "fame-shame" culture.[1] Did you notice that subtle shift from honor-shame to fame-shame? Crouch connects this change to social media—"What if they don't like my post? How many likes did I get? Who defriended me? Did it go viral? Time to check again."

Honor, of course, does the exact opposite of shame; it unites the family, the community, and even the nation. Social acceptance and social acknowledgement reign. This brings contentment and security—"I'm part of the community!"

The essence of the above led companion-scholar Thigpen to conclude that keeping voice (primary orality) with digital technology (secondary orality) was a way to expand their learning while ensuring their honor. Person-connected learning raises the honor of adult learners with limited formal education.

The author also recognizes much more can be accomplished when all this is done through the faith community. That is because the community of faith offers connection through relationships horizontally and vertically—both of which offer healing. Trusted relationships through trusted religion

---

1. Crouch, "Return of Shame," 32–41.

will assist in expanding learning while bringing honor to the community of learners not just abroad, but at home as well.

One goal on my bucket list, I wrote companion-scholar Thigpen in a recent email, is to send her a quote on orality she has not already seen. After reading this masterpiece on adult learners with limited formal education, which I was privileged to chair, you will understand why this may be more difficult than it might sound. There are always some students that far surpass their teachers. You are about to meet one of them!

Tom Steffen

Professor Emeritus,
Cook School of Intercultural Studies,
Biola University

Preface

"You don't know what you don't know," the old adage goes. So, what do we not know about oral learners, about how adults with limited formal education (ALFE) learn? Prior to the research presented here, I missed the obvious, as have others. First, I never realized highly literate people who can analyze text and learn from it are a definite minority across the globe. The majority? People who do not prefer to learn by reading—people like some of our refugee friends, our immigrant neighbors, like most of the people in the villages of the world and quite a few urban dwellers. Explore chapter 1 for the startling statistics.

I have worked in both worlds—in the US and Singapore, Central America and India, and then in Cambodia and Southeast Asia. Very little in my background prepared me for the stark contrast between the world of the literate minority and the majority of the world who learn by a different means—through connected or relational learning. I muddled along for a number of years in a non-reading environment by focusing on narrative and drama, but I desperately wanted to learn more. Surely someone else had traveled the same path, worked with oral learners, and possessed knowledge I lacked. Finally, I discovered those wise travelers at Biola University, in professors who had spent countless years overseas, who taught us how to explore, research, and value differences. Drs. Steffen, Starcher, and McEwen mentored me through the product you now hold; and I am grateful to these three professors and more for the roles they played during the dissertation process.

As much as I learned from my interaction with professors and print, I learned even more from oral learners themselves, from the participants in this study. Even though I had taught some and walked with them along their learning journeys, I had never asked the deeper questions about their learning experiences and preferences. The resource you hold represents their world—their thoughts and words, their joys and sorrows. Each interview was a precious window into a different way of thinking from my own. I am grateful for the hospitality I was extended, the seat at the table with my friends, the confidences shared, and for the chance to cry together over lost opportunities and intense struggles. Tears stain the original manuscripts and what I did not know shocked me.

Following the format of a standard qualitative dissertation, this text first introduces the lacuna in orality scholarship, then analyzes the relevant literature, presents a suitable research method and process, then provides findings, implications, and conclusions. Do not let this format discourage you. If you are as inquisitive as I was but not interested in qualitative research, please feel free to skip chapter 3. If you only want the conclusions, read chapter 1, then skip right to chapters 4 and following. However, orality proponents will want to take note of the relevant literature, some from areas outside the obvious. Educators will not want to miss the discussion surrounding the Learning Quadrants. I hope you will all learn as much as I did and make wise application of connected learning to your training efforts with the ALFE you serve. A grave inequity in the learning realm may finally begin to be corrected.

During my years of immersion in Cambodian culture and our work there, family, friends, and colleagues played a large role in allowing me to complete this endeavor. I am especially grateful to Woody and Bethany Thigpen, to colleagues Iv SiYee and Julie Martinez, to my church family, and to some very special leaders in the IMB. You all enriched and paved the way for this book to come into fruition. Finally, as a person of faith, I traveled through this sacred excursion on my knees in prayer. I sought not only knowledge, but also understanding and wisdom to apply to serving connected learners better. God provided so much that I lacked. *Soli deo Gloria*.

Lynn Thigpen

July 31, 2019
Phnom Penh, Cambodia

1

Research Purpose and Questions: The Setting

"Enter a stream at the turn; enter a boat at the port; enter a country according to its customs."

—CAMBODIAN PROVERB

WHILE I ATTENDED UNDERGRADUATE school and spent late nights studying for exams, a young Cambodian woman experienced a different kind of test. Born in the same year as I, she had only six years of schooling, was already married, and had two sons. Pol Pot and his cadre ruled her country at that time, and in the ensuing years my friend watched her parents, husband, and two sons succumb to painful deaths. Roughly two million Cambodians lost their lives during those years of atrocity.[1] No formal schooling, no bedtime stories, no sense of normality existed—only grasping for survival. The effects linger to this day.

War interrupts formal education, as do poverty, learning disabilities, illness and physical difficulties, misconceptions, and many trials in life. I remember the first time I met an older Cambodian lady who had never attended school. She confided that parents in her era withheld schooling because they feared their daughters would compose love letters if they were literate. Other Khmer (Cambodian) friends could not attend school because they had to supplement the family income or their families lacked funds for books, uniforms, and obligatory payments to teachers. Many others attended only a few precious years and thus found reading painful. These stories

1. Mueller, "Expert Has New Numbers."

represent the norm in much of Cambodia. In fact, Rosenbloom reported nine of fourteen million Khmer or more than 63 percent lacked adequate training in literacy at the time of her research.[2]

What happens when a highly educated and highly literate teacher encounters adults who never learned to read or who read at a basic level? Like many teachers across the globe, I was not prepared to train such adult learners when I arrived in Cambodia on the last day of 1999. Oblivious to differences in mindset and learning needs, I proceeded to teach in the manner I had been taught only to discover even the simplest studies were an educational disaster. I was not trained in appropriate pedagogies and could not relate to these adult learners nor fully understand their learning needs and strategies. I resonated with Smith's eloquent explanation of my dilemma:

> The gap between the two [orality and literacy] can sometimes be a yawning chasm into which no one is more likely to tumble than the scholar who ventures into the realm of orality without first shedding the bundle of literate preconceptions he habitually carries about with him.[3]

As a teacher in a cross-cultural setting, I lamented the effects of this socially constructed chasm. I understood the benefits of literacy but felt keenly the woes of those who had no schooling opportunities or those who had tried literacy and failed. The haunting questions in my mind were, "Why make them change? Why force literacy on them? How do they learn in their present situation, without reliance on print resources?" Much literature portrays illiteracy as a wretched situation, a problem needing eradication. Relating to healthcare and issues dealing with children, Parker chastised this adult population: "People who are illiterate are threats to themselves, their families and others."[4] Is this view correct? Before this modern age heavily skewed toward print learning, would society have agreed that illiteracy was a menace?[5]

Even though this study focuses on adult learners in the kingdom of Cambodia, lack of literacy and limited access to formal education is not confined to Least Developed Countries (LDCs). According to Kutner et al., ninety-three million Americans or 43 percent of the US population at that time could not follow directions using a map.[6] In the most recent reports,

---

2. Rosenbloom, "Adult Literacy in Cambodia."
3. Smith, "Worlds Apart," 6.
4. Parker, "Adult Perspectives," 2.
5. Roman, "Illiteracy and Older Adults."
6. Kutner et al., *Literacy in Everyday Life*.

half the population still could not identify the author of a book.[7] Moreover, the International Orality Network and Lausanne Committee for World Evangelization estimated four billion people over the age of fifteen or "two-thirds of the world's population are oral communicators"—people who cannot read or prefer not to read, people with a different learning preference than one relying on print alone.[8]

Goodman et al. delineated six proficiency levels in literacy research—Below Level 1, Level 1, Level 2, Level 3, Level 4, and Level 5.[9] In a recent PIAAC (Program for the International Assessment of Adult Competencies) study, 49 percent of the western population operated at Level 2 or below.[10] In her research in the United States, Parker reported: "Functionally illiterate persons comprise 68 percent of those arrested, 85 percent of unwed mothers, 79 percent of welfare dependents, 85 percent of dropouts, and 72 percent of the unemployed."[11] Why is this the case and must it continue to be true?

In the same PIAAC study mentioned earlier, "across all countries only 2 percent of adults performed at Level 5 on many of the variables in the literacy and numeracy scales."[12] Highly proficient readers—those who have studied at advanced levels—are a tiny minority across the globe, yet the majority of research focuses at this level. Moreover, most teaching and learning is based on the use of print technology when most of the world's population cannot or would rather not read. It is grossly unfair to give so much focus to 2 percent of the world's population when the majority of adults face a different situation. Who will focus a proportional amount of research on the learning needs and strategies of the majority of the world's population?

Moreover, as increasing numbers of immigrants with low levels of literacy in their first languages change residences, their teachers experience the same challenges I did, being unaware of these adults' ways of learning. Scholars in the field of teaching English as a second language, such as Condelli and Wrigley, DeCapua and Marshall, and the Low-Educated Second Language and Literacy Acquisition (LESLLA) symposium, have begun to develop culturally appropriate pedagogies and study educational issues related to the instruction of students from traditionally oral

---

7. Rampey et al., *Skills of US Unemployed*.
8. ION and Lausanne Committee, *Making Disciples*, 3.
9. Goodman et al., *Literacy, Numeracy, and Problem Solving*.
10. Goodman et al., *Literacy, Numeracy, and Problem Solving*, 4.
11. Parker, "Adult Perspectives," 31.
12. Goodman et al., *Literacy, Numeracy, and Problem Solving*, 3.

backgrounds.[13] They call these learners SLIFE—Students with Limited or Interrupted Formal Education.

Because I work with adults who are not engaged in formal study and are not therefore students, I struggled with terminology. I felt I could not refer to those I interviewed as SLIFE. Some missiologists call them "oral preference learners"[14] and have discovered that even those with higher levels of education can be oral learners,[15] just as did Sweeney in a study of Malay university students.[16] However, West disagreed with the term "oral preference learner," claiming orality is not "a 'preference' (as if an insider cultural participant could choose or not choose oral style), but . . . an identity."[17] Gee explained, "Saying that someone is in an 'oral culture' does not mean that they and other members of their culture are not literate; it means only that their culture retains a strong allegiance to thematically based, culturally significant face-to-face storytelling."[18] Continuing, Gee noted,

> Along with storytelling, though, the pervasiveness of orality may be signaled by interpersonal interactions of manifold everyday kinds not limited to storytelling alone, and not necessarily being restricted to face-to-face contact. For example, people's social media interactions may well show characteristics that suggest the workings of "oral" more than "literate" culture.[19]

As Ong affirmed, "Oral formulaic thought and expression ride deep in consciousness and the unconscious, and they do not vanish as soon as one used to them takes pen in hand."[20]

West referred to oral learners as "oralists" and described them "as experiential, gestural, actional, and holistic in nature over those *habitus*-shaping effects that literacy-contingent models produce, e.g., 'compartmentalized, passive, cerebral, isolationistic, elitist, and professionalization-biased.'"[21] Having worked over a decade in Cambodia at the time, I observed these learners needed more than auditory instruction. They also benefited from

---

13. See Condelli and Wrigley, "Instruction, Language and Literacy"; DeCapua and Marshall, "Serving ELLs"; "Students with Limited Education"; Wall and Leong, "Tradition Continues."

14. Moon, "Discipling"; "Understanding Oral Learners."

15. Moon, "Encouraging Ducks to Swim"; "Teaching Oral Learners."

16. Sweeney, *Full Hearing*.

17. West, "Re-Eventing," 1.

18. Gee, "Discourses In and Out," 59.

19. Gee, "Discourses In and Out," 59.

20. Ong, *Orality and Literacy* (1982), 26.

21. West, "Re-Eventing," 1.

visuals, from observational learning, and from interaction, drama, ritual, hands-on activities, and real-life experiences.

Thus, to call this group simply *oral learners* seemed troubling to me, an incomplete description, and a simplification that obscured the complete picture of their learning strategies. Similarly, Finkelstein explained, "As for the tribal society, it was not 'oral' and 'auditory.' The tribesmen had keen, observant eyes and skillful hands as well as sensitive ears."[22] They learned by more than just oral means, so why label them as such?

In addition, to call these adults *preliterate* or *nonliterate*—as Thompson did in her recent dissertation[23]—thereby defining this population by what they do not possess, also seemed ethnocentric, treating and labeling non-readers as other.[24] Street concurred:

> The study of the transition from orality to literacy in "other cultures" tended to be a study of how far "they" were becoming like "us": since "we," with our forms of literacy, have achieved such technological marvels as putting men on the moon, the acquisition of literacy by others means that it is only a matter of time until they "catch up." It is in this fundamentally ethnocentric sense that literacy has tended to be viewed almost entirely in positive terms.[25]

How do we deal with this sort of othering, the hegemony of literacy? According to Foley, "Orality alone is a 'distinction' badly in need of deconstruction, a typology that unfairly homogenizes much more than it can hope to distinguish; it is by itself a false and very misleading category."[26]

Since I work with a mixture of people—some nonliterate, some barely literate, most lacking formal education, all having common characteristics, but learning by other than exclusively oral means, I was dissatisfied with the labels. Cambodians are not primary oral learners because they have a written script and print materials, yet the vast majority of the population has had limited access to formal schooling. Their reading and writing abilities vary widely, but most seem to have a common oral identity. Because adults in Cambodia typically are not involved in formal education situations and are not usually students, I chose to adapt the SLIFE term (Students with Limited or Interrupted Formal Education) coined by DeCapua and Marshall

---

22. Finkelstein, *Sense and Nonsense*, 37.
23. Thompson, "Perceptions of Teaching."
24. Hegel, *Philosophy of Mind*.
25. Street, *Social Literacies*, 74.
26. Foley, "Word in Tradition," 170.

and call the participants *Adults with Limited Formal Education* (ALFE).[27] In the course of this study of ALFE learning strategies, I also hoped to locate a more positive term for the participants and describe them according to their preferred way of learning.

Ethnographically, what characterizes the learning experiences of Cambodian adults with limited formal education (ALFE)? How do they learn best? It is certainly more involved than using auditory approaches. Only by entering the life world of adults with limited formal education can we truly understand their learning strategies. Few have embarked on this journey.

As for existing literature, there is some research on education in Cambodia related to public school education and training[28] and vocational education.[29] However, studies on learners with limited formal education in Cambodia are scarce.

Outside Cambodia, Fingeret studied illiterate adults in the United States.[30] Fanta-Vagenshtein concentrated on learning channels—basically contrasting institutional learning and experiential learning.[31] Diouf, Sheckley, and Kehrhahn questioned, "What, when, why, how, and from whom do adults in African villages learn?"[32] while Kilpatrick and Johns researched how farmers learned and approached change.[33] Merriam and Ntseane analyzed transformative learning and culture in Botswana.[34] Vautrot probed why Appalachian illiterates did not participate in literacy efforts.[35] Finally, Thompson conducted a Delphi study with those who teach nonliterates.[36] However, who will seek to understand the learning strategies of adult learners with little education?

27. DeCapua and Marshall, "Students with Limited Education."

28. See Ayres, *Anatomy of a Crisis*; "Tradition"; Benveniste et al., *Teaching in Cambodia*; Berkvens, "What International Aid Organizations Can Learn"; Courtney, "Effective Components In-Service Training"; Courtney and Gravelle, "Switching Sides"; Dawson, "Tricks of the Teacher"; "Private Tutoring"; Gravelle, "Dilemmas in Development"; Reimer, "Local Negotiation."

29. Cheng, "Case Studies of Integrated Pedagogy"; "Re-modelling and Reconceptualising."

30. Fingeret, "Illiterate Underclass."

31. Fanta-Vagenshtein, "How Illiterate People Learn"; Fanta-Vagenshtein et al., "Technological Knowledge."

32. Diouf et al., "Adult Learning," 32.

33. Kilpatrick and Johns, "How Farmers Learn."

34. Merriam and Ntseane, "Transformational Learning in Botswana."

35. Vautrot, "Why Don't They Come?"

36. Thompson, "Perceptions of Teaching."

In the field of missiology, ION publishes *The Orality Journal*, which features articles mostly dealing with applied orality. Publications on the use of narrative in biblical training are growing in number,[37] but little research has been done on the general learning strategies of non-readers and low literates. A few dissertations in the last decade have focused on orality in cross-cultural biblical training.[38] The recommendations and instructional models offered for teaching oral learners have majored on the use of narratives, proverbs, and the arts. Among his many orality-focused articles, Moon penned one entitled "Understanding Oral Learners," the result of studies with seminary students, many seeming to be oral learners.[39] Moon made several recommendations for educators but did not address learners outside formal school settings.

Finally, what one culture views as a disability others consider unnecessary. Expressing an alternate viewpoint, a few educational researchers view western teaching and learning, along with literacy training, as instruments of colonialism and oppression.[40] Some educational scholars reject the advantages of literacy and the belief that illiteracy is directly associated with poverty and other social ills.[41]

Whatever one's paradigm, most would agree those who cannot or do not read should not be ignored. Their ways of learning must be researched, for they represent such great numbers—a majority of the world's population, as mentioned earlier.[42] Watson eloquently summarized these ideas and the knowledge gap that exists:

---

37. See Ansre, "Crucial Role of Oral Scripture"; Box, *Don't Throw the Book at Them*; Brown, "Communicating Effectively"; "Designing Programs"; "Make Oral Communication More Effective"; Evans, "Matters of the Heart"; ION and Lausanne Committee, *Making Disciples*; Jagerson, "Hermeneutics and Methods"; Klem, "Dependence on Literacy Strategy"; Lovejoy, "Extent of Orality"; "Extent of Orality: 2012 Update"; Moon, "Discipling"; Prior, "Orality"; Slack et al., "Chronological Bible Storying"; Steffen, "Storying the Storybook"; *Reconnecting God's Story*; "Journey to Narrative Evangelism"; "Pedagogical Conversions"; Thompson, "Discipleship at Arm's Length?"; Wilson, "What It Takes"; "Let the Earth Hear."

38. See Anderson, "Implicit Rhetorical Theory"; Fellows, "Training of Semiliterate"; Hartnell, "Oral Contextualization"; Koehler, *Telling God's Stories*; Lee, "Bible Storying"; McIntyre, "Using Ceremonies to Disciple"; Moon, "Using Proverbs"; Norwood, "Developing a Course"; Yoakum, "Spoken Word."

39. Moon, "Understanding Oral Learners."

40. Battiste and Henderson, *Protecting Indigenous Knowledge*; Courtney and Gravelle, "Switching Sides."

41. Pattanayak, "Literacy."

42. ION and Lausanne Committee, *Making Disciples*.

The notion that traditional cultures living in harmony with an orally-toned worldview are characteristically quite distinct from cultures that have fully embraced the technologies and affordances of literacy, and that these distinctions might have relevance for literacy and academic instruction of students from oral environments, is a notion that has largely escaped the attention of educational researchers and policy makers.[43]

PROBLEM STATEMENT

During a period of turmoil, June 19, 1980, was proclaimed "Cambodia's National Day of Struggle against Illiteracy" and a program initiated for the "liquidation of illiteration [sic]."[44] Despite much effort, however, illiteracy has not been "liquidated." Reportedly, nearly half of all Cambodian children cease their education at the primary level.[45] Oral learners, adults with limited access to formal schooling (ALFE), are a definite majority in the Cambodian context. However, Duke and Hinzen opined that "a long and familiar trend has yet to be reversed: Youth and adult education and learning ... are almost neglected in the international development agenda."[46] Speaking at a Harvard commencement, Bill Gates avowed, "Humanity's greatest advances are not in its discoveries, but in how those discoveries are applied to reduce inequity."[47] We cannot afford to continue the inequity of overlooking the learning strategies of a majority of the world's population.

As Watson explained earlier, the ways of learning and the needs of this majority have escaped the notice of many in the academic world.[48] In contrast to this hegemony, Bigelow and Watson advocated exploring a profound question: "How can orality be privileged pedagogically as a linguistic strength and cultural norm?"[49] To even begin to approach their question and the scarcity of this kind of research, one must enter the world of these oral learners, adults with limited formal education, and explore their preferred ways of learning. How oral Cambodian adults with limited formal education learn is largely unknown.

43. Watson, "Interpreting across the Abyss," 109.
44. Ayres, *Anatomy of a Crisis*, 139.
45. Brinkley, *Cambodia's Curse*, 208.
46. Duke and Hinzen, "Adult Education," 20.
47. Gates, "Remarks of Bill Gates."
48. Watson, "Interpreting across the Abyss."
49. Bigelow and Watson, "Role of Education Level," 470.

PURPOSE STATEMENT

The purpose of this ethnographic grounded theory study was to understand the ways of learning of oral Cambodian adults or those with limited formal education, that is, how Cambodian ALFE learn or acquire new knowledge, beliefs/values, or skills.

RESEARCH QUESTIONS

The central research question guiding this study was how do oral Cambodian adults with limited formal education (ALFE) learn or acquire new knowledge, beliefs/values, and skills?

The following sub-questions were also explored:

1. How do ALFE in Cambodia approach the acquisition of new knowledge, beliefs, values, and skills?
2. What role do other people (society, teachers, family, and others) play in the learning of ALFE in Cambodia?
3. What role does context/environment/setting/time play in the learning of ALFE in Cambodia?
4. What role do media (such as print, audio, video, pictures, narrative, music, drama) play in the learning of ALFE in Cambodia?
5. What role does self play in the learning of ALFE in Cambodia?
6. What role does religion play in the learning of ALFE in Cambodia?

DEFINITIONS

I used the following working definitions in this study:

- *Informal education* is often known as socialization or everyday learning.
- *Learning* has been defined in multiple ways in the literature. In fact, Knowles, Holton, and Swanson believed "it is doubtful that a phenomenon as complex as adult learning will ever be explained by a single theory, model, or set of principles."[50] However, for the purpose of this study *learning* is the complex, often ubiquitous, cognitive/psychomotor/social/affective process of gaining knowledge, skills, values, and beliefs which includes "interaction between what is known" and what is yet to be acquired.[51] Maintaining problem solving should also be

50. Knowles et al., *Adult Learner*, 1.
51. Jarvis, "Learning to Be a Person"; Wray, "Teaching Literacy."

included, Harel and Koichu gave an operational definition of learning "as a continuum of disequilibrium-equilibrium phases manifested by (a) *intellectual needs* and *psychological needs* that instigate or result from these phases and (b) *ways of understanding* or *ways of thinking* that are utilized and newly constructed during these phases."[52]

- *Literacy* is "the ability to understand and employ printed information in daily activities, at home, at work and in the community—to achieve one's goals, and to develop one's knowledge and potential."[53]
- The *low literate* is a person "who has attended school, but has a reading level below the average primary school level."[54]
- *Narratives (stories)* "are *intentional-communicative artifacts*,"[55] "stylized communication patterns of symbols with pictures in the mind transferred to others so that awe and imagination take center stage, accenting cognition and volition."[56]
- *Non-formal education* is learning that is functional and practical, such as in a seminar or workshop environment, whereas *formal education* is academic and often involves credentials.
- While *pedagogy* is "any conscious activity by one person designed to enhance learning in another,"[57] *oral pedagogy* is a set of methods for effectively assisting oral learners with their learning efforts.
- *Orality*, "as analytic concept, involves a mindset, a whole attitude towards reality and experience."[58] Orality is a complex cultural construct much broader than a state of non-reading and whose learning patterns I hope to more fully comprehend through this study.
- *Primary orality* is the condition of persons never schooled in writing. Primary oral cultures have no written language.[59]
- *Secondary orality* is the "literate orality of popular culture" or communication delivered orally but based on text, such as news broadcasts.[60]

---

52. Harel and Koichu, "Operational Definition of Learning," 116.
53. OECD, *Literacy in the Information Age*.
54. Craats et al., "Research," 8.
55. Currie, *Narratives and Narrators*, xvii.
56. Steffen, "Foundational Roles of Symbol," 480.
57. Watkins and Mortimore, "Pedagogy," 3.
58. Botha, "Letter Writing," 24.
59. Ong, *Orality and Literacy*.
60. Ong, *Rhetoric, Romance, and Technology*.

- *Storying* or *Chronological Bible Storying* (CBS) is a way of presenting biblical narratives, often in chronological sequence. Sessions include recounting a biblical story along with dialogue and discussion. According to Madinger, *storying* is an application of the principles of orality.[61]
- *Traditional orality* is the situation of persons who may know how to read and write but prefer oral learning in daily life.[62]

SCOPE

This study concentrated on adult learners in the Cambodian context who had limited formal education. The participants, therefore, included people who never learned to read, low literates, and some who learned to read. Interviews were conducted with adults aged eighteen and older who studied six grades or less. According to Slack, those who have less than eight grades of education are sometimes considered functional illiterates and have yet to move into full literate competency.[63]

I conducted interviews in the country of Cambodia with native Khmer people. I did not interview Cambodians residing in other countries. In addition, I did not include other ethnic groups who might consider themselves to be Cambodian (such as the Kampuchea Krom, the Western Cham, members of hill tribes, and Vietnamese speakers residing in Cambodia). This exclusion was made in order to maintain a homogeneous study of the learning of one specific ethnolinguistic group.

LIMITATIONS

Learning can be a highly internal, implicit process. Illeris maintained there are two processes involved in learning—one external and one internal.[64] Cohen and Scott and Reimer also found some learning strategies "occur on a cognitive level and are thus not observable."[65] As a researcher, I can only ask questions and make observations to understand the inner workings of those interviewed. Investigating learning strategies turned out to be a difficult endeavor. Some participants could not articulate how they learned or whether they continued to learn. Like Parker, I found some of the broad research questions were difficult for some participants. I was forced to begin with more concrete questions and then offer opportunity

---

61. Madinger, "Coming to Terms with Orality," 204.
62. Sample, *Ministry in an Oral Culture*.
63. Slack et al., *Memory and Recall*.
64. Illeris, "Comprehensive Understanding," 8.
65. Cohen and Scott, "Synthesis of Approaches"; Reimer, "Learning Strategies," 9.

for elaboration when I stumbled on pertinent data.[66] "We can know more than we can tell," according to Polanyi.[67] In this case, I was thankful I had included observation and living as an oral learner (phenomenology or identification) in the research process.

In an effort to diversify the pool of participants, I interviewed in a variety of urban and rural locations, thereby providing a broad sampling; but the study cannot be extrapolated to represent the entire population of Cambodians with limited formal education. In addition, because Cambodia has a written language and is therefore not a primary oral culture, these results may not apply to the learning of adults with no written language.

In the beginning of this research I felt that not being Khmer or that being a woman interviewing might be a limitation in exploring this sensitive topic, but it was not. People were open to my questions and shared their stories in a surprisingly personal manner. In addition, I learned that the presence of a Khmer informant during the interviews was comforting to the participants. She assisted in clarifying questions and understandings in the Khmer language and we experienced no roadblocks in obtaining interviews as two females working together, most likely because she was an ALFE herself.

My major purpose in this study was to examine in a positive light how oral adults learn, the learning culture of ALFE. Consequently, I did not examine the negative aspects of illiteracy. Those aspects have already been widely covered in the literature, and while important issues for consideration, they are not the focus of this study.

SIGNIFICANCE STATEMENT

Oral learners or adults with limited formal education represent a majority of the world. Many live in rural areas, face poverty and other challenges to further education, and have been quite overlooked. This study explored how ALFE learn and sought a more positive term for their ways of learning. This kind of research raises awareness for that neglected but significant group of people. Exploring how Cambodian adults with limited formal education continue to learn has potential to influence literacy efforts, adult education and Christian education, lifelong learning, missiology and orality, theological education, and second language acquisition. Research of this nature is also important in contributing to practice and theory.

In the area of practice, many literate people travel to foreign lands to work with oral peoples. Cambodia plays host to a large number of such

---

66. Parker, "Adults' Perspectives," 114.
67. Polanyi, *Tacit Dimension*, 4.

visitors each year. These teachers are typically well-versed in their topics but often have yet to study the cultural context or educational status of their students and begin the journey toward understanding orality. The results of this study can point them to efficient ways to direct their practices. Even though there have been a few studies relating to education and development in Cambodia, this study also serves to inform those working with non-governmental organizations and teachers in rural settings. The grounded theory developed here can also inform policy makers addressing the educational needs of oral learners in their present contexts and educators creating curriculum.

After enduring the Khmer Rouge regime, invasion by Vietnam, and war through the 1970s and 1980s, Cambodia has been no stranger to relief and development efforts subsequent to the 1991 Paris Peace Accords and the United Nations' intervention. In 2015, the World Bank alone financed over $232 million USD in projects.[68] As Suarez and Marshall observed, "Cambodia is one of the most aid dependent countries in Asia."[69] Because of the influx of overseas donor funds, much of the influence on education and training has been western and highly literate. If the country is to become mature and self-sufficient, her leaders need to be encouraged, acknowledged with a listening ear, and developed through the best means possible. Inquiring how ALFE learn in the present is a significant step in informing the practice of adult education, literacy efforts, non-formal and formal theological education, as well as leadership development.

In considering theory, Courtney and Gravelle made an engaging case for the lack of student-centered public education in Cambodia and elaborated on the clash of such pedagogies with national identity.[70] They urged education be conducted in a contextually appropriate manner. This study fills a gap in the literature related to understanding such perspectives. Finally, because this study fits in the academic domain of non-western teaching and learning, it fills a gap in the literature in regard to the lifelong learning of oral adults. The grounded theory developed here could advance the fields of orality and adult learning by providing a researched analysis of the learning strategies of ALFE in Cambodia.

According to the UNDP, the "mean years of schooling" for Cambodians is 4.4 years, and 80 percent of the population lives in rural locations.[71] In 2013, the UNDP website listed the mean years of schooling as 5.8, and

68. World Bank Group, "Cambodia."
69. Suarez and Marshall, "Capacity in the NGO," 182.
70. Courtney and Gravelle, "Switching Sides."
71. UNDP, "About Cambodia."

Slack's research agreed, ascertaining the average educational level of the pastors he interviewed to be less than six grades.[72] Thus, these statistics have not improved over the last decade. In addition, the numbers of literacy classes, literacy learners, and "re-entry class learners" have declined.[73] With a population of 15.2 million as of 2014, these statistics translate to millions of Cambodians lacking both formal schooling and non-formal opportunities for learning.

Even though Cambodia adopted the United Nations' 2030 *Agenda for Sustainable Development*, which includes the goal to "promote lifelong learning opportunities for all,"[74] education for millions of Cambodian adults may not improve without a better understanding of their present learning strategies and addressing their learning needs in the ways they desire to learn. To begin this study, the following chapter examines pertinent literature dealing with the situation in Cambodia, especially educational research, as well as general literature on orality.

---

72. Slack et al., *Memory and Recall*.
73. MoEYS, "Non-Formal Education."
74. UN, *Transforming Our World*, 14.

2

Introductory Literature Review: The Context and Construct

"Then the book will be given to the one who does not know books, saying,

'Please read this.' And he will say, 'I do not know books.'"

—Isaiah 29:12 (NASB)

IN THIS CHAPTER I discuss the context, conceptual framework, and complex construct of this study. In other words, I frame the current study of how Cambodian adults with limited formal education (ALFE) learn, provide the background of previous educational and cultural studies in Cambodia, and examine writings related to orality, literacy, and lack of formal education.

In 1967 Glaser and Strauss advised those embarking on grounded theory research not to review literature prior to their studies lest their findings become "tainted." Later, Glaser conceded and recommended a cursory look at the literature before research if necessary.[1] Creswell listed three uses of literature: "to frame the problem in the introduction to the study," as a separate section, or to compare and contrast findings at the end of the study, a strategy used frequently in grounded theory.[2] I have chosen, therefore, to conduct a "split literature review," following the advice of Andrews, who mentions doing two literature reviews—one to put "the study into some context and the

---

1. Glaser, "Staying Open."
2. Creswell, *Research Design*, 27.

16   Connected Learning

other one used as data to fully integrate the theory."[3] This chapter serves to frame the research problem and situate the study.

While analyzing the related literature, as is true with many grounded theory studies, I recognized a definite gap related to the learning of adults with limited formal education, or the learning of adults with an oral identity, as discussed earlier. Figure 1 locates the focus of this study at the intersection of four elements—the cultural context, the context of age, the construct of orality, and the content of proposed learning. The cultural or anthropological context of this study was Southeast Asia and the Khmer people of Cambodia, while the context age-wise for the study centered around adult learners. My research problem sits in the realm of adult learning and non-western teaching and learning. The construct to be considered was orality, especially in those with limited formal education, and the content of ALFE learning in this context ranged from gaining vocational skills, gathering religious/spiritual knowledge, to learning English as a second language.

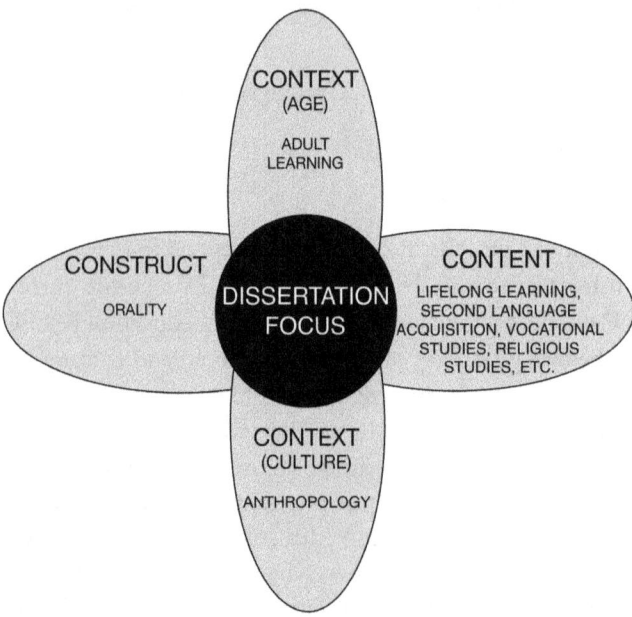

Figure 1. Dissertation focus at the intersection of contexts, construct, and varied content.

According to McMenamin, "A literature review must establish the intellectual geography of the dissertation and locate the dissertation's project

3. Andrews, "Literature in Grounded Theory," 32.

within it."[4] As Dunne advised, this kind of review serves to "contextualize" the research before data sourcing,[5] thus this dissertation explored the intersection of sociocultural and contextual factors and how ALFE learn. In particular, then, this chapter examines literature relating to the cultural context—Cambodia—as well as the construct of orality and any intersections of the two. The chapter, then, becomes more of a "state-of-the-art review."[6]

I briefly mention some studies related to learning and orality in this section but will examine pertinent studies more fully after data analysis. In addition, as this topic intersects the fields of literacy, learning, and oral communication, I thought it prudent to interact with research in those fields when discussing the research findings. In that section, I also examined any additional issues that arose during the study.

THE CONTEXT: CAMBODIA

The central research question guiding this study was how do oral Cambodian adults with limited formal education (ALFE) learn or acquire new knowledge, beliefs/values, and skills? The problem involved understanding the ways of learning of Cambodian ALFE who have an oral identity. Therefore, this section describes the context of the research (Cambodia) and examines studies related to culture and education in Cambodia, as well as orality and literacy in that kingdom. I exclude from this section studies related to Cambodians living outside the country unless the works provide insight into native Cambodian culture.

The Cultural Context in Cambodia

Cambodia is a Southeast Asian nation with a traumatic past. A country of twenty-five provinces and municipalities, Cambodia was once popularly known as the "pearl of Asia" and the "Paris of the East." The Vietnam War and a period of genocide at the hands of Pol Pot and the Khmer Rouge (Red Khmer) changed that glamorous image. Yale University's Cambodian Genocide Program estimated 21 percent of the population died during the years of the "Killing Fields," when the Marxist Khmer Rouge sought to return the country to "year zero" and its supposed former agricultural glory.[7] Educated Khmer were exterminated, families disrupted, and citizens evacuated to rural locations and put to forced labor. To this day, many of

---

4. McMenamin, "Process and Text," 135.
5. Dunne, "Place of the Literature Review," 121.
6. Jesson et al., *Doing Your Literature Review*.
7. Yale University Genocide Studies Program, "Cambodian Genocide Program."

Cambodia's over fifteen million people (at the time of this research) still suffer in some way from those atrocities.

Officially a Buddhist nation, Cambodia's majority actually holds to an amalgamation of animism, Buddhism, and Brahmanism, commonly known as folk Buddhism. Bit noted, "The merging of classical Buddhist thought with animistic and Brahmanist traditions produces patterns which are quite atypical of Buddhism as practiced elsewhere."[8] There have been some fascinating recent works in this area—on the practice of Buddhism,[9] conflict style,[10] the use of spirit houses,[11] the role of Khmer mediums,[12] rituals surrounding death,[13] animism and the practice of the "calling of the souls,"[14] general sociocultural issues,[15] narratives and Buddhist ethics,[16] and spirit cults.[17] Most of these works, however, do not touch on learning, orality, or lack of formal education, except for Hansen's treatment of traditional narratives.[18] Hansen, however, did not delve into oral transmission of Khmer narratives. Likewise, Harris had an entire chapter on literary traditions, but did not consider the transmission of that knowledge to non-readers.[19]

In an intriguing study more related to adult learning, Eisenbruch researched the work of traditional healers (*kru*—a phonetic rendering of the Khmer word)[20] and their relationship with patients and the spirit world.[21] The knowledge of the *kru* was transmitted through apprenticeship-style education and often determined by descent or family lines or special birth characteristics.[22] The curriculum of the *kru* came from palm leaf manuscripts as well as the memory of the mentors and their notes. Additionally,

---

8. Bit, *Warrior Heritage*, 21.
9. Harris, *Cambodian Buddhism*.
10. Bagdasar, "Khmer Conflict Style."
11. Baeq, "Spirit House."
12. Bertrand, "Therapeutic Role."
13. Davis, "Treasures of the Buddha"; Holt, "Caring for the Dead."
14. Ang, *Brah Ling*; "Place of Animism"; *People and Earth*; Thompson, *Calling the Souls*.
15. Abdulgaffar, "Understanding the Khmer."
16. Hansen, *Ways of the World*; "Image of an Orphan."
17. O'Lemmon, "Spirit Cults and Buddhist Practice."
18. Hansen, *Ways of the World*; "Image of an Orphan."
19. Harris, *Cambodian Buddhism*.
20. Please see Appendix A and Table A1 for all Khmer terms in this document written in Khmer font.
21. Eisenbruch, "Ritual Space."
22. Eisenbruch, "Ritual Space."

the *kru* sometimes used pseudo-script and language not understood by the shaman or the patient.[23]

As for more recent research on Cambodia in general, writings of more international concern abound, such as studies on domestic violence, human trafficking, and children's rights;[24] gender issues;[25] leadership and patron-client issues;[26] mental health, healthcare, and traditional medicine;[27] politics;[28] and socio-economics, development, and nongovernmental organizations.[29] None of these works, however, broached the topic of orality or adult learning in Cambodia, except for inferences from Miller and Rodgers's discussion of the correlation between "mother's education and children's nutritional status" and findings that "median educational attainment for adult women" was less than three years.[30] Additional research by Springer discussed legal land ownership in light of oral law, oral history, and verbal agreements in Cambodia.[31]

The Educational Context in Cambodia

What are schooling and lifelong learning like in the Cambodian context? Turning to examine the educational context in Cambodia, this section first covers the history of Cambodia's educational system. Then I examine the present situation of schooling and lifelong learning and any other literature relevant to the study of ALFE learning in Cambodia.

---

23. Eisenbruch, "Ritual Space."

24. Gourley, *Middle Way*.

25. Brickell, "We Don't Forget"; Knodel and Zimmer, "Gender and Well-Being."

26. See Kimura, *Developing Christian Relief*; Ledgerwood, "Social Hierarchy"; Ma, "Leadership Traits"; Pak et al., *Accountability and Neo-Patrimonialism*; Selvarajah et al., "Effect of Cultural Modeling"; World Concern, "Khmer Leadership"; Zepp, "Perceptions of Leadership."

27. See Chhim, "*Baksbat* (Broken Courage)"; Lipsky, "Khmer Women Healers"; Miller and Rodgers, "Mother's Education."

28. See Ann, *Patron-Clientelism*; Jacobsen and Stuart-Fox, *Power and Political Culture*; Ledgerwood and Vijghen, "Decision-Making in Rural Khmer."

29. See Batchelor, "Christian and Secular Approaches"; Berkvens, "What International Aid Organizations Can Learn"; Fforde and Seidel, "Cambodia—Donor Playground?"; Jonsson, "Healthy Houses"; Matthews, "Internal Control"; Eng et al., *Social Accountability*; O'Leary, "Influence of Values"; Pearson, "No Visible Difference"; Rudengren and Ojendal, *Learning by Doing*.

30. Miller and Rodgers, "Mother's Education," 134.

31. Springer, "Illegal Evictions?"

CAMBODIA'S PAST EDUCATIONAL CONTEXT. Even before Cambodia's years of tragedy, formal education was not widespread. Ayres's work delineated the history and culture behind Cambodia's present educational state, especially the "web of patronage and clientship," with absolute power at the top of various hierarchies.[32] Not surprisingly, Ayres's book is entitled *Anatomy of a Crisis*. He recounted that the village *wat* (Buddhist monastery) was the traditional center of education, providing learning only for males.[33] In 1918, when the French who colonized the country finally proposed a system of education for Cambodia, the following objections to schooling arose and are still applicable: "Few children remained at school longer than three years," parents preferred temple education, culture constrained girls' involvement, teachers were few, students could not travel easily to the nearest school, and "the public was largely apathetic to the system."[34]

The first high school in Cambodia was established in 1935, long after surrounding nations. In 1939, only 294 students out of 60,000 passed their primary school exams.[35] At the time of Cambodia's independence from France in 1953, only eight high schools and no higher education institutions existed. King Norodom Sihanouk, considered the "father of education" in Cambodia, began expanding schooling at that time. Ultimately, however, numbers of graduates increased while employment did not. Education for girls began as well, but few enrolled.[36]

Then came war and genocide with very little opportunity for anything, much less education. After the years of devastation subsided, the whole Cambodian infrastructure needed rebuilding. In 1991, the United Nations Transitional Authority (UNTAC) brought peacekeeping forces, and in 1993, the nation finally had her first election after the war.[37] Created during that time, Article 68 of the constitution pronounced, "The State shall provide primary and secondary education to all citizens in public schools."[38]

CAMBODIA'S PRESENT EDUCATIONAL CONTEXT. Life has improved for the country but is still difficult for the rural majority. The present educational system consists of six years of primary school (*bah-tom-ah-suk-sah*), three years of lower secondary (*ah-noot vee-jee-ah-lie-ee*), and three years of upper

---

32. Ayres, *Anatomy of a Crisis*, 11.
33. Ayres, *Anatomy of a Crisis*.
34. Ayres, *Anatomy of a Crisis*, 24.
35. Ayres, *Anatomy of a Crisis*.
36. Sopheak and Clayton, "Schooling in Cambodia."
37. Chandler, *History of Cambodia*.
38. *Constitution of Cambodia*.

secondary education (*vee-jee-ah-lie-ee*). Very few Cambodians attend preschool (*t'nak may-tay*) or kindergarten, which is considered part of a primary education. There are exams after grades nine (for receiving a *dee-plome*) and twelve, when students receive the *bah-dope*. Besides the government schools, there is presently a proliferation of private institutions as well.

Students who do not have the opportunity to complete twelve grades of education can study and take an exam, the *svay-run*, for those who did not attend secondary school and the *bomb-payn moke-vee-jee-ah* or *vee-jee-ah-sah put* for those who had attended some secondary school. Students who did not complete nine grades of education may also take the ninth-grade exam to receive *dee-plome* status.

The Ministry of Education, Youth, and Sport (MoEYS) ascribed to the worldwide "Education for All" initiative, but accessing that education is not easy for most Cambodians. Sopheak and Clayton recorded an enlightening "day in the life of a rural girl in Cambodia today," delineating the difficulties and diligence of Khmer students trying to survive and learn at the same time.[39] Add to this kind of life the needs and trials of adults and there is no time for lifelong learning. The MoEYS promotes non-formal education (NFE) but reported a decline in the number of literacy learners in recent years.[40]

Presently, the MoEYS has only one national training center for secondary teachers, six for lower secondary teachers, eighteen teacher training colleges for primary teachers, and only one national college for pre-school teachers.[41] Over 70 percent of primary teachers have only a secondary education or less.[42] In fact, most teachers have only a bit more education than do their students.[43]

THE SURVEY OF RELEVANT EDUCATIONAL LITERATURE. Since the years of devastation in Cambodia, educational infrastructures have been in a state of flux and formation. The western world rushed in with aid and well-meaning advice. In fact, Fforde and Seidel called Cambodia a "donor playground."[44] Reportedly, over half the budget for education is from foreign sources.[45] Additionally, according to Courtney and Gravelle, foreigners imposed their

39. Sopheak and Clayton, "Schooling in Cambodia," 54.
40. MoEYS, "Non-Formal Education."
41. Richardson, "Diffusion of Technology Adoption."
42. Kim and Rouse, "Reviewing the Role."
43. Ayres, *Anatomy of a Crisis*.
44. Fforde and Seidel, "Cambodia—Donor Playground?"
45. Courtney, "What Are Effective Components."

ways on Cambodian education in the form of student-centered pedagogies.[46] These educational researchers viewed the lack of success in teacher training and educational improvement as a controversy between western learner-centered teaching methods and Khmer thinking. In agreement with other researchers, such as Needham,[47] a UNESCO study maintained, "The international community has done much good and also considerable harm to Cambodia" because "donor preferences continue to dominate the allocation of education spending."[48] These researchers, along with Reimer, argued "child-friendly pedagogies" have not been successful because the ideas conflict with Khmer culture.[49]

Similarly, Needham studied the learning of Khmer refugees in the United States. Although outside the realm of this study, Needham made some significant and pertinent conclusions.[50] She described the meeting of two very different pedagogies, each reflecting the philosophy of its originating country—a contrast between the active learning, student-centered pedagogy of the west versus Khmer rote memory and "choral recitation"—one pedagogy attending to the individual versus another that is group oriented.

Interestingly, Needham discussed orality and the need for "correct recitation" in "oral transmission of knowledge" in Khmer traditional culture.[51] She related that Buddhist texts were often transmitted orally and chanted, thus the connection to the meaning of the word *study* in Khmer—*ree-un sote*—*ree-un* meaning *to study* and *sote* meaning *to chant* or *recite*. Her conclusion was as follows:

> Because active and passive are culturally bounded, they should not be used to characterize the teaching techniques of social groups who do not share an active and doing cultural orientation. The education practices negatively labeled "passive learning" are, from the Cambodian point of view, a model for society and the most effective way for children to learn.[52]

Wisely, Needham concluded that learning styles are culturally situated, and refused the common hegemony of viewing Asian pedagogy as other or as a less effective way of learning.

46. Courtney and Gravelle, "Switching Sides."
47. Needham, "'This Is Active Learning.'"
48. UNESCO, "Education and Fragility in Cambodia," 43–44.
49. Reimer, "Local Negotiation."
50. Needham, "'This Is Active Learning.'"
51. Needham, "'This Is Active Learning,'" 31.
52. Needham, "'This Is Active Learning,'" 45.

Needham's viewpoint, however, is in stark contrast to that of researchers clamoring to improve Cambodia's educational situation. Recent education-related studies in Cambodia dealt with the Education for All initiative,[53] contract teachers,[54] corruption and education,[55] early childhood education,[56] fragility and development,[57] girls and schooling,[58] higher education,[59] interjecting more learner-centered pedagogies and "Child Friendly Schools,"[60] parental involvement,[61] professional development and teacher training,[62] school leadership and educational policies,[63] teacher status and teaching,[64] teaching English as a second language,[65] tradition and education,[66] and vocational education and integrated pedagogy.[67] In his analysis, Cheng's research in vocational education used a "three-tier approach to creating an empowering environment," a holistic model of education suited for Cambodia.[68] Other organizations would do well to

53. Ai, "Educational Movement"; Kim and Rouse, "Reviewing the Role."

54. Geeves and Bredenberg, "Contract Teachers in Cambodia."

55. See Dawson, "Tricks of the Teacher"; "Private Tutoring"; Heyneman, "Education and Corruption"; *Buying Your Way*.

56. Rao and Pearson, "Early Childhood Care."

57. Raun-Linde, "International Narratives"; Un, "Comparative Study"; UNESCO, "Education and Fragility."

58. Filmer and Schady, "Getting Girls into School."

59. Kreng, "Factors Influencing College Students'"; Locard and Ang, "Higher Education in Cambodia"; Nash, "Using Student Evaluations"; Om, "Harnessing the Hope"; Walker, "Cambodia's Postgraduate Students."

60. Ginsburg and American Institutes for Research, *Active-Learning Pedagogies*; Ginsburg, "Improving Educational Quality"; Nith et al., "Active-Learning Pedagogies"; Nonoyama-Tarumi and Bredenberg, "Impact of School Readiness"; Ogisu, "Cambodian Pedagogical Reform"; Tek, "Barriers to Implementing."

61. Eng et al., "Cambodian Parental Involvement."

62. Berkvens, "Developing Effective Professional Learning"; Berkvens et al., "Improving Adult Learning"; Courtney, "What Are Effective Components"; Duggan, "Education, Teacher Training."

63. Ai, "School Leadership and Management"; Morefield, "School Leadership Development"; Tan, "Educational Policy."

64. Benveniste et al., *Teaching in Cambodia*; Knight and MacLeod, *Integration of Teachers' Voices*.

65. Krzeszewski, "Poverty, English, and Evangelism"; Skilton-Sylvester, "Should I Stay."

66. Ayres, "Tradition."

67. Cheng, "Case Studies of Integrated Pedagogy"; Husum et al., "Training Prehospital Trauma."

68. Cheng, "Case Studies of Integrated Pedagogy," 441.

study Cheng's educational model that integrates the classroom, the playground, and the workshop.

Most recently, Courtney and Gravelle implemented and analyzed a reading intervention in rural schools, finding "most teachers in Cambodia use a one-strategy approach to teaching reading but that reading competence remains poor."[69] These two educational researchers trained teachers in a multi-strategy approach that reportedly resulted in improved student reading ability. In addition, Wagner et al. researched the training of village health guides in diabetes education.[70] They mentioned very little about pedagogy. Rather, the curriculum seemed to focus on three simple areas—eating properly, walking, and getting enough sleep. The guides used true/false pre- and post-tests "given the low educational attainment of most guides," and read the questions to participants.[71]

Also dealing with "low educational attainment," Smith-Hefner presented a study on "Khmer education, gender, and conflict." Researching Cambodian refugees in the US, she found many lacked formal schooling, and "most rural Khmer women over the age of 40" were illiterate.[72] Interestingly, Smith-Hefner concluded this lack of education for women was a face-saving mechanism designed to preserve female purity.

Finally, Tan presented a succinct summary of the present educational status in Cambodia.[73] Her more recent examination of education through the lens of Johnson's "trajectories of educational change and policy transfer" (telling, rebelling, compelling/selling, and gelling) compared educational policy in Cambodia and Singapore.[74] In line with Tan's conclusions, Reimer's extensive study on Child Friendly Schools and Cambodian worldview maintained Cambodian education has not "gelled" with "transnational influences" because of worldview and traditional practices.[75] Unlike other educational studies, Reimer's included a discussion on orality, examined in the next section.

Orality and Literacy in Cambodia

At the intersection of the Cambodian cultural context and the construct of orality, very little research exists. Of the 1325 digital education resources

---

69. Courtney and Gravelle, "What Makes The Difference?," 416.
70. Wagner et al., "Training Cambodian Village."
71. Wagner et al., "Training Cambodian Village," 163.
72. Smith-Hefner, "Education, Gender, and Generational Conflict," 137.
73. Tan, "Education Reforms."
74. Tan, "Educational Policy."
75. Reimer, "Local Negotiation."

available on the Royal University of Phnom Penh (RUPP) website in March of 2015, none related to orality.[76] Predictably, a number of these sources did address literacy. Rosenbloom gathered statistics on literacy, as have various aid and governmental agencies.[77] As mentioned earlier, Rosenbloom's research reported that nine million Cambodians needed literacy instruction. Hyde's study of Cambodian Christian church leaders ascertained nearly three-fourths of the population had "only a primary education or no education" and the average formal educational attainment was eight grades.[78] Similarly, according to the Cambodian government's 2008 census, 80 percent of heads of household had a sixth-grade education or less.[79]

As with most countries and the global effort to arrive at accurate numbers of non-readers, findings can be contradictory.[80] Definitions of literacy differ widely. A UNESCO/UNDP survey revealed only 36 percent of Cambodians "literate in terms of being able to use their literacy skills in everyday life."[81] Historically, those with the lowest levels of literacy and education tend to be female. According to the Cambodian government's National NFE (Non-Formal Education) Action Plan (2003-2015), "Only 12 percent of women over twenty-five have more than a primary education on which to build subsequent literacy, life management, or income generation."[82] Matthews also reported many poor and illiterate women had to rely on patrons with literate skills for their financial well-being.[83]

While Matthews's study concentrated on finances and the rights of the poor and illiterate, he covered some interesting information management concepts related to oral society.[84] Bit concurred, "For the weak and helpless in society, a patron offers security in a very personalized form."[85] Lee et al. reported on participatory action research with a Cambodian NGO and an apprenticeship program that removed women from unhealthy workplaces to study in the hotel industry.[86] Their work incorporated literacy training,

---

76. Royal University of Phnom Penh (RUPP) website (http://119.82.251.165:8080/xmlui), March of 2015.

77. Rosenbloom, "Adult Literacy in Cambodia."

78. Hyde, "Missiological and Critical Study," 101.

79. Hyde, "Missiological and Critical Study," 102.

80. Lovejoy, "Extent of Orality."

81. UNESCO, *Global Education Digest*, 3.

82. MoEYS, "Education Strategic Plan 2009-2013," 3.

83. Matthews, "Internal Control."

84. Matthews, "Internal Control."

85. Bit, *Warrior Heritage*, 21.

86. Lee et al., "Creating New Career Pathways."

but with little discussion of the results. Certainly, a plethora of organizations, such as Freedom from Hunger, Health Unlimited, and the like, work with ALFE in Cambodia; however, most do not directly address orality as such. Many do deal with the issues of training and teaching those with limited education and low literacy. For instance, Mobile Health Without Borders from Stanford University stated they used a "train-the-trainer approach," and that their "education will be structured to reflect the average level of education," using "symbols for illiterate individuals."[87] Any other related literature unearthed will be discussed in later chapters.

Culturally, Reimer advised: "Khmer views of the teaching and learning process differ not simply in form but [also] at a more fundamental level, and this difference must be carefully considered when devising (importing, adapting) international pedagogical standards and practices."[88] She researched the educational situation in Cambodia and discussed Khmer culture, giving a cursory look at orality, but providing an excellent discussion of Khmer philosophy of education.

In 2007 Trans World Radio conducted a survey of orality resources in Cambodia and gathered a listing of the various organizations working in the area.[89] They concluded 33 percent of Cambodians in the three provinces of Battambang, Prey Veng, and Siem Reap had no opportunity for schooling and 65 percent of rural Cambodians in those provinces could not read. Reportedly, the other 35 percent could read only a bit. TWR's statistics are contrary to those of the government and various agencies because of differing definitions of literacy; however, TWR's results are in line with my experience working with many Cambodians and observing their lack of functional reading ability.

Kalab reported improved literacy after a 1964 campaign in a Kampong Cham village.[90] However, Ebihara, in her early study of the village Svay, concluded three-quarters of males over eighteen had "minimal literacy" and all the adult females were illiterate.[91] In contrast to that period, the Cambodian government now plans to

> ensure that all children, youth, adults, poor people and those with disabilities realize their rights to a basic education and

---

87. Mobile Health without Borders, *Health Literacy*, 2.
88. Reimer, "Local Negotiation," 256.
89. TWR, personal communication with the author, August 6, 2013.
90. Kalab, "Study of a Cambodian Village."
91. Ebihara, "Svay," 530.

lifelong learning. Another objective is to provide opportunities for youth and adults to access life skills and become literate.[92]

So, it would seem some progress in realizing the importance of education has been made over the decades.

In her moving dissertation, Hagadorn explored imagination and memory in the process of change in Cambodia.[93] Gathering narratives from Khmer Rouge survivors, she promoted social *phronesis* (wisdom), an intensive community-based alternative to traditional development efforts. Two additional studies touching on narrative were Ly's conceptualization of carvings in Cambodian temples as "storytelling in stone"[94] and Agger's et al. study of the healing power of "testimonial therapy."[95] The intersection of narrative studies and Cambodian culture warrants further research.

Ayres took a glance at orality and noted, "Prior to the arrival of the French, literacy . . . was very low among the peasantry."[96] According to him, cultural heritage was learned through folk tales, didactic poems, and epics, each of which he overviewed, concluding these teaching devices reinforced tradition. In the same light, Hansen examined the use of narrative for ethical purposes in the traditional *Gatilok* ("ways of the world") stories but did not discuss their transmission.[97] In a surprising historical study, Chigas and Mosyakov delineated the literacy and educational efforts of the Khmer Rouge and noted their goal in the 1970s was to "abolish illiteracy" and re-educate the rural populace.[98]

Turning to post-Khmer Rouge literature, various other researchers studied Khmer folktales (e.g., Jacob),[99] a crucial endeavor for studies in oral tradition. One work related to narrative and orality in Cambodia was Than's thesis, a study of the contemporary use of oral folktales.[100] Similar to a study of Khmer folktales I conducted for a doctoral course, Than discovered nearly half of interviewees were unfamiliar with local legends.[101] The minority who could recite traditional stories were older villagers. Expected in a country crushed by the ravages of war, the younger generation missed the recounting

92. MoEYS, "Non-Formal Education."
93. Hagadorn, "Khmer Rouge Survivors."
94. Ly, "Storytelling on Stone."
95. Agger et al., "Testimony Ceremonies in Asia."
96. Ayres, *Anatomy of a Crisis*, 13.
97. Hansen, *Ways of the World*.
98. Chigas and Mosyakov, "Literacy and Education."
99. Jacob, "Short Stories."
100. Than, "Status of Oral Folktale Narration."
101. Than, "Status of Oral Folktale Narration."

of folktales. Cambodian culture, then, has diverged from the norm of traditional societies that preserve their historical narratives (legends and folklore) by transmitting them orally from generation to generation. This is an interesting area for further study.

Even though the Khmer Rouge destroyed many works of literature, the nation does have a well-established written script and literature; therefore, Cambodia is not a primary oral culture according to Ong's definition mentioned in chapter 1.[102] Rather, the kingdom of Cambodia has faced poverty, war, and genocide, and has historically not been as concerned with formal education as have neighboring nations.[103] To be expected, agricultural workers, who are a majority in Khmer society and who struggle just to survive, expressed having far too many concerns to invest time in reading and writing or allowing their children to do the same. For instance, McIver et al., in studying "diarrheal disease" in Cambodia, also found that "educational factors such as school attendance and adult literacy may be of greater significance in protecting against diarrheal disease than access to improved water, sanitation, and hygiene facilities."[104] Unfortunately, many who work with ALFE divert the conversation to literacy instead of helping ALFE learn according to their interests.

Turning to the realm of ethnodoxology, veteran missionary Compain chronicled an important resource related to oral learning—the Cambodian hymnal.[105] Refugees in border camps during the Pol Pot era created most of the original tunes recorded in that resource. Similarly, Mam and Hutchinson related the importance of song to Cambodian Christians.[106] As Arrington concluded from her research with the oral Lisu, hymns were essential for the continuation of the Christian faith among that people.[107] I have also witnessed the importance of the Khmer hymnal and Alice Compain's work in this area.

Few studies exist related to Christianity and orality in Cambodia, however. One of the most significant works was Johnson and Campbell's book on church planting among oral cultures.[108] Pioneers in the field of orality in Cambodia, Johnson and Campbell mentored many in the art of

---

102. Ong, *Orality and Literacy*.

103. Ayres, *Anatomy of a Crisis*.

104. McIver et al., "Diarrheal Diseases and Climate," 584.

105. Compain, "Born across Borders."

106. Mam and Hutchinson, "Communicating the Gospel."

107. Arrington, "Hymns as Theological Mediator"; Arrington, "Hymns of the Everlasting Hills."

108. Johnson and Campbell, *Worldview Strategic Church*.

storytelling and training oral learners. Although others had used storying in Cambodia prior to Johnson and Campbell, the duo were catalysts for the orality movement to gain momentum in the country.

Following their lead and learning from storying work in the Philippines, I noticed Cambodia's oral learners needed audio and visual resources, so I created *The Oral Bible School* curriculum.[109] Since that time, a plethora of organizations have begun creating storying sets, doing Chronological Bible Storying (CBS), and working with oral learners in the country (e.g., D. Jones).[110] However, it is beyond the scope of this study to mention or critique them all.

Researchers with the IMB, Slack and Maroney conducted a church planting assessment in Cambodia in 2001.[111] Studying Southern Baptist-related church planters and leaders, they identified their average educational grade level as less than six grades. Presently, the "mean years of schooling" in Cambodia is 4.4 years, according to the UNDP.[112] However, in 2013 the mean listed on their website was higher—5.8 years.[113] In 2001, Slack and Maroney concluded the infrastructure for radical improvements did not exist and a significant turnaround would be long in coming. They were correct.

Present government statistics still show 57 percent of women and 41 percent of men aged 15 to 49 have little or no education.[114] If those over fifty were added to this mixture, the statistics would be even higher. For instance, in his research with over 168 church leaders across Cambodia, Hyde calculated 71 percent of rural church leaders had little or no education.[115] All these statistics lead to the strong conclusion that Cambodia is an environment ripe for studying the needs of oral learners and adults with limited formal education.

THE COMPLEX CONSTRUCT: ORALITY AND ALFE LEARNING

Orality is by no means a simple construct. This section delves into the complexity that is orality, focusing especially on available research involving adult learning and limited formal education. I also introduce a conceptual

---

109. Thigpen, "Oral Bible School."
110. Jones, "Moving towards Oral Communication."
111. Slack and Maroney, *Church Planting Movement*.
112. UNDP, "About Cambodia."
113. UNDP, "About Cambodia."
114. National Institute of Statistics, *2010 Demographic and Health Survey*, 2.
115. Hyde, *Portrait of the Body*.

framework for exploring the literature on ALFE ways of learning and for exploring the research questions.

Bigelow and Watson maintained orality could be traced back to Saussure's Course on General Linguistics from 1916 because of "what he called the semiological facts of any human society, including diachronic versus synchronic language studies, paradigmatic versus syntagmatic approaches, linguistic register studies, and the key distinction between written and oral language."[116] After that time, various scholars began comparative studies between literacy and the lack thereof.[117] Others, such as Havelock, Lord, Parry, as well as Finnegan and Foley, all inspected oral literature.[118] Research then spilled over into media and communications studies.

Nasser reported a slightly different beginning of the interest in orality, the rise of McLuhan and Ong, and the story behind the Great Divide—the dichotomous contrast between literacy and orality.[119] Tracing the references used by Ong and McLuhan (Ong's professor), Nasser discovered two other controversial works influenced McLuhan's *The Gutenberg Galaxy*, written in 1962. First, Prince, researching "brain fag [fatigue] syndrome in Nigerian students," mentioned a Freudian type of orality,[120] and second, Carothers's dealings in ethnopsychiatry in Africa stimulated a frenzy of writing.[121]

On the other hand, according to the Google Books Ngram Viewer online, the word *orality* was not used much before the 1950s. I found one of the earliest mentions of the word in an 1818 study of British history by John Hughes, quoting Edward Williams's *Poems, Lyric and Pastoral* from 1794. Hughes upgraded Williams's English text[122] as follows:

> The Bards and Druids (both one and the same people) of ancient Britain had, before letters were known, reduced the arts of memory and oral tradition into a well-systematised science. Song was one of their methods of giving permanency or fixation to orality: songs, skillfully composed on interesting subjects, were learned with avidity; they soon became popular; they could

---

116. Bigelow and Watson, "Role of Education Level," 461.

117. See Goody and Watt, "Consequences of Literacy"; Jousse, *Oral Style*; Levi-Strauss, *Savage Mind*; Luria, *Cognitive Development*.

118. See Havelock, *Preface to Plato*; Lord, "Perspectives on Recent Work"; Parry, *Making of Homeric Verse*; Finnegan, "Response from an Africanist"; Foley, "Word in Tradition."

119. Nasser, "Great Divide."

120. Prince, "'Brain Fag' Syndrome," 559.

121. Carothers, "Culture, Psychiatry, and the Written Word."

122. Williams, *Poems, Lyric and Pastoral*.

be transmitted, without the aid of letters, from one person, time, or place, to another, though ever so remote.[123]

Since Williams discussed orality and oral tradition as early as 1794, I imagine there remains much more to be researched in this area.

Traditionally, the seminal text usually examined in discussions on orality is Ong's *Orality and Literacy*, along with works related to his.[124] Before delving into the realm of orality *viz* Ong et al., we can now locate many other works intersecting with orality, as researchers have begun to recognize the issue affects everything from teaching English as a second language to finance and developmental issues.

Technical writers have discovered orality.[125] Clinical neuropsychologists and scientists have discovered orality.[126] Even social workers have entered the conversation,[127] as have practitioners involved in micro-finance, aid, and development.[128] For instance, the non-profit Freedom from Hunger reported on their website that their education modules were created in such a way that "illiterate women can participate fully in each session."[129] A number of organizations have also implemented and researched entertainment education opportunities for those with low literacy.[130]

Additionally, in the medical and health education fields, trainers and educators have long been concerned with communicating effectively with patients. For example, *Teaching Patients with Low Literacy Skills* by Doak et al. might provide useful for teaching in other situations,[131] as would *Helping Health Workers Learn* by Werner and Bower.[132]

Organizing the wealth of literature related to orality alone would be quite a feat, as the complex construct crosses many disciplines. Table 1 is an attempt at dividing the various fields into specializations and listing some notable contributors in each of those specializations. The table is not exhaustive by any means. Orality intersects with anthropology and the

---

123. Hughes, *Horae Britannicae*, 196.

124. Ong, *Orality and Literacy*.

125. See Cibangu, "Oral Communication"; Woerkum, "Orality and the Process."

126. See Ardila et al., "Illiteracy"; Montgomery and Kumar, "Telling Stories."

127. Tsang, "Orality and Literacy."

128. See Bogale et al., "Reaching Hearts"; Matthews, "Internal Control"; UNESCO, *Harnessing the Potential*.

129. Freedom from Hunger, "Education Modules."

130. See Booth, "Radio Soap for Health Education"; Hernandez and Organista, "Entertainment-Education?"; Papa et al., *Journal of Communication*.

131. Doak et al., *Teaching Patients*.

132. Werner and Bower, *Helping Health Workers*.

study of culture, with communication, history, literature, biblical studies, performance, missiology, and with education. Oral tradition, discourse analysis, speech act theory, performance theory, ethnopoetics, and ethnodoxology have risen as relatively new specializations. Finally, the areas of missiology and biblical studies have also produced a great deal of literature, most with a practical bent.

Table 1.

General fields of orality divided into specializations, with sample contributors for each.

General Field	Specialization	Contributors
Orality	Orality in General	Ong, Sterne, Winger
Orality & Culture	Primary Orality	de Vries, Finnegan, Shuter
	Orality, Culture & Worldview	Cutz, Draper, Finnegan, Hurteau
	Socialization, Sociolinguistics	Mazamisa
	Ethnopoetics, Ethnomusicology, Indigenous Media	Akesson, Hynes, Klem, Mushengyezi
Orality & Communication	Oral Communication, Media, Technology, Media Criticism,	Innis, Goody, Jousse, Loubser, McLuhan, Ong, Sienaert, Wootton
	Secondary/New Orality	Lamberti, Ong
Orality & History	Oral Tradition, Oral Literature	Foley, Finnegan, Kaartinen, Klem, Lord, Pobee, Rubin
	Orality in Antiquity, Middle Ages	Alexander, P. Botha, Clanchy, Carruthers, Goody, Havelock, Hezser, Small, Stock
	Bible History (Jewish & NT) & Canon	Achtemeier, Alexander, P. Botha, Harvey, Ong, Walton, Zachman
Orality & Literature, Bible	Orality & Literature Studies, Textuality	P. Botha, Cambron-Goulet, Furniss, Goody and Watt, Goody, Havelock, Klem, Long, Ong, Oreck

General Field	Specialization	Contributors
	Bible Study, Interpretation, Oral Hermeneutics & Bible as Oral Literature	Bryan, Draper, Foster, Iverson, Klem, Naude, Swearingen, Winger
Orality & Performance	Orality, Performance, Rhetoric & Homiletics	Anderson, Hadisi, Hearon, Rhoads, Schechner
	Discourse Analysis, Speech Act	J. Botha, P. Botha
Orality & Missiology	Orality & Mission Strategies	Alberts, Hartnell, Steffen, Yoakum
	Orality & Bible Translation	Noss, Sogaard, Sundersingh, Wendland
	Ethnodoxology	Akesson, Arrington, Schrag
Orality & Education	Non-Western Ways of Knowing	Avoseh
	Teaching & Leadership Development Biblical (Practical)	Enns, ION, Jagerson, Lee, Marmon, Ponraj, West, Zahniser
	Orality & Teaching—Biblical (Researched)	Fellows, Klem, McIntyre, Moon
	Brain, Memory, Cognition, Neuroscience	Ardila, Dehaene, Sienaert
	Teaching, ESL & Culture	Condelli and Wrigley, DeCapua and Marshall, Freeman, Kern, Li
	Patient/Health Education	Doak et al.
	Orality & Learning	Avoseh, Durodeye, Lillard, Moon
Literacy	Literacy, New Literacy Studies	Gee, Heath, Stock, Street

Because the phenomenon of orality intersects with so many fields, I needed to focus my efforts by using a conceptual framework. I present one framework for examining the literature related to ALFE and orality below. De Vries maintained three debates surround orality and literacy: the linguistic (styles of writing), the anthropological (cultural differences), and the philological (oral derivatives of textual material).[133] His ideas will be discussed further; however, in my understanding, the ways of orality and ALFE learning involve a number of other important factors:

- Ways of being (ontology) or identity,[134]
- Ways of knowing or epistemology[135] and storing information,[136]
- Ways of transferring/transmitting knowledge (communicating or teaching), and
- Ways of taking knowledge from the environment or learning.[137]

Figure 2 depicts this framework and the direction for the following discussion.

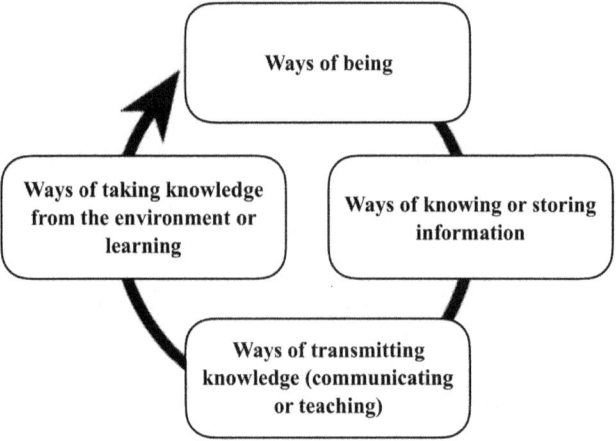

Figure 2. Conceptual framework for exploring literature on orality and ALFE learning.

---

133. Vries, "New Guinea Communities."
134. West, "Re-Eventing."
135. Belenky et al., *Women's Ways of Knowing*; Bradt, *Story as Knowing*.
136. See Hiebert, *Anthropological Insights*; *Transforming Worldviews*; Hiebert cited in Ponraj and Sah, "Communication Bridges"; Hiebert et al., *Understanding Folk Religion*.
137. Heath, "What No Bedtime Story Means," 49.

Orality, ALFE Learning, and Ways of Being

Ways of being and ways of knowing—or ontology and epistemology—have direct impact on teaching, communicating, and learning. As mentioned previously, West viewed orality as a sociocultural identity, one into which learners are socialized.[138] Possessing literacy or not possessing literacy skills could be seen as a way of being, as the two worlds seem to differ on several levels, including their pedagogies. Both Li and Cutz analyzed this kind of "sociocultural discourse,"[139] Li calling it a "cultural mismatch"[140] and Cutz an "emic-etic conflict."[141] Watson delved into "interpreting across the abyss" in her "hermeneutic exploration" of English students with limited formal schooling, noting the wide socio-cultural differences in identity across the continuum.[142]

Similarly, Aterianus-Owanga entitled her research article on orality and music, "Orality Is My Reality," noting the Gabonese youth involved constructed identities that are distinctly and proudly orally based.[143] Parker[144] and Waters[145] investigated the lived experience of illiterate adults in the US and their studies related the situation of oral learners to literate scholars. However, just how different are readers and non-readers? The classic work examining this issue was written by Ong in 1982.

ORALITY, ONG, AND OTHERS. A number of works preceded Ong's seminal *Orality and Literacy*, but his emerged as the most influential.[146] According to Chandler,[147] works by Goody, Goody and Watt, Havelock, Levi-Strauss, McLuhan, and Ong brought the idea of orality to greater attention.[148] McLuhan's *Gutenberg Galaxy* focused on media, while Goody's *Domestication of the Savage Mind* included media and cognition. Ong provided an extensive bibliography but omitted one notable figure—Innis

---

138. West, "Re-Eventing."
139. Li, *Culturally Contested Pedagogy*, 185.
140. Li, *Culturally Contested Pedagogy*, 196.
141. Cutz, "Emic-Etic Conflicts," 64.
142. Watson, "Interpreting across the Abyss," 1.
143. Aterianus-Owanga, "Orality Is My Reality."
144. Parker, "Adults' Perspectives."
145. Waters, "Exploration of the Lived Experiences."
146. Sterne, "Theology of Sound."
147. Chandler, "Biases of the Ear."
148. See Goody, *Interface*; Goody and Watt, "Consequences of Literacy"; Havelock, *Muse Learns to Write*; Levi-Strauss, *Savage Mind;* McLuhan, *Gutenberg Galaxy*; Ong, *Orality and Literacy.*

and *The Bias of Communication*, along with his other works.[149] In addition, many of Ong's ideas stemmed from Jousse's work, mostly ignored by scholars because of its French origins.[150] Figure 3 displays the influences on Ong's writing and thought.

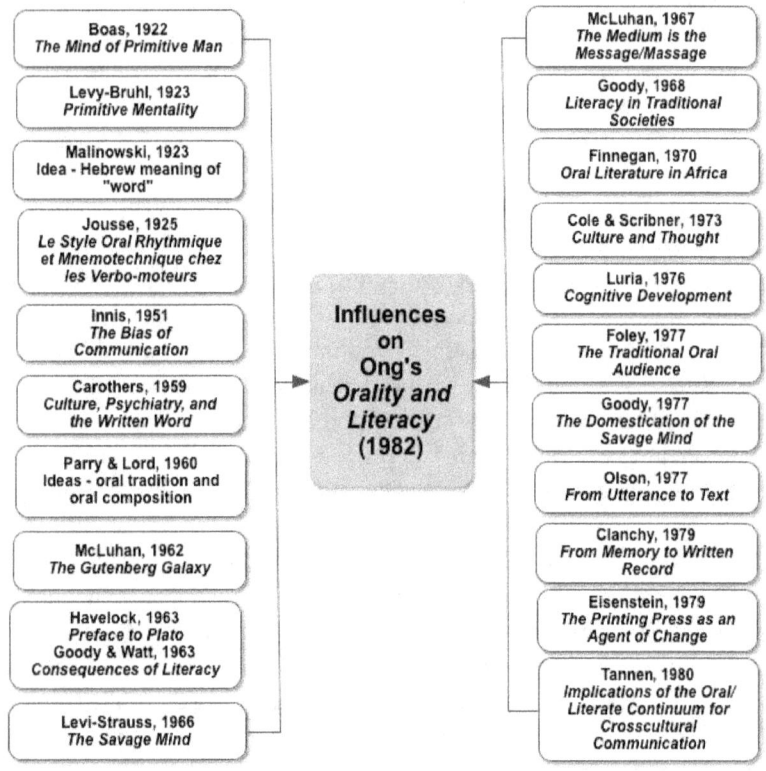

Figure 3. Influences on the work of Ong (1982).

Ong's work greatly influenced writings on orality—to the point many pieces seem to be a repetition of his thoughts—like Ongites spouting Ongese.[151] In describing this phenomenon, I mean no disrespect but rather desire to emphasize the dearth of original research with oral learners. Ong's important thought was not produced from long hours of empirical study with oral learners. A literature professor, he only developed a conceptual study. Cruikshank had similar misgivings, stating, "I recall reading Ong, Havelock, and Innis years ago, intrigued by their arguments but troubled

149. Ong, *Orality and Literacy*.
150. Jousse, *Oral Style*.
151. See Draper, "Confessional Western"; Farrell, "Walter Ong's Thought."

that none of these theoretical giants had actually spent much time talking with oral storytellers."[152]

Ong explained that his writing described primary oral cultures,[153] which is not the situation in Cambodia. Here we have a mixture of illiterate with functionally illiterate, of poverty and lack, of difficulties with memory, of those not accustomed to memorizing the oral epics of some tribes. What happens in the mind of the almost literate, the no longer oral? That phenomenon remains to be studied. Ong believed that "it takes only a moderate degree of literacy to make a tremendous difference in thought processes."[154] That may be true; however, Ong was not a neuroscientist and not qualified to make that claim. On the other hand, neuroscience researchers Kosmidis et al. determined "semantic processing strategies" to be equivalent in literates and nonliterates.[155] Dias et al. also recognized both schooled and unschooled participants could "reason from unfamiliar premises" with prompting.[156]

Repeating the idea of dichotomy, Chandler contrasted those who prefer to learn with their ears (speech) with those who prefer to learn with their eyes (writing).[157] Ong's work is filled with those contrasts, of which many like to quote. Havelock, a contemporary of Ong, concluded people were not naturally readers and writers but were natural oral communicators.[158] Defending the dichotomy for purposes of scholarship and understanding, Swearingen maintained,

> Contrary to charges of ethnocentrism or even racism which have been brought against the literate-oral dichotomy, the ongoing investigation of that dichotomy can focus on cultural similarities as well as differences and in so doing correct ethnocentric bias. What significant cultural, cognitive, or linguistic features divide those who are literate and those who aren't?[159]

Alternately, de Vries summarized Ong's oft-quoted "picture of primary orality" as consisting of "the additive parataxis from the linguistic debate, the context-bound concreteness from the anthropological debate, and the formulacity from the philological debate."[160] Studying a true primary oral

152. Cruikshank, "Orality and Literacy," 712.
153. Ong, *Orality and Literacy* (2002), 6.
154. Ong, *Orality and Literacy* (1982), 50.
155. Kosmidis et al., "Semantic and Phonological Processing," 818.
156. Dias et al., "Reasoning from Unfamiliar."
157. Chandler, "Biases of the Ear."
158. Havelock, "Alphabetic Mind."
159. Swearingen, "Oral Hermeneutics," 150.
160. Vries, "New Guinea Communities," 399.

culture first hand, de Vries debunked quite a number of Ong's findings, stating that Ong's

> qualifications as a rule did not emerge from empirical study of specific primary oral societies in their historical unicity but seem to result from universalistic projections on these societies, of pictures from various academic debates such as the Homeric debate, the debate of written versus oral style in English, and the anthropological debate on cognitive dichotomies.[161]

The only characteristic de Vries noticed to be true in his study was the "intention and action nature of primary oral metalanguage."[162]

McLuhan asserted that a shift to literacy in Africa made "a sharp division in experience, giving to its user an eye for an ear, and freeing him from the tribal trance of resonating word magic and the web of kinship."[163] Now, however, the differences are no longer limited to a dichotomy. Three "eras" have been introduced: oral, literate, and electronic;[164] so, a number of types or levels of orality and literacy exist. Street argued the previous descriptions of literacy followed an "autonomous model"—as if literacy stood alone from other influences—and one that imposed "western conceptions of literacy on to other cultures or within a country, those of one class or cultural group onto others."[165] Instead, Street touted the idea of "multiple literacies." The literature on functional illiteracy and semi-literacy is sparse and much research needs to be conducted in these areas.

As Shuter noted, "Few field studies have been conducted on oral societies. . . . Reported studies on orality have been limited to ethnographic and historical analysis of oral literature and investigation of oral traditions."[166] Even thirty years after Shuter's work, definite gaps in field research on orality still exist. His older research on the communication patterns of Hmong refugees I find more reliable and more intriguing than Ong's exploration based on literature studies. For instance, Shuter created an orality continuum of sorts, comparing the exclusively oral with "high-residual orality" and "low-residual orality," one of the primary differences being whether "words, objects, and events" were inseparable, closely connected, or separate.[167] Shuter

---

161. Vries, "New Guinea Communities," 397.
162. Vries, "New Guinea Communities," 403.
163. McLuhan, *Essential McLuhan*, 122.
164. See Ong, *Orality and Literacy*; Sterne, "Theology of Sound."
165. Street, "Autonomous and Ideological Models," 2.
166. Shuter, "Hmong of Laos," 103.
167. Shuter, "Hmong of Laos," 108.

related that both literate and oral Hmong communicated in "oral stylistic patterns" and referred to this phenomenon as "residual orality."[168]

In a similar vein, Motty proposed, "To be oral is to be relational and people-oriented."[169] In this regard I appreciate Fasheh's piece on "How to Eradicate Illiteracy without Eradicating Illiterates," in which he dealt with feelings of being highly educated, working at Harvard University, and having an illiterate mother.[170]

Ong maintained his work dealt with cultures having no written language.[171] Street, on the other hand, appraised various cultures and multiple literacies.[172] We do find that one does not understand the other, but they are not a simple dichotomy. While oral people can become literate, those who are highly literate cannot revert to being "oral." Street maintained the "autonomous model of literacy" assumes literacy is the hero of the poor and illiterate, a belief which, he maintained, "disguises the cultural and ideological assumptions that underpin it so that it can then be presented as though they are neutral and universal."[173] Literacy reigns, then, as a definite hegemonic figure.

If the Great Divide were guilty of making literacy autonomous, did Ong also err in using an autonomous or even a juxtaposed model of orality? Collins and Blot would reply in the affirmative.[174] Finnegan avowed, "The accumulating empirical evidence . . . demonstrates that the postulated characteristics of each type simply do not always predictably follow."[175] Finally, Biakolo gave sage advice: "Several scholars seem unable to make any serious theoretical sense of orality except in contrast to literacy" and "until clarity is achieved at these preliminary level, the discourse of orality and literacy will continue to be bedeviled by the sort of cyclical reasoning we have seen so far."[176]

ORALITY, ALFE LEARNING, AND OTHERNESS. In development and educational arenas, orality or illiteracy is often portrayed as something to be fixed versus a situation to be embraced as it is.[177] Many seem to view orality/

---

168. Shuter, "Hmong of Laos," 106.
169. Motty, "Contextualizing Theological Education," 155.
170. Hu, "Eradicate Illiteracy."
171. Ong, *Orality and Literacy.*
172. Street, *Social Literacies.*
173. Street, "Autonomous and Ideological Models," 1.
174. Collins and Blot, *Literacy and Literacies.*
175. Finnegan, *Literacy and Orality,* 313.
176. Biakolo, "Theoretical Foundations," 62.
177. Maddox, "What Good Is Literacy?"

illiteracy as merely a liminal state on the path to literacy. While lack of education has been related to poverty and ill health[178] and reportedly costs $1.19 trillion USD yearly,[179] is illiteracy the disability it has been portrayed as? Ardila et al., in a literature review of "the neuropsychology of cognition without reading," recounted four reasons to study illiteracy, none of which were to better teach the learners in the situation in which they presently live.[180] Nearly all studies assume movement toward literacy at some point. Literates creating this sense of "otherness" in regard to lacking literacy, labeling it as something other than the norm, seems harsh.[181] Fingeret's dissertation agreed:

> Definitions of literacy are used to sort people into categories of "literate" or "illiterate." As such, they are normative; "literacy" represents an ideal state. The sorting process occurs in the dominant class, and the criteria, therefore, represent dominant-class norms.[182]

While I do not disagree that there are benefits to learning to read and illiteracy has historically traveled hand in hand with poverty, I do see the road to literacy as long and arduous, sometimes paved with defeat and reversion.[183] I am a proponent of literacy studies. However, my main concern is for oral learners in their present moment. How do they learn without reading skills right now? How can we teach in an effective manner according to the ways they naturally learn, whether a person chooses the road to literacy or not? It seems most would rather talk about renovating the situation than entering the oral world as it already is—this world belonging to millions of people.[184]

Heath, in her seminal study of the reading habits of three societal groups, noted, "Strict dichotomization between oral and literate traditions is a construct of researchers, not an accurate portrayal of reality across cultures."[185] Ong's dichotomy was not created consequent to field research but rather largely through his analysis of literature—most notably his study of Ramus as well as a supposed difference in Hebrew and Greek

---

178. Miller and Rodgers, "Mother's Education."
179. Cree et al., *Economic and Social Cost*.
180. Ardila et al., "Illiteracy."
181. See Borrero et al., "School as a Context"; Hiebert, "Western Images of Others."
182. Fingeret, "Illiterate Underclass," 83.
183. Lovejoy, "Extent of Orality."
184. Barrett et al., "Christian World Communions."
185. Heath, "What No Bedtime Story Means," 73.

thought.[186] I find this concerning, giving impetus to research oral/ALFE ways and compare findings.

Approaching the idea of more of a continuum between orality and literacy, Slack delineated several steps on the educational ladder:

1. The primary orality described by Ong, then

2. Functional illiteracy, where "competency is somewhere between first grade and the eighth grade," next

3. Semi-literacy, in which individuals have not yet completed their high school education, and finally

4. Literacy.[187]

However, even this listing assumes a progression toward literacy and away from primary orality.

Alternately, the International Adult Literacy Survey, conducted in over twenty-three countries from 1994 through 1998, proposed five levels of literacy, with Level 3 being the minimum for functioning in literate society.[188] Finally, Ong proposed the states of primary orality and the secondary orality of modernity in his contrast with literacy,[189] while Rao preferred the term "contemporary orality" for non-primary oral participants in India.[190] According to Swearingen, the problems with "the Great Divide hypothesis" and the oral-literate dichotomy promoted by Ong and others involve issues of ethnocentricity, discourse, and setting.[191] In reality, the world cannot be divided neatly and simply into readers and non-readers.

Orality, ALFE Learning, and Ways of Knowing

Finnegan inquired, "Does non-literacy have consequences for modes of thinking? Do non-literates *ipso facto* think differently from literates?"[192] Comparing oral literature and that composed by literates, Finnegan viewed orality as a "huge and complicated subject—far too complex to be reduced to trite classifications or the categorization implied when we facilely define

---

186. See Ong, *Presence of the Word*; Soukup, "In Commemoration"; Sterne, "Theology of Sound."
187. Slack et al., *Memory and Recall*, 6.
188. OECD, *Literacy in the Information Age*, xi.
189. Ong, *Orality and Literacy*.
190. Rao, "Contemporary Orality," 7.
191. Swearingen, "Oral Hermeneutics."
192. Finnegan, "Literacy versus Non-Literacy," 112.

certain groups as 'non-literate' and unthinkingly go on to assume consequences from this for the nature of their thought."[193]

Hiebert et al. delineated three means of storing information,[194] but listed a large number in other works, stating, "In oral societies, knowledge is stored in the forms of stories, parables, songs, aphorisms, proverbs, riddles, poems, creeds, and catechisms that can be easily remembered. It is also stored in rituals that are living reenactments of primordial events."[195] This section addresses the intersection of orality and the literature in two major areas—narrative and non-narrative means of storing knowledge.

NARRATIVE STUDIES. Bradt described story as a way of knowing.[196] Similarly, Steffen discussed the "foundational roles of symbol and narrative in the (re)construction of reality and relationships."[197] Bruner proposed two modes of thought—paradigmatic and narrative.[198] Indeed, narrative can be a way of knowing, a way of storing knowledge, a way of transferring knowledge (teaching and/or communicating), and a way of forming worldview and identity within social relationships.[199] Neuroscience research has highlighted the influence of stories on brain processes.[200] Indeed, stories are powerful. Narratives embody truth and carry embedded secrets. Stories can change lives and worldviews—whether one is literate or non-literate.

Works on storytelling and the use and power of narrative are equally abundant—in the fields of neuroscience, science, communication, management, persuasion, development, qualitative research, and education as well as teacher education and professional development.[201] Applied orality

---

193. Finnegan, "Literacy versus Non-Literacy," 144.
194. Hiebert et al., *Understanding Folk Religion*.
195. Hiebert, *Anthropological Insights*; *Transforming Worldviews*, 116.
196. Bradt, *Story as a Way of Knowing*.
197. Steffen, "Foundational Roles of Symbol," 477.
198. Bruner, *Actual Minds*.
199. Steffen, "Tracking the Orality Movement," 145.
200. See Brennan et al., "Syntactic Structure Building"; Hasson, "I Can Make Your Brain Look Like Mine."
201. See Andrews et al., "Storytelling as an Instructional Method: Descriptions"; Andrews et al., *Storytelling as an Instructional Method: Research*; Baskin, "Complexity, Stories, and Knowing"; Brennan et al., "Syntactic Structure Building"; Carter, "Place of Story"; Clark, "Narrative Learning: Its Contours"; Clark and Rossiter, "Narrative Learning in Adulthood"; Fisher, "Narration as a Human"; "Narrative Paradigm"; "Clarifying the Narrative Paradigm"; Gartner et al., "Power of Narrative"; Gershon and Page, "What Storytelling Can Do"; Green and Brock, "Role of Transportation"; Harbin and Humphrey, "Teaching Management"; Hasson, "I Can Make Your Brain Look Like Mine"; Haven, *Story Proof*; Linde, "Narrative and Social"; McQuiggan et al., "Story-Based

proponents in the field of missiology have also latched onto narrative with fervor and rightly so. Works on storying come from Boomershine, Bradt, Colgate, Corcoran, Koehler, Loewen, Lovejoy, McIlwain, Norwood, Pederson, Reinsborough and Canning, Robinson, Salisbury, Singerman, Slack et al., So, Stahl, Steffen, and Terry, besides numerous popular works on storying, biblical storytelling, and Chronological Bible Storying as well as Bible storying sets worldwide.[202]

In a critical examination of the literature surrounding orality in Christian circles, one would not be amiss in concluding many of those writing seem to equate orality with the use of narrative. However, orality involves much more. In fact, even the word *orality* seems problematic, an attempt to supply an antonym for the word *literacy*. In my years of experience with oral learners, I have noticed they are not exclusively oral. They can be quite visual or kinesthetic. They can also be social and observational in their learning. What of other approaches? Does the Christian use of orality strategies have only one string on which to strum? As Wilson related,

> Those already using the chronological method and the narrative approach to evangelism and Bible teaching need also to understand the role and validity of orality—the oral counterpart of literacy and literariness. It is one thing to recognize the value of recounting the Great Story as a mission strategy; but we also need to pay attention to the oral context.[203]

I inspect strategies beyond storying and the use of narrative in the next section.

Learning"; Mello, "Power of Storytelling"; Montgomery and Kumar, "Telling Stories"; Mott et al., "Narrative-Centered Learning"; Rossiter, "Narrative Approach to Development"; Rossiter, *Narrative and Stories*; Schrader, "Performing Narrative"; Slater and Rouner, "Entertainment-Education"; Strothmann, "Narrative Persuasion"; Swap et al., "Using Mentoring"; Vitz, "Use of Stories"; Willis, "Scheherazade's Secret"; Yackley, "Storytelling."

202. See Boomershine, "Biblical Storytelling"; *Story Journey*; Bradt, *Story as a Way of Knowing*; Colgate, "Part I"; "Part II"; Corcoran, "Biblical Narratives"; Koehler, "Telling God's Stories"; Loewen, "Bible Stories"; Lovejoy, "Chronological Bible Storying"; McIlwain, *Firm Foundations*; Norwood, "Developing a Course"; Pederson, "Biblical Narrative"; Reinsborough and Canning, *RE:Imagining Change*; Robinson, "Gospel as Story"; Salisbury, "Testing Narrative Theory"; Singerman, "Orality Observations"; Slack et al., "Chronological Bible Storying"; Slack et al., "Realities of Orality"; Slack et al., *Memory and Recall*; So, "Theological Institution Prepare Students"; Stahl, "Telling Our Stories Well"; Steffen, "Storying the Storybook"; "Foundational Roles of Symbol"; *Reconnecting God's Story*; "My Journey"; "Pedagogical Conversions"; "Chronological Communication"; "Chronological Practices"; Steffen and Terry, "Sweeping Story of Scripture"; Terry, "In Defense of 'Storying.'"

203. Wilson, "Let the Earth Hear," 154.

BEYOND STORYING. An array of literature, some practical and some researched, represent these oral ways of knowing and storing information beyond the use of narrative. Much of the literature in this area comes from the field of missiology. Madinger's treatise on orality rightly proposed a more holistic approach, including more than storytelling.[204] His diagram incorporated elements he called "seven disciplines of orality" that should frame oral content. However, I see his diagram as more of an outsider's etic approach to orality than one directly incorporating researched elements from the emic world of an oral person and their needs.

Dyer's dissertation proposed the use of storytelling, song, and drama "in health education, evangelism, and Christian maturation."[205] Avoseh, Keysser, McIntyre, Moon, and others examined ways of using proverbs, drama, rituals, and ceremonies with oral peoples.[206] Arrington discovered the Lisu retained their Christian faith through their hymns,[207] which functioned as "storage language"[208] for "biblical abstractions."[209] Aikman investigated the ways of knowing of the Arakmbut and recognized they acquired knowledge through experience, through dreaming, and through their elders.[210] Could these strategies also contribute to the ways of learning for Cambodian ALFE?

One often neglected expert on orality, Marcel Jousse, pronounced, "I began my publications with the *Oral Style* in 1925 . . . so much so that I am now considered the discoverer of the oral style."[211] Jousse's *Le Style Oral [The Oral Style]: Rhythmique et Mnemotechnique chez les Verbo-moteurs* was written in 1925, well before Ong's classic. Focusing on the anthropology of gesture, Jousse had experience with illiteracy, contrary to Ong. His mother and most in his birthplace were non-readers. Fortunately, West revived Jousse's ideas in a recent presentation urging the "re-eventing" of theological education.[212]

In regard to movement and knowing, researchers Ardila et al. discovered "illiterates demonstrate poorer performance in a diversity of motor tests,

204. Madinger, "Coming to Terms with Orality."

205. Dyer, "Use of Oral Communication Methods."

206. See Avoseh, "Proverbs as Theoretical Frameworks"; Keysser, *People Reborn*; McIntyre, "Using Ceremonies to Disciple"; Moon, "Using Proverbs"; "Discipling"; "Rituals and Symbols"; "Using Rituals to Disciple."

207. Arrington, "Hymns as Theological Mediato"; "Hymns of the Everlasting Hills."

208. Havelock, *Muse Learns to Write*.

209. Arrington, "Hymns as Theological Mediator," 157.

210. Aikman, *Intercultural Education*.

211. Jousse, *Oral Style*, s.v. "Introduction," para. 3.

212. West, "Re-Eventing."

including reproducing movements and sequences of movements, alternating movements with both hands, and imitating meaningless movements."[213] This research would lead one to suppose that while hand motions may serve a literate audience as memory aids, they might add a difficult additional learning layer for oral learners. Ardila's literature review also presented a summary of research related to "visuoperceptual and spatial abilities," as well as memory and illiteracy. In the end the writers stated, "It is not totally accurate to assume that people with low levels of education are somehow 'deprived.' It may be more accurate to assume they have developed different types of learning, more procedural, pragmatic, and sensory oriented."[214]

There is more to reading and illiteracy than just words on a page. Hvitfeldt discussed the difficulties of using visual aids with preliterate peoples.[215] She related "reading" pictures can require additional perceptive ability, depending on the type of visual used—whether abstract or not. She also referred to Bruner's three modes of information processing—enactive (learning through the use of tools), iconic (learning through the senses), and symbolic (learning that is more abstract).[216] Similarly, Bradley et al. delved into visual literacy, a corollary concern to the study of orality and how oral adults learn.[217] Their four studies concluded visual literacy varies just as much as print literacy does.

Finally, Abadzi explored "brain architecture" and adult illiteracy and promoted "visuospatial training," such as the kind used by participatory rural appraisal (PRA) facilitators when helping "the poor articulate their existing knowledge" and in "working collectively and producing materials such as maps, calendars, matrices, and diagrams."[218] Robinson-Pant considered PRA to be a "*new literacy*, where ideas are represented visually through symbols."[219] She discussed the use of "diagramming methods as specific skills which are being introduced to non-literate, and literate, villagers"[220] and maintained "the visual aspect of PRA is seen to be a bridge between the

---

213. Ardila et al., "Illiteracy," 697.

214. Ardila et al., "Illiteracy," 707.

215. Hvitfeldt, "Picture Perception."

216. Bruner, *Actual Minds*.

217. See Bradley, *How People Use Pictures*; Bruski, "Do They Get the Picture?"; Morain, "Visual Literacy"; Smith, "Visual Art and Orality."

218. Abadzi, "Adult Illiteracy," 4.

219. Robinson-Pant, "PRA," 78.

220. Robinson-Pant, "PRA," 78.

oral and written ways of communicating and means of sharing the power usually limited to literate groups of people."[221]

In considering other elements besides storying, Keysser recounted using the "acted out Word" successfully when preaching was not well received in New Guinea in the early part of the century.[222] Moreover, Moon maintained we "look for discipling methods in all the wrong places" in dealing with oral learners.[223] In his work with West Africans, Moon investigated the use of rituals.[224] His dissertation researched using proverbs,[225] and he quipped, "We become what we hum," "rituals drive meaning to the bone," and "drama stands the Word of God on its feet."[226] Similarly, McIntyre directed his dissertation toward using ceremonies with oral people in Bangladesh.[227] In his popular work, Sample described living in an oral culture where importance was placed on "proverbs, stories, and relationships."[228]

Mission Frontiers concentrated on the emerging field of ethnodoxology in their September/October 2014 edition. Krabill authored an ethnodoxology handbook[229] and Goold provided an insightful article on using creative arts with oral learners.[230] He avowed, "For oral learners, art-making is not an optional aesthetic experience."[231] Ethnomusicologists and others have long understood the value of "indigenous media" and modes of communication.[232] Mushengyezi explained, "Communication planners should not overlook the significant role indigenous forms such as popular theatre, drumming, village criers, storytellers, orators, etc., have played—and continue to play—in communication among rural, poor communities."[233] According to Foster, African songs function as the carriers of oral theology.[234] As mentioned earlier, Arrington discovered

---

221. Robinson-Pant, "PRA," 80.
222. Keysser, *People Reborn*, 7.
223. Moon, "Discipling," 127.
224. Moon, "Understanding Oral Learners"; "Using Rituals to Disciple."
225. Moon, "Using Proverbs."
226. Moon, "Discipling," 129–32.
227. McIntyre, "Using Ceremonies to Disciple."
228. Sample, *Ministry in an Oral Culture*, 3.
229. Krabill, *Worship and Mission*.
230. Goold, "Envisioning a Model."
231. Goold, "Envisioning a Model," 1.
232. See Akesson, "Oral/Aural Culture"; Mushengyezi, "Rethinking Indigenous Media."
233. Mushengyezi, "Rethinking Indigenous Media," 107.
234. Foster, "Oral Theology."

hymns to be the means of perpetuating faith among the Lisu in China.[235] Kaartinen recognized the Bandanese in Indonesia learned and performed traditional songs as "part of producing social relationship," making for "shared experiences that unfold through time."[236]

Besides narrative, song, and drama, storing knowledge can also involve poetry, symbol, and ceremony. Zahniser, in his seminal study of ceremony and its use in Christian discipleship, did not address orality per se, but it described yet another way of knowing and storing knowledge.[237] Ethnopoetics is an emerging field intersecting with orality as well. Chetrit inspected the indigenous knowledge of illiterate women in Morocco.[238] He discovered the women possessed a broad base of "poetic and narrative oral texts" which served as carriers of wisdom in and through their performance.[239] Fuller evaluated the memory work, recitation, and chanting of monks learning ancient texts from their gurus—simple rote learning.[240] Some used no written materials at all, no kinesthetic helps, and no mnemonic devices. Their memory work was phenomenal.

Orality, ALFE Learning, and Ways of Transmitting Knowledge

A great deal of literature addressed oral ways of transferring, transmitting, or conveying knowledge, whether in ancient or modern times.[241] In this section I investigate orality and ALFE learning as it relates to communication and teaching in areas with literature relating to orality—such as applied orality in second language acquisition and biblical studies.

ORAL COMMUNICATION. Much writing in biblical studies and missiology has dealt with ways of communicating and/or teaching, methods and issues related to "applied orality."[242] Contra Ong, Finnegan described oral communication as "multiplex" and "multimodal," involving gesture and non-verbal

---

235. Arrington, "Hymns as Theological Mediator"; "Hymns of the Everlasting Hills."

236. Kaartinen, "Handing Down," 388.

237. Zahniser, *Symbol and Ceremony*.

238. Chetrit, "Textual Orality."

239. Chetrit, "Textual Orality," 101.

240. Fuller, "Orality, Literacy and Memorization."

241. See Chiang and Lovejoy, *Beyond Literate Western Practices*; Hezser, "Oral and Written Communication"; Thompson, "Nonliterate and Transfer"; Winger, "Spoken Word."

242. Madinger, "Applied Orality."

cues.[243] Departing from a simple dichotomy, she maintained oral expressions could be:

> Read, recited, sung, cantillated, chanted, declaimed, multimodally performed, communicated through audio recordings or the web, experienced in the sonic memory. They can be individually or collectively enacted, informal or liturgical, public or private, announcements by one person or dialectical engagement.[244]

In addition, both Weber's and Klem's classic studies discussed communication methods.[245] Could all these ideas inform oral Cambodian ways of learning?

Ong's classic work dealt not only with ontology, the ways of being of oral learners, but also with the characteristics of their literature, communication, and thought.[246] In this area, referring to Ong's dichotomized listings contrasting orality and literacy seems to be a standard mantra. A number of works addressed communication and orality—dealing with Bible translation, communication style, culture, preaching, and use of media.[247]

APPLIED ORALITY AND SECOND LANGUAGE ACQUISITION. The impact of orality studies has been widespread, entering the education arena—teaching English as a second language (TESOL), second language acquisition (SLA), and biblical studies. A number in academia have reported being enlightened to an oral approach—for example, Dinkins, Marmon, Moon, and Steffen.[248]

Apart from the above-mentioned literature and studies of orality as a mode of communication or literary process, the field most serious of late about the concept seems to be that of Teaching English to Speakers of Other Languages (TESOL), Teaching English as a Foreign Language (TEFL), and Second Language Acquisition (SLA).[249] Concerned educators have pondered

---

243. Finnegan, "Orality and Literacy."

244. Finnegan, "Response from an Africanist," 9.

245. Weber, *Communication of the Gospel*; Klem, *Oral Communication of the Scripture*.

246. Ong, *Orality and Literacy*.

247. See Botha, "Potential of Speech Act Theory"; "Mute Manuscripts"; "Living Voice"; Hartnell, "Oral Contextualization"; Maxey, "Bible Translation as Contextualization"; Noss, "Oral Story"; Sundersingh, "Toward a Media-Based Translation"; Thornton, "Orality and Theological Education"; Wendland, "Towards an 'Oratorical' Bible"; Winger, "Orality as the Key."

248. See Dinkins, "Presenting Orality"; Marmon, "Teaching through the Lenses"; Moon, "Rituals and Symbols"; "Understanding Oral Learners"; Steffen, "My Journey."

249. Bigelow, "Orality and Literacy"; Kern and Schultz, "Beyond Orality."

their new predicament in receiving many learners with limited formal education and now have a body of research related to illiteracy/orality.[250]

Researchers in the field of teaching English as a second language (TESOL) have produced a body of literature on teaching those who have had limited access to education. Their pragmatic teaching strategies attempt to be culturally sensitive but have yet to address how oral adults learn. DeCapua and Marshall urged, "What is needed is an overall reconceptualization of the education" of this type of learner.[251]

In the sensitive climate of western education, one concern has involved naming oral learners, a concern I also expressed in chapter 1. Brod used the term "non-readers."[252] Alcala, Gunn, McPherson, and Tarone used "preliterate."[253] Colter added the term "low literacy" for the situation of those with some reading ability.[254] Freeman et al. used the term "students with limited formal schooling."[255] A symposium on "Low Educated Second Language and Literacy Acquisition" (LESLLA) began in Canada in 2005.[256] Finally, DeCapua and Marshall dubbed these learners "students with limited or interrupted formal education" (SLIFE), an acronym which seems to have stuck.[257] All these educators are rightly concerned with pragmatic strategies for teaching their new audience, and many may be transferable to work with oral learners in other settings.

In researching "adult learners of English with little formal education," Ramirez-Esparza et al. recognized "the socio-interactive practices required in formal classrooms limit their ability to learn."[258] The researchers considered introversion and extraversion. However, I believe exploring cultural cues would have been more productive, as DeCapua and Marshall have

---

250. See Burt et al., "Working with Adult Learners"; Condelli and Wrigley, "Instruction, Language and Literacy"; DeCapua and Marshall, "Serving ELLs"; "Students with Limited"; DeCapua et al., *Meeting the Needs*; Freeman et al., "Keys to Success"; Ramirez-Esparza et al., "Socio-Interactive Practices"; Vinogradov and Bigelow, "Using Oral Language Skills"; Weinstein, "Literacy and Second Language Acquisition."

251. DeCapua and Marshall, "Serving ELLs," 51.

252. Brod, *What Readers Need to Know*.

253. See Alcala, *Preliterate Student*; Gunn, "Opportunity for Literacy?"; McPherson, *Modes of Delivery*; Tarone, "Second Language Acquisition."

254. Colter, "Audience."

255. Freeman et al., "Keys to Success."

256. See Craats et al., "Research on Literacy Acquisition"; Wall and Leong, "Tradition Continues."

257. DeCapua and Marshall, "Students with Limited."

258. Ramirez-Esparza et al., "Socio-Interactive Practices," 542.

done.²⁵⁹ Ramirez-Esparza et al. concluded low-education learners "behave in more introverted ways" and have more to learn than others.²⁶⁰ This is an obvious conclusion for anyone who has worked with oral learners, especially in a cross-cultural situation. In addition, Ramirez-Esparza et al. acknowledged, "Low-education learners need to learn the socio-interactive practices of how to participate and what to attend to in the classroom"—also an obvious conclusion that can be gleaned from social learning.²⁶¹ Students growing up attending western schools have already been socialized to understand the hidden curriculum of the classroom setting, which would be quite unfamiliar to those from other countries or those not exposed to classroom learning.²⁶² Rightly, however, Ramirez-Esparza et al. also surmised,

> Adult language-learning students without a great deal of experience with formal education have likely experienced learning in this apprentice-mentor or socialization model in which observation and learning through practice allows one to move from legitimate peripheral participation to fuller participation through contextualized practice.²⁶³

So, what would be wrong with utilizing these students' preferred learning methods?

Written before the research just discussed, DeCapua and Marshall addressed those foundational issues and that very question.²⁶⁴ DeCapua and Marshall have worked hard to meet the needs of SLIFE, but opined,

> Through classroom observation and mentoring teachers, we have identified reasons why SLIFE may not succeed, despite these excellent recommendations and strategies. We argue that these are only pieces of a larger puzzle. What is needed is an overall reconceptualization of the education of SLIFE.²⁶⁵

Does this sound familiar? They continued, "When SLIFE enter the US schools, they are confronted with a contrasting way of approaching learning

---

259. DeCapua and Marshall, "Students with Limited."
260. Ramirez-Esparza et al., "Socio-Interactive Practices," 564.
261. Ramirez-Esparza et al., "Socio-Interactive Practices," 562.
262. See Jarvis, *Adult Learning*; LeCompte, "Learning to Work"; Main, "'Other Half.'"
263. Ramirez-Esparza et al., "Socio-Interactive Practices," 544.
264. DeCapua and Marshall, "Students with Limited."
265. DeCapua and Marshall, "Students with Limited," 51.

and organizing knowledge."²⁶⁶ What happens when expatriates go to other cultures in teaching capacities? Something similar happens in reverse.

As a prescriptive measure, DeCapua and Marshall developed the "Mutually Adaptive Learning Paradigm" (MALP), practices of which those who work in cross-cultural settings would do well to note.²⁶⁷ Including the ideas of "immediate relevance, interconnectedness, shared responsibility, oral transmission, and pragmatic tasks," MALP has rightly become very popular with TESOL educators and others teaching students from various cultures.

APPLIED ORALITY AND BIBLICAL STUDIES. Even though the body of research related to orality and education is large in the TESOL/SLA fields, as Ong observed, "Orality-literacy theorems challenge biblical study perhaps more than any other field of learning, for over the centuries, biblical study has generated what is doubtlessly the most massive body of textual commentary in the world."²⁶⁸ Turning to review literature related to orality in fields related to biblical studies, one discovers a plethora of writings. Most of the work in this field does not discuss having limited formal education. The situation of ALFE is included in the concept of orality, not separating non-readers, those with limited reading ability, from those who are proficient readers but prefer oral methods in learning or those who are readers but not yet proficient.

The majority of these writings are practical, relating to applied orality.²⁶⁹ The International Orality Network has produced a great deal of material in this area in the form of their *Orality Journals* and their compilations of meetings dealing with theological education.²⁷⁰ The remaining literature can be divided loosely as follows:

- Academia and higher education²⁷¹
- Applied orality and missiology²⁷²
- Audio communication²⁷³

266. DeCapua and Marshall, "Students with Limited," 52.

267. DeCapua and Marshall, "Students with Limited."

268. Ong, *Orality and Literacy* (1982), 169.

269. Madinger, "Applied Orality."

270. See Chiang and Lovejoy, *Beyond Literate Western Models*; *Beyond Literate Western Practices*.

271. See Dinkins, "Presenting Orality"; Marmon, "Teaching through the Lenses"; Moon, "Encouraging Ducks to Swim"; "Teaching Oral Learners."

272. Steffen, "Orality Comes of Age."

273. See Klem, "Dependence on Literacy Strategy"; Starling, "Audio-Communications"; Wilson, "Let the Earth Hear."

- Bible translation and Scripture engagement[274]
- Church planting[275]
- Contextualizing approaches with oral peoples, designing appropriate educational endeavors, worldview perspectives, and communication[276]
- Evangelization, evangelism, discipleship, and Christian maturity[277]
- Hermeneutics/interpretation[278]
- Homiletics instruction[279]
- Leaders, leadership training, and development[280]
- Missiology[281]
- Oral transmission, oral tradition, and canon construction[282]

274. See Ansre, "Crucial Role of Oral Scripture"; Dye, "Scripture in an Accessible Form"; Franklin, "Part II"; Green, "Orality Strategy"; Leatherwood, "Case and Call for Oral Bibles"; Porter, "Using the Non-Print Media"; Sogaard, "Emergence of Audio-Scriptures"; Wafler, "Interrelationship of Orality."

275. See Arlund, "Church Planting Movements"; Bowman, "Communicating Christ"; Bush, "Effective Church Planting"; Ponraj and Sah, "Communication Bridges."

276. See Abraham, "Contextualized Theological Education"; Adeney, "Feeding Giraffes"; Brown, "Designing Programs"; "Communicating Effectively"; Hill, "Conversations about Orality"; Klem, *Oral Communication of the Scripture*; Morales, "Worldview and Learning Perspective"; Motty, "Contextualizing Theological Education"; Naylor, "Towards Contextualized Bible Storying"; Wiher, "Worldview and Oral Preference."

277. See Atkins, "Multiplying Disciples"; Brown, "Communicating Effectively"; "How to Make Oral Communication More Effective"; Chiang, "Oral Reality"; Davis, "Is That Really God?"; DeNeui, *Communicating Christ*; Dyer, "Use of Oral Communication Methods"; Franklin, "Part I"; Lovejoy, *Making Disciples of Oral Learners*; Lucien, "Relationship of Illiteracy"; McIlwain, *Firm Foundations*; McIntyre, "Using Ceremonies to Disciple"; Moon, "Using Proverbs"; "Discipling through the Eyes"; Nguyen, "Orality—A Tool"; Sells, "Discipleship Revolution"; Smither, "Celtic Approach"; Steffen, *Reconnecting God's Story*; Weber, *Communication of the Gospel*; Weerstra, "Editorial"; Wilson, "What It Takes to Reach People."

278. See Bryan and Landon, *Listening to the Bible*; Rynkiewich, "Mission, Hermeneutics, and the Local Church."

279. Anderson, "Implicit Rhetorical Theory."

280. See Balingnasay, "Training in the Philippines"; Bekker, "Empowering Oral Learners"; Evans, "You Think in Lines"; Howell, "Memorization and Maturation"; Overstreet, "Fruitful Labor"; "Theological Education."

281. See Alberts, "Catholic Written and Oral Cultures"; Prior, "Orality"; Yoakum, "Spoken Word."

282. See Bjoraker, "'People of the Book'"; Carr, "Torah on the Heart"; Fishman, "Guarding Oral Transmission"; Harvey, "Orality and Its Implications"; Hezser, "Oral and Written Communication"; Jaffee, "Rabbinic Ontology"; Klem, "Bible as Oral Literature"; Walton and Sandy, *Lost World of Scripture*.

- Prayer[283]
- Socialization studies and curriculum development[284]
- Theological education and Bible study or Bible teaching[285]
- Theology, oral[286]

Sheard proposed a plan for "Biblical Oral Pedagogy" and delineated his success in teaching non-narrative passages, helping oral learners with theology and using "parabolic engagement," and more oral-friendly teaching strategies.[287] His short book is worth considering for missionaries and those involved in grassroots theological education.

Noticeably lacking, however, are a few types of studies, such as the history of orality in missions. Steffen and Terry analyzed the flow of McIlwain's work in biblical storying[288] from the Philippines outward, but there is scant research on the use of narrative in mission work through the centuries.[289] Missing as well are works in areas like oral hermeneutics or ways for oral learners to study non-narrative Bible portions. The only examples at present are Swearingen[290] and Chifungo.[291]

Even in surveying mission history, it would seem Christian workers were slow in adapting their methods for teaching those who could not read. In testimonies of missionaries using stories or drama, workers seemed almost apologetic.[292] Many appeared to operate from a presupposition that people must learn to read in order to understand the Bible and become church leaders.

Considering orality and Biblical studies, Dewey maintained that few in the early days of Christianity were readers, literacy not being essential for the

---

283. Wootton, "Freedom of the Spirit."

284. Steffen, "Socialization among the Ifugao."

285. See Chan, "Storytelling Seeking Understanding"; Chiang and Lovejoy, *Beyond Literate Western Models* and *Beyond Literate Western Practices*; Chemengich, "Case of Africa"; Dinkins, "Objections and Benefits"; Fellows, "Training of Semiliterate"; Irving, "Orality Applied"; Kwabena, "Narrative Theology in Dialectic"; Steffen, "What if?"; Thompson, "Helping Adults Learn"; Thornton, "Constructivism"; Verghese, "Oral Bible Story Telling"; Walker, "Africa Theological Seminary."

286. See Naude, "Theology with a New Voice?"; Pobee, "Oral Theology."

287. Sheard, *Orality Primer*.

288. McIlwain, *Firm Foundations*.

289. See Steffen, "Orality Comes of Age"; "Tracking the Orality Movement"; Steffen and Terry, "Sweeping Story of Scripture."

290. Swearingen, "Oral Hermeneutics."

291. Chifungo, "Oral Hermeneutics."

292. See Keysser, *People Reborn*.

daily living of the majority.²⁹³ According to Dewey, in those days letters were designed to be read aloud to groups and professional traveling storytellers abounded.²⁹⁴ These kinds of historical studies serve to inform this research and situate the Scriptures among people much like those in Cambodia, a people "of the earth" and with no perceived need for reading.

Orality, ALFE, and Ways of Learning

In her classic study, Heath advised understanding how "different social groups 'take' knowledge from the environment."²⁹⁵ Aikman researched the ways of knowing of the Arakmbut and identified they acquired knowledge through experience, through dreaming, and through their elders, as mentioned earlier.²⁹⁶ She compared the context, medium, content, and structure of their informal learning with that of traditional schooling. DeCapua and Marshall discovered SLIFE (Students with Limited or Interrupted Formal Education) "have different priorities and different, nonacademic ways of perceiving and construing the world around them; and they are used to seeing learning as being of immediate benefit or relevance."²⁹⁷ Ways of taking knowledge and ways of learning included aspects surrounding cognition, delivery, environment, religion, self, and society, each represented in the conceptual framework in Figure 4 I created for exploring the research questions at hand.

---

293. Dewey, *Orality and Textuality*; "Textuality in an Oral Culture."
294. Dewey, "Textuality in an Oral Culture."
295. Heath, "What No Bedtime Story Means," 74.
296. Aikman, *Intercultural Education and Literacy*.
297. DeCapua and Marshall, "Students with Limited," 52.

Introductory Literature Review: *The Context and Construct* 55

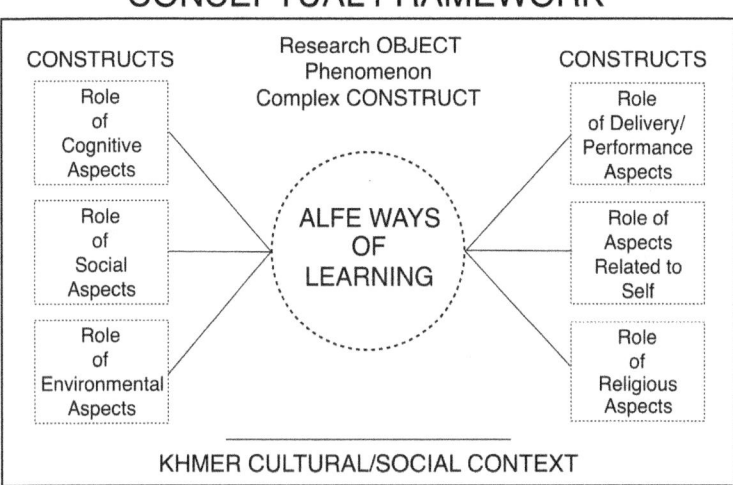

Figure 4. Conceptual framework for researching oral/ALFE ways of learning.

While Heath researched three different societal groups and their ways with books, she advised using ethnography to understand this idea of taking knowledge.[298] Some groups relied on "literacy events" and some did not. Heath asserted: "'Ways of taking' from books are a part of culture and as such are more varied than current dichotomies between oral and literate traditions and relational and analytic cognitive styles would suggest."[299] Basu et al., in the arena of economics, made a case for the vital social aspects of a non-literate having access to a literate person for reading assistance, a practice common historically before widespread schooling in the western world.[300] They maintained, "Literacy . . . is something like a public good in that a literate agent confers a positive externality on the illiterate agents in the household by sharing the benefits of his or her literacy."[301] Therefore, in their estimation drawn from data in Bangladesh, the idea of proximate (proximal) illiteracy versus isolated illiteracy was of major importance. Their wise concept for group-oriented cultures could bring an efficient strategy to literacy programs, helping target households with no access to one literate person, as opposed to trying to teach every person to read.

298. Heath, "What No Bedtime Story Means."
299. Heath, "What No Bedtime Story Means," 49.
300. Basu et al., *Isolated and Proximate Illiteracy*.
301. Basu et al., *Isolated and Proximate Illiteracy*, 2.

Most closely related to ways of learning, Fanta-Vagenshtein concentrated on learning channels, intersecting with my proposed study.[302] That work began with an exploration of learning and touched briefly on illiteracy, while I do the opposite. Diouf, Sheckley, and Kehrhahn questioned, "What, when, why, how, and from whom do adults in African villages learn?"[303] My study concentrated on the how and from whom. Kilpatrick and Johns investigated how farmers learned, approached change, and whom they consulted.[304] Thompson's study considered "preparing the western-educated literate to be effective in the transfer of knowledge in traditional West African nonliterate communities."[305] Merriam and Ntseane inspected transformative learning and culture in Botswana,[306] while Merriam and Mohamad examined "how cultural values shape learning in older adulthood" in Malaysia.[307] For those Malaysian participants, "'school' is not seen as a place for learning once one has become an adult."[308] Later, Merriam and Mohamad's results will be compared with the research findings of this study.

Additional research most directly relevant to the study of oral ways of learning include Avoseh and the study of proverbs in Africa;[309] Klem's classic work on "oral communication of the Scripture";[310] Merriam[311] and Merriam and Kim's[312] exploration of "non-western perspectives on learning and knowing"; along with Ong,[313] Slack's discussions stemming from Ong's work,[314] and Weber's accounts.[315]

According to research, non-print learners and print learners think differently.[316] In probing ways of learning, Lado delineated "ways in which Spanish-speaking illiterates differ from literates in an ESL classroom."[317]

302. Fanta-Vagenshtein, "How Illiterate People Learn."
303. Diouf et al., "Adult Learning," 32.
304. Kilpatrick and Johns, "How Farmers Learn."
305. Thompson, "Nonliterate and the Transfer," 4.
306. Merriam and Ntseane, "Transformational Learning in Botswana."
307. Merriam and Mohamad, "How Cultural Values Shape Learning."
308. Merriam and Mohamad, "How Cultural Values Shape Learning," 52.
309. Avoseh, "Proverbs as Theoretical Frameworks."
310. Klem, *Oral Communication of the Scripture*.
311. Merriam, *Non-Western Perspectives*.
312. Merriam and Kim, "Non-Western Perspectives."
313. Ong, *Orality and Literacy*.
314. Slack et al., "Realities of Orality"; Slack et al., *Memory and Recall*.
315. Weber, *Communication of the Gospel*.
316. Castro-Caldas and Reis, "Neurobiological Substrates"; Castro-Caldas et al., "Illiterate Brain"; Castro-Caldas et al., "Neuropsychological Aspects."
317. Lado, *Ways in Which Spanish-Speaking Illiterates*, 1.

Also significant in taking stock of ways of learning, Watson delved into "interpreting across the abyss" in her "hermeneutic exploration" of English students with limited formal schooling.[318] She offered assistance navigating between the literate world and its oral counterpart. Likewise, Parker's dissertation filled a gap by giving perspective to the lives of illiterate adults in the United States.[319] Similarly, Waters considered "the lived experiences of illiterate African American adults" in the United States as well.[320] However, none of these studies addressed how adults with limited formal education learn, especially in the Cambodian context.

In regard to literate practices, Ong claimed, "Writing and reading . . . are solo activities (though reading at first was often done communally). They engage the psyche in strenuous, interiorized, individualized thought of a sort inaccessible to oral folk."[321] Like many in the applied orality community, Lovejoy insisted: "What sets orality apart is *reliance* on spoken language. To the extent that people rely on spoken communication instead of written communication, they are characterized by 'orality.'"[322] Is this true? Abney created an orality assessment for considering such "learning styles."[323] Oddly enough, the document is only in written format at present.

Is the auditory channel the only way oral peoples learn? Is the major difference along the continuum between the preference for using the eye or for using the ear?[324] This study examines that question. Regarding the ways oral peoples learn, Wilson urged, "Attention ought to be given, therefore, to the traditional learning styles, which are 'context-oriented' and by apprenticeship—'learning by example through experience.'"[325] Similarly, highly literate Fasheh pondered his own illiterate mother's world and way of thinking. He noted she learned by "observing, doing, reflecting, relating, and producing," and that "her knowledge sprang from life and was connected to life."[326] Insightfully, he added, "We need to look not only at what literacy adds . . . but also at what it subtracts or makes invisible"[327] and proposed an important point:

318. Watson, "Interpreting across the Abyss," 1.
319. Parker, "Adults' Perspectives."
320. Waters, "Exploration of the Lived Experiences."
321. Ong, *Orality and Literacy* (1982), 150.
322. Lovejoy, "Extent of Orality," 12.
323. Abney, "Orality Assessment Tool."
324. Chandler, "Biases of the Ear."
325. Wilson, "Scripture in an Oral Culture," 41.
326. Hu, "Eradicate Illiteracy," 53.
327. Hu, "Eradicate Illiteracy," 48.

Education is one way to learn; those who are comfortable with it should be supported. Those who are comfortable with other ways of learning should also be supported by providing them with means and facilities (including resources) that help them learn. This implies an end to the era of "education for all" and, instead, providing diverse ways of learning where we do not produce useless people (including dropouts) and blame them for it.[328]

In summary, even the body of research that most closely deals with oral ALFE ways of learning did not address my research question and sub-questions. Moreover, studies producing theory in each of the areas are few. This cursory examination of relevant literature serves to expose the gap and provide reason for a study of this nature—an exploration of the learning strategies of millions of overlooked adults in Cambodia, people who are seldom provided intentional opportunities to learn.

CHAPTER SUMMARY

In conclusion, in this chapter I examined the literature related to the context of Cambodia, specifically any literature related to education and orality in Cambodia. As with most ethnographic grounded theory studies, this examination unearthed very few works intersecting with the study of orality or ALFE learning in Cambodia.

The second half of the chapter dealt with literature touching on the complex construct of orality. In seeking a paradigm for the study of such a large body of literature, I created a conceptual framework concentrating on the ways of orality—ways of being, ways of knowing and storing knowledge, ways of transmitting knowledge (communicating and/or teaching), and ways of learning or acquiring knowledge. Much writing exists on the first three aspects, but as for researched oral ways of learning, there is more of a lacuna. I created a second conceptual framework for ways oral adults learn, examining aspects related to delivery, self, religion, cognition, society, and environment. The same conceptual framework is used to address the research questions in the next section.

---

328. Hu, "Eradicate Illiteracy," 52.

3

Research Method and Design: The Quest

"You will never really understand a person until you consider things from his point of view."

—Harper Lee, *To Kill a Mockingbird*

The purpose of this chapter is to delineate the research methods and procedures chosen for understanding how Cambodian adults with limited formal education (ALFE) learn. First, I explain the research approach used in this study and the rationale for the approach. Then I provide an explanation of the data sourcing strategy, the strategy for data analysis, ethical considerations for my study, and appropriate validation strategies.

OVERALL RESEARCH APPROACH

To begin this chapter on investigating how Cambodian ALFE learn, I find the Contextual Constructs Model (CCM) conceived by Knight to be a helpful framework. Knight approached studies in phases, listing them as *conceptual, philosophical, implementation,* and *evaluation*.[1] At the heart of her model lies the theory that research involves both a context and constructs. A discussion of each phase follows.

Conceptual Phase and Conceptual Framework for Research

During the conceptual phase, the researcher considers the study itself (the phenomenon to be considered and the research questions), the discipline of

---

1. Knight, "User Perceptions," 41.

the study and where the study is situated in the literature, as well as the theoretical lens of the researcher in the study. The previous two chapters covered the research and research discipline portion of the conceptual phase.

In positioning myself in this study, I operated with the theoretical lens of a respectful ethnographic researcher. I conducted interviews in the Khmer language. As someone working with a faith-based non-governmental organization (NGO), I approached participants with respect, compassion, and understanding and conducted the study in such a way as to treat them as people with great value. I took a non-judgmental, accepting stance honoring Cambodian learners. I did not ascribe to an agenda to bring literacy to the learners but rather only a quest to understand how Cambodian ALFE viewed learning and did so in their situations. My axiology or values included honoring the voice of the participants as well as respecting indigenous and cultural aspects of Khmer society. This value does not mean I agree with every aspect of Cambodian culture, but that I approached the Khmer people with an understanding and respectful point of view.

Also, because I am part of a faith-based humanitarian organization and familiar with Khmer culture and religion, I did not want to shy away from exploring or addressing faith and spirituality in this study. Spirituality has become a much-discussed topic in adult learning,[2] one in which adults reportedly wish to be engaged,[3] and an important "dimension of educational practice."[4] Traditionally, "to be Khmer is to be Buddhist," so I thought I might have difficulties being a Christian and interviewing Buddhists, but that was not the case. Buddhists were just as willing to share about their learning experiences as were Christians. Even though I have lived in the country over a decade and a half, I also learned a great deal during the times I observed Buddhist devotees at local *wats* (temples). I was graciously allowed to observe and ask questions even though they knew I was not Buddhist. As expected, however, I did note that younger Cambodians were not as interested in practicing or learning Buddhist precepts as were older adults. Therefore, only conversations with older Cambodians gave much insight into learning Buddhist dharma and precepts.

Considering how the theoretical lens affects a study also aligns with the purposes of a conceptual framework. Maxwell succinctly summarized the linkage of goals, research questions, conceptual framework, methods, and validity in one helpful diagram displaying the mutual interactions between

---

2. Tisdell, "Spirituality and Adult Learning."
3. Battiste, "Nourishing the Learning Spirit."
4. Hunt, "Long and Winding Road."

the factors.[5] Although Maxwell tended to equate the conceptual framework with the literature review, he also made clear the conceptual framework was built or created, a model of what was researched. In the previous chapter, I explored the context of the research—Cambodian oral learners—and the complex construct of orality. Given the gap in the literature related to ALFE learning in Cambodia and given the findings from the literature review, I found creating a framework surrounding the research questions quite helpful. In Figure 4 (presented in the previous chapter), the complex construct being studied—ALFE ways of learning—is again pictured within the cultural and social context of Cambodia. I explored six constructs based on the research questions: the role of self, cognitive components, and delivery/performance as well as social, environmental, and religious aspects involved in the learning of Cambodian ALFE.

Philosophical Phase

According to Knight, during the second phase of research, the researcher reflexively shares his/her ontology and epistemology or assumptions about being and knowledge.[6] As many have discussed,[7] research methodology stems from these roots, and the resulting elements must be congruent.

In my personal struggle to choose one epistemology, I felt conflicted. Ultimately, I resonated most with Starcher,[8] Knight and Cross,[9] and Cupchik[10] in adhering to a novel combination of realism/post-positivism and social constructivism. Starcher proposed the use of "functional relativism, functional constructivism, and a Christian theoretical lens."[11] Knight and Cross chose critical realism, stating it was pluralistic and "embraced the absolutes of positivism and the recognized bias of interpretivism."[12] Cupchik proposed an alternative known as constructivist realism, aspects of which I also found appealing.[13] He described a holistic qualitative process reflecting "an empathic understanding as if the structure of the social

---

5. Maxwell, *Realist Approach*.

6. Knight, "User Perceptions."

7. See Annells, "Grounded Theory Method"; Creswell, *Research Design*; Greckhamer and Koro-Ljungberg, "Erosion of a Method"; Urquhart, "Encounter with Grounded Theory"; "Evolving Nature."

8. Starcher, "Qualitative Research in Missiological Study."

9. Knight and Cross, "Using Contextual Constructs."

10. Cupchik, "Constructivist Realism."

11. Starcher, "Qualitative Research in Missiological Study," 61.

12. Knight and Cross, "Using Contextual Constructs," 47.

13. Cupchik, "Constructivist Realism."

world is seen through the eyes of the participants," and one that is "constructive, in that meaning is generated from a world that is observed and understood."[14] Whatever the name applied, I embraced the philosophical "middle way" elaborated below.

I believe Ultimate Reality and a God's Eye View exist, but finite and limited human beings are incapable of fully grasping either. In my estimation, people do construct their own perceptions of reality socially and culturally; thus, multiple perspectives on reality exist in the minds of those around us. No two people see life the same way; however, people come to understand the nuances of their own cultures' shared symbols and languages.

Those understandings or constructions of reality may or may not agree with Ultimate Reality or even my own version or understanding of reality but can be examined through immersion in the lives of the participants, through coming to comprehend the nuances of their shared symbols and languages, and through empathetic interviewing. Although long-term in my field of interest and very familiar with Khmer culture, I still sought an emic understanding through the shared process called research. In that process, I did not see myself constructing meaning with the participants; rather, I believe they had already constructed their own realities through the complicated process known as life. Together, we delved into and deconstructed particular aspects of their lived experiences. While exploring their learning, the participants were my guides and curators, assisting in deconstructing and interpreting their reality so I could appreciate its individual facets. Until those facets were exposed and polished, the beauty of their learning remained a mystery to me as an outsider. During and after this deconstructive and illustrative joint process, I had the privilege of exploring the elements of the participants' understanding, labeling their ideas, coding and writing memos about them, and raising conceptualization until a central understanding of the participants' constructed reality emerged.

Implementation/Methodological Phase

Moving to discuss the actual research phase, I found qualitative research and the grounded theory approach in particular provided an excellent framework for exploring "interaction grounded in the views of participants in a study."[15] In the case of the present research problem, my emphasis was on developing an understanding or theory of how Cambodian ALFE learn. This kind of study required relational observation, not objective measurement. The search necessarily involved descriptions as opposed to

14. Cupchik, "Constructivist Realism," 6.
15. Creswell, *Research Design*, 13.

the kind of numerical data gained from quantitative study. The research was also exploratory. Given the need for the inductive process of theory building and developing an understanding in a relatively unresearched field, a qualitative paradigm was most appropriate.[16] As Bloomberg and Volpe concurred, "Qualitative research is pragmatic, interpretive, and grounded in people's lived experiences."[17]

Among the various qualitative research strategies, the most logical methodology for theory building where none exists is grounded theory (GT), first proposed by Glaser and Strauss.[18] According to the originators, the method involves "the discovery of theory from data systematically obtained from social research."[19] One of the most used research methods, GT involves concurrent data sourcing and analysis, a process of coding leading to increasing abstraction of the data in an openness to the central concern of the participants, memoing the thoughts of the researcher throughout the study, constant comparison of findings, and theoretical sampling.[20]

Choosing from the various forms of GT and their philosophies, some researchers prefer to conduct their studies rather than enter the arguments.[21] Omitting personal philosophy is a possibility, as Breckinridge et al. explained: "Classic grounded theory . . . is essentially ontologically and epistemologically neutral."[22] Holton concurred,[23] but not everyone agrees. As a result, like Babchuk,[24] I chose to employ emergent grounded theory because of the emphasis on allowing a central understanding to emerge from the major concern of the research participants.

Entering this methodological phase meant opening a door to a new world. Smith called the difference between oral and literate worldviews a "chasm"[25] and Watson referred to an "abyss."[26] Although I had lived in Cambodia for over sixteen years at the time and had worked with many ALFE, I had not sought to fully understand their ways of learning or identify with their experiences. To enter their world and truly understand

16. Merriam, *Qualitative Research in Practice*.
17. Bloomberg and Volpe, *Completing Your Qualitative Dissertation*, 30.
18. Glaser and Strauss, *Discovery of Grounded Theory*.
19. Glaser and Strauss, *Discovery of Grounded Theory* (2012), 2.
20. Artinian et al., *Glaserian Grounded Theory*, xv.
21. Heath and Cowley, "Developing a Grounded Theory."
22. Breckenridge et al., "Choosing a Methodological Path," 68.
23. Holton, "Coding Process."
24. Babchuk, "Grounded Theory."
25. Smith, "Worlds Apart," 6.
26. Watson, "Interpreting across the Abyss."

it as a literate person, I used a three-stage approach for rich and relative data collection: (a) an identification stage, (b) an observation stage, and (c) an interview stage. I explain each more fully in the following sections. This kind of multi-stage approach allowed me to identify more deeply with Khmer learners by entering their world and experiencing their life situation firsthand. The identification and observation phases enriched interview times and allowed for deeper conversations and better understanding, resulting in a good triangulation of data.[27]

IDENTIFICATION STAGE. To begin this process, I lived for five days as an oral learner and recorded my experiences on a digital audio recorder. I avoided all written communication and reading material, including text messages. After recording my experiences, I transcribed the files and uploaded them in MAXQDA 12. Although I am not an oral Cambodian and escaped some of the difficulties they face during my own identification stage, I felt this step to be a necessary one prior to interviewing. The experience assisted me in entering an oral world from an emic perspective and in more clearly identifying with the participants. As Wolcott urged,

> Not everybody in education needs to go seeking after culture, but we cannot hope to achieve a full or balanced understanding of what we are up to or how we are going about it if the cultural dimensions of human behavior are ignored or obscured because of our own traditional and psychologically dominated "ways of looking."[28]

As someone using ethnographic techniques to study an educational process, my understanding was enriched through this first experience. Unexpectedly, I had great difficulty during the identification stage, and I discuss this more fully in chapters 5, 6, and Appendix B.

OBSERVATION STAGE. After that rich immersive experience, I began conducting qualitative observations in settings where oral Cambodians were involved in learning—at Christian trainings, Buddhist meetings, work places, and in everyday situations. In conducting these observations, I followed an observation protocol when possible. Tope et al. compared the effectiveness of various qualitative methods and identified participant observation to be "the queen of methods," giving rich data and coverage

---

27. Bloomberg and Volpe, *Completing Your Qualitative Dissertation*.
28. Wolcott, "Ethnographic Intent," 54.

in comparison to interviews and non-participant observation.[29] In some cases, such as classes I conducted, I was a participant and an observer. At other times, I was merely an observer. Like Charmaz, I was involved in "seeking data, describing observed events, and answering fundamental questions about what was happening."[30] My resulting field notes were transcribed into MAXQDA 12 for coding and writing memos. These observations factor in the findings in chapter 5.

As a long-term worker in Cambodia, I constantly sought an emic perspective. I did not wish to merely study insiders but rather to cooperate and collaborate with them in the journey of jointly deconstructing their reality, exploring their learning experiences, and examining the facets of this one aspect of their lives. Elaborating on the work of Simmel,[31] Collins discussed the concept of being an "outsider within," someone immersed in a situation but never becoming an "insider."[32] As a long-term cross-cultural teacher in Cambodia, I identified with this view. I had "been around" long enough to change perspective, and I tasted the benefits of being like Simmel's "stranger who stays."[33] As Collins added: "Outsiders within occupy a special place—they become different people, and their difference sensitizes them to patterns that may be more difficult for established sociological insiders to see."[34] I gained much insight by observing in this, my perpetual liminoid state.[35]

As a resident stranger, most of my time in Cambodia had been spent working with ALFE in conjunction with a faith-based NGO. However, beginning July 2015 we offered certificate level studies in conjunction with Gateway Seminary's Contextualized Leadership Development program. Designed for working rural leaders, classes filled one Saturday each month. Four of the twenty initial students in the program could read well enough to engage in class but were not able to write well. Two were not really able to learn by reading. These four became participants in this research. I observed and assisted them from July 2015 through June 2016 in multiple settings that provided rich data.

My previous sixteen years of experience and participation in various educational and informal settings provided much insight and ethnographic

29. Tope et al., "Benefits of Being There," 490.
30. Charmaz, *Constructing Grounded Theory*, 25.
31. Simmel, "Sociological Significance."
32. Collins, "Learning from the Outsider."
33. Simmel, "Sociological Significance."
34. Collins, "Learning from the Outsider," s29.
35. Turner, "Liminal to Liminoid."

data, which I recorded in a dissertation journal for analysis. As Paradise wisely shared and I discerned to be true, "The insight into a behavioral ethos that this approach offers probably is not available from ethnographic interviews with informants."[36] In some respects, these first two stages offered as much data as did the interviews. Chapter 5 includes that discussion.

INTERVIEW STAGE. After identifying phenomenologically through a non-reading immersive experience as well as being continually involved in observation, I began conducting interview conversations with Cambodian ALFE.[37] In the latter half of 2015 and early 2016, I conducted face-to-face interviews in the Khmer language with thirty-eight participants ranging from nineteen to eighty-three years of age.[38] Fourteen participants were male and twenty-five were female. Eighteen of the participants were Buddhist, fifteen self-identified as Christian, and five were unsure, wavering between both religions. In Appendix C, I list participants in thirty groupings because conducting lone interviews in a group-oriented culture was not always the norm. On numerous occasions I had onlookers—whether children of participants or other ALFE. In the end, I interviewed ten of the thirty-eight participants in one of three groups. Most interviews were an hour or more in length, but with some ALFE, interviews were too brief but gave bits of data, so I listed them as informants in a separate table—Table D1 in Appendix D.

I did not need to look far to find adults with limited formal education, whether in the city or in rural areas. Using criterion sampling, I purposefully selected adults over eighteen who met the criterion of having studied no more than six grades. Attending to homogeneous sampling, I chose only ethnic Khmer participants. In my search, I talked with more than the thirty-eight participants and eight informants in the process of discovering suitable participants. I also conversed with an equal number of adults of two other kinds—those who studied more than six grades and did not qualify for this study and those who had very few responses about their learning. In other words, I met a number of Cambodians who felt they could no longer learn, whether due to age, visual difficulties, or lack of opportunity or time. Attempting to question them, I was met with no means to consider how they learn because they could not readily identify anything they were learning. In observing this population, I noticed that even though they expressed being stagnant in learning, they did gather information and have

36. Paradise, "Learning Through Social Interaction," 44.
37. Charmaz and Mitchell, "Grounded Theory in Ethnography."
38. Creswell, *Qualitative Inquiry*.

new experiences, however limited they felt them to be. My insights on how they learned in reality coincide with those from participants I was able to interview and are expressed in chapters 5 and 6.

Besides live interviews, I also obtained six archival recordings conducted in 2013 by the NGO Resource Development International. Three female garment factory workers and three monks who trained novices participated in those recordings. These are listed as informants in Appendix D, Table D1.

I conducted interviews until achieving theoretical saturation, selecting participants with the potential to inform the research questions until no new data emerged (i.e., theoretical or theory-based sampling). During the process, I also revisited some participants and settings for further study and clarification. I conducted interviews in a variety of settings where learners could be found, including a mix of locations, with a mixture of ages and genders, as I engaged in random purposeful sampling as well.

Conducting semi-structured interviews, I used as ideas the open-ended questions in the interview guide in Appendix E. However, I also realized the need to follow the main concerns of participants in GT interview conversations. In keeping records, I recorded demographics and other pertinent information, assigning pseudonyms to each participant. I conducted interviews in the Khmer language, then translated and transcribed the audio files, including peer review of translation and member checking of understanding. In my interview process I included a cultural informant, and during the transcription process, I included two additional Cambodians. As with all data in this study, each interview was recorded digitally when possible and transcriptions imported into qualitative data analysis software.

Evaluation Phase

The final phase of the CCM research process is evaluative. Knight included data analysis and the recording of findings in this phase.[39] The remainder of this chapter discusses data analysis and elements related to accomplishing this process, while the following chapters focus on findings and application.

DATA ANALYSIS STRATEGY. No matter the philosophical slant, any true GT study has certain agreed-upon fundamentals. Sbaraini et al. listed these essentials as openness throughout the course of the study, immediate analysis of data beginning with data collection, constant comparison and coding during data analysis, memo-writing, theoretical sampling, the striving for theoretical saturation during data collection and analysis and resulting

39. Knight, "User Perceptions."

substantive theory.[40] Figure 5 diagrams my own approach used in following these essentials.

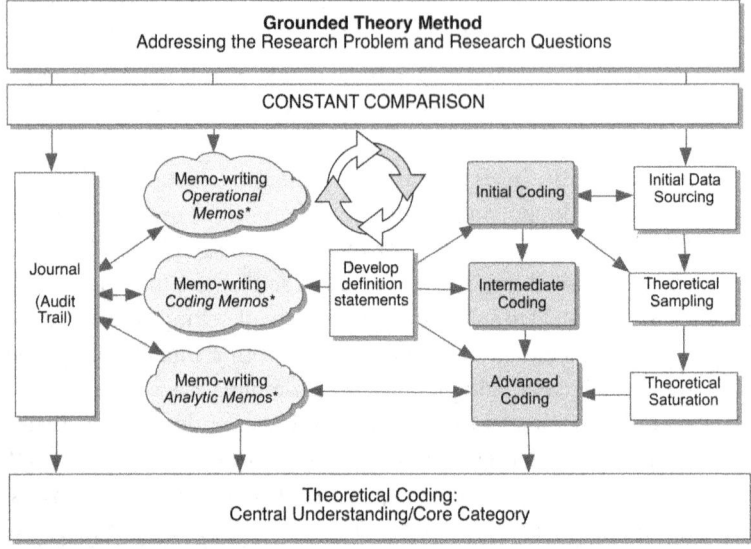

Figure 5. Schematic of grounded theory method to be followed in addressing the research problem and research questions in this study.

Data analysis covers all the areas to the right of data sourcing in the schematic in Figure 5. The GT method involved sampling and sourcing, coding, writing memos, and journaling until I uncovered no new information and a central understanding emerged. I constantly compared data throughout the sourcing and analysis, so that process figures prominently at the left side of the schematic. The following section discusses my plan for coding and memoing as well as a proposed addition to this emergent GT study.

CODING AND MEMO WRITING. In GT methodology, data analysis is an ongoing, iterative process concurrent with data gathering; so, I coded from the first interview. GT researchers offer various names for the codes at each level of abstraction along the path to seeking a central understanding. I used Birks's and Mills's terminology that follows the coding stages: *initial, intermediate,* and *advanced*.[41] While inputting data into qualitative data analysis software, I began initial coding line by line, then moved toward more

40. Sbaraini et al., "Grounded Theory Study," 3.
41. Birks and Mills, *Grounded Theory*.

substantive or intermediate coding by locating common themes and issues. At that point, coding was more analytical and theoretical.[42] My intermediate codes are visualized in Figure F1 in Appendix F. Finally, in the advanced stage of coding, a central understanding emerged from a thorough and iterative conceptual analysis of the data. The central understanding and themes are portrayed in Figures 10 and H1.

During the process of data collection and analysis, I wrote memos to track my insights.[43] The backbone of GT analysis, memos function as essential sets of thoughts that chronicle the research and inform the final product. Birks and Mills referred to memo writing as "the cornerstone of quality" and the lubricant of the GT "machine."[44] Hutchison et al. outlined their own use of memos consisting of a research diary of conceptual development and general events, reflective memos, conceptual memos, emergent questions, and explanatory memos related to literature, technical matters, and model descriptions.[45] My memos became somewhat of the same mixture, also including diagrams.

DATA ANALYSIS AND THE DIKW HIERARCHY. Giving freedom to espouse or adapt GT, Glaser and Strauss commented: "Our principal aim is to stimulate other theorists to codify and publish their *own* methods for generating theory."[46] In keeping with that advice, I propose a modified form of emergent GT, interjecting what is commonly known as the data-information-knowledge-wisdom (DIKW) hierarchy.[47] The schematic in Figure 6 and the commentary in the following paragraphs introduce this integrated approach.

---

42. Urquhart, "Encounter with Grounded Theory."
43. Creswell, *Qualitative Inquiry*, 289.
44. Birks and Mills, *Grounded Theory*, 40.
45. Hutchison et al., "Using QSR-NVivo," 287.
46. Glaser and Strauss, *Discovery of Grounded Theory* (1967), 8.
47. See Ackoff, "From Data to Wisdom"; Rowley, "Where Is the Wisdom"; "Wisdom Hierarchy."

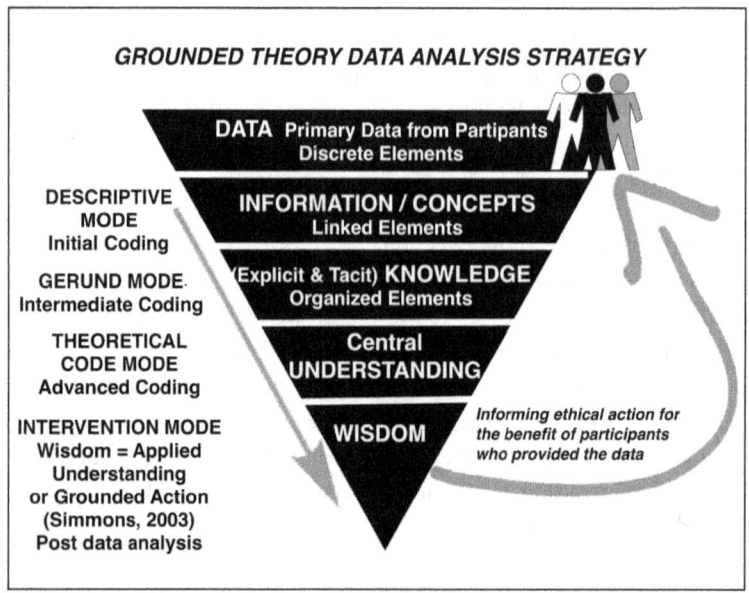

Figure 6. Integration of conceptual model for data analysis with modes of grounded theory (Artinian, 2009) and levels of abstraction in coding (Birks and Mills, 2011).

The elements of Ackoff's DIKW hierarchy sound much like the steps in the process of data analysis and approaching a central understanding in GT.[48] Walter, mentored by Ackoff, renamed the hierarchy WUKID (reversing DIKW and including understanding) and defined each element and the process as follows:

> Data is the raw stuff of the world, information provides structure for data, knowledge is actionable information, understanding is seeing patterns in knowledge and information, and wisdom is going beyond the levels of understanding to see larger scale systems.[49]

As Glaser observed, "The comparative process constantly raises the conceptual level of the study, which gives the research a continually transcending perspective, a constantly larger and less bounded picture."[50] Ackoff aptly summarized arriving at this succinct premise: "There is an old adage to the effect: *the better a phenomenon is understood, the fewer variables are*

48. Ackoff, "From Data to Wisdom."
49. Walter, "Knowledge versus Information."
50. Glaser, "Future of Grounded Theory," 840.

required to explain it (Recall E = mc²)."[51] The distillation in Figure 6 illustrates how "data can gradually transform itself into findings,"[52] the process of data analysis as I perceive it, including Birks's and Mills's coding stages[53] and Artinian's modes.[54]

Traditional GT ends with a central understanding or theory; however, I propose going one step further—delineating wise approaches to applying that understanding for the benefit of the participants from which the data came. Grounded theorists Artinian[55] and Simmons and Gregory proposed something similar in the form of intervention/action following GT.[56] I propose this possibility in the next section.

ETHICAL CONSIDERATIONS

I wanted to gain an understanding of how oral Cambodians learn in order to approach their education with wisdom, to inform culturally appropriate teaching practice, and to champion the needs of learners with limited access to formal study. Therefore, I utilized a number of means for valuing, protecting, and benefiting the participants.

Valuing Participants

During each interview and observation, I treated the individuals and their data respectfully, assuring ethical validation of the process.[57] I treated the learners with dignity in person, and in writing the findings, I provided a "true-to-life" understanding of their pedagogical lives and needs, allowing their voices "to shine through" in the written study. This research was a sincere attempt to understand in order to advocate for ALFE, to discover their ways of learning in order to better inform curriculum design and teaching. I informed participants beforehand that their responses would be used to gain insight into Khmer ways of learning. The impetus behind proposing wisdom-focused GT was based on valuing the participants, keeping the benefit of the participants in constant view, a logical extension of conducting ethical research.

---

51. Ackoff, "From Data to Wisdom," 5.
52. Knight and Cross, "Using Contextual Constructs," 52
53. Birks and Mills, *Grounded Theory*.
54. Artinian, "Overview of Glaserian Grounded Theory."
55. Artinian, "Overview of Glaserian Grounded Theory."
56. Simmons and Gregory, "Achieving Sustainable Change."
57. Angen, "Evaluating Interpretive Inquiry."

Protecting Participants

As with every kind of responsible qualitative research, I gave participants the opportunity to refuse interviews.[58] I resonate highly with the concept of reciprocity proposed by Creswell;[59] therefore, I did not coerce anyone into involvement. I also sought to minimize power distance between each person and myself by avoiding interviews with anyone I supervised.

Prior to each interview, I obtained verbal permission to conduct and record them. See Appendix G for the *Verbal Informed Consent Form*, the content of which was told to potential participants. Formal agreements, such as written permission, would only have served to alienate the participants and cause them anxiety. In addition, such documents would be inappropriate for non-readers. As Knowlton related when working with "illiterate and marginally literate populations":

> Not infrequently the act of having to read a document and sign it removes the research from the space of ordinary interactions ... to equivalent acts of signing forms in formal society, where generally something is at risk. As a result, the act itself generates suspicion and distrust. Instead of generating informed consent it can generate outright hostility, fear of loss, and suspicion about the broader concerns of the researcher. It changes the nature of relationships and interactions, not infrequently in ways that can make research impossible.[60]

Like Jimison et al., I proposed recorded verbal affirmation as an alternative to signed informed consent.[61] Moreover, I followed Biola University's PHRCC (Protection of Human Rights in Research Committee) guidelines and received approval.[62] In addition, I sought to protect the rights of the participants at all times. As Creswell advised, I did "not put participants at risk, and respect[ed] vulnerable populations."[63]

Protecting participants, I assigned pseudonyms to maintain confidentiality and made sure they were not identifiable in the presented research. When elaborating findings, I endeavored to quote participants in context, retaining the essence of their thoughts. During the research, I also maintained a journal as an audit trail and transcribed that data into MAXQDA

---

58. Creswell, *Research Design*.
59. Creswell, *Research Design*.
60. Knowlton, "Informed Consent and Ethnography," 36.
61. Jimison et al., "Use of Multimedia."
62. Protocol #SS15-004_AC, June 4, 2015.
63. Creswell, *Research Design*, 89.

12. For security purposes, I stored files on a password protected computer hard drive, on a password protected external hard drive, and uploaded files to a secure remote file storage account.

Benefiting Participants

Why collect these enormous amounts of data without benefiting the participants? I propose that final step creates a full circle of responsible and ethical research. The field of social work embraces "practice wisdom."[64] Artinian, a GT researcher, developed an intervention mode.[65] Simmons and Gregory developed grounded action. In this vein, I recommend wisdom-focused GT, going one step beyond developing theory to proposing wisdom for addressing learning needs of ALFE.[66]

Many researchers affirm knowledge alone is insufficient to tackle complex social problems.[67] In that vein, Rowley advised wisdom, "the capacity to put into action the most appropriate behaviour, taking into account what is known (knowledge) and what does the most good (ethical and social considerations)."[68] Baiget, a professor in knowledge management, proposed "wisdom management" as "the last frontier" in her field.[69] In the case of this research, this final component involves wisdom in applying the GT central understanding ethically and practically to the learning needs of ALFE in Cambodia.

The model in Figure 7 integrates the DIKW hierarchy in conjunction with the essential elements of grounded theory, showing the process of arriving at a central understanding, then gaining practical wisdom for ethically and effectively addressing the learning needs of Cambodian ALFE. Quoted earlier, Bill Gates wisely advised, "Humanity's greatest advances are not in its discoveries, but in how those discoveries are applied to reduce inequity."[70] Wisdom takes research and applies it to the stark inequities unearthed. It is my deepest desire that studying and working with oral learners, Cambodian ALFE, and relating their concerns and their ways of learning will aid in reducing the inequities they face in our modern literate world.

---

64. Dybicz, "Inquiry."

65. Artinian, "Overview of Glaserian Grounded Theory."

66. Simmons and Gregory, "Achieving Sustainable Change."

67. See Ardelt, "Wisdom as Expert Knowledge"; Bierly et al., "Organizational Learning and Wisdom"; Sternberg, "What Is Wisdom."

68. Rowley, "Where Is the Wisdom," 257.

69. Baiget, "Wisdom Management."

70. Gates, "Remarks of Bill Gates."

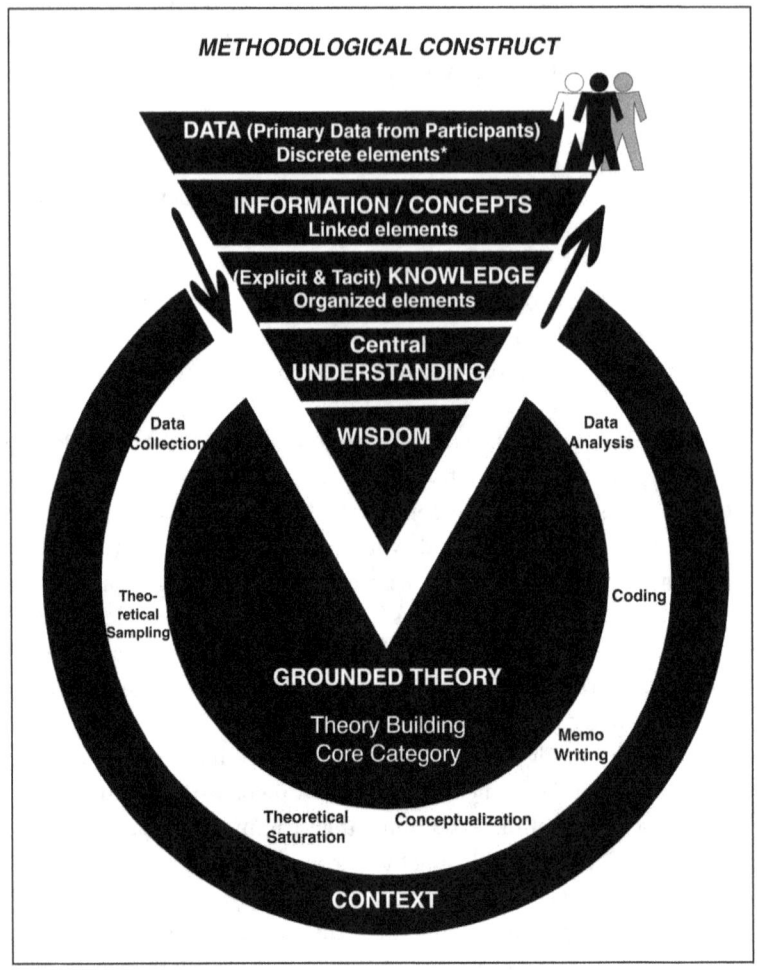

Figure 7. Conceptual model integrating grounded theory with Rowley's (2007) modified DIKW hierarchy.

VALIDATION STRATEGIES

Creswell advised qualitative research should include at least two validation strategies.[71] In this section I discuss seven strategies I employed to ensure valid results—"clarifying researcher bias" or reflexivity, keeping an audit trail or journal, ensuring triangulation of data, conducting peer debriefing

---

71. Creswell, *Qualitative Inquiry*, 253.

and member checks, using rich description in reporting, and being involved for long periods in the field.[72]

First of all, I understand researchers must make clear their process of reflexivity. I dealt with researcher bias by explaining any preconceptions and misconceptions during the journey and how those changed through my own learning process. From the outset, I acknowledge I brought the mindset of a literate person. I could not enter my mother's womb and become oral once again. I realized my limitations, but I could certainly research empathically to understand the lifeworld and needs from an emic perspective. Moreover, as a second language learner, I could readily identify with the functionally illiterate in a few respects, especially in the struggle to read difficult texts to gain information. From that humble stance, I entered the process of learning from and accurately representing the perspectives of the participants.

Along this journey I also made clear areas of concern or conflict, feelings and questions, made journal notes about my thoughts, allowed the participants to respond to any suppositions this process might expose in my thinking, and presented any contradictory ideas or results and how I dealt with them. I assumed at the beginning of this research that Cambodian ALFE continue learning throughout their lives, but that was not the case for some I interviewed. Even with that assumption, however, there were enough oral adults learning some skills and information that I could probe their experiences and perceptions of learning.

I employed six additional strategies to ensure valid results. I kept an audit trail not only for clarifying my position as researcher but also as a journal of the process of data collection and analysis. In triangulating data, I used different methods of data collection in three stages (identification, observation, and interviews), multiple sites for collecting data, theoretical sampling, as well as returning to participants for questions and clarification. I also used field notes from multiple sites and sources, gathered through multiple observations.

Additionally, even though I was fluent in speaking the Khmer language (American Council on the Teaching of Foreign Languages or ACTFL Advanced High) and had been in the country over sixteen years, I consulted Cambodian nationals to confirm my understanding and translation of interviews conducted in the Khmer language (peer debriefing). I employed experienced Cambodian translators to make certain the English text accurately reflected the participants' words. I re-read any translations and transcriptions to verify accuracy.

---

72. Creswell, *Qualitative Inquiry*, 250–53.

Finally, I used "rich and thick description" during the narrative reporting of findings, quoting participants in context.[73] In this way I hoped to accurately represent ALFE in the Cambodian context. Obtaining this kind of description entailed "prolonged engagement and persistent observation," which I did throughout this study.[74] In addition, I feel my previous years in the country and my immersion in the culture and language also contributed to reliable findings. Finally, I found Glaser and Strauss's decades' old advice in this area still apropos and worth quoting in full:

> If there is only one fieldworker involved, it is he himself who knows *what* he knows about what he has studied and lived through. They are his perceptions, his personal experiences, and his own hard-won analyses.... He has been living with partial analyses for many months, testing them each step of the way, until he has built his final substantive theory. What is more, if he has participated in the social life of his subjects then he has been living by his analyses, testing them out not only by observation and interview but also in daily livable fact. Hence by the close of his investigation, his conviction about his theory would be hard to shake—as most fieldworkers would attest. This conviction does not mean that his analysis is the only plausible one that might be based on his data, but only that the researcher himself has high confidence in its credibility.[75]

After this concentrated time of research added to my years of field experience, I felt I had grown in my understanding of ALFE learning.

CHAPTER SUMMARY

Heath and Cowley advised researchers choose a form of GT that fits their thinking styles.[76] Learning from a previous research project, I discovered I resonated most with emergent GT. To follow the tenets of this qualitative research methodology, I proposed using computer software, recording interviews, establishing rapport with participants, and using conceptual models, contrary to the original version of GT. Striving to be an ethical and responsible researcher, I chose to integrate a hierarchy that directed my efforts after research back to the participants from which the data came—a full circle of holistic and ethical activity, an endeavor that focused on producing a central understanding and wisdom for application.

73. Creswell, *Research Design*, 191.
74. Creswell, *Qualitative Inquiry*, 250.
75. Glaser and Strauss, "Discovery of Substantive Theory," 8.
76. Heath and Cowley, "Developing a Grounded Theory," 149.

In summary, I entered the realm of adult Cambodian learners with limited formal education with an aim toward using an emergent GT method modified to include the following:

- The gathering of ethnographic data as a rich source for analysis;[77]
- A focus on the phenomenon of orality in its context;[78]
- An aim for a central understanding surrounding the learning habits and needs of oral Cambodians, those with limited formal education; and
- An honest search for wisdom that would inform future grounded action.[79]

The following chapter analyzes the results of this study and this quest for wisdom to apply to those who participated in the study and the millions more like them. Initially, the reporting of the findings follows the research questions and conceptual framework. Chapter 4 answers the research questions, while chapter 5 begins the exploration of the central understanding and surrounding themes.

---

77. Merriam, *Qualitative Research in Practice*.
78. Merriam, *Qualitative Research in Practice*.
79. Simmons and Gregory, "Achieving Sustainable Change."

4

Data Analysis: Mining for Knowledge

> "How has this man become learned having never been educated?"
> —John 7:15 (NASB)

In the next three chapters I analyze the resulting research data. First, this chapter examines the comments gleaned from participants through the lens of the conceptual framework and research questions. (See Figure 4 in chapter 2.) In chapters 5 and 6 I explore the main concerns of the participants, synthesize the data including observations and my phenomenological experiences, make interpretations, and introduce corollary participant themes and the central understanding. In the final two chapters I delve into the implications of these findings, draw conclusions, and propose a number of wise recommendations—actions mentioned in the previous chapter that will take the grounded theory research one step further to apply the findings and central understanding in ways that could benefit ALFE in Cambodia.

CHAPTER OVERVIEW AND BACKGROUND

In this section I examine the data according to the conceptual framework and research questions. The purpose of this ethnographic GT study was to understand the ways of learning of oral Cambodian adults or those with limited formal education—that is, how oral Cambodian ALFE learn or acquire new knowledge, beliefs/values, or skills. The research sub-questions to be addressed remained as follows:

1. How do ALFE in Cambodia approach the acquisition of new knowledge, beliefs, values, and skills? (Role of Cognitive Components)
2. What role do other people (society, teachers, family, and others) play in the learning of ALFE in Cambodia? (Role of Social Components)
3. What role does context/environment/setting/time play in the learning of ALFE in Cambodia? (Role of Environmental Aspects)
4. What role do media (such as print, audio, video, pictures, narrative, music, drama) play in the learning of ALFE in Cambodia? (Role of Delivery/Performance)
5. What role does self and experience play in the learning of ALFE in Cambodia? (Role of Self)
6. What role does religion play in the learning of ALFE in Cambodia? (Role of Spirituality)

In discussing each aspect in the following sections, I chose one participant's words to present as a vignette that seemed to typify the findings; however, each vignette will obviously include many other aspects of ALFE learning. In sharing the participant stories, however, I felt the words did not convey sufficiently the emotions attached to them at the time. Therefore, I also attempt to interject the weight of the affective dimension throughout the final chapters by including rich description, quoting the participants in context, and including my responses, as the emotional element was a surprising inclusion for me during this research.

To recap, in order to explore the learning world of Cambodian ALFE, I used a three-stage approach: (a) an identification stage, (b) an observation stage, and (c) an interview stage. In this chapter I focus mainly on interview data and elaborate on the identification stage and observations in later chapters. Participants included thirty-eight people, ten of which were interviewed in three different groups listed in Appendix C. Fourteen participants were male and twenty-five were female. They ranged in age from nineteen to eighty-three years.

In addition, because I had brief interview conversations with and observed many more people, I listed any pertinent encounters, along with past encounters, in a table of informants in Appendix D. Finally, I had access to six 2013 Resource Development International (RDI) archival videos in which they interviewed three garment workers and three monks. I include a listing of these six informants in Appendix D as well.

During the beginning phases of evaluation, I coded, organized, and analyzed the data according to the research questions and conceptual framework. In the process of analyzing the participants' data, I used a combination of qualitative data analysis software and old-fashioned paper and pen strategies. Initially, I attempted using NVivo 10 and MAXQDA 12 in a comparison study. I discovered I preferred MAXQDA 12 and finally defaulted to that software for coding and writing memos. I also noticed I preferred a more tactile approach to the data, so I printed the initial 387 codes and 124 memos and physically worked with them via paper and pen while organizing and searching for themes and a central understanding. In this iterative process moving toward intermediate coding, I created the visual in Appendix H. Advanced or substantive coding resulted in the schematic presented in chapter 5.

RESEARCH SETTING AND BACKGROUND OF PARTICIPANTS

In order to find suitable participants for interviews, I had to converse with a great deal more people than I first imagined. Appendix C provides a final listing of participants and their pseudonyms, and Appendix D lists informants and their pseudonyms. Like Lave, I had assistance in locating suitable participants, asking "peripheral acquaintances . . . as intermediaries who vouched for us to peripheral acquaintances of theirs as a means of recruiting . . . participants."[1] In the end, the best interview conversations were with friends or relatives of interviewees in the presence of a Khmer national who accompanied me. I felt these adults related the most information, perhaps because of the initial relationships and the ease of sharing with those known contacts.

In the end, I discovered I had three sub-groups of participants—one which I call incidental learners with seemingly no hope or aspirations to learn, according to their own words; one which I call maintenance learners, who made the most of the little education they had and plodded along; and another group, purposeful learners, who struggled through their limitations with self-proclaimed hope and purpose to learn, becoming readers and some becoming writers. Figure 8 delineates these three types of participants. I discuss their characteristics in more detail in the following as well as subsequent chapters.

---

1. Lave, *Cognition in Practice*, 194.

Data Analysis: Mining for Knowledge 81

Figure 8. Groups of ALFE in Cambodia.

Group 1 self-identified as non-learners and included sixteen participants. However, as with most of the participants, they seemed to equate learning with schooling and literacy. Having neither, they felt they were no longer involved in learning. As I explored their learning strategies, I came to understand that the Khmer word for learning, *ree-un,* conjured up thoughts of neat rows of wooden desks, students in uniforms, a teacher at a blackboard, and the group chanting their lessons in unison—formal learning. Supposedly, studying was for the young, for those who had time for such matters. For these, their lives had no room for another activity called learning something new. They seemed to face many obstacles, such as visual or learning difficulties, or health problems; but in observing their everyday lives, I did see evidence of learning. For instance, seventy-year-old Ms. Terina consulted church members on how to respond to neighbors who shamed her for her Christian faith—what to do and what to say. During Khmer New Year, I observed she also learned to play new games as part of the festivities.

Group 2 (maintenance learners) included eleven participants, and Group 3 (purposeful learners) had nineteen. The focus of both their learning consisted of just-in-time help when needed, such as learning to use a phone or other device, asking for advice and exploring options, and job-related learning needs. A key difference in Groups 1 and 3 seemed to stem from spirituality, as the participants reported. Surprisingly, nearly all the participants in Group 3, whether Buddhist or Christian, wanted to learn more about their faith, and this purpose reportedly drove them to return to attempt learning—in many cases learning to read and write. A large number of them were successful. All but five of those in Group 3 could write in varying degrees.

Finally, during my observations, I also watched participants in Group 3 actively assist those in Groups 1 and 2 in their learning efforts. Of Khmer I have watched teach in Cambodia over the last decade and a half, this group seemed to be most successful in helping their colleagues and most relevant in their teaching.

Moreover, I discovered in the interviews that my initial open-ended questions were difficult for many of the participants to process and understand. Adapting, I began to ask them to tell me about their lives and learning experiences and to interject my own exploratory questions at pertinent points. Any first questions about learning were usually answered with experiences about schooling. Even though this information was not associated with adult learning, the impact of those years was significant and followed them their whole lives. The affective consequences of less than positive experiences in the first few grades of school seemed to discourage lifelong learning and invoke a negative self-concept. This phenomenon is discussed further in the following chapters.

To usher the reader into my journey with the participants, I would like to relate the situation of fifty-three-year-old Ms. Amie. One weekday morning, Ms. Sona took me to meet her. We walked through an area nearly an hour north of Phnom Penh where workers haul fish to be processed from the Mekong River. A distinctive odor met us as we walked by concrete areas for collecting, cutting, and loading the precious commodity. The smooth areas are washed daily; but the section closest to the Mekong, surrounded by wooden houses on stilts, was littered with trash. In this setting, I spied Ms. Amie sifting through discarded plastic bags. She recovered the ones still intact, gathered them, and took the awful mass to the fish processing area. There she washed each bag in the muddy water from the Mekong. Then she proceeded to take the whole lot one by one—scores in various colors of yellow, green, blue, and pink—and place them on wire strung between two poles. The day was steamy and the bags sopping wet and heavy, but she lifted the whole mass of all the wet bags and the wire and tied the wire high on a pole. They were then left to dry in the wind. My heart broke for this widow who could find no other way to make a living. She confided, "I don't know what else to do, but sometimes I make 5000 riel [$1.25 USD] a day."

Data Analysis: Mining for Knowledge   83

With her job complete and the bags flapping in the breeze, we traversed down a steep alleyway to a tall wooden house on stilts. The house had been fashioned from wood reclaimed from a previously dilapidated dwelling in the area. The two-room building, housing five people, sat perilously near the floodwaters and had an unusually high and precarious stairway. I struggled to maneuver the narrow steps to the entrance. Inside were some of the usual decorations of a typical Cambodian home—a television, an altar with flowers and food, pictures of family hung high on the walls. We proceeded to sit on a floor made of wooden slats and talk about life, about how she lost her loving husband, how she worked hard every morning, how she was in ill health, and how she struggled to deal with her six children, the youngest of whom had mental difficulties due to falling from their stilted house. Learning was the last thing on her mind. Did she want to do something else besides wash bags every day? She could not think of anything else to do, and she did not have time. She related, "I was twelve years old during the Khmer Rouge and I only finished the fifth grade. I did not get to study anymore, so I forgot how to write. I can read unless it's bad handwriting."

The image of her life is emblazoned forever in my mind. In fact, the life situations of each person I interviewed still burden my heart. I watched those working in construction—women carrying heavy loads of bricks—heard people talking about suffering in garment factories, listened to widows who learned to make desserts to sell along dusty streets. Some had hope; others had none. Their learning stories are represented in the following.

RESEARCH QUESTION FINDINGS AND DESCRIPTIVE VIGNETTES

In this section I examine the interview findings according to the research questions and conceptual framework mentioned earlier—the role of cognitive components, social components, environmental aspects (context, time, etc.), delivery/performance (media), self (experience and affect), and spirituality. In exploring each aspect related to ALFE learning, I include one applicable vignette along with pertinent background of the participant and context.

Question 1: Role of Cognitive Components in ALFE Learning

Research sub-question 1 asked, "How do ALFE in Cambodia approach the acquisition of new knowledge, beliefs, values, and skills?" This question majored on the cognitive aspects of learning. If I were to choose one Khmer word a number of the participants used repeatedly to describe their cognitive abilities, I would choose the word *l'ngong*, meaning *ignorant*. Even those who learned to read felt they were not so *poo-kie-ee*, not so clever at learning when they were younger. Ms. Veta shared,

> I was not so good at studying. (*K'nyom ree-un aht so poo-kie-ee tay*.) I didn't really care so much then. I tried but I was just not as good at studying as everyone else. I was always last in the class. Now the difference is I follow Jesus. He has helped me. I know it is not because of my own ability that I am doing well now.

When I asked Ms. Tari, who is representative of Group 1, about her learning experiences, she replied, "Really, I do not have any idea because I do not know. I am illiterate. I do not have a lot of ideas. If I were literate, then I would have ideas and think about the future." In contrast, Ms. Yoshie was learning at the age of forty-five and chatted about her learning with hope and confidence:

> Some people say I'm too old to learn. But I'm not too old. I've watched foreigners. Even though they are old, they still learn—over sixty years old. We need to look at their example. They try hard to learn even if they are seventy years old or older—like reading Khmer or learning Khmer. I've seen them. We can't let them beat us! We need to study, too. We don't have to study a lot—just a little. We can try hard and rest also and get it done. If we have the opportunity, we can do it. My husband says, "You're studying. You're old already." But I want to study. I want to learn, to know. I am going to keep trying until I know how to do it [sewing]. And when I don't know, I will try hard to learn—for about a year. I think I can keep trying and do it.

Sometimes, however, the cognitive was affected by war, poverty, and lack of time in formal schooling. Ms. Amie recounted her experience during the war:

> I was twelve years old during the Khmer Rouge and I only finished the fifth grade. I did not get to study anymore because we had to work during Pol Pot times. They would not let us study, so I forgot how to write.

As mentioned in the opening chapter, much of the generation aged fifty and above never had an opportunity to learn or have a normal upbringing. Many who only had a few grades of education and were only just beginning to learn to read lost what precious knowledge they had gained—like Ms. Amie above. Even though her lack of education was due to no fault of her own, she still felt shame and embarrassment over her reading and writing skills.

As a foreigner steeped in an educational emphasis on self-esteem, I had great difficulty with participants calling themselves names and even more mental angst when others sitting with them called them *l'ngong* (ignorant or stupid) during interviews. I did not interview anyone who seemed to have an intellectual disability, but I quickly realized how deficient the participants felt because of their lack of education. The Cemented Ladies, a group working in construction, commented: "We don't know what to learn because we don't know anything." In fact, many people with whom I conversed but did not interview felt they were too old to learn. Ms. Mei, an informant who sold fruit, explained with a sense of pride: "We use our strength, not our brains."

All the participants in Groups 1 and 2 complained about learning, saying, "*Ree-un aht jole*"—the learning would not go into their minds. Mr. Kirby in the vignette below was one of those people. Age nineteen, he had attended six grades of school but could read only what he described as "50 percent." Athletic and adept at soccer, he worked in a garment factory. He said no matter how long he went to school or who tutored him, what he tried to learn would not enter his brain (*ree-un aht jole*).

Of the eleven maintenance learners and sixteen incidental learners, I felt at least five—Vania, Nestor, Tari, Tova, and Kirby—might have learning disabilities. They did not seem to have intellectual disabilities but expressed sincere difficulties in learning to read. No one had ever talked with them about visual problems or learning disabilities like dyslexia, so I introduced them to these issues, explaining a problem in which one might confuse letters or find reading difficult. All five seemed to gain hope that they might not be mentally impaired but simply have "a problem with letters" or their vision instead. After these interviews, I also researched further about dyslexia and reading difficulties.

After my first interview with Mr. Vania, who expressed wanting to commit suicide because of his inability to learn to read, I returned to chat further and test my suspicions about dyslexia. He did need glasses, and after trying a few techniques advised for learners with dyslexia, I ascertained he preferred a larger, 36-point font, of which the Battambang font was easiest for him to process, and that he preferred having words separated, contrary to the usual practice of written Khmer. In addition, Mr. Vania viewed text more easily through a pink overlay. This kind of work with those who may have dyslexia is certainly an area ripe for further study.

Cognitively, some participants mentioned learning bit-by-bit, learning through recitation or through repetition and memorization. Ms. Yoshie related, "It's very important to repeat words over and over again, to *tune tee-un* [memorize/review/recite]." Needless to say, Ms. Yoshie numbered among the purposeful learners. The vignette below originates with Mr. Kirby, an athletic nineteen-year-old who worked at a garment factory.

Question 1: Descriptive Vignette, Mr. Kirby

I would walk to school from home; but when I was there, I would never stand and read, so the teacher would hit me, so I felt angry with that teacher. I couldn't learn to read. I finally studied outside of class time with an older man to help me. If I couldn't get it, I didn't have to pay him. He was trying to help me read from the first—word by word, sentence by sentence but I couldn't get it [*ree-un aht jole*]. I can now read about 50 percent.

When I started working at the garment factory, I didn't do it well. I did it wrong, and then I would hit myself, but I had to keep learning and trying myself to get it. I was angry with myself that I couldn't do it! That's why I hit myself. I didn't understand why I couldn't learn how to do the work. The boss would say bad things to me and then I would do better after he scolded and berated me. He said things like, "You've been here a month. Why don't you know how to do this?"

In one day, we are required to complete twenty-four garments. Now I can do it. I started when I was sixteen. Now I know how to do this job well. There are many different jobs, but I don't know how to do a different job. Some of the other jobs are harder and mine is easier. I'm not afraid to learn something new. This is just easier, and I know how to do it.

My friends make fun of me. It makes me angry, so I berate them back when they scold me. They look down on me.

Question 2: Role of Social Components in ALFE Learning

Mr. Kirby's vignette leads us to research sub-question 2: "What role do other people (society, teachers, family, and others) play in the learning of ALFE in Cambodia?" Nearly every person with whom I talked expressed they learned from others—*ree-un pee gay*—or they watched others in order to learn—*mull gay*. For instance, I asked Mr. Vania how he learned to do his work. His reply was typical of many others: "I watched people—*mull gay*—then I tried to do what they did. I had to sneak and watch others do the work."

During the interview with Mr. Vania, an older female friend would interject thoughts that seemed very degrading to me. These are included below to show the frank and shaming nature of many comments made to ALFE in Cambodia. During a number of these kinds of interviews, I encouraged the participants, complimented them, and tried to give them dignity—especially in front of those who had berated and shamed them.

What about the role of the teacher? Teachers were not often mentioned in the interviews in relation to adult learning, except for complaints about teachers the participants had in their early grades of study. Unfortunately, the majority of those comments were negative. Even though the experiences might have been many years prior, they were still raw in their minds, with much emotion attached. Ms. Sona confided: "In school if you cannot read, the teacher will beat you. I was beaten often because I couldn't read. I cried at school; but when I came home, I did not tell my parents about it." Similarly, as Mr. Kirby revealed above, "I would never stand and read, so the teacher would *wie-ee* (hit) me, so I was angry at the teacher." Shaming in school was evident, as was a general lack of concern for the learning of each individual. Ms. Sona added, "In the first grade, the teacher did not help the students learn to read well. Even if you had very low grades, still they would allow you to pass." Unfortunately, I heard about too many unfortunate situations like these and how often the system had failed these learners.

The vignette that follows illustrates the situation of a thirty-seven-year-old man who wanted to learn how to do construction work, but his co-workers would not allow him to watch, lest they lose their jobs in such a competitive environment. Not being able to read at all, Mr. Vania could not consult a book or the Internet but sought instead to observe others in order to learn. Given the choice of learning from people or from print, the ALFE I met overwhelmingly chose people as a means and source for learning. Even those who learned to read and write had a community they consulted for learning purposes.

Question 2: Descriptive Vignette, Mr. Vania

> I do not know how to write or read at all. My mother used to send me to school, but I always left and went to other places to have fun instead of going to school. So, I did not study at all. I am thirty-seven years old and I was born in Kompong Thom province. Now I live with my brother here closer to Phnom Penh and I work in construction.
>
> *An older female friend interjected*: "Excuse me. I want to talk about him a little more. He can only call others on his phone. He cannot check a missed call or a text or anything else on the phone. He cannot write down a phone number or get a number from someone else. I know because he asks me for help often. He does not know how to use a phone really. He only

knows how to answer and call people he knows and numbers he remembers. He does not know enough. He needs help."

I would like to learn but I am too busy with my work. If there are any places that have construction, I will go there to find work. When they call me, I go wherever they need me in order to work.

The first time I went to work I did not know how to do anything. I just had to watch others [*mull gay*] and see how to do the work and then I would try to do it myself. At first, they called me stupid or ignorant because I did not know how to do anything. But I would try to sneak and watch others working in order to learn.

First, I worked just as a helper for others, doing whatever they told me to do—carrying things or whatever. But now I can do the work myself because I observed others that were able to build. I tried at home so many times on my own to copy what I had seen others do. I practiced a lot until I could do it by myself. I would get wood and a measuring tape and try some things at home after I watched others do it at work. Then I learned to measure and do the work.

Now they allow me to do the work myself because I know how to do it. In the beginning I tried to learn but they would not teach me. I would ask the boss but only until he saw I could do the work would he let me do it. If I could do it well and not ruin the materials, I was allowed to do the work. Also, if I could do it fairly quickly, that was important, too.

I have worked on houses and in a housing community to lay brick and flooring. When I worked as a helper, I was paid only a small amount—about 20,000 riel a day ($5 USD). If you know more, you can make more—like $15 USD a day.

I can mix cement, lay brick, and make the foundation of a small building. I started working when I was nineteen and I chose this work because it is the only way for me to earn money. I felt I could not learn at school.

I do not really have time to learn anything else, but I have not become a main boss or anything like that. I have a hard time understanding and learning. I get my information from my relatives—especially from my older brother.

When I first started working, it was very hard. It was not easy at all. I wanted to learn but no one would teach me. I had to sneak and watch others in order to learn. When I asked, no one would tell me, or they would lie to me! There is a lot of competition for jobs, so people will not share their knowledge because they are fearful of losing their jobs to someone who knows more. I like this work. It is enough for me and I can do it.

The older female friend interjected again: "It is not that he likes it so much as it is what he can do. If you cannot read and write, what kind of work can you do? You have to do manual labor like this—like working with cement or something."

For an illiterate person like me I must try hard to study or observe from others carefully. If I could do anything I wanted to do, I would like to be a businessman and sell things.

The older female friend interjected once more: "How could you do that work without being able to read and write? That would not work!"

How could I do the work with the writing and the numbers? I would use my physical strength to do the heavy work, but I would depend on my wife to help with writing, calculating, setting the prices, etc. My wife can read and write.

Question 3: Role of Environmental Aspects in ALFE Learning

Turning to consider other factors, research sub-question 3 explored: "What role does context/environment/setting/time play in the learning of ALFE in Cambodia?" Many learners were so busy with work and life they reported not having margin for anything else, no real time to learn. The Cemented Ladies, who traveled extensively doing construction work, confided, "We do want to learn, but we don't have time." They wanted to learn English, and even though they were not able to be involved in more formal learning, I noticed they had learned a great deal in their travels. They learned to navigate new towns and villages and find sources of food, etc. I noticed they had learned to do this not in a solo fashion but with one another, traveling from place to place as a united group. This is quite common and to be expected in Cambodia's group-oriented culture.

A number of The Cemented Ladies complained, "We do want to learn but we don't have time now. We didn't get to learn because it was during the Pol Pot regime. It was very difficult then." Mr. Eli explained how his environment affected his learning: "I studied until grade two. Because my mother was a widow and we did not have money for me to keep going to school and there was no one to watch the cows, so I had to work."

Mr. Cyril also confided, "I want to go to class but I don't know where to go. And I can't afford to learn. I want to learn from the example of others. I prefer watching them and practicing." Likewise, small business owner Ms. Lisha, only twenty-five years old and a mother of two, lamented,

I don't know what to do. I only depend on my own knowledge and selling all of this stuff and trying to find things on my own. It's too late for me if I want to learn more so we don't have time to learn anymore. Now it's the time that we have to do whatever we can to find money for our children. I'd love to, but I don't have time to learn. I want to know how to do everything, but I just don't have time to study, I only have time to work in order to make money.

The vignette below illustrates the life of a fifty-two-year-old woman who can read a bit but cannot write.

Question 3: Descriptive Vignette, Ms. Lela

My life is difficult. I did not get to do a lot of school. When I was in the first or second grade, my life was hard. My parents were very poor. That is why all of us did not get to study. Before I went to school, I had to go cut vegetables to sell. I was punished because I was always late for school. I had to stand on one leg in the sun as a punishment or I had to run around the flag. If I didn't sell vegetables, I couldn't afford to buy books for school. Sometimes I cried while standing outside the class watching others study. Sometimes I passed out.

In the third grade there was an exam for bright students. I passed the exam. I didn't have the proper clothes to wear to the ceremony, so the teacher had to raise funds for me. When I went for another exam at a different school, I saw a lot of nice-looking people and their parents with them, and I started to cry. When the teacher handed me the exam, I wrote on the paper, "I have been poor my whole life, and I can't study anymore." When I looked around, everybody was very nice. The teacher asked why I didn't write something else. I told them, "When I looked on my left and right, I saw rich people with their parents to support them. I am the only one that no one came to support except my teacher." It was break time, but I didn't go outside. I stayed in the classroom and stared at the board. I saw a list of smart students and I started to realize that I needed to try really hard for the next test. I needed to focus and not to worry if people looked down on me or teased me.

After the exam, my mom sent me to live with other relative. I never even finished the third grade. The person that I lived with was very kind, but I didn't have time to study because there were a lot of plates for me to wash because I worked in a restaurant. Later, all the teachers at my school went to my mom to ask if she wanted to send me back to school because they had a scholarship for me, but my mom did not care. She didn't seem to like me as much as my other six siblings. She would buy clothes for all my siblings except for me. I had to buy my own. When I was in school, I would buy lotus seeds to eat with my friends. My teeth were always chewing on lotus seeds. I didn't have money to buy anything else to eat.

I regret not being able to carry on with my studies. If I could have finished grade five, I probably would have a better job; but thank God, He blessed me to be able to read. I think I was twelve or thirteen years old when I had to stop going to school. I kept wondering why my mother did not love me. I pictured myself being a doctor or a professor. My cousins that went to school with me are now doctors and nurses.

Later, I grew up and sold vegetables, then I worked in the garment factory for three years and got married, but my husband treated me very badly. When I got home, my husband abused me and drank a lot. We never had money left. I used to have a lot of gold, but my husband took it all.

I had an uncle come to visit from another country. When I saw him, I greeted him and told him my story and that I could not bear to be with my husband anymore, and I wanted a divorce. I told him I didn't know how to change my husband. He abused me mentally.

When I want to go somewhere, I can't. That is why now I try to work even though I am really sick. I don't want to depend on my husband anymore. I am working as a construction worker, carrying cement and sand so I can have money.

Question 4: Role of Delivery/Performance in ALFE Learning

Turning to a completely different matter, research sub-question 4 explored, "What role do media (such as print, audio, video, pictures, narrative, music, drama) play in the learning of ALFE in Cambodia?" How accessible are technologies for ALFE learning?

Surprisingly, in our modern world of internet, smart phones, and computers, the majority of learners across the globe find them beyond their use.[2] In a study conducted in India, Chudgar revealed: "Actual mobile phone ownership and the ability to dial a phone number using the phone . . . is however low. In fact, even those who currently own a mobile phone . . . report that

---

2. See Chudgar, "Promise and Challenges of Using Mobile Phones"; Medhi et al., "Beyond Strict Illiteracy"; Medhi et al., "It's Not *Just* Illiteracy"; Medhi et al., "Text-Free User Interfaces."

they need help to use their phones."³ Seven of the participants I interviewed use smart phones—all but one of which were among the purposeful learning group. Additionally, those seven had learned how to use Facebook for sharing and gaining information. Most of the rest of the participants used simple Nokia phones, which they call "push button and flashlight" phones because the user presses buttons to make calls and most include a flashlight. One step above that basic phone is one with an SD card slot, adding memory for listening to audio files and radio. Many, however, did express difficulties using their phones and needed to ask for assistance.

As for learning from radio or television, only five learners related they learned best from listening to the radio. Some of these reported listening at night or while they worked. Mr. Nestor commented that he could not read the Bible, but he learned more about Christianity from the radio. Most of the others preferred watching television in order to learn from technology, but some did not have time for television viewing. Mr. Claude, who works two jobs, said he preferred to read his Bible rather than watch television or listen to the radio. Mr. Claude, a purposeful learner, used a smart phone and showed me how he learned by recording video of something he was taught and watching it repeatedly.

In regard to using various technologies, one restaurant worker from the men in the KC Group shared,

> I can use Facebook. My phone has Khmer on it. Some people use expensive phones to get information, but I use a basic (*toe-mah-dah*) phone because I don't need to have a special phone. I don't have a lot of money, so I must think about my family and don't need a special phone.

This young man could operate a phone but chose economics over prestige. Not all participants thought the same. Some chose prestige and owned a more complicated phone than they could use. In navigating these devices, Ms. Tal explained,

> When I first bought the phone, I did not know how to use it. So, I asked others questions like, "How do you use this? How do you share the photos?" Then they would tell me, "This is how you share your photos, and this is how you play on the internet."

The vignette below comes from Ms. Lidia, a fifty-five-year-old lady who took part in our certificate-level courses. She can read but cannot write. She discussed how she learns best.

---

3. Chudgar, "Promise and Challenges of Using Mobile Phones," 27.

Question 4: Descriptive Vignette, Ms. Lidia

> When I got here [to the certificate-level Bible course], I told the teacher that I did not know anything, so when I registered the teacher helped me write down my information. I know how to write; but it takes me a long time, so I did not think I could keep up with the class. It was very difficult for me, so I started to pray to God, "Please help me learn." In my heart I was afraid and thought, "How can I keep up with this class?" I sat next to Pisey [pseudonym], the pastor's wife, and when the teacher spoke, she never stopped writing. It was intimidating to watch her, so I thought it would be impossible to keep up. I could read but it was difficult to pronounce the words fluently. I studied to the tenth grade [in the French system], which is the third grade nowadays. I did not know how to read well until I knew Christ. If there are pictures, I can see and learn—like telling stories. Whenever I go to the workshops and the teacher tells stories once or twice, I can remember about 50 percent, and when the teacher comes to tell the story again, I can remember about 80 percent. I thank the Lord that when the teacher asks for someone to go up and retell the stories, I raise my hand. Retelling stories is easy for me. I can remember; but as for writing, I cannot do it.

Question 5: Role of Self in ALFE Learning

Moving on from technology, research sub-question 5 examined: "What role does self play in the learning of ALFE in Cambodia?" The name-calling related to cognitive abilities or lack thereof and beliefs about one's self were a surprising aspect of ALFE learning. Even those in the purposeful learning group expressed they had done poorly in the few years they experienced formal schooling; however, those in groups 1 and 2 did not fare well in the area of self-efficacy.

Since so many of the participants seemed to equate learning with schooling and literacy and so many made comments they were *l'ngong*, these adults seemed to suffer in a painful and perpetually liminal state created by their failure in school or their lack of formal education and literacy. Benjamin recounted: "I don't have high education, so I can't think far. I can only work using physical ability and use little knowledge." He also described his childhood and lack of education:

> So we were striving to survive. I had to work. That is why my education was low. When I saw kids go to school, I really wanted to go, but I couldn't. Then I tried really hard to save money to

buy books so that I can study by myself because I couldn't afford to go to school.

The shame associated with lack of education and lack of literacy was surprisingly strong, and the sense of complete worthlessness astounded me. Ms. Shu, who was abandoned by her family, lamented: "I had no one left to help me. I was embarrassed (*k'mah gay*). Even if I was not wrong, they hit me." Similarly, Ms. Saphira confessed,

> Sometimes I feel small talking to people who get to go to school and sometimes people look down on me and tell me that I am stupid. . . . Sometimes I get really angry with my kids because they don't want to study, and they procrastinate. I have to yell at them so that they do their homework because I don't want them to be stupid like me.

I spent much time during interviews encouraging and trying to help my informants have a sense of worth and dignity, trying to bestow my own estimation of their great value. Contrary to what I imagined the interviews would be like, there were many tears and times of consoling. The emotions I experienced have forever changed my understanding of and dealings with oral learners. At one point, when I was encouraging and consoling Ms. Tova, whose younger sister persisted in called her *l'ngong*, I touched her and looked right at her, declaring firmly her worth as a human being. We were both in tears as she remarked happily, "I have goose bumps." Ms. Tova has since changed jobs and has been involved in learning new skills. I am thankful for the opportunity I had not only to learn from her but also to encourage her in her life journey.

The vignette below presents the sincere words of a twenty-nine-year-old man working in agriculture. His words brought me to tears as well.

Question 5: Descriptive Vignette, Mr. Nestor

> I was born in the year of the dragon. I think I am almost thirty years old. My hometown is in Kandal province near Kampong Speu. I moved here to this area of Kandal when I was seventeen years old. I work for a local NGO [non-governmental organization] in agriculture. I chose agriculture because I already knew a little bit about it, and it does not require a lot of reading and writing. I learned a little bit all along the way and I learned more from watching others. It is my favorite work and something I can learn quickly.

If I want to learn new information, I ask others I know, those who know how to do it. I only ask trusted people, as I have been lied to before.

I wanted to learn when I was in school. I went six years, but I could not get it (*ree-un aht jole*). I really do not know why I could not learn. When I came home from school, I even went for tutoring. I really did not know anything. The teachers would just pass us even though we did not know the material. Nowadays I learn by listening to the radio. I go to church and I listen to God's Word on the radio. I cannot read the Bible, but I like to listen. I feel sad and disappointed when I go to church because I cannot read like everyone else. I am married now, and my wife tried to help me, but now I feel I am too old to learn, and I feel I still will not be able to learn. My brain just cannot get the information.

I believe teachers should pay attention to poor students and help them even more than other students. If teachers do not really try to help them, they will never learn. They should not push them without helping them first, otherwise they will never learn. Now whenever I see the alphabet, I feel so full of the information and cannot get it to go into my head. As for other work, I feel I can do it. Other work needs strength, but not a lot of knowledge, but if I could be anything or do anything, I would love to be a policeman. However, I cannot do this because I would need to read and write, but this is a dream of mine.

The truth is—in regard to my feelings—when I can see that others can read and write well, I feel really sad and even think of committing suicide, but after I believed in Jesus, I do not feel quite so bad. I love books but because I cannot read, they are hard to look at. You can only hug them while you are sleeping.

When I was younger, if the teachers really cared about me—especially in kindergarten and first and second grade—they should have taught us clearly until we understood the consonants and vowels. They should not just pass people without them knowing how to read—like me. I want to learn but I no longer have the will or the endurance to try.

Question 6: Role of Spirituality in ALFE Learning

Turning to examine spiritual, research sub-question 6 asked, "What role does religion play in the learning of ALFE in Cambodia?" As mentioned earlier, religion played a large role in determining who was in group 1, the incidental learning group, and in group 3, the purposeful learners. All those who overcame obstacles to learn to read attributed the success to their faith—whether Buddhist or Christian. The Christians talked about praying and God helping them learn to read and understand text. One of the ladies in The Bridge Group confided,

> I know how to read now. Before I believed in Jesus, I didn't know how to read at all! I didn't have the chance to study at all. I lived in the time of Pol Pot. I used to know how to make this dessert a long time ago; but when I didn't have any work or anything, I prayed, "Lord help me know what to do." I have been selling desserts for a year now. God helped me learn to read. Now I can read the Bible. At night I read the Bible now.

Older Buddhists like The Devout Three who lived on the temple grounds shared, "We learned to chant bit-by-bit, line-by-line, even if we could not read the sacred words." Their desire to grow in their spirituality seemed to be the incentive they needed to try harder, to overcome obstacles. Christians seemed to find their impetus seeking help from God. Ms. Terina related:

> I feel like when I want to do something I need to pray to the Lord. I do not know. I worship Him and tell Him that I do not read. I ask, "Please send me grace to help me to understand a little bit more." I can pray, and it is answered.

Along these lines, the vignette below represents part of the learning journey of a twenty-two-year-old who works with an NGO (non-governmental organization). She has learned to become a very proficient teacher.

Question 6: Descriptive Vignette, Ms. Sona

> I was not so clever at studying. (*K'nyom ree-un aht-so poo-kie-ee tay.*) I didn't really care so much then. I tried but I was just not as good at studying as everyone else. I was always last in the class. Now the difference is I follow Jesus. He has helped me. I know it is not because of my own ability that I am doing well now and that I did well on the twelfth grade exam [but she did not pass it].
>
> The teacher would just teach by writing the lessons on the white board. After she finished writing on the white board, she asked the students to copy the information down in their notebooks. While the students copied, the teacher had free time and would leave. The smart students could get the information, but the poor students could not.
>
> I wanted to learn, but I stopped going to school about the sixth grade because I could not see the white board. The teachers did not believe me and thought I only wanted to sit near the

front. They put me on the last row. Thankfully I had a friend with the same problem, but who could see better than I could, so she helped me and allowed me to copy from her. I quit school after that.

How did I learn to read and write finally? When I started believing in the Lord, I started to learn how to read the Bible. The pastor announced that if people would read the whole Bible in one year, they would get a gift from the church. I was not thinking about the gift. I wanted to have a Bible like everyone else. I wanted to know what they were talking about, so I asked for a Bible, but there were none left. They had given them all away. I found an old Bible no one was using and read it. I spent a lot of time reading the Bible because I did not go to school anymore and had a lot of free time. I was the first one to finish reading the whole Bible.

I just looked at other people and how they read, and I started reading. I did not really know how, but when I started to read the Bible, God just gave me the ability to read. There were words that I could not understand—like royal words for addressing the king, so I wrote down the words that I could not understand and would go and ask those who know more than I do what those words mean. God gave me the ability to read but I did not understand what I read. Before I started to read the Bible, I would pray and ask God for wisdom and the right way to read the Bible and what He wanted to tell me through the Bible. After that, I could do it.

CHAPTER SUMMARY

In examining the participant data according to the research questions and conceptual framework, I recognized the role of others, the role of self, and the role of spirituality to be more prominent than I expected. The affective dimension of ALFE learning took me by surprise, changing my heart forever toward those who have few opportunities to learn. I imagined my research would be a more of a cognitive journey, but it was an emotional one from the first interview onward.

On one occasion, I met with the four learners who struggled most in our certificate-level leadership development courses. We talked for a whole day about their lives and their learning experiences. Afterward while traveling home, we passed a sign at a school that seemed to summarize what that learning group discovered and what I hope the others can as well: "*Ree-un howey, ree-un tee-ut, ree-un ah muy jee-vwit,*" in other words "Learn. Learn a bit more. Learn all your life." The ALFE that I interviewed certainly embodied these words of lifelong learning—especially those in group 3.

In the next section I examine, interpret, and synthesize all the data from the participants as well as data from my observations, memos, and time spent identifying with ALFE as a non-reader. I also discuss the resulting themes on the road to discovering the central understanding of the participants. Finding that people, religion, poverty, and shame were all unexpectedly looming larger in my study than I would have imagined, I returned to the literature for additional analysis.

5

Interpretation and Synthesis: The Central Understanding

> "Imagine yourself in a situation where you are alone, wholly alone on earth,
>
> and you are offered one of the two, books or men....
>
> I knew nothing of books when I came forth from the womb of my mother,
>
> and I shall die without books, with another human hand in my own.
>
> I do, indeed close my door at times and surrender myself to a book,
>
> but only because I can open the door again and see a human being looking at me."
>
> —MARTIN BUBER, *BOOKS AND MEN*

THE RESEARCH QUESTIONS HAVE been answered through the participants' words in the previous chapter, but that knowledge does not yet portray the whole story of the main concerns of the participants, my observations and participation with ALFE learners, nor my phenomenological experiences as a non-reader. This chapter, along with chapter 6, seeks to synthesize and interpret the findings, integrating and considering literature related to those findings, and present the central understanding and corollary themes. As mentioned in the literature review in chapter 2, the discussion in the following chapters will also incorporate additional pertinent literature related to the central understanding and themes discovered in this GT study. In this chapter, I present a list of inclusive themes, then focus the discussion on the central understanding. In chapter 6, I continue the discussion of four corollary themes.

CENTRAL UNDERSTANDING AND INCLUSIVE THEMES

As I analyzed the data, I found one major idea that succinctly explained how ALFE in Cambodia learn. Surrounding that central understanding were four inclusive and accompanying themes. In response to the central research question, "How do oral Cambodian adults with limited formal education (ALFE) learn or acquire new knowledge, beliefs/values, and skills?" the one-word answer would be *connection*. The central theme that emerged was one of connected or relational learning or learning by socialization. The themes listed below include that core idea plus four additional themes unearthed during the research.

- Connected learning was found to be a relational or social process, with a preference for observing and learning from known, trusted, and/or successful people. ALFE preferred learning from people instead of learning from print.

- Connected learning was also a reflexive process in regard to one's self as learner. This kind of learning was connected to self and self-image in all of life's dimensions—cognitive, affective, and physical (psychomotor). Connected learning depended heavily on self-efficacy and honor or dignity. Any resulting relational and cultural shame due to failure, therefore, was a definite deterrent to successful learning.

- Connected learning was a redemptive process, learning that was highly connected to one's faith or spirituality as a source of aspirational hope,[1] purpose, and assistance.

- Connected learning was a relevant process. This kind of learning was highly related to one's context and culture and was experience based and practical.

- Connected learning was repackaged learning or packaged differently from print learning. This kind of learning included connection with accessible technologies and other portable vehicles of connection, such as stories, parables, metaphors, drama, art, and the like.

1. Wydick and Lybbert, "Poverty."

Interpretation and Synthesis: The Central Understanding 101

Figure 9 and H1 (Appendix H) visually depict these connected ways of learning embraced by ALFE in Cambodia and are discussed more fully in the following chapters. The next sections of this chapter focus solely on the first point above, the central understanding.

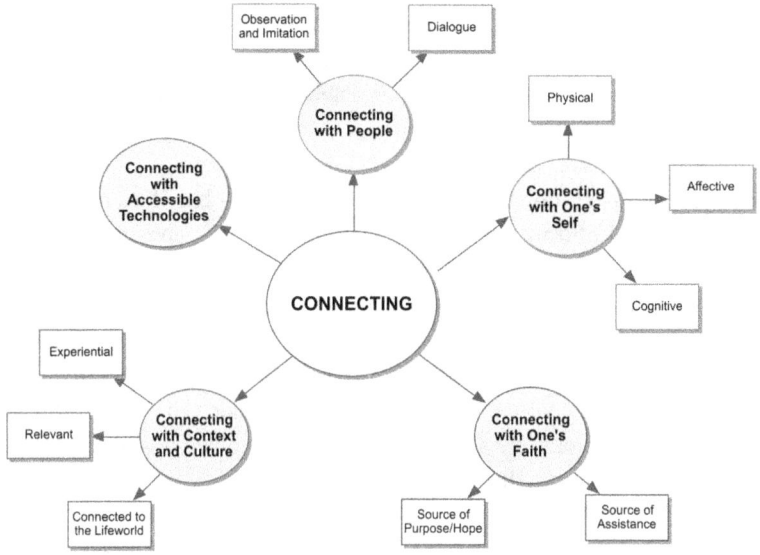

Figure 9. Connected Learning Schematic.

CONNECTED LEARNING: LEARNING THAT RESEMBLES SOCIALIZATION

In this section, I discuss the central understanding derived from my three stages of interaction with ALFE learning (identification, observation, and interview stages). First, I examine connected learning or social/relational learning and synthesize the thoughts into quadrants charting means of learning and funds of knowledge. Then I consider learning from people by watching or observation, imitation, and the discussion that follows such learning. Finally, I explore this default kind of learning, comparing thoughts on socialization by Berger and Luckmann[2] with thoughts on oral communication by Ong.[3]

---

2. Berger and Luckmann, *Social Construction of Reality*.
3. Ong, *Orality and Literacy*.

Social/Relational/Connected Learning

ALFE's major way of learning was shown to be by means of people, with a preference for observation. A relational process, connected learning involved known, trusted, and/or successful people. As I explored their desired way of learning, I noticed it resembled the natural process of socialization. I had never thought of people as being central to the learning process. Cambodian ALFE preferred learning from people instead of learning from print. When this kind of learning was not available, ALFE seemed to be at a great loss for finding opportunities to learn.

Scholars have proposed many types of learning—observational, dialogical, conversational, experiential, and problem-based, to name just a few. Each kind of learning focuses on the means and tends to ignore the vehicle by which the learning is accomplished. By contrast, ALFE seemed to concentrate heavily on the vehicle—the person—in learning. When considering dialogical and conversational learning, researchers focused on the questions and answers, the conversations or dialogue. Similarly, when considering observational learning, researchers tended to focus on the act of observation—not the primacy of the people involved or the connection and relations built into the process.

Previously, I did not consider the primacy of the person as a vehicle for learning. I only thought of them as part of the milieu, merged with the setting surrounding the main event of learning. ALFE, however, viewed people as the means and the source of learning—the principal actors and focus of the drama. Figure 10 below depicts connected learning as an integration of learning by experience, by observation, through discussion, even in the midst of the need to solve problems, all revolving around deep and central spiritual needs, and driven by social, relational, cultural, and affective elements. It does not ignore already existing learning strategies in the literature. For the participants, connected learning seemed to be a holistic inclusion of all these forms of learning with an emphasis on relationship or connection.

Interpretation and Synthesis: The Central Understanding 103

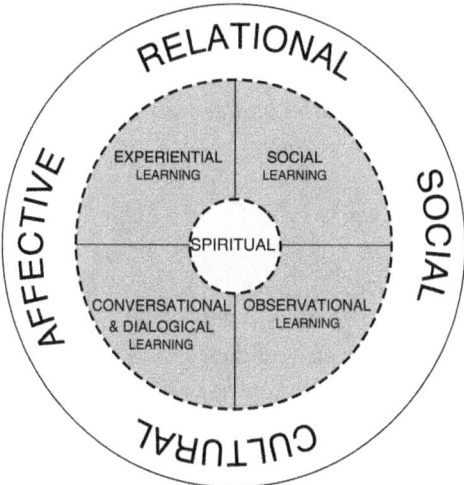

Figure 10. Components of connected learning.

I came to understand connected learning more clearly when I spent nearly a week living as a non-reader, identifying with ALFE. I include an evocative autoethnography with reflection in Appendix B. During those excruciating days of being denied access to print, the only way I could gather information was from other people. I had to hound them for assistance. I know my husband would testify to suffering as much as I did during the time I abstained from using print resources. The experience was intensely painful for me. The level of dependence and need for trust in others, the sense of powerlessness, the frustration, the feeling that the world was unwelcoming to me as a non-reader, the boredom, and the anger were all surprising results. Without connection to living, breathing people, life was difficult, if not impossible. Experiencing this intense need for people instead of print or other technologies, I came to understand first-hand all these themes and more, discussed further in chapter 6.

For ALFE, people were a preferred fund of knowledge[4] and a preferred means by which that knowledge was acquired. Introducing the term in an anthropological study, Velez-Ibanez and Greenberg described various available "bodies of information" as *funds of knowledge*.[5] Moll et al. utilized the term in an educational study to broaden the base of available knowledge in school settings through ethnographic exploration of students'

---

4. See Moll et al., "Funds of Knowledge"; Rodriguez, "Power and Agency"; Velez-Ibanez and Greenberg, "Formation and Transformation."

5. Velez-Ibanez and Greenberg, "Formation and Transformation."

homes.[6] They defined the concept as "historically accumulated and culturally developed bodies of knowledge and skills essential for household or individual functioning and well-being."[7] Oughton described how the term *funds of knowledge* was used in adult education for the knowledge individuals bring to their own learning.[8]

Contrary to Rios-Aguilar et al., I do not use the term *funds of knowledge* "for describing capital in lower income and immigrant communities."[9] I believe each person in every stratum of society has access to different funds of knowledge; therefore, I use the term for those who are literate as well as for those who do not choose to learn through print resources. Jousse called these important people and their oral tradition "the living press."[10] They are valuable containers or holders of knowledge that can be accessed through relational means.

During my week of living as a non-reader, I realized how my funds of knowledge tended toward text. Most ALFE feel excluded from that source. Explaining the use of a readily available fund of knowledge, Diouf et al. described how one informant in their study initiated the process of learning from a village elder:

> You know a person who holds a specific knowledge that you want to get, and you start a process of letting him know that you are interested in learning what he holds if he is willing to transmit it to you.... Nobody can get valuable knowledge without showing devotion to the holder as a sign of respect and of recognition of his achievement.[11]

Oughton asked a poignant question along these lines: "Whose knowledge counts?"[12] As I learned in this study, ALFE took advantage of others as funds of knowledge, much as a literate person might consult a library book or search the internet. They preferred a warm, human connection when learning. People were the vessels holding a precious commodity, a living library. As Sfard proposed,[13] ALFE seemed to view learning as participation and not as mere acquisition, much like the difference between formal schooling and that which occurs in informal and non-formal learning

6. Moll et al., "Funds of Knowledge."
7. Moll et al., "Funds of Knowledge," 133.
8. Oughton, "Funds of Knowledge."
9. Rios-Aguilar et al., "Funds of Knowledge," 179.
10. Jousse, *Oral Style*, 135.
11. Diouf et al., "Adult Learning," 40.
12. Oughton, "Funds of Knowledge."
13. Sfard, "Two Metaphors for Learning"; "Moving between Discourses."

Interpretation and Synthesis: The Central Understanding 105

settings.[14] Thus, academics might prefer funds of knowledge portrayed in research journals, whereas most ALFE might default to being engaged in warm conversation while learning from a person.

All human beings desire connection. Some, however, prefer to connect via print and technology. Others do not. As Cambron-Goulet noted, "Letters make the absent present."[15] However, non-literates do not experience this print connection, preferring rather very present, face-to-face encounters, unless another person reads print for them. As Einstein explained,

> Knowledge exists in two forms—lifeless, stored in books, and alive in the consciousness of men. The second form of existence is after all the essential one; the first, indispensable as it may be, occupies only an inferior position.[16]

When Belenky et al. researched procedural knowledge, they proposed connected knowing as opposed to separate knowing.[17] As Marrs and Benton related, the foundation of such an emphasis is relational.[18] However, what emerged from this study was more holistic than merely applying connected knowing to ALFE learning.

As I researched the term *connected learning* after arriving at the central understanding, I discovered connected learning is a term beginning to be used for "learning that is socially embedded, interest-driven, and oriented toward educational, economic, or political opportunity," an approach directed toward young people.[19] Ito and a group of educator–researchers initiated a Connected Learning Research Network. Additionally, while exploring "mentoring relationships between nurses," Ryan et al. also discovered a theme of relational learning.[20]

The way I observed this connected/relational/social learning emulated was much like Bandura explained: "In the social learning system, new patterns of behavior can be acquired through direct experience or by observing the behavior of others."[21] Bentley and O'Brien defined this kind of social learning as "learning by observing and interacting with others."[22]

---

14. Oughton, "Funds of Knowledge."
15. Cambron-Goulet, "Orality in Philosophical Epistles," 151.
16. Einstein and Calaprice, *Ultimate Quotable Einstein*, 439.
17. Belenky et al., *Women's Ways of Knowing*.
18. Marrs and Benton, "Relationships."
19. Ito et al., *Connected Learning*, 4.
20. Ryan et al., "Wise Women," 183.
21. Bandura, *Social Learning Theory*, 3.
22. Bentley and O'Brien, "Tipping Points," 298.

Rendell et al. saw social learning as "learning that is influenced by observation of or interaction with another individual, or its products."[23] Brown and Adler maintained:

> Social learning is based on the premise that our *understanding* of content is socially constructed through conversations about that content and through grounded interactions, especially with others, around problems or actions. The focus is not so much on *what* we are learning but on *how* we are learning.[24]

Similar to the concept of social learning, Browning and Solomon advised a relational learning approach in medical education.[25] Holloway and Alexandre discussed the importance of relational learning in doctoral study.[26] As I returned to the literature excluded from chapter 2, I discovered DeCapua and Marshall also insisted on a number of my same conclusions, one being the importance of relationship. They emphatically declared, "The cornerstone of learning is the unity of people and knowledge."[27]

In his study of Thai Christians' understanding of God, Taylor concurred with the findings of this study: "The Thai have a tradition of learning from people rather than from books."[28] In the 2013 Participate study of "people's experiences of living in poverty," the researchers found that relationship was a key to sustainable development.[29] Similarly, Bigelow explained in her study with a Somali diaspora group, "Orality does not just denote communicating through listening, speaking, orating, and reading poetry; in the deepest sense, it refers to a way of life entirely organically fashioned on face-to-face human relations."[30]

Rhoads also described "predominately oral cultures" as having "commonly-held social knowledge . . . that is, for almost everyone there was little or no experience of impersonal writing on a scroll unassociated with a person. Life was relational and social—face to face."[31] Additionally, Shuter related, "The Hmong culture relies strictly on people and groups to transmit information and consequently places inordinate value on these

---

23. Rendell et al., "Cognitive Culture," 68.
24. Brown and Adler, "Minds on Fire," 18.
25. Browning and Solomon, "Relational Learning."
26. Holloway and Alexandre, "Crossing Boundaries."
27. DeCapua and Marshall, "Students with Limited," 164.
28. Taylor, "Study of Relationship," 118.
29. Participate, *People's Experiences of Living in Poverty*, 1.
30. Bigelow, "Orality and Literacy," 55.
31. Rhoads, "Biblical Performance Criticism," 157.

sources of information."³² Finally, Kilpatrick and Johns found in their study of how farmers learn: "Informal learning sources in the form of experts, observation, and experience, and other farmers were the most frequently used learning sources for change."³³

In the emerging fields of study, social neuroscience and social physics, researchers Jones et al. chronicled "how different probabilities of positive interaction from distinct peers rapidly influence social learning."³⁴ Studying diffusion of ideas, Young noted, "Neighbors were listed as the *most influential in deciding whether to implement*."³⁵ Taylor et al. examined a successful adult classroom and ascertained it involved collaboration of peers, a distinct classroom socialization process, and social learning behaviors.³⁶ Merrifield and Bingman "conducted twelve in-depth profiles with adult men and women in four states in Appalachia and the West Coast" and recognized the learners had "other-oriented learning strategies," which included visual strategies (watching others, having someone model a skill) and oral strategies (dialogue), and cooperative learning.³⁷ These strategies definitely resemble connected learning.

Of course, not all learning is positive. Some learning experiences can be quite negative, even in the presence of connection and relationship. Learning experiences nevertheless, discussion of these is beyond the scope of this study. Subsequent attempts at education can cause disconnection and are discussed in these two chapters. However, when connections are absent or broken, the affective becomes highly charged and shame enters the stage. An important aspect of ALFE learning unearthed in this study, shame is addressed later.

This kind of informal and "implicit learning has attracted far less attention than its explicit counterpart, even though it is thought to be at least as ubiquitous as explicit learning and can dramatically influence our behavior and social perception."³⁸ Chavis reiterated:

> Social learning theory is one of the most influential theories of learning and human development and is rooted in many of the basic concepts of traditional learning. The theory focuses on learning that occurs within a social context and that people learn

32. Shuter, "Hmong of Laos," 104.
33. Kilpatrick and Johns, "How Farmers Learn," 161.
34. Jones et al., "Behavioral and Neural Properties," 5.
35. Young, "Innovation Diffusion," 1917.
36. Taylor et al., "Collaborative Practices."
37. Merrifield and Bingman, "Living and Learning," 181.
38. Hudson et al., "Implicit Social Learning," 1.

from one another; however, the theory adds a social element. It proposes that people can learn new information and behaviors by observing other people. Thus, the use of observational learning, imitation, or modeling explains a wide variety of human behaviors using social learning theory and approach.[39]

This ethnographic grounded theory sought to extend the ideas of social and relational learning in different ways as presented in the following.

Learning Quadrants

From which do ALFE prefer to learn—from people or print? Overwhelmingly, the participants shared they learned from people. Even as I observed those with limited formal education who became readers, I witnessed a sense of community, rich times of talk, an emphasis on relationship and connectedness, and their strong affinity for people as resources. From learning together to teaching together, fervent personal connection abounded. For instance, Ms. Pia recounted:

> Whatever we learn, we go together to teach. We help each other out. If she does not know something, I will add and if I don't know something, she will add. But we have documents; we will teach using those documents. She will know some and I will know some. When I go out to teach, I always learn something as well.

When intent on learning, for instance, Ms. Talia confided, "I tried to sneak and watch others (*mull gay*). After I watched for awhile and learned, then the boss took me as a worker." The phrases *mull gay* (to watch others/them) and *ree-un pee gay* (to learn from others/them) were scattered repeatedly throughout the interviews—like strategic breadcrumbs leading me to the central understanding and emphasizing the importance people played in their learning.

Coomaraswamy and Coomaraswamy agreed: "From the Indian point of view, a man can only be said to *know* what he knows *by heart*; what he must go to a book to be reminded of, he merely knows of."[40] Similarly, Enbar and Flombaum at the Flatiron School, creators of "an online learning platform," emphatically retorted, "Learning does not come from content. Learning comes from connecting people through content. No one remembers their college textbooks or class lecture slides. People remember their classmates. Their study groups. Their teachers." Their blog

---

39. Chavis, "Social Learning Theory," 471.
40. Coomaraswamy and Coomaraswamy, *Essential Coomaraswamy*, 59.

shouted a message of connection to their learning community: "You may be online, but you are not alone."[41]

As mentioned in chapter 2, Hiebert recorded numerous means of storing knowledge, such as stories, symbols, and rituals.[42] His list, however, neglected the participants' most important information storage—people. In contrast, literates rely on knowledge found in print media. Examining the "worldviews of small-scale oral societies" and "peasant worldviews" and accompanying orality, Hiebert agreed, "Oral communication is highly relational,"[43] "immediate and face-to-face."[44] He admonished all who delve into the strategic area of bridging the abyss between the two ways of storing knowledge as follows:

> We who are literate tend to think only in terms of storing and communicating the gospel in spoken and written forms. We fail to realize that oral societies are not "illiterate." They have, in fact, a rich supply of cultural knowledge and many different ways of storing it. In such societies we must use these media to present the gospel in concrete ways that the people will recall.[45]

People comprise an integral role in the oral cultural milieu. Not peripheral to the drama in ALFE learning, they proved to be center stage for the storage and funneling of knowledge.

As I worked with Cambodian ALFE, I came to understand which people they would consult and trust. Literate westerners tend to favor expertise gained by education, following and trusting textual funds of knowledge. When I interjected my knowledge in the mix with my acquaintances, I discovered expertise was not important to them. The only thing that mattered was relationship. For instance, Ms. Kelis's legs cramped when she slept. I talked to her about the need for calcium, what had helped me, and what I knew medically about this problem (as a laboratory scientist). A glazed look greeted my words. They meant nothing to her. Even though I had been her husband's teacher, my advice was not revered. I was not very relationally close to her. So where did she turn? Her mother, living in another village nearly eight hours away, told her about a massage chair able to cure her ills. That was the fund of knowledge she trusted—advice from her mother. Another participant, Mr. Morris, confided how he got information: "I ask my older sister. She studied longer than I did, and she helps me."

41. Enbar and Flombaum, "Learn.co."
42. Hiebert, *Anthropological Insights*; *Transforming Worldviews*.
43. Hiebert, *Transforming Worldviews*, 116.
44. Hiebert, *Transforming Worldviews*, 128.
45. Hiebert, *Transforming Worldviews*, 162.

In an older work, Mayers referred to this concept as "the prior question of trust" or PQT.[46] In my interaction with Ms. Kelis above, I had not built sufficient trust with her; therefore, my attempt to advise the use calcium was spurned. Trust reigned over expertise or knowledge. In all likelihood, family would be trusted more than outsiders in group-oriented culture, so what does this information mean for those bearing an important message or teaching in this context? How can we come to be trusted? An important question outside the scope of this research, the idea of trust in learning is worthy of further study.

People or print, knowledge gained through schooling or knowledge from trusted people—which one is the preferred means? In an exploration of the literature, I unearthed many studies in agreement with my findings. Aikman related that for some "knowledge came from written texts and from the teacher, while for others knowledge came from experimentation and the elders."[47] Hardman also related that Cambodians studying ESL in the US took advantage of classmates as "knowledge holders" or "funds of knowledge,"[48] as Moll and Greenberg also described.[49] Parker discovered students related better to teachers who behaved like parents, with close and caring connections.[50] In a study of HIV/AIDS prevention messages in Ethiopia, Bogale et al. revealed, "Social-oriented presentation formats, such as discussion between women" were more readily received than "expert-oriented presentation formats, such as an interview with a male doctor."[51]

Merriam and Mohamad considered "how cultural values shape learning in older adulthood" in Malaysia.[52] For their participants, "'school' is not seen as a place for learning once one has become an adult."[53] In their literature review, they related several studies that reiterated this theme of connection and the need for relationships in old age. They also noted "learning is communal" and "intertwined with family relationships." As I pondered this theory of connected learning, the participants' words, my observations, and time of identifying with non-readers, I sketched the two ideas so integral to learning—the means or process of learning versus funds of knowledge or the preferred seat of authority and trust—in the form of four different

---

46. Mayers, *Christianity Confronts Culture*, 7.
47. Aikman, *Intercultural Education and Literacy*, 125.
48. Hardman, "Community of Learners."
49. Moll and Greenberg, "Creating Zones of Possibilities."
50. Parker, "Adult Perspectives," 97.
51. Bogale et al., "Reaching the Hearts," 2.
52. Merriam and Mohamad, "How Cultural Values Shape Learning."
53. Merriam and Mohamad, "How Cultural Values Shape Learning," 52.

Interpretation and Synthesis: The Central Understanding 111

quadrants. Figure 11 portrays those resulting Learning Quadrants, with discussion in the following section.

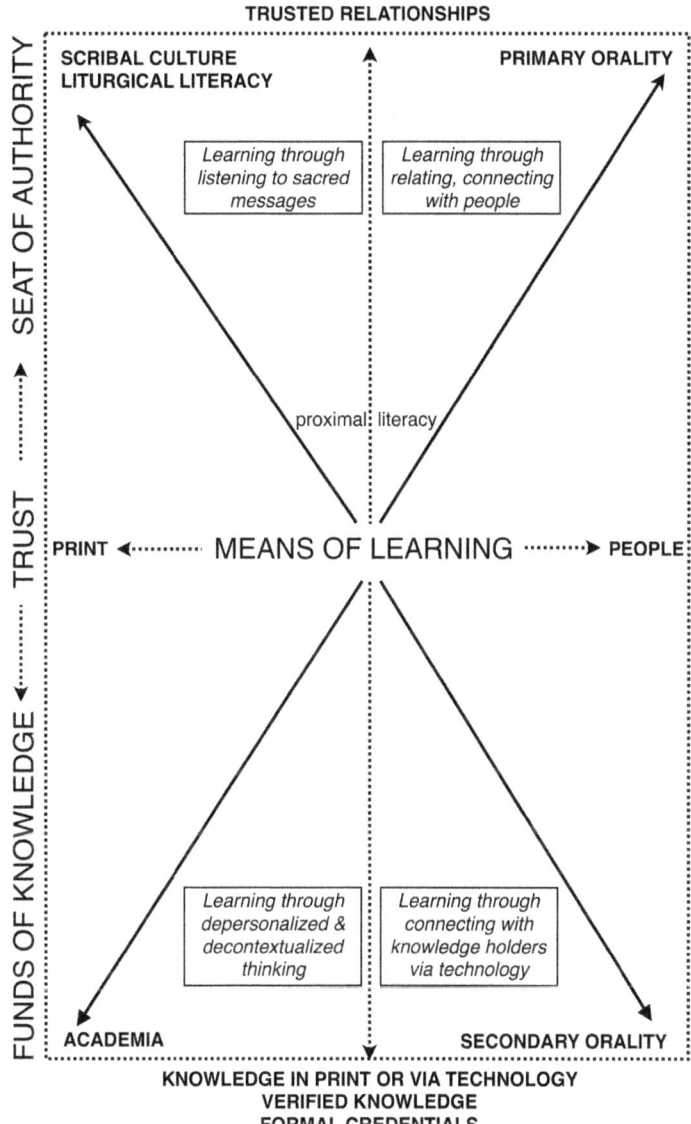

Figure 11. Learning Quadrants.

MEANS OF LEARNING. The horizontal axis of the grid represents the means of learning. Does the person prefer to learn from people or from print? We all begin life by attaching to our mothers or our primary caregivers. We watch those people intently and learn from them. We are neurologically wired to gather this information, process it, and learn from it. We continue on this journey of learning from people until we die. It is a form of socialization, as I consider below.

For some, however, the journey takes a different trajectory. Some pursue formal schooling and begin to learn from print. The left side of the figure represents that means of learning. According to neuroscience researchers such as Dehaene, learning from print is not a natural form of human learning.[54] In examining various time periods in history—from orality to literacy—Pettitt maintained, "The natural flow of communication was interrupted by the print phase."[55] Shifting from the natural learning depicted in the upper right quadrant requires a cultural and unnatural resocialization.

Because of the shift required in moving toward literacy and formal schooling, I did not position learning from people on the left and extend learning from print to the right, which would portray a sort of progression from illiteracy to literacy. Learning from print is an entirely different trajectory, while learning from people is a lifelong and natural means of acquisition. However, learning from print has been elevated to important status through such well-meaning organizations as UNESCO.

As we have seen throughout this study, the process of formal schooling and learning from print can fail. As Klem observed, cultural values and knowledge can be transmitted via personal or impersonal means, with preferences along the continuum.[56] Similarly, Stock maintained: "Oral society has faith in one type of text. Literate society in another."[57] Historically, our contemporary global culture as a whole (but not all individual cultures) has moved from orality to reliance on print, as a sort of "Gutenberg galaxy," according to McLuhan,[58] or historically as a "Gutenberg parenthesis," according to Sauerberg[59] and Pettitt.[60]

In her ethnographic study of Hmong adults in an ESL program, Hvitfeldt ascertained relationship to be primary.[61] However, as Hvitfeldt disclosed, "Success in our educational system necessitates for the Hmong learner, a

54. Dehaene, *Reading in the Brain*.
55. Pettitt, "Gutenberg Parenthesis."
56. Klem, *Oral Communication of the Scripture*, 143.
57. Stock, *Listening for the Text*, 146.
58. McLuhan, *Gutenberg Galaxy*.
59. Sauerberg, "Encyclopedia and the Gutenberg Parenthesis."
60. Pettitt, "Gutenberg Parenthesis."
61. Hvitfeldt, "Traditional Culture."

Interpretation and Synthesis: The Central Understanding 113

paradigm shift from a familiar learning paradigm to the unfamiliar, formal educational learning paradigm."[62] The two ends of the spectrum are "two conflicting learning paradigms."[63] Indeed, as Fingeret also noted,

> Illiterate adults in this study identify a risk connected to learning to read and write. They may become alienated from network members and subcultural conventions. . . . Illiterate adults know, however, that as they learn to read, all of their network relationships must shift.[64]

Therefore, this leap from learning from people to learning from print involves an intentional change in culture, the result of an intentional resocialization effort. As seen in this study, not everyone can or does make that leap.

Some learners become proficient in the print mode of learning and come to prefer it. Some like the isolation of escaping into a book, while those who prefer the warmth of learning through relations and face-to-face contact may feel print cold and impersonal—as untrusted or unreliable. Thao related in his study of Hmong adults: "They said that a primarily oral person could take their knowledge with them everywhere they go, whereas a literate person has to depend on books. A literate person does not function well without books."[65] He is exactly right. As a literate person, I did "not function well without books" in the first stage of this research study.

Rogoff et al. contrasted formal schooling with informal learning by referring to formal schooling as "assembly-line instruction" versus "intent participation," observational learning that occurs naturally in socialization—the difference between the learning in the primary orality quadrant and the academic quadrant in the Learning Quadrants diagram presented earlier.[66] Educators

> see the two traditions as descriptions of *processes*, whereas the informal/formal dichotomy is often applied to *places*. Our distinction is not applied to locales or setting. . . . The processes of intent participation and assembly-line instruction are not necessarily tied to the type of activities or domain of knowledge (such as practical versus theoretical endeavors or concrete

---

62. Hvitfeldt, "Traditional Culture," 4.
63. Hvitfeldt, "Traditional Culture," 4.
64. Fingeret, "Social Network," 144.
65. Thao, "Voices of Mong Elders," 242.
66. Rogoff et al., "Firsthand Learning."

versus abstract information). The distinction is in the form of involvement, not in the subject.[67]

It would seem we need to take informal means into formal places so more people can learn in the manner most suited to their ways of learning.

FUNDS OF KNOWLEDGE. On the vertical axis dissecting the learning process or means of learning lies consideration of source—the locus of authority or fund of knowledge, as discussed earlier. In my interaction with ALFE, I noted the emphasis and importance of the locus of authority. Who or what is considered an expert from whom we can learn? Who or what is trusted? Upon whom should one rely? Many who prefer print trust academic authorities, experts who have analyzed a body of knowledge and conducted research. Others shun such supposed knowledge and prefer a relational authority, someone trusted or someone older and wiser.

QUADRANTS. Traditionally, quadrants in a Cartesian coordinate system are labeled numerically, beginning with the top right as the first, then moving counterclockwise to the other three quadrants. Examining the corners of each quadrant, we see the extremes—the academic who values print learning and bodies of knowledge, experts who have been educated for years and are authorities in their fields in the third quadrant (lower left). This quadrant receives a great deal of attention in the literature, and unfortunately, as Glazer noted, this kind of education "has become grounded in disconnection."[68]

In the upper right or first quadrant is the natural, traditional state of humankind, learning from people, trusting the wisdom of the aged—the situation of the primary oral culture without access to written language. As Fanta-Vagenshtein related, "A population that does not know how to read and write acquires knowledge and skills through learning agents and other channels that bypass literacy-based learning."[69] In additional research, Fanta-Vagenshtein and Chen observed, "In traditional culture, knowledge in general and technological knowledge in particular is amassed via interpersonal dialog"[70] or "informal frameworks featuring interaction with the practical sphere."[71]

---

67. Rogoff et al., "Firsthand Learning," 184.
68. Glazer, *Heart of Learning*, 9.
69. Fanta-Vagenshtein, "How Illiterate People Learn," 45.
70. Fanta-Vagenshtein et al., "Technological Knowledge," 290.
71. Fanta-Vagenshtein et al., "Technological Knowledge," 299.

Interpretation and Synthesis: The Central Understanding 115

The second or top left quadrant depicts the situation of people respectful of a sacred book or sacred teachings but relying on relational experts in order to hear them—"scribal culture,"[72] the living Torah of the Jewish rabbi or the "master as living text,"[73] the Indian *guru*, the master teacher in Confucianism, or the chanting Buddhist monk, for example. This respect for knowledge stored in print but reliance on people can fall along a continuum, extending from proximal literacy, a situation in which those who cannot read have access to those who can, to the kind of learning imparted by priests like Ezra in Nehemiah 8:2–6. Pieter Botha described a "dynamic interaction between oral and written communication," between a "culture familiar with writing but in essence still significantly, even predominantly, oral."[74] He wisely concluded, "Learning *to read* is different, moreover, from learning *by reading*."[75]

Of course, people can learn from sacred texts in any quadrant and that is reflected in the complexity of this diagram. Learning involves more than a dichotomy between orality and literacy. Those who prefer the first quadrant would not hold a sacred text and read it. Instead, they might listen to recordings or live storytelling sessions. Others learning in the third quadrant might delve into hermeneutics and the ancient origins of the texts, exploring Greek, Hebrew, Pali, Sanskrit, or Arabic meanings. Lastly, learners in the fourth quadrant would major on the use of technology, in which the learner might listen to podcasts or live streaming events to connect with others of like faith.

Does this diagram portray the old Great Divide controversy?[76] The answer is most certainly not. As discussed previously, differences exist in the worlds of those learning from people and those learning from print, with differing ontologies and social epistemologies. Ong and others proposed a dichotomy—literacy versus orality.[77] These quadrants, along with the possibility for many Cartesian coordinates, display a situation far more complex than one dichotomy. Many options lie along each of the horizontal and vertical axes.

Finally, the fourth (lower left) quadrant depicts the combination of knowledge and relationship—the technological learning that comes from

72. Botha, "Mute Manuscripts."
73. See Carr, "Torah on the Heart"; Jaffee, "Rabbinic Ontology."
74. Botha, "Mute Manuscripts," 42.
75. Botha, "Mute Manuscripts," 42.
76. See Furniss, *Orality*; Goody and Watt, "Consequences of Literacy"; McLuhan, *Gutenberg Galaxy*; Raven, "How Not to Explain"; Snyder, "Case Study in Defining Literacy"; Street, *Social Literacies*.
77. Ong, *Orality and Literacy*.

YouTube and Facebook, the "secondary orality" of Ong. Papacharissi spoke of a secondary orality and a "secondary visualism," as well as "digital orality."[78] Rao referred to the same idea as "contemporary orality."[79] Papacharissi maintained, "Orality is used to describe forms of storytelling and knowledge sharing that characterize every epoch. . . . Orality describes the form, the texture, the tonality that communication takes on."[80] I would, however, maintain connection or relationship and *connected learning* more clearly explains this phenomenon. Schrage, in his Merrill Lynch Forum blogpost, made an astute conclusion in relation to learning in this quadrant:

> The biggest impact these technologies have had, and will have, is on relationships between people and between organizations. *The so-called "information revolution" itself is actually, and more accurately, a "relationship revolution."* Anyone trying to get a handle on the dazzling technologies of today and the impact they'll have tomorrow, would be well advised to re-orient their worldview around relationships.[81]

Indeed, this strategy involves connection with people through technology on a wide scale.

Each quadrant of this diagram serves to contrast the learning in various lifeworlds or cultures. The lifeworld in the second quadrant values sacred print delivered through sacred people, while the one in the first quadrant values learning through people in face-to-face encounters, a culture of primary orality. Those in the third quadrant dwell in the academic world with a penchant for print and expertise, and the lifeworld in the fourth quadrant depicts that of the many modern learners who value connection and knowledge gained through technology. Learners in each quadrant desire connection and validation. Culturally, they desire it in different ways.

Neurologically, infants are already prepared to learn early after birth. They learn socially and observationally by watching the face of mother and father. A delicate, synchronized dance begins between the loving gazes of mother and child—one that creates an intense feeling of attachment,[82] the genesis of connected/social/relational learning.[83] Aragon et al., in researching the brain's ability to mirror the actions of another, disclosed, "We have neural

---

78. Papacharissi, "Unbearable Lightness of Information."
79. Rao, "Contemporary Orality," v.
80. Papacharissi, "Unbearable Lightness of Information," 4.
81. Schrage, "Relationship Revolution."
82. Schore, "Minds in the Making."
83. See Cozolino, *Social Neuroscience of Education*; Loder, *Transforming Moment*; Loder, *Logic of the Spirit*; Schore, "Minds in the Making"; Siegel, *Mindsight*.

systems that support this connection and understanding."[84] Children learn through observation and imitation for some time.

For some of those individuals, however, a new way of learning and a new culture is introduced, one that is foreign to learning by connection, foreign to natural learning, and early life-on-life socialization in a family atmosphere. Primary oral cultures do not transition to schooling. They continue to learn life skills and are sometimes apprenticed to an expert for further learning. Aikman related:

> In contrast to formal schooling, where solo performance is crucial—the social transaction itself is the fundamental vehicle of education. . . . Through their own culturally and socially patterned learning practices the Arakmbut acquire an understanding of the world in which they live.[85]

By contrast, many children across the globe leave home at a tender young age to be socialized and schooled into a new culture by means of an institution—one based on print. As Vygotsky noted, "The nature of man's education, therefore, is wholly determined by the social environment in which he grows and develops."[86] Mazamisa rightly called this entrance into "textuality" "resocialisation."[87] It is difficult to move from primary orality to literacy or the reverse. As Motty related:

> I came from a small village. . . . Orality is part of who I am, even though I received literate training from Western educators. I "un-learned" my orality in attaining formal education, but rediscovered it . . . when I was . . . trying to connect a life-saving message with my people.[88]

This journey from non-reading to literacy involves a special feat. Cognitive neuroscience researchers such as Bouhali et al.,[89] Dehaene,[90] Dehaene and Cohen,[91] Dehaene et al.,[92] and Glezer and Risenhuber[93] have examined the portion of the brain most used when experts read, the visual word form area

84. Aragon et al., "Modulations of Mirroring Activity," 1762.
85. Aikman, *Intercultural Education*, 122–24.
86. Vygotsky, *Educational Psychology*, 211.
87. Mazamisa, "Reading from This Place," 72.
88. Motty, "Spreading the Word," 9.
89. Bouhali et al., "Anatomical Connections."
90. Dehaene, "*Reading in the Brain* Revised."
91. Dehaene and Cohen, "Unique Role."
92. Dehaene et al., "Illiterate to Literate."
93. Glezer and Risenhuber, "Individual Variability."

or VWFA. Reportedly, when learning to read, a new process called "neuronal recycling" begins in our brains, in which "part of this neuronal hierarchy converts to the new task of recognizing letters and words." Surprisingly, Dehaene et al.,[94] Knowland and Thomas,[95] and others have also revealed that the brain area used for reading is the same area used for face perception, and when one learns to read, "face perception suffered in proportion to reading skills."[96] As Dehaene revealed in his article title, "learning to read changes your brain."[97] Knowland and Thomas also discovered:

> Those participants in the Dehaene study who had learned to read in adulthood (the ex-illiterates) also showed substantial activity in the VWFA in response to faces, suggesting the written words had not come to dominate the area to the same extent as in those who learned to read in childhood. This may represent a limit on brain plasticity, supporting the notion that when a system has specialized (in this case to face), it becomes increasingly hard to re-specialise (to words).[98]

Before I learned this interesting fact, I had already created the quadrants with the opposing sides of learning from people versus learning from print. They are indeed different ways of learning even according to neurological studies.

Along the paths toward the center of this grid, there are many points at which there can be combinations of means of learning and funds of knowledge. For instance, in researching the Lisu in China, who have had access to a script and written materials, Arrington observed them still retaining "oral thought patterns and the related communal social structure."[99] One major word she used to describe their focus was the word *together*—reiterating the findings of this study. Their relationship with literacy was one based on hymnody, something Arrington termed "liturgical literacy."[100]

In conclusion, each quadrant is neither good nor bad, even though some tend to dominate or receive more attention than others, some tend to be researched more than others, and sadly, in some situations, some seem to be valued more than others. To judge or pronounce one side of the continuum or one quadrant as bad or deficient is to miss the point of this study

---

94. Dehaene et al., "Learning to Read."
95. Knowland and Thomas, "Educating the Adult Brain."
96. Dehaene et al., "Learning to Read," 1364.
97. Dehaene et al., "Learning to Read."
98. Knowland and Thomas, "Educating the Adult Brain," 106.
99. Arrington, "Hymns of the Everlasting Hills," 5.
100. Arrington, "Hymns of the Everlasting Hills," 245.

and to join the hegemony that would exclude some or label some as other[101] or as deficient.[102] That view could be construed as oppressive and marginalizing. According to Shuter,

> Literacy threatens the very fabric of Hmong oral society, its group-centeredness, and it is another major obstacle to acculturation. For older Hmong, the very concept of independent study is alien to them, since learning always occurred in the present with cohesive groups of community people. Learning in groups of strangers, homework, independent study—hallmarks of literacy—run counter to the group-centered value of the Hmong.[103]

Imposing literacy and formal schooling can sometimes be seen as harmful. In fact, Montandon called for abandoning the formal, informal, and non-formal labels because they make schooling the ideal form and foster hegemony.[104] Diouf et al. likewise opined, "Equating 'education' with 'formal schooling,' reflects epistemological ethnocentrism by suggesting that the educational traditions in Africa—which are informal, are tied to the social life of the community . . . are not 'legitimate' forms of education."[105] Montandon proposed a different model or typology examining content and context and listed twenty-eight dimensions of types of education.[106] I tend to agree with her. Perhaps formal learning should be referred to more specifically as "institutionally-directed learning" and other forms "learner-directed," as most people engaged in formal learning cannot direct their entire learning process. ALFE did have more control over theirs as far as initiating learning projects.

Observation, Then Discussion

As mentioned previously, a key aspect of connected/relational/social learning was observation, watching others and learning from them. Participants repeatedly told me that in order to learn something they would *mull gay* (watch others), and I witnessed them doing so.

Several participants, however, when asked how they would learn something new, responded that they would learn by themselves, on their

---

101. See Hiebert, "Western Images of Others"; Borrero et al., "School as a Context."
102. See DeCapua and Marshall, "Students with Limited"; Irele, *African Imagination*.
103. Shuter, "Hmong of Laos," 106.
104. Montandon, "Forme Sociales," 237.
105. Diouf et al., "Adult Learning," 33.
106. Montandon, "Forme Sociales."

own (*clue-un iyng*). That was confusing to me. How could they learn without print or people, just on their own? Then I realized they were indeed still learning from people. They were just emphasizing the fact that the process would be self-directed. Someone else would not consciously teach them. The learner would not seek an institutional solution in which a teacher would direct their study. The learner would seek a personal model, observe that person's actions, and then mimic in trial-and-error fashion. Sometimes discussion would follow.

After observing this, I began re-reading research on learning and development in childhood—especially in traditional societies—research by Aikman,[107] Gaskins,[108] Rogoff,[109] and Rogoff et al.[110] This kind of learning is initiated by the person, is highly visual, and involves acute powers of observation, not necessarily verbal instructions from the one possessing the skill. Then I realized ALFE simply continued to learn and develop in the same way they did from childhood—following a natural life process that had never been interrupted by formal education, never interrupted by teaching or analysis or consulting printed material.

Gaskins explained the phenomenon as "open attention":

> A distinct, habitual way of taking information from the present environment that is strikingly different from the common Euro-American way of observing. Based on our own ethnographic research and a reading of other accounts, we believe that this pattern of attention is regularly found in cultures that highly value observation as a more general source of knowledge for everyone in the community, but that has been overlooked or underreported in the past.[111]

She elaborated: "Learning through observation in daily life is a universal learning strategy in childhood and beyond."[112] Relating the widespread nature of this type of learning, Dijksterhuis remarked:

> Imitation, and especially imitation of complex behavioral patterns, constitutes the "social glue" that makes us successful social animals. . . . Imitation is of such importance because it can be conceived of as default social behavior. Imitation is not

---

107. Aikman, *Intercultural Education*.
108. Gaskins, "Children's Daily Activities."
109. Rogoff, *Apprenticeship in Thinking*.
110. Rogoff et al., "Firsthand Learning."
111. Gaskins, "Open Attention," 3.
112. Gaskins, "Open Attention," 1.

Interpretation and Synthesis: The Central Understanding 121

something we only occasionally engage in. Instead, we *usually* imitate—automatically—and not doing it is the exception.[113]

The apostle Paul in the New Testament urged believers to imitate him (1 Cor 11:1; 4:16). There is something to be said for the merits of this kind of mentoring relationship especially for ALFE.

Others exploring traditional cultures have noticed this need for observation to be true as well. In studying African ways of learning and knowing, Ngara expounded, "Social observational and vicarious learning is culturally acknowledged in indigenous cultural wisdom."[114] Fanta-Vagenshtein concluded the number one learning channel for the Ethiopian adults in his study was visual.[115] In regard to non-western learning and knowing, Merriam and Kim explained:

> Given that learning is embedded in the context of everyday experience, active participation in everyday activities and the rites and rituals of a community are seen as conduits to learning. Learning occurs through observation of others and through practicing what is being learned.[116]

In studying women learning to weave in India, Venkatesan observed "most people learn the various processes involved in mat-weaving by watching and imitating others."[117] Likewise, Aikman noted, "Unlike classroom practice in the school, neither verbal explanation nor didactic demonstration was given. Nor was any comment made on the results of the girls' labours."[118]

Studies in this area are numerous. For instance, DeCoker, while learning Japanese traditional calligraphy, discovered the process involved "a great deal of nonverbal communication."[119] Gaskins, in studying Mayan children, expressed, "Mayan understandings of responsibility also promote careful social observation."[120] In an older study on working with Native Americans, Cazden and John concurred, finding "their style of learning is more visual than verbal, more learning by looking than learning through language."[121] In working with the Dene people, Goulet discovered they "expect learning to occur through

---

113. Dijksterhuis, "Why We Are Social Animals," 208.
114. Ngara, "African Ways of Knowing," 13.
115. Fanta-Vagenshtein, "How Illiterate People Learn."
116. Merriam and Kim, "Non-Western Perspectives," 77.
117. Venkatesan, "Learning to Weave," 168.
118. Aikman, *Intercultural Education*, 123.
119. DeCoker, "Seven Characteristics," 69.
120. Gaskins, "Children's Daily Activities," 384.
121. Cazden and John, "Learning in American Indian Children," 256.

observation rather than instruction, an expectation consistent with the Dene view that true knowledge is personal knowledge."[122]

Meltzoff learned "human children can imitate hand movements in the first six months of life," that "newborns imitate facial acts," and that "brief exposure to a novel act is enough to sear it into the memory of a toddler."[123] Once this process begins in infancy, it never seems to stop in the healthy human learner. Gaskins and Paradise decidedly confirmed that observational learning "is not an age-specific form of learning."[124]

In addition, actions we observe have been shown to impact our brains neurologically. "Neuro-physiological experiments demonstrate that when individuals observe an action done by another individual their motor cortex becomes active, in the absence of any overt motor activity," according to Rizzolatti and Graighero.[125]

As I observed the participants, I realized their process of learning was highly visual. Goulet noticed in learning a skill from traditional people, she was "not going to go very far by asking questions."[126] Like natural participant observers, people learn from others often by being silent watchers. I observed in my research that only when a participant wanted to learn information, such as Buddhist chants or Christian Scriptures, was much knowledge transmitted orally.

Turning to consider connected learning, Ong pronounced previously, "Language . . . is paramount."[127] By contrast, according to the participants in this study, relationship or connection with people was paramount. Ong majored on the study of communication and seemed to neglect the communicators, the vehicles driving the process. For the participants and their lifeworlds, the contrast was not between orality and literacy, between oral communication and text, but between learning from people and learning from print. Learning from people involved watching, listening, then talking.

In this process of learning, however, Jordan and Davis-Floyd[128] and Paradise and Rogoff[129] noted dialogue played a secondary role to observation and imitation. Ms. Shu, one of the participants, learned not by discussion, but by watching and listening to commands:

122. Goulet, *Ways of Knowing*, 27.
123. Meltzoff, "Elements of a Developmental Theory," 23, 29.
124. Gaskins and Paradise, "Learning through Observation," 89.
125. Rizzolatti and Graighero, "Mirror-Neuron System," 174.
126. Goulet, *Ways of Knowing*, 31.
127. Ong, *Orality and Literacy* (1982), 6.
128. Jordan and Davis-Floyd, *Birth in Four Cultures*.
129. Paradise and Rogoff, "Side by Side Learning."

> My parents died, and my brothers and sisters would hit me. I had to fend for myself. There was no one to help me. I just had to depend on myself, cook for myself even at a young age. If I wanted to learn something, I asked and they would show me and tell me what to do, every step, every little step of how to make a certain dish. When they told me, I remembered.

In comparing the use of talk in formal and informal settings, Rogoff et al. discovered,

> The contrast is not whether or not words are used, but the embeddedness or isolation of the word from the endeavors being referred to. In intent participation [observational learning], talk is used *in the serve of* engaging in the activity, augmenting and guiding experiential and observational learning; in an assembly-line lesson, talk is *substituted* for involvement.[130]

Of course, in connected learning, there could be talk or discussion. Kolb et al. wrote about conversational learning, calling it "experiential."[131] Fanta-Vagenshtein and Chen discovered, "In traditional culture, knowledge in general and technological knowledge in particular is amassed via interpersonal dialogue."[132] Even though the participants did not mention dialogue, discussion, or conversation in my interviews, I observed much talk in our courses. Participants often engaged in question and answer sessions as a means of clarification. Most of all, however, this talk worked as a form of connection that facilitated learning. Learners had a tendency to consult only a close, trusted leader. They met in small, familiar groupings during breaks and lunch for these extended question and answer sessions.

The Default Learning Process: Father Ong Meets Dr. Berger

How are humans socialized into our first lifeworlds? We attach to our mothers or significant primary caregivers. We watch. We mimic. From the moment we are born, we fixate on the faces of our caregivers. That process of watching people does not cease. Reading faces does not stop with infancy. Neurobiologically humans begin a trajectory at birth. From the first moment babies look into the eyes of their caregivers and begin to look for feedback and expressions, they start a learning process, a process of socialization that never stops.

---

130. Rogoff et al., "Firsthand Learning," 195.
131. Kolb et al., "Conversation as Experiential Learning."
132. Fanta-Vagenshtein et al., "Technological Knowledge," 290.

In primary socialization, we learn our own culture, our own social mores. In secondary socialization, we learn the intricacies of other worlds, such as our schools and workplaces, and incorporate their hidden curricula into our internal schema. However, we never "turn off" learning from people, watching them, amassing sensory details about how they act, how they dress, what they say.

At each stage, learning occurs quite unconsciously through people watching. We become so adept at observing cultural cues and reading faces that we even make snap judgments.[133] Profoundly affected by social influences, humans have been known to become "caught up" in social epidemics, the herd mentality, viral ideas, and the like.

In formal and work settings we also learn the hidden curriculum even though no one teaches it, much of it through observation and social learning.[134] Mossop et al. devised a cultural web map to delineate "issues contributing to the hidden curriculum" in many school and work settings.[135] These involved rituals, symbols, routines, stories, power structures, organizational control, control systems, and core assumptions.[136] Yuksel added that the "hidden curricula" are "messages that are not specifically stated but that students are expected to learn," as well as "unintended learning outcomes."[137] We learn these by means of observation and experience. Extending the idea further—to the world of neuroscience—Olson wrote of "the invisible classroom," or "the microscopic neural connections inside all of us and the hidden human connections among us. These webs of neurological and interpersonal connections create the context for teaching, learning, and living."[138]

We observe. We learn from others. We adopt fashion trends and word usage. In fact, "studies indicate that students' significant learning experiences come from their friends rather than books."[139] This is socialization. This is learning—no conscious teaching, just assimilation, learning what we want when we want. This simple, ubiquitous kind of learning is how ALFE seemed to prefer to continue learning in later life—in a natural, self-directed process that resembles socialization, learning by connecting, observing, trying,

133. Bar et al., "Very First Impressions."
134. See Jackson, *Life in Classrooms*; Jarvis, *Adult Learning*; Lingenfelter and Lingenfelter, *Teaching Cross-Culturally*; Snyder, *Hidden Curriculum*.
135. Mossop et al., "Analysing the Hidden Curriculum."
136. Mossop et al., "Analysing the Hidden Curriculum," 137.
137. Yuksel, "Role of Hidden Curricula," 95.
138. Olson, *Invisible Classroom*, xx.
139. Brown, *Buddhist in the Classroom*, s.v. "Community in the Classroom," para. 10.

repeating without the pain or shame associated with the formal learning in a school environment. For instance, a "non-literate" Ugandan man in Openjuru's study expressed a desire to learn to repair vehicles or drive a car—not by attending vocational school and not by becoming literate but rather through apprenticeship, learning from a person by observation.[140]

Mazamisa concurred, stating, "African orality must be seen as socialisation [sic]."[141] Likewise, Furniss asserted: "The oral is a set of communicative conditions apparent in *all* societies and it is the implications of those conditions which have been obscured by the focus on the so-called 'advances' purportedly engendered by 'writing.'"[142] Also commenting on this global nature of oral socialization, Ballantine et al. taught:

> As a species, we are remarkable in how many aspects of our lives are shaped by learning—by socialization. Human socialization is pervasive, extensive, and lifelong. We cannot understand what it means to be human without comprehending the impact of a specific culture on us. . . . Without social interaction, there would not even be a self. We humans are, in our most essential natures, social beings.[143]

"This internalization of society, identity and reality is not a matter of once and for all. Socialization is never total and never finished," according to Berger and Luckmann.[144] Arnett concurred, stating, "Socialization clearly continues through emerging adulthood."[145] Additionally, Luong et al. defined *socialization* as involving "processes through which individuals internalize experiences from their social world in ways that alter their behavior, beliefs, health, and emotions."[146] Clearly, this resembles what ALFE did during their connected learning efforts.

Following primary socialization, secondary socialization, or the process of learning in work, "is the acquisition of role-specific knowledge" and "the character of such secondary socialization depends upon the status of the body of knowledge concerned."[147] According to Diamond,

---

140. Openjuru, "Adult Literacy and Development Link."
141. Mazamisa, "Reading from This Place," 71.
142. Furniss, *Orality*, 141.
143. Ballantine et al., *Our Social World*, 99.
144. Berger and Luckmann, *Social Construction of Reality*, 157.
145. Arnett, "Socialization in Emerging Adulthood," 87.
146. Luong et al., "Multifaceted Nature," 110.
147. Berger and Luckmann, *Social Construction of Reality*, 159.

> In traditional or primitive societies . . . the actual process of learning was rarely, if ever, subject to careful and informed scrutiny. Learning in such societies is embedded in socialization. That is, the learning of skills and attitudes has not been functionally rationalized in segregated institutions; it takes place in a network of personal relations based on the paradigm of kinship. . . . Formal schools in primitive societies would be as strange and as repugnant as jails. Primitive learning, on the contrary, is an instrumental-cognitive-affective enterprise . . . a process that never ends—for the journey from childhood to maturity and death.[148]

Paradise and Rogoff called this process "a panhuman phenomenon," "an integrated learning tradition," and "a cultural tradition of humanity."[149] They commented on the process as follows:

> What is called informal learning is often taken to be learning that everyone engages in "naturally," by virtue of being human; its grounding in sociocultural practices and their social institutions goes unnoticed. Although it is not simply prefabricated in "human nature," we believe that is it so compatible with everyday cultural life in a wide array of family and community settings that it tends to become "second nature." The tendency to conceive of informal learning as natural or simple also reflects a cultural school-centric bias that has impeded understanding of its social and cultural organization. Among highly schooled people, informal ways of learning outside of school through observation and participation are often considered inherently less conceptual or cognitive than formalized school learning.[150]

Likewise, Ventura et al. in their study of Portuguese learners, noticed:

> Given that unschooled Portuguese people also seem to adopt a holistic style, our results suggest that this style does not derive from socialization within an Asian culture. One may tentatively suggest that the "default" processing style is the holistic one.[151]

---

148. Diamond, "Epilogue," 301.
149. Paradise and Rogoff, "Side by Side Learning," 132.
150. Paradise and Rogoff, "Side by Side Learning," 102.
151. Ventura et al., "Schooling in Western Culture," 86.

Ong explained the situation of being a non-reader as representing "orality—the 'primary modeling system'—as an anachronistic deviant from the 'secondary modeling system' that followed it."[152]

Thompson stated, "The only way that culture is transmitted in oral cultures is through oral means."[153] Indeed, oral tradition and the recounting of stories is a conduit for transmitting much cultural knowledge; however, according to Berger and Luckmann, one absorbs culture through socialization, which involves more than oral communication.[154] Unfortunately, just as shown in Figure 11, "socialization and education are in competition" because:

> Education—the inculcation of standardized knowledge and skills by standardized and stereotyped means—is the predominant mode of shaping the mind in social systems in which nonkinship and *universalistic* considerations are of primary significance.[155]

The fact that students also learn the hidden curriculum of formal schooling shows the power of socialization enduring seemingly by stealth throughout life. This behind-the-scenes expectation to perform, behave, and dress in certain ways causes conflict with the worldviews of those who do not seem to require formal education.[156] Life and school become at odds with one another, and in many instances, life wins.

CHAPTER SUMMARY

One of the participants, Ms. Veta, offered great wisdom that helps summarize this chapter. She advised:

> I have a lot of experience teaching the Vietnamese. They know Khmer very much but can't read. In order to teach them, we have to understand and care about them and know about their life situation and their abilities, etc. Sometimes people just come to class, but you have to know what kind of things they have to do at home. They may have to work and take care of their families. Sometimes they are abused. For a student that doesn't know how to read, and for people that can learn how—they do it not just by just listening. The teacher can't just talk and talk and talk and

---

152. Ong, *Orality and Literacy* (1982), 12.
153. Thompson, "Perceptions of Teaching," 7.
154. Berger and Luckmann, *Social Construction of Reality*.
155. Levinson, *Schooling the Symbolic Animal*, 96.
156. Illich, *Deschooling Society*.

stop. It's also by watching and by doing—there are three parts that are necessary, so if we prepare lessons, we have to include all three of those points in order to help people.

In her text on adult learning, MacKeracher also related: "Two basic approaches to learning are available: self-directed or autonomous learning and other-connected or relational learning."[157] My research revealed something different. Even though nearly all the participants talked about learning from others, many also mentioned learning by themselves. Those two juxtaposed ideas confused me until I returned to examine socialization.

When we are young, we observe others—those close to us—but the young are the ones who initiate the observation and hold the strong desire to learn. In this type of connected learning, as with observational learning and learning in traditional settings, the desire comes from the learner, but it is strongly connected to relationship—both self-directed and relational or other-connected at the same time. In agreement with the findings of this study, Preece, in studying lifelong learning and development, maintained:

> I have also argued that philosophical perspectives that embrace concepts of connectedness, communalism, interdependency and subjectivity are potential resources for emphasizing a more holistic interpretation of lifelong learning than the dominant, instrumental focus on skills enhancement. The more holistic interpretation would embrace the notion of communal embeddedness and connectivity of a person to other persons rather than the western concept of the individual self existing separately or independently from other.[158]

This study was conducted with Cambodian ALFE, a people who tend to be group-oriented. This orientation could highly influence connected learning as a preferred means of learning. It would be interesting to conduct this study with ALFE in individualistic-oriented cultures, such as in some parts of the United States. Past research examined earlier, however, has already shown that these adults also preferred a relational approach to learning.

In summary, Gee, in analyzing the work of Heath and others, maintained, "What is at issue . . . is different ways of knowing, different ways of making sense of the world of human experience, that is different social epistemologies."[159] If connected learning indeed comes from a differ-

---

157. MacKeracher, *Making Sense of Adult Learning*, 19.
158. Preece, *Lifelong Learning*, 156.
159. Gee, "Orality and Literacy," 734.

ent social epistemology than that of print learners, then beliefs, values, religion, and worldview would all certainly affect and be affected by the socialization process. Some of these values, beliefs, and worldview issues influencing connected learning—the corollary themes—are discussed in the following chapter.

ated or contribution would be reading, which, as our expert of course, I saved

6

Interpretation and Synthesis: The Inclusive Themes

"Connection is why we're here. We are hardwired to connect with others."

—Brené Brown, *Daring Greatly*

CONTINUING WITH THE INTERPRETATION and synthesis begun in chapter 5, this chapter discusses the four inclusive themes connected to the central understanding and depicted in Figure 9. As in the former chapter, I introduce and consider pertinent literature in conjunction with the themes surrounding the central understanding of this GT study. The chapter concludes by summarizing these holistic and integrated concepts.

CONNECTED LEARNING INCORPORATED THE SELF

As mentioned in chapter 5, connected learning was shown to be a highly social process. Beyond relating with others, connected learning was also reflexive in regard to one's self as learner embedded in a sociocultural context—the relational or connected self.

The ALFE learning process was shown to be strongly connected to self and self-concept in all of life's dimensions—i.e., cognitive, affective, and physical. Indeed, as Clifford commented on Leenhardt's research, "A personage without concrete participatory supports was adrift . . . alienated, and closed to communitas,"[1] a difficult situation for learning. For Leenhardt,

---

1. Clifford, *Person and Myth*, 185.

working in Melanesia, "the *kamo*, or authentic person, was a participatory personage existing in relationship."[2] This next section inspects the relational self and AFLE learning.

Connected Learning Included Cognitive Processes

Participants mentioned using a variety of cognitive devices to learn—reciting, reviewing, listening, memorizing, dramatizing, drawing, and some even reading and writing. Basing their work on older studies in the area of high and low context cultures, DeCapua and Marshall believed there are

> two types of cognitive thinking . . . "pragmatic" and "academic" orientations . . . for members of HC [high context] cultures with a pragmatic orientation, the meaning of messages must be embedded in context. The concept of "knowledge for knowledge's sake" has no relevance because "knowledge" in an HC culture entails immediate relevance and/or application.[3]

The idea that learning must be relevant for those with limited formal education was also true for Cambodian ALFE. Many Cambodians I know and have taught made a great distinction between practical learning relevant to life versus learning in school. I discuss this concept further in the following.

Moreover, the most noticeable issue that arose during the interviews was not the ways people chose to remember but rather the strong attachment to self-efficacy and self-concept during the process of learning (to be discussed later). Ms. Tari confided: "I am often upset with myself, asking, 'Why was I born illiterate while others were not?'"

So many factors in life seemed to affect the cognitive side of learning for these participants—poverty, margin, time, money, self-efficacy, hope, purpose, etc. Mere daily living was enough to create cognitive overload. The ladies in the Bridge Group shared,

> Learning is difficult. Even my grandchildren, they have a difficult time concentrating. Maybe because the mother and father are poor or there was a lot of domestic violence in the family. Then, the children recall the events and have a hard time learning. The children who go to school to study, they also had a hard time. Some of them do not have the supplies for learning.

Add to this milieu the fact that a number of the participants seemed to have lurking undiagnosed learning disabilities, and we find the perfect storm for

2. Heekeren, "'Don't Tell the Crocodile.'"
3. DeCapua and Marshall, "Students with Limited," 162.

difficulties with formal education. Tanner spoke of the "conundrum of failure" among adult dyslexics, and that 5–10 percent of adults "who are of average or above average intelligence, had adequate schooling and yet struggle to decode the written word despite educational intervention."[4] I observed this conundrum in the lives of many I interviewed. The repeated phrase *ree-un aht jole*—"the learning/study would not go in"—forever echoes in my mind. These were the words used to explain this cognitive failure to process learning, especially when trying to learn to read.

Orenstein described such adults as "uneven learners, people who are gifted in some areas but seemingly incompetent in others."[5] Undiagnosed learning disabilities (ULD) often seemed to initiate this "conundrum of failure." Additionally, "because the learning disability has not been validated, they may never achieve . . . in their areas of strength. . . . Therefore, no matter how successful they are, they fail to meet their own expectations and are left feeling incomprehensibly flawed."[6]

Connected Learning Included Affective Processes

This feeling of being "incomprehensibly flawed," stemming from failure in formal schooling or failure in learning at work, seemed to have lasting impact on the affect and served to deter learning for many Cambodian ALFE. In some instances, the impact was so long-lasting the participants felt overwhelming shame, a sense of "global inadequacy."[7]

One of the first to discuss shame in anthropology, Benedict described the emotion as being "associated with the feeling of not having lived up to one's standards and aspirations."[8] As Rasmussen noted in an "anthropological study of emotion in relation to shame": "Shame is particularly challenging to study since it is situated betwixt and between—on the border between the personal and the social."[9] Shame involves deep emotion but is tainted and directed by cultural and social values. What is shameful in one culture might not be in another. Along these lines, Bartlett taught:

> While the concepts of psychological and emotional capital certainly have their utility, my work reveals that they are somewhat limited. . . . As anthropological studies of emotions

---

4. Tanner, "Adult Dyslexia," 785.
5. Orenstein, "Picking Up the Clues," 35.
6. Orenstein, "Picking Up the Clues," 36.
7. Flanders, *About Face*.
8. Benedict, *Chrysanthemum and the Sword*, 274.
9. Rasmussen, "Revitalizing Shame," 233.

have demonstrated, emotions are utterly cultural and social. . . . People learn feeling. . . . Socio-interactionally produced emotions like shame play an important role in the cultural production of inequality.[10]

Tangney and Dearing described shame as "an extremely painful and ugly feeling that has a negative impact on interpersonal behavior."[11] Lewis elucidated the phenomenon as "an acutely painful emotion that is typically accompanied by a sense of shrinking or of being small and by a sense of worthlessness and powerlessness."[12] Scheff proposed, "Shame is the master emotion of everyday life but it is usually invisible in modern societies because of taboo."[13] Finally, Brown defined shame as "the intensely painful feeling or experience of believing that we are flawed and therefore unworthy of love and belonging," adding that shame also involves "the fear of disconnection."[14]

This cultural, social, and psychological lack of honor, dignity, "worth or value of persons both in their eyes and in the eyes of their village, neighborhood, or society" was pervasive for many of the learners in this study.[15] As Kaufman explained, "Shame is the principal impediment in all relationships."[16] The status of dishonor associated with shame or "the loss of good fame in the eyes or mind of the other is the central feature of the experience."[17] In agreement, Peristiany felt "honour and shame are the constant preoccupation of individuals in small scale, exclusive societies where face to face personal, as opposed to anonymous, relations are of paramount importance."[18]

Other studies also found a strong association between illiteracy and shame.[19] "One of the words frequently associated with 'illiteracy' is 'shame,'" according to Bartlett.[20] Hayes recognized low self-confidence and social dis-

---

10. Bartlett, "Literacy, Speech and Shame," 551.
11. Tangney and Dearing, *Shame and Guilt*, 3.
12. Lewis, *Shame and Guilt*, 18.
13. Scheff, "Shame in Self," 239.
14. Brown, *Daring Greatly*, 69.
15. Neyrey, *Honor and Shame*, 15.
16. Kaufman, *Psychology of Shame*, 7.
17. Lewis, *Shame and Guilt*, 69.
18. Peristiany, *Honour and Shame*, 11.
19. See Boyden and Bourdillon, "Reflections"; Kaufman, *Shame*; Fingeret, "Illiterate Underclass"; Kaufman, "Social Network"; Johnson, "Shame and Implications"; Minz, "Hope amidst Hopelessness"; Narayan, *Voices of the Poor*.
20. Bartlett, "Literacy, Speech and Shame," 547.

approval as "deterrents to participation in adult basic education."[21] A study by Wolf et al. provided the following findings:

> Fifty-one percent of patients had low literacy skills (less than or equal to sixth grade) and 27 percent were assessed as having marginal literacy (second-eighth grade). Half (47.6 percent) of patients reading at or below the third-grade level admitted feeling ashamed or embarrassed about their difficulties reading.[22]

Lewis expounded on the holistic nature of this burden of shame and dishonor, this lack of worth in one's social sphere as follows:

> Shame is the product of a complex set of cognitive activities: the evaluation of an individual's actions in regard to her standards, rules, and goals and her global evaluation of the self. The phenomenological experience of the person is that of a wish to hide, disappear or die. . . . This emotional state is so intense and has such a devastating effect on the self-system that individuals presented with such a state must attempt to rid themselves of it. However, since shame represents a global attack on the self, people have great difficulty dissipating this emotion.[23]

Taking different forms in different cultural settings, shame is painful, an emotion and a cultural condition that serves to ostracize and withhold honor from its unfortunate suspects. As DeYoung declared, "Shame in all its forms is relational."[24]

To be expected, "higher levels of hopelessness and depressive symptoms" surface, according to Lee et al.[25] These feelings and the enormity of their impact surprised me. Ms. Tari recounted her early experiences working in the garment factory:

> They criticized me. They asked why did I not know when they had already taught me the first time? I felt upset also because I thought to myself, "Why after what they taught me, could I not remember?" I thought maybe it was because I was dumb. They scolded me, but I still couldn't remember. They would say, "It's a simple task! Why can't you use the calculator?" So, I am upset with myself. I always am upset with myself because I am just a

---

21. Hayes, "Typology of Low-Literate," 3.
22. Wolf et al., "Patients' Shame and Attitudes," 721.
23. Lewis, *Shame*, 75.
24. DeYoung, *Understanding and Treating Chronic Shame*, 18.
25. Lee et al., "Potentially Traumatic Experiences," 47.

human being. I also think, "I was born with good features, but why am I illiterate?"

The lack of self-efficacy while involved in cognitive learning directly impacted self-concept.[26] The sense of shame and complete worthlessness, the fear, the lack of self-confidence, the name-calling by self and others dominated so much that it took a great perseverance, tenacity, and determination to overcome and proceed to learn. In other words, students who were not efficacious in learning to read and write tended to hold an overall negative self-concept. As Waters and Harris learned, early experiences "lay the groundwork for the development of a long continuum of abilities that expedite future success."[27] Waters and Harris also discovered nearly all their participants had negative experiences in school—findings similar to this research.

This negative self-concept affected all of life and any further learning attempts. Because of failed attempts in formal schooling, the participants in this study found no desire to return to anything that remotely resembled that arena. For some, schooling and literacy equaled failure. They felt shame and worthlessness, existing in a liminal state of feeling as if they failed to meet cultural norms and expectations. Mr. Odis confided: "When I saw others, I hated myself and was not able to learn that well. Why was it so easy for others to learn, but difficult for me?"

Positioned next to feeling shame loomed the cultural act of shaming. Unfortunately, many cultures—especially group-oriented or honor/shame cultures—practice shaming in order to prod others to attend to certain values, beliefs, and norms of society.[28] "Shaming individuals for their poor academic performance, therefore may be not only anticipated by all within-group members but also culturally accepted by the society," according to Lee et al.[29] One of the participants, Ms. Naida, who could read a bit, frankly commented on how she felt about her sister, who could not read at all. I witnessed the following harsh words spoken about and in front of her sister Ms. Tova:

> It's very difficult. I tried to guide her to learn what she does not know so she can be smart. It's shameful. Some people do not read, but they are smart. But my sister is illiterate and very dumb. She only knows how to spend money. She does not even know the

26. Schunk, *Learning Theories*.
27. Waters and Harris, "Exploration of the Lived Experiences," 254.
28. See Fung, "Becoming a Moral Child"; Pellissery, "Persistence of Shaming"; Schoenhals, *Paradox of Power*; Wong and Tsai, "Cultural Models."
29. Lee et al., "Potentially Traumatic Experiences," 48.

alphabet. I ask, "Why don't you learn so you can be smart? Will you not know your whole life, until you are old?" That's what I think to myself. That's what I told her. For those who do not read, there is guidance and teaching. After a while, they can learn. For me, I do not know how to write, so I ask so I can know how to write word. My sister is not brave. She is illiterate and dumb. She lacks strength of will and speaks little. Her whole life she is sheepish. Some people are illiterate, but their speech sounds like they are literate. That is why I instructed my sister, "Please learn to speak." Study, so you will know. Otherwise, you will always stay dumb. If you don't learn to put words together, you will not be able to speak your whole life. You always stay dumb.

Coming from an individualistic western culture but also having lived in Asia nearly twenty years, I was still appalled by the words spoken in the presence of many ALFE I interviewed. The chastisement quoted above included some of the most caustic comments, words difficult to hear. The labels and stigma, the shaming words overflowed with raw emotion, disconnection, exclusion, and cultural isolation.

After interviewing the two and hearing these caustic words, I spent a great deal of time affirming Ms. Tova in the presence of her sister and the others seated around us. Being affirmed publicly was a new experience for her. We sobbed as she shared she had goose bumps and had never felt such so much joy. She has since attempted to learn a new trade with the help and encouragement of others in her village. Over the last few years, her life has transformed.

Because of these emotions as well as the feelings of those close to the participants, most ALFE who proceeded to learn had to first contend with their own self-concept and with societal shame. This dimension seemed to be a key area in the process of ALFE learning. Only by experiencing success in some form of learning did the participants seem to begin to experience self-worth, self-efficacy, and a tiny bit of honor and dignity. Those small successes in learning seemed to lead to more successes and even more learning by providing aspirational hope.[30] Those who did not have these experiences remained in groups 1 and 2.

Interestingly, I observed that outward symbols of prestige seemed to be greater or out of proportion among these learners. Therefore, a positive connection with one's self, especially in the affective dimension seemed essential to the internal and external process of ALFE learning. After observing their emphasis on modern dress and style, their desire for flashy technology despite

---

30. Wydick and Lybbert, "Poverty."

not being able to use it, I came to understand the need to portray external status and honor in the midst of absent internal and social accolades.

In other words, looking at the affective dimension of the experience of these learners through an anthropological lens, lacking the ability to obtain honor or to bring honor to one's family through culturally appropriate means, such as succeeding in school, ALFE experienced a perpetual cycle of shame. Unfortunately, society is ill-prepared to restore the dignity of ALFE once they have left formal schooling. Some of those who did learn to read, who began reading sacred texts, and those who studied and passed the ninth-grade exam seemed to feel accepted in the view of society. The rest of the participants not involved in these activities seemed to retain the stigma of being *l'ngong* (ignorant or stupid), to feel marginalized and shamed by their failure or their lack of opportunity in comparison to others in the culture.

In the face of this cultural opposition, the affective dimension of connected learning required a great deal of perseverance and tenacity. ALFE also showed remarkable determination despite the effects of poverty on their education. When I asked Ms. Veta how she learned to work in the garment factory, she affirmed,

> It came from the strength of my heart. When we love people, we want to help them. I loved my mother, so, I wanted to help her, to make sure she had some money, so, I had to learn. At the factory, they gave me a test, but I did not know how to sew. But I had a strong will, a strong desire to help my mother, so when they gave me the test, I couldn't really sew all that well with the foot pedal. I would start and stop. Some people who don't know how to sew, they just step on the pedal and go but I thought you should at least stop sometimes. It was hard. I studied only about an hour before they called me for the test. I explained, "I don't know how to do this!" I just started and stopped when using the foot pedal [she explained with motions the halting way she tried to sew] and they said they thought I could learn. They thought I could understand later how to operate the machine, so they chose me to work there. They taught me so that I could move ahead. I can sew myself now. I can sew clothes now. I could do it because I loved my family and wanted to help them. At that time, I had hope, but I didn't understand or consider myself, so I worked hard. I didn't really understand about life at that time. This came from love, a love to help others. We have to have to help ourselves so that we can help others. If I had not worked at the factory, I would not have been able to help others a lot, so I changed.

Ultimately, shame caused many other ALFE to shrink back, to disconnect themselves from groups, and tend toward isolation. Only with great effort or hope for connection did ALFE avoid this natural, cultural, and social response. Brown agreed, stating, "Shame unravels our connection to others. I often refer to shame as the fear of disconnection—the fear of being perceived as flawed and unworthy of acceptance or belonging."[31]

Connected Learning Included Physical Processes

When we think of learning, we often default to cognitive understanding. However, the kinds of learning in which Cambodian ALFE were involved included other dimensions, including physical processes and the senses. According to neuropsychologists Ardila et al.,

> School attendance, however, does not mean that educated people simply possess certain abilities that less-educated individuals lack. It does not mean that highly educated people have the same abilities as less-educated individuals, plus something else. The individual with no formal education mostly likely has acquired knowledge, skills, and values that educated people have not. . . . Neither literacy nor school attendance is a simple and linear variable.[32]

Embodying their learning, some participants needed to use a sense of taste and smell in cooking, the feel of objects as they sewed or weaved or did construction work. Some needed to be physically aware when learning a sport, for example. Regarding his previous trade, Mr. Eli explained:

> I was a wood worker but now that my eyes are weak, I can't do it anymore, so I'm a farmer in Preah Vihear now. If my eyes were still good, I would still do woodworking. It's too hard to read now even with glasses. Listening to the radio is easier in order to learn.

There is so much involved in learning that is not oral, that is connected to dimensions other than hearing or speaking, especially the physical and other senses. Learning can be somatic or embodied,[33] the kind "that transpires from the 'doing' of the task."[34] While Ong majored on literature and

---

31. Brown, *I Thought It Was Just Me*, s.v. "Courage, Compassion and Connection," para. 6.
32. Ardila et al., "Illiteracy," 692–94.
33. Nguyen and Larson, "Don't Forget about the Body."
34. Timma, "Experiencing the Workplace," 163.

communication,[35] even those areas must take into consideration non-verbal communication, used extensively by ALFE. According to Hadisi, "One characteristic that is missing from Ong's inventory of orality's psychodynamics is the aesthetic nature."[36] Paradise and Rogoff described this aspect of connected learning as involving

> highly symbolic and precise meanings carried through sensitive and coordinated use of gesture, posture changes, timing, and the information available in shared action. . . . Rather than restricting communicative possibilities, communication that relies less on speech and verbal explanation may open up the possibility of learning through many channels that are either systematically ignored or excluded in teaching and learning situations that rely relatively exclusively on verbal explanation.[37]

Jousse, whose mother was unable to read, wrote *The Oral Style* well before Ong's classic and believed "all is gesture."[38] Jousse referred to one who did not read as *verbomoteur*, which West defined as "a person whose socialization and identity is immersive in a concrete, relational, gestured and actional way"[39]—definitely a connected learner. Arrington found the Lisu hymn singing, a precious event in that community, to be "participatory performance," a "communal activity" that also created "a sense of belonging."[40] She maintained this kind of participating "through sound and motion" resulted in "inclusiveness, social bonding."[41]

Likewise, Fanta-Vagenshtein detected "several different learning channels that are employed by illiterate populations: visual . . . imitative . . . practice-based . . . enacting . . . apprenticeship" and explained,

> Oral culture has developed ways of bypassing literacy-based learning, employing non-symbolic learning channels that do not require the ability to read and write. Non-symbolic learning channels are based on hands-on experience acquired through direct interaction with the real world . . . the main learning methods of oral culture as concrete, sensory-motor based, and dependent on activity and interaction with the environment.[42]

35. Ong, *Orality and Literacy*.
36. Hadisi, "Exploring the Performance," 450.
37. Paradise and Rogoff, "Side by Side Learning," 117–18.
38. Jousse, *Oral Style*, 8.
39. West, "Re-Eventing."
40. Arrington, "Hymns as Theological Mediator," 154.
41. Arrington, "Hymns as Theological Mediator," 155.
42. Fanta-Vagenshtein, "How Illiterate People Learn," 31.

Diouf et al. discovered the farmers they researched also preferred "hands-on learning," experiential and active sociocultural learning.[43]

CONNECTED LEARNING INCORPORATED FAITH OR SPIRITUALITY

Connected learning was also a redemptive process, learning highly connected to one's faith as a source of purpose, hope, and assistance. ALFE could be strongly influenced by the positive aspects of hope and purpose in their learning—especially in the spiritual domain. A connection with faith or spirituality proved to be essential to breaking free from cognitive and affective limitations in learning, thus connected learning was redemptive. Through these faith journeys, the lives of ALFE changed, redeemed from shame.

For those in group 3 (purposeful learners), prayer, hope, and purpose resounded as reasons for learning success. Without a connection to God, in the case of Christians, or to other devotees or sacred persons, in the case of Buddhist followers, these ALFE seemed to lack hope, purpose, and aspirations. Older Buddhist followers found purpose in learning to chant Buddhist precepts in the community of the temple whether they could read or not. In the case of Christians, prayer, receiving help from God, connection with Him in their striving to learn—especially in learning to read—became a constant explanation for their success in learning. One of the ladies in The Bridge Group related:

> I prayed, "Please God, help me read!" I felt if I couldn't read, I would be like ignorant people, people that don't know anything at all, so I tried to study. I would look and forget and look and forget. Finally, little by little I would learn a little and forget. Finally, I could remember and only forget a little. Nobody taught me the alphabet. It was just God and me. I know that I can't win without depending on God. What I know now, I learned from the Bible. I like to look at the stories. They are like my life, too.

Ms. Veta, on the other hand, asserted that she called on her community of faith for assistance in learning:

> When I left school, I couldn't remember anything at all. I forgot a lot, but what was important was that we tried to read the Bible. When we read, we didn't know what we were reading. When I got to a hard word, I would ask someone who knew what it meant. "How do you say that word?" I would ask. Sometimes we would not understand the meaning—especially in the Old

---

43. Diouf et al., "Adult Learning," 42.

> Testament because there are hard words. It is really different from how we started learning to read. I listened to the radio like others, too. I had strength after that. I would start writing down verses that I liked—and write them in a book. That helped us.

Similarly, Ms. Yoshie confided:

> I couldn't read well, so I prayed for wisdom from God. God helped me read. I can write, too, and learn songs/hymns. I prayed with tears and cried out to God. God answered! When I read something I don't understand now, I ask someone who does know—especially my husband. He knows. But every time I ask him, he says, "Why don't you know that?" That's why I read and cry. I want to learn/know more.

On the other hand, a contest at church motivated Ms. Sona to learn (as mentioned earlier):

> I wanted to know what they were talking about in the Bible, so I asked for a Bible but there were no Bibles left. They had given them all away. There was an old Bible no one used, so I used it. I read the Bible every day. I spent a lot of time reading the Bible because I didn't go to school anymore, so I had a lot of free time to read the Bible.

In describing the participants earlier, we noted the contrast between groups 1 and 3. Group 1 seemed to have no hope or aspirations, while group 3 possessed hope and aspiration in abundance. The difference seemed to lie in this area of connected learning—in their faith and spirituality, whether Buddhist or Christian. Studying hope, Wydick and Lybbert divided the attribute into two types—wishful and aspirational.[44] Group 3 definitely displayed aspirational hope. For Christians, there seemed to be no learning without a connection to God and to a learning community of faith. For Buddhists, there seemed to be no learning without connection to special funds of knowledge, to people who held the content of chants and Buddhist teaching.

CONNECTED LEARNING INCORPORATED CONTEXT

A relevant and practical process, ALFE learning is highly connected to context and culture and is very experience-based. Everything ALFE learned had to be relevant—of necessity. With limited time and resources, they did not possess the margin to learn anything extraneous. Learning directed largely toward amassing work skills in context and by experience.

---

44. Wydick and Lybbert, "Poverty."

However, this endeavor was accomplished in ways connected to culture and the ways of learning espoused by Cambodian ALFE. For instance, if rote learning or recitation worked best, that method prevailed. If observation was traditionally used, that method was chosen. The idea of learning for learning's sake was completely foreign for Cambodian ALFE. Their learning seemed pragmatically connected to some purpose. In their thinking, if literacy was irrelevant,[45] why bother?

As Rogers explained,

> Adults (as distinct from children) learn best through doing things in their own lives for real—they learn cooking by (real) cooking, they learn farming by (real) farming, they learn parenting by parenting, they learn literacy skills by using literacy for real. It is not a "learn first, then do" model, but a "learn through doing for real."[46]

As I returned to the literature, I found most of those studying traditional cultures agreed that learning is experiential, holistic, cooperative, and communal.[47] DeCapua and Marshall found in working with immigrants: "Learning is immediately incorporated into daily life or has practical relevance for tasks to be performed. . . . Knowledge is utilitarian not theoretical."[48] Similarly, learning was experiential, learning "by doing, by following a role model, by operating with a context, and by obtaining feedback."[49]

Hvitfeldt, in a "microethnographic study of the classroom behavior of Hmong adults in an ESL program" ascertained that the "learning paradigm" of the Hmong seemed in conflict with that of formal schooling—even if they were literate.[50] As we saw earlier, learning had to be relational and it had to be "immediately incorporated into daily life."[51] Literature in adult education clearly points to relevance as a core factor in adult learning.[52]

This type of learning contrasts with formal education, which can be decontextualized and detached from practice.[53] As Brown et al. noted, "Learning methods that are embedded in authentic situations are not merely

---

45. Knowles et al., *Adult Learner*.
46. Rogers, "Literacy Comes Second," 238.
47. Parker, *Cultural and Academic Stress*.
48. DeCapua and Marshall, "Students with Limited," 164.
49. DeCapua and Marshall, "Students with Limited," 166.
50. Hvitfeldt, "Traditional Culture."
51. Hvitfeldt, "Traditional Culture," 6.
52. See Knowles et al., *Adult Learner*; MacKeracher, *Making Sense of Adult Learning*; Merriam and Bierema, *Adult Learning*.
53. Denny, "Rational Thought."

useful; they are essential."⁵⁴ Adult learning must be authentic, purposeful, and connected to life. Merriam⁵⁵ and Merriam and Kim also described non-western learning and knowing as "communal, lifelong and informal, holistic."⁵⁶ Fanta-Vagenshtein et al. added:

> Traditional knowledge systems are integrated and holistic while modern knowledge systems are reductionistic.... Learning by doing and experiencing versus learning through formal education.... Traditional knowledge systems symbolically represented orally or visually in stories, rituals, arts, and riddles versus modern knowledge systems represented in writing ... derived through rational conscious process plus experiential, intuitive, and spiritual cognitive processes versus derived and validated through rational conscious process only ... included knowledge, technologies, philosophies and concepts, skills, arts and practices, values, and spiritual/religion versus includes knowledge, technologies and concepts.⁵⁷

Denny remarked,

> Western thought has only one distinctive property separating it from thought in *both* agricultural and hunter-gatherer societies—decontextualization. Decontextualizing is the handling of information in a way that either disconnects other information or backgrounds it.⁵⁸

I have taught both ways—through experience and stories and through literate means that were quite decontextualized. I observed that participants with the least formal education struggled most with those kinds of literate methods.

In further confirmatory studies, Deyo,⁵⁹ Corbett,⁶⁰ Jordan and Davis-Floyd,⁶¹ Shuter,⁶² Paradise and Rogoff,⁶³ and Ziegahn⁶⁴ all published

54. Brown et al., "Situated Cognition," 37.
55. Merriam, *Non-Western Perspectives*.
56. Merriam and Kim, "Non-Western Perspectives," 77.
57. Fanta-Vagenshtein et al., "Technological Knowledge," 291.
58. Denny, "Rational Thought," 66.
59. Deyo, "Perspectives on Learning."
60. Corbett, "'It Was Fine.'"
61. Jordan and Davis-Floyd, *Birth in Four Cultures*.
62. Shuter, "Hmong of Laos."
63. Paradise and Rogoff, "Side by Side Learning."
64. Ziegahn, "Formation of Literacy."

similar findings. Studying a fishing community in Nova Scotia, Corbett discovered, "Many informants viewed formally educated people as lacking life skills."[65] They viewed school as "a pale shadow of life, an unreal place where one was infantilized and where 'nothing really happened.'"[66] Ultimately, Corbett observed:

> Rural schooling sought to do the "missionary" work of cultural elevation in a "backward space." Yet dropout rates remained high, resistance was common, and people remained committed to staying where they were and to gaining practical knowledge about places at hand rather than theoretical knowledge about places they had never seen.[67]

Likewise, Shuter perceived in working with Hmong transplanted in the United States from Laos: "For many literate Hmong, the printed word is an inadequate mode of communication, a poor substitute for the oral, experiential learning of the traditional society."[68] Additionally, Malicky and Derwing discerned that Cambodians transplanted in the United States were also involved in "mastery learning," needing to completely absorb every aspect of the lessons they were taught.[69] Learners assumed every detail was equally important, equally relevant, and none could be omitted.

CONNECTED LEARNING INVOLVED SPECIAL PACKAGING

Connected learning must be repackaged in suitable formats, especially where media are concerned. The process of ALFE learning included connection with accessible technologies and other portable vehicles of connection, such as stories, parables, metaphors, drama, art, etc. Tremblay believed McLuhan interpreted media as "extensions of the human body."[70] I discovered firsthand decontextualized learning did not work with ALFE. Learning must connect and be repackaged into formats ALFE prefer. The desire to connect is strong, especially in shame-based relational cultures, and media can facilitate that connection—if the forms are accessible.

Elmholdt ascertained that those involved in information and communication technology (ICT) used two metaphors in their learning—both

---

65. Corbett, "'It Was Fine,'" 460.
66. Corbett, "'It Was Fine,'" 458.
67. Corbett, "'It Was Fine,'" 466.
68. Shuter, "Hmong of Laos," 106.
69. Malicky and Derwing, "Literacy Learning of Adults."
70. Tremblay, "From Marshall McLuhan to Harold Innis," 565.

cognitive acquisition and social participation.[71] Learners wanted to stay connected via technology and they intended to do so as much as is possible in their situations. However, ALFE found some media quite inaccessible and experienced a dearth of suitable media for learning. Ms. Tari explained,

> Before I could not use a phone. I had to use a simple Nokia phone. But a friend taught me by showing me, "Here's the numbers and here's how to use the numbers and colors." I didn't know English. I had to ask all the time, "What does this mean?"

When I lived for five days as an oral learner, I felt technology led as one of the most frustrating obstacles I encountered. At every turn, I longed to create technology that would assist non-readers—like phones that were more user-friendly—instead of technology filled with barriers. As mentioned earlier, Ms. Tari explained about learning to use her smart phone,

> When I first bought the cell phone, I did not know how to use it, so I asked others things like, "How do you use this? How do you share photos?" Then they would tell me, "This is how you share your photos and surf the Internet."

During my research, I observed a pair of night guards who told me they were too busy to learn anything new. In the evening when they had a few moments to spare, they shared time with a young child who knew how to use a portable computing device and they learned—the younger generation teaching the older in a great role reversal.

Cohen noted low-literates benefit from video/television; if that is not available, they benefit more from using pictures and audio as opposed to solely oral presentation.[72] Many participants responded that they watched television, and only a few preferred radio. Those who preferred listening to the radio were too busy with work and family to spend time in front of a television or only had time to listen to the radio while they were working or before they went to bed. Mr. Nestor, a busy worker, husband, and father, recounted, "My habit is to listen to the Word of God on the radio."

Finally, this special packaging included other portable vehicles of connection, such as stories, parables, metaphors, drama, art, etc. As I observed the learners in our certificate course, beyond an affinity for community with others, they also seemed to have a preference for the use of visuals and stories. They did not seem to be able to reproduce or re-teach other content lacking these visuals and narratives.

71. Elmholdt, "Metaphors for Learning."
72. Cohen, "Alternative Instructional Strategies," 64.

The stories or narratives of which missiologists and those who teach on orality[73] are so fond function as vehicles of connection, with characters that draw us into identification with them. "Storytelling is a universal human activity, found in all cultures."[74] According to neurobiological research, stories actually create a connection between the listener and the narrator, called brain-to-brain coupling.[75] Similarly, "previous studies have shown that during free viewing of a movie or listening to a story, the external shared input can induce similar brain activity across different individuals."[76] These portable vehicles of connection become powerful educational tools. Larkey and Heckt fashioned a thought-provoking case for the use of "culture-centric narratives" in "health promotion."[77] The possibility of transportation or "being carried away" and identifying with narratives make them universally engaging. Finally, as mentioned in chapter 2, there is much literature on narrative in education and in philosophy;[78] however, the intersection between narrative and connected learning merits future study.

CHAPTER SUMMARY

Upon arriving at the central understanding of connected learning during this ethnographic grounded theory study, I felt I had reached a fuller grasp of my experiences over the previous decade and a half with adult learners in Cambodia. I had been guilty of not focusing on connecting with my students in the ways they needed. In the past, I believed the key was telling stories when, in fact, the need was greater—it was connecting, connecting in every area of life. This way of learning needed to include all the elements in the Connected Learning Schematic in Figures 9 and H1 (in Appendix H), and the Learning Quadrants in Figure 11.

---

73. See Boomershine, "Biblical Storytelling"; Boomershine, *Story Journey*; Bradt, *Story as a Way of Knowing*; Corcoran, "Biblical Narratives"; Madinger, "Coming to Terms with Orality"; Pederson, "Biblical Narrative"; Steffen, "Foundational Roles of Symbol"; *Reconnecting God's Story*; "My Journey"; "Pedagogical Conversions"; "Chronological Communication"; "Chronological Practices"; Steffen and Terry, "Sweeping Story of Scripture."

74. Kvernbekk and Frimannsson, "Narrative," 571.

75. Hasson, "I Can Make Your Brain Look Like Mine"; Hasson et al., "Brain-to-Brain Coupling."

76. Stephens et al., "Speaker-Listener Neural Coupling."

77. Larkey and Heckt, "Model of Effects."

78. See Bruner, *Making Stories*; Clark, "Narrative Learning"; Clark and Rossiter, "Narrative Learning in Adulthood"; Rossiter, "Narrative Approach to Development"; Rossiter, *Narrative and Stories*; Rutten and Soetaert, "Narrative and Rhetorical Approaches"; Smith, *Moral, Believing Animals*; Taylor, *Sources of the Self*.

Connected learning proved to be a relational or social process in which learners retain a preference for observing and learning from known, trusted, and/or successful people. Also relational in regard to self as learner, connected learning entailed sensitivity to cultural nuances and expectations, a process subject to shame in face of failure. A redemptive process, successful connected learning involved redemption from shame through faith searches as well as the embracing of spirituality, giving aspirational hope and purpose. In the case of Christians, connection with God as a personal and relational being seemed to also give hope and assistance. In the case of Buddhists, learners majored on connection with those versed in Buddhist dharma. As already shown in adult learning literature, the process of connected learning reveals itself through a relevant, contextual, and experiential package. Finally, connected learning is learning that has been packaged for those with limited formal education, providing connection through accessible technologies and other portable vehicles of connection, such as stories, parables, metaphors, drama, and the like. As Innis taught, "In oral intercourse the eye, ear, and brain, the senses and the faculties acted together in busy co-operation and rivalry each eliciting, stimulating, and supplementing the other,"[79] an integrated social process, with human beings playing center stage.

Figure 11, displaying the Learning Quadrants, illustrates two important concepts in adult learning—the chosen means of learning (either people or print) intersecting with funds of knowledge or the seat of authority. Do the learners trust print and formal credentials or do they rely on trusted relationships? The resulting quadrants display various lifeworlds, diverse ways of connecting, from primary orality to secondary orality, to academia, to scribal cultures that do not necessarily read but have reverence for sacred texts.

As Shinil discovered, there is a distinct difference in the schooling perspective versus the learning perspective, a distinction between formal education as opposed to informal and non-formal education.[80] One seems to dominate most thinking and research. That exclusion and disproportionate emphasis saddens me. Shinil concluded: "Learning . . . is oriented to develop connectedness in whole life."[81] And this dominant form of learning embraced by the majority needs to be promoted, according to ALFE.

Moon considered the differences in oral learners' and print learners' preferences in the categories of dialogue, oral art, experience, holism,

---

79. Innis, *Bias of Communication*, 105.
80. Shinil, "Learning Perspective."
81. Shinil, "Learning Perspective," 3.

mnemonics, and participation.[82] One can see these categories more clearly in the connected learning schematic. Without the foundation of connection as opposed to solely emphasizing oral communication, many of these dichotomies fall short. Fanta-Vagenshtein and Chen's contrast between traditional knowledge systems and modern knowledge systems, for instance, was much more comprehensive.[83]

To summarize, ALFE learned through connection with a myriad of kinds of learning encompassed in one integrated theory of connected learning as shown in Figure 10. Cambodian ALFE did not learn simply by oral means. Their kind of connected learning ALFE integrated preferred learning strategies, including autonomous learning, conversational learning, dialogical learning, embodied learning, everyday learning, experiential learning, holistic learning, incidental learning, informal learning, lifelong learning, peer learning, observational learning, oral learning, participatory learning, self-directed learning, situated learning, social or relational learning, spiritual learning, as well as tacit learning—all in one comprehensive holistic process.

82. Moon, "Understanding Oral Learners."
83. Fanta-Vagenshtein et al., "Technological Knowledge."

7

Conclusions: The Practical Wisdom

"What's it all about, Alfie?"

—Burt Bacharach and H. David, 1966

THE PURPOSE OF THIS ethnographic, wisdom-focused grounded theory (GT) study was to explore the ways of learning of Cambodian adults with limited education (ALFE). The answer to the question of how Cambodian ALFE learn can be expressed in one word: *connection*. The central understanding that surfaced from analyzing the data was an emerging theory of connected or relational learning. Cambodian adults with limited education learn through social and relational connections, a holistic process that resembles socialization, begins at birth, and continues until death. This theory of connection is the core or foundation of how Cambodian ALFE learn—not merely by oral/aural means, as the term *orality* might suggest.

In chapter 3, I proposed modifying ethnographic and emergent grounded theory and adding an important final step after coming to a central understanding: to make wise application of the findings to the lives of the research participants and others like them. Applying wisdom to this theory of connected learning should result in a number of practical conclusions and recommendations. I elaborate on the conclusions in this chapter after discussing two products of this research—the prime product of *phronesis* or practical wisdom and the by-product of empathetic *Verstehen* (understanding). I hoped to discover a grounded theory that elaborated on the learning strategies of this group of people. I did not imagine the research would impact me in even more ways.

This chapter presents phronetic conclusions, wisdom gleaned from the participants and wisdom to address their learning needs. In the next chapter I also delineate recommendations for educators, faith communities, and policy makers, present ideas for further research, and provide a final reflection. First, however, I share an unexpected byproduct of this research. I searched for understanding and wisdom (*phronesis*). I not only found both but also encountered empathy.

EMPATHETIC *VERSTEHEN* (UNDERSTANDING): AN UNEXPECTED BY-PRODUCT

At the beginning of my dissertation journey, I thought I had embarked on a cognitive course to discover how Cambodians with limited formal education learn. Instead, my halting questions met tearful responses from hurting and broken people, emotionally fragile adults filled with shame and loss of face in their cultural context. One felt such a negative self-concept that he openly expressed the desire to commit suicide. These emotions rattled my objective mind and marked my research with tears. I thought I cared deeply about ALFE before I began this study. Indeed, I began this research because of my concern for ALFE. After listening to hours of confessional conversation, I now empathize at a level too deep for words. I will never forget the first day of interviews and the mutual tears that flowed from my eyes. A great compassion overtook my heart that day.

Exploring that deep compassion, I stumbled upon the somewhat misunderstood concept of *Verstehen*. Giddens and Turner defined *Verstehen* as "empathic understanding of the outlook and feelings of others."[1] The term "empathetic *Verstehen*" denotes a "meaningful understanding," a concept that entails entering into another's life world and seeking to grasp his/her point of view. Reflexively, after experiencing life as a non-reader, interviewing ALFE, and observing them for some time, I have finally come to a fuller understanding of their learning processes. Nowak would additionally label my experience as "empathy," or "the manifestation of a symbiotic fusion between affective and cognitive responses to another's condition whereby a sense of understanding, kinship and engagement occurs naturally and on a level playing field."[2]

---

1. Giddens and Turner, *Social Theory Today*, 2.
2. Nowak, "Introducing a Pedagogy," 52.

American shame and vulnerability researcher Brown discerned "empathy fuels connection; sympathy drives disconnection."[3] The results from the study and the emotions emerging in myself as researcher created an important synergy with these ALFE. They drew me into connection. Wiseman, a nursing scholar, delineated four qualities of empathy: perspective taking, staying out of judgment, recognizing emotion in other people, and communicating that understanding.[4] As Brown explained, "Empathy is feeling *with* people"[5] and "what makes something better is connection."[6] Connected learners do not need our sympathy—it is not the right prescription for their concerns. The appropriate prescription is the kind of empathy that majors on connection, the wise response that says, "You do not have to learn to read before you can learn."

During the research, I connected with the participants and they connected with me in a way unlike prior to this research journey. I learned from them. And I did not do so selfishly. I attempted to encourage the hurting, to give dignity, to assist and advise, and to check for visual problems and learning disabilities. These kinds of remedial responses to ALFE learners remain a necessity.

As someone who has taught ALFE for over a decade, I discovered I had neglected several key areas. In teaching ALFE, I used visuals and stories, drama and metaphors, orality principles; but after discovering how they really learn, I felt my teaching lacked important elements. I adapted to what I thought was their learning style and culture, but I have not yet adapted sufficiently. In order to learn most effectively, ALFE need a number of things I had not been giving them. I need to focus more on relationship and connection. I need to realize the sensitive nature of the ALFE psyche and the strong need for kindness and encouragement. Successful learning in small amounts is much preferred over other options. I wonder how many other educators have overlooked these same teaching strategies.

Anthropologically, I feel that connection with understanding produced empathy, which, in turn, promoted a feeling of connection in the other person, gracing those who formally in the throes of cultural shame and loss of face with a restored sense of honor and dignity. As I experienced in the group interview with Ms. Tova, my connecting with her, validating her, and showing empathy and understanding in a public setting seemed to restore honor and dignity to her and allow her to save face in her sociocultural context.

---

3. Brown, "On Empathy," 0:15.
4. Wiseman, "Concept Analysis of Empathy," 1166.
5. Brown, "On Empathy," 0:48.
6. Brown, "On Empathy," 2:36.

I would love to see all those I interviewed learn to read or read better. For many of them, that venture is no longer possible. Some felt they were too old or could not see well enough. The younger ones with other issues explained, *"Ree-un aht jole"* (the learning would not go in), settling any further course of action. However, I have come to believe another way exists. If we care about the plight of non-readers as much as we should, we as educators will adapt to *them* and not vice versa. Throughout this study, I lamented time after time, "Where is learner-centered education when it comes to those who cannot or do not read?" Empathetic *Verstehen* would provide a better plan.

PHRONESIS (PRACTICAL WISDOM): A SOUGHT-AFTER PRIME PRODUCT

During my quest for wisdom, the affective by-product of empathy should not have come as a surprise. According to Meeks and Jeste, several of the agreed-upon components of wisdom include empathy, social cooperation, and altruism.[7] Promoting phronetic social science, Flyvbjerg et al. defined one kind of wisdom—Aristotelian *phronesis*—as "practical wisdom on how to address and act on social problems in a particular context."[8] In addition to knowing how to act, Leathard and Cook proposed the necessity for attentive presence and relationality (spiritual practice) combined with experiential learning in order to acquire, proceed, or act in a wise manner.[9] Finally, Flyvbjerg et al. explained that this important kind of engaged research—phronetic social science—should "make a difference in people's lives by focusing on what it would really take to make that difference in the issues that matter to them most."[10]

Schwartz, also examining Aristotle's work on *phronesis*, maintained, "Acting wisely also demands that we are guided by the proper aims or goals of a particular activity. Aristotle's word for the purpose or aim of a practice was *telos*."[11] Given the findings of this study, what efforts would most benefit the participants of this study? One wise aim or *telos* would be to facilitate or promote connected learning for Cambodian ALFE. The discussion that follows elaborates on wise principles toward those ends.

---

7. Meeks and Jeste, "Neurobiology of Wisdom," 357.
8. Flyvbjerg et al., *Real Social Science*, 1.
9. Leathard and Cook, "Learning for Holistic Care," 1321.
10. Flyvbjerg et al., *Real Social Science*, 20.
11. Schwartz, "Practical Wisdom," 5.

WISDOM APPLIED: PHRONETIC CONCLUSIONS

As mentioned in chapter 3, I proposed a novel form of wisdom-focused grounded theory, a method extending the central understanding toward practical wisdom for use with the participants from whom the data was gathered and for others like them. In this section I consider what *phronesis*, or the practical wisdom of Aristotle, might promote given the findings of this research. Along these lines, Flyvbjerg et al. proposed the kind of wisdom emanating from phronetic social science, something "that comes from an intimate familiarity with the contingencies and uncertainties of any particular social practice."[12] Crapanzano, writing the preface to Leenhardt's *Do Kamo*, praised Leenhardt's approach to anthropology, as "a way toward wisdom that depended on grasping the essential outlook of others ... with the reverence and real understanding due."[13]

Applying wisdom to the theory of connected learning would result in a number of practical conclusions. I propose five such phronetic conclusions related to the Connected Learning Schematic in Figure 9 and one additional conclusion concerning the term *orality*. I discuss each of these in the following sections.

1. First, given the findings of this research, wisdom would conclude *orality* is an unfortunate misnomer masking other principal ways ALFE truly learn and the global and holistic ways incorporated in connected learning.

2. Having discovered the core of ALFE learning involves relationship or connection, a process begun at birth and never ending, the default learning system of humans, and one that has been largely ignored, wisdom would conclude connected learning should be promoted on a wider scale, making allowances for those who learn best in ways that resemble this natural process of socialization.

3. Having found connected learning is reflexive in regard to the self as learner, connected to self and self-image in all of life's dimensions—cognitive, affective, and physical, for example—wisdom would conclude ALFE require learning settings that promote self-efficacy, honor, dignity, and validation, settings in which they are not shamed, in which they do not lose face or fail due to poverty, stigma, or learning disabilities. Wisdom would promote "no failure" learning (see below), put an end to Othering[14] in education, and thereby end cultural shame

---

12. Flyvbjerg et al., *Real Social Science*, 1.
13. Leenhardt, *Do Kamo*, xv.
14. See Borrero et al., "School as a Context"; Hiebert, "Western Images of Others."

and stigma. Wisdom would also conclude some ALFE need tender, experienced, and immediate attention to any undiagnosed learning disabilities.[15]

4. Having discerned that connected learning is a redemptive process and highly connected to one's faith or spirituality as a source of aspirational hope,[16] purpose, and assistance, wisdom would conclude faith communities are ideal for serving as spaces in which damaged self-concepts can be healed and those who have experienced cultural shame and loss of face due to failure in formal learning might be graced with honor.

5. Having also discovered connected learning is a relevant process, highly connected to one's context and culture as well as being experienced-based, wisdom would conclude connected learners should be offered these types of learning experiences with an understanding that learning can occur apart from or before literacy.

6. Finally, having observed that connected learning is learning that must be repackaged or packaged differently from print learning, that connected learners need accessible technologies and other portable vehicles of connection, such as stories, parables, metaphors, drama, art, and the like, wisdom would conclude companies and institutions should work to provide appropriate technologies and foster research to make media that do not exclude this important majority.

How can we trust these are wise conclusions? One way is by examining the opposite, what might be considered unwise given the findings of this research. As a result of this study, I would consider it unwise to continue to muddy the waters with the term *orality* without redefining it. I would consider it unwise to sidestep learning in favor of teaching literacy first. It would also be unwise to ignore the theory of connected learning and the repercussions of this type of ongoing learning. In considering the millions in the world who live without learning by print, it would be unwise to continue to exclude technologies that would assist ALFE in learning. Finally, it would be unwise to ignore the shame associated with lack of formal education, the benefits of spirituality on learning, the existence of undiagnosed learning disabilities, and the continued sense of failure some experience in formal learning settings.

15. Orenstein, "Picking Up the Clues."
16. Wydick and Lybbert, "Poverty."

Phronetic Conclusion 1: Orality Is an Unfortunate Misnomer

"For Marshall McLuhan, Walter Ong, and their followers, oral consciousness is a sonic consciousness, and the difference between orality and literacy is based on the difference between the eye and the ear."[17] It is unfortunate that Ong and others chose to make the dichotomy eye versus ear, orality versus literacy, throwing us off the scent of the myriad of ways ALFE learn, of natural learning, social learning, learning through trusted relationships and connections. While the principles of orality have been helpful and indeed revolutionary, the name would seem to be a misnomer, an incomplete explanation of this type of learning.

This study shows that ALFE in Cambodia do not learn exclusively through oral/aural means. Most humans can and do learn by hearing unless they are hearing impaired. However, as Innis taught, "In oral intercourse the eye, ear, and brain, the senses and the faculties acted together in busy co-operation and rivalry each eliciting, stimulating, and supplementing the other."[18] Therefore, this study now proposes using the term *connected learner* for those who do not prefer learning by means of print and *connected learning* for the process in which they engage in their lifeworlds.

By contrast, in regard to the two terms *orality* and *literacy*, Killingsworth explained:

> As opposing pairs of terms—product *versus* process, literacy *versus* orality—they bear a special relationship to one another, one that resembles a ratio: *Product is to literacy as process is to orality.* *Product* and *process* are code words for a set of generalizations in the history of composition, while *literacy* and *orality* represent similar structures in the history of culture.[19]

Furniss concurred, stating:

> In the contemporary world of increasingly global oral communication the relegation of the "oral" to the tendentious and unhelpful paradigm of the Ongian binary classification of types of society is no longer appropriate. The oral is a set of communicative conditions apparent in *all* societies and it is the implications of those conditions which have been obscured by the focus on the so-called "advances" purportedly engendered by "writing" and by the relegation of the oral as a feature of western antiquity. . . . The features of these communicative conditions

---

17. Sterne, "Theology of Sound," 210.
18. Innis, *Bias of Communication*, 105.
19. Killingsworth, "Product and Process," 26.

for the constitution of human societies—the power of the spoken word—are evident wherever we turn.[20]

However, Finnegan once asked the provocative question, "What is orality—*if anything*?"[21] Wanting to avoid stereotypes, sweeping generalizations, and indefinite answers, her reply was, "*Nothing.*"[22] In light of this study and countless other experiences literates have had with ALFE, I disagree. Finnegan did conclude, saying, "The term nevertheless can perform a useful function, provided we go about it with care, in directing us to certain kinds of investigations and insights, labeling and identifying certain aspects of human behaviour."[23] Contrary to Finnegan, I believe there is something to orality, something literates encounter when they meet those with limited education, something that causes us literates to stumble, to fall short in appropriate teaching skills, something we need to label appropriately so that we can adjust to this type of learning we have forgotten.

What term would I choose instead? West rejected the term "oral preference learner," as he believed people are not privileged to choose their first and foundational way of learning, to have a preference.[24] I agree with him that orality is an identity, one that we all seem to have at the beginning of our lives. West chose another term, explaining: "As a more useful term, I offer French anthropologist Marcel Jousse's *verbomoteur* to describe oralists as experiential, gestural, action and holistic in nature over those *habitus*-shaping effects that literacy-contingent models produce."[25]

As I learned from the participants, Cambodian ALFE do not learn solely by oral or auditory means, instead they retain their primary or foundational ways of learning from childhood. I do not want to generalize my findings and say that all oral learners are the same as Cambodian ALFE; however, I believe if this study were replicated in other areas, other researchers might also find the idea of connection or relationship to be vital in this type of learning. The concept seems so obvious to me now that I have completed the research, yet I never noticed it before. In addition, the existing literature seems to strongly agree with my findings.

If we also examine literature in the field of neuroscience, we find that from infancy, we as humans are involved in observing and attaching to our caregivers, a type of learning that affects us at the neural level. We watch, we

---

20. Furniss, *Orality*, 141.
21. Finnegan, "What Is Orality," 146.
22. Finnegan, "What Is Orality," 147.
23. Finnegan, "What Is Orality," 148.
24. West, "Re-Eventing."
25. West, "Re-Eventing," 1.

observe, we listen, we feel. This way of learning seems to ripple from observing our first caregivers to observing our families, then our peers, then a wider audience. Our eyes play just as much a role as do our ears, and the process necessarily depends heavily on the presence of people.

As mentioned earlier, Merrifield and Bingman named what they observed in this kind of learning "other-oriented learning strategies."[26] Paradise and Rogoff called this "a panhuman phenomenon," "an integrated learning tradition," and "a cultural tradition of humanity."[27] Ventura et al. referred to "the 'default' processing style."[28] Knighton added: "Orality, far from being primitive and savage, is pervasive and cohesive."[29] Even Ong believed orality to be "the primary modeling system."[30] I actually think this latter term a better, more inclusive description.

I value highly the work being done in the field of orality. I simply have a problem with the term "orality," as it focuses on only one way in which these learners might gather knowledge. As the literature has shown and I found in this study, these adults learn by more than oral means. Of course, we could tease out socialization, informal learning, social learning, conversational learning, observational learning, etc. from this process, but I observed ALFE learning to be more holistic and integrated than separating the various parts.

Therefore, I propose referring to this construct some have called "oral preference learning" as "primary," "foundational learning," or even, if you will, "connected learning," should the theory be found as pervasive among other cultures. This way of learning is not merely oral but also visual, social, and holistic. Beginning to use the terminology I mention, we avoid the Great Divide and the dichotomies of the past because we all begin learning in the first (upper right) quadrant of the Learning Quadrants diagram. As someone has said, "we" are "them," and "they" are "us." However, I believe we must be careful to avoid placing stigma on those who continue to learn from people, those who remain foundational or connected learners, and avoid withholding appropriate learning opportunities from them; but these are concepts for further discussion. Wisdom would conclude we should focus on the learning, the holistic process, and the content as well as all the means through which these are accomplished, including but not limited to oral channels.

26. Merrifield and Bingman, "Living and Learning," 181.
27. Paradise and Rogoff, "Side by Side Learning."
28. Ventura et al., "Schooling in Western Culture."
29. Knighton, "Orality," 149.
30. Ong, *Orality and Literacy*.

Since the term *orality* will most probably not cease to be used and another take its place, in terms of adult learning, I would now define *primary orality* as an identity in which indigenous knowledge is learned through holistic and relational (or connected) means. Since humans begin learning from infancy by relational or connected means, this kind of learning can and does persist throughout life, especially in those with limited education. Ong referred to this as "oral residue" or "residual orality."[31] A more positive term might be *persistent orality*. Additionally, *secondary orality* is a preference in which global knowledge is learned through holistic and integrated connections with a preference for oral, visual, and digital communication.

Phronetic Conclusion 2: The Core of ALFE Learning Is Connection

As this study revealed, ALFE learning is relational or connected, a process beginning at birth and never ending for most. This process is connected not only to people but also to all areas of life. These ways of learning do not end at some definable point known as the end of socialization. These ways continue into adulthood for those who do not pursue formal education. As mentioned earlier, this type of learning is the default system of humans, one that has been largely ignored by those doing research with adults.

I watched many of the group 3 (purposeful) learners walk beside those in groups 1 and 2 as if they were mothers and fathers. They knew how to teach them. They understood how they learned. They worked in pairs and in groups. People were scaffolds. They provided models. They taught bit by bit. They contextualized and situated. They provided on-the-job, just-in-time training. They allowed for observation and shared the best tools. They corrected when necessary. In researching non-formal education in Ethiopia, Abiy et al. discovered the process was "very much family-and community-based" and did "not depend very much on the presence of literacy skills."[32] Hardaker and Sabki, in exploring Islamic pedagogy and orality, noticed facilitating learning was "not a matter of simple methods and technique but as a holistic approach that deals with the capacity to form the human person."[33] Whether learners are oral or have limited formal education, orality encompasses "the way of life and verbalization of past communities. It refers to social bonds characterized by emotional cohesion, depth, continuity, and fullness of communities that perceive the oral tradition as the pith and

---

31. Ong, *Orality and Literacy* (1982), 35.
32. Abiy et al., "Developing a Lifelong Learning System," 648.
33. Hardaker and Sabki, "Islamic Pedagogy," 873.

marrow of communication," according to Mazamisa.³⁴ In agreement, Hiebert asserted, "Oral communication is highly relational."³⁵

Smith-Hefner evaluated the role of education in Christian conversion of Khmer refugees.³⁶ Predictably, she noticed Khmer pastors transplanted in the United States operated under traditional leadership styles, became patrons to their congregations, and thus some experienced moral shortcomings due to new temptations in their positions. She also found church members sometimes switched churches in pursuit of better patrons. However, Smith-Hefner related Christian conversion in the Khmer community with a loss of ethnicity and identity. She concluded her study by explaining, "One of the most important sociological features of Khmer conversion . . . may have less to do with belief, ritual, or morality than with education."³⁷ Noting that a larger number of Christian Khmer attend college than the general Khmer population, Smith-Hefner related their success to educational youth programs and fellowships in churches. However, I believe the reason for success lies more with the impact of social relationships than with education, the programs merely functioning as the means or conduit of providing the social glue integral to Khmer society, offering role models and a support system, connections that propelled these youth to more successful futures than the norm. As Leenhardt found, the influence of the group reigns supreme, the self relationally identified inextricably with the whole: "This can be apprehended only through a relationship which we define as communal rapport, that is, a personal rapport maintaining person-to-person participation."³⁸

Hasson et al. investigated "brain to brain coupling" and explained, "During successful communication, the speaker's and listener's brains exhibited joint, temporally-coupled, response patterns. . . . On average, the listener's brain responses mirrored the speaker's brain responses with some temporal delays."³⁹ So, we observe that connection occurs even at the neurological level.

In conclusion, what should this type of learning look like? It would be personal and close, allowing for observation. It would include the kind of communication and teaching that connects at the neural level, providing personal examples as well as shared narratives and other means of storing

---

34. Mazamisa, "Reading from This Place," 70.
35. Hiebert, *Transforming Worldviews*, 116.
36. Smith-Hefner, "Ethnicity and the Force."
37. Smith-Hefner, "Ethnicity and the Force," 32.
38. Leenhardt, *Do Kamo*, 168.
39. Hasson et al., "Brain-to-Brain Coupling," 5.

knowledge delivered in close community. In other words, school needs to visit the village and take notes.

Phronetic Conclusion 3: We Must Promote "No Failure" Learning

Gray posed a thought-provoking question: "What if medicine's first principle were also education's?"[40] Medicine's widely known first principle is "first, do no harm." For a number of participants in this study, education unfolded as a difficult, if not hurtful, experience, one associated with intense shame and leaving permanent emotional scars. Gray presented a number of studies showing the negative aspects of formal schooling—from increased stress levels to the experience of intense trauma.[41] Even some of those in the study who completed formal schooling recounted less than ideal schooling situations. Schooling was often associated with failure or poverty, both resulting in shame. In teaching, I thought I could simply focus on content and culturally appropriate delivery, but those alone prove insufficient. The affective domain holds a prominent place in ALFE learning and must be considered.[42]

Unfortunately, the present schooling situation in Cambodia has created a situation in which many fail, often through no fault of their own, as seen from this research. Some failed due to poverty and the need to leave formal school for work, others because of undiagnosed learning disabilities. In a group-oriented culture with a formal education system, this kind of failure can cause personal and family shame and loss of face. I discuss this cultural construct further in the following phronetic conclusion dealing with spirituality and connected learning.

Studying poverty and education, Boyden and Bourdillon related, "Emphasizing success at school as a criterion for success in life can be debilitating for those whose interest and aptitudes lie elsewhere, and who are stigmatized as failures on account of their school performance."[43] As Nathanson explained, "This business of being unable to decipher what's on the printed page has huge consequences for a child's self esteem."[44] Shelton researched this kind of "school-induced shame" and reported: "Early childhood experiences of school failure shape a person's identity that lasts

---

40. Gray, "Medicine's First Principle," para. 1.
41. Gray, "Medicine's First Principle."
42. Schunk, *Learning Theories*, 146.
43. Boyden and Bourdillon, "Reflections," 273.
44. Nathanson, "Dr. Donald L. Nathanson."

not only across the school years but throughout adulthood," creating "an educational wound that diminishes a person's feelings of self-efficacy and competence."[45] Pattison observed as well: "Education and schooling can reinforce feelings of inferiority and incompetence."[46]

In contrast, Childs and Greenfield found learning to weave in Zinacanteco to be "an example of 'no failure' learning."[47] This situation prompted them to wonder why, given available resources in formal schooling settings, failure prevails. They lamented, "If we knew something about a successful process of informal education, we could perhaps use this knowledge to remedy problems in formal educational systems."[48]

Likewise, Aikman observed in studying Arakmbut informal learning, "The teacher ensures that the child does not 'fail.'"[49] Most likely, this situation is common worldwide. Childs and Greenfield also noted all Zinacanteco weavers succeeded at learning their skill.[50] Failure to learn is foreign in traditional cultures.[51] In a similar vein, Spindler and Spindler described the learning of the Arunta people:

> No one failed in the rites of passage among the Arunta. But minorities fail in formal educational settings. . . . The school experience early on defines them as potential failures or even learning disabled, and there is always the implication that even if they put up with such definitions and endure the school, they are not assured of a positive gain at the end. The long initiation ritual of the school is for many minorities a long drawn out degradation ritual.[52]

Paradise concurred, asserting even more strongly:

> The drive to learn in humans is something so strong, so defining of human nature according to anthropologists, that it should still amaze us as truly remarkable that we have been able to design a social institution that can teach children to fail at learning.[53]

---

45. Shelton, "Heart of Literacy," 3–4.
46. Pattison, "Shame and the Unwanted," 15.
47. Childs and Greenfield, "Informal Modes of Learning," 285.
48. Childs and Greenfield, "Informal Modes of Learning," 285.
49. Aikman, *Intercultural Education*, 122.
50. Childs and Greenfield, "Informal Modes of Learning."
51. Childs and Greenfield, "Informal Modes of Learning," 269.
52. Spindler and Spindler, *Fifty Years of Anthropology*, 187.
53. Paradise, "What's Different," 276–77.

This persistent tendency toward failure must end. Merriam and Brockett maintained, "Shame interrupts maturity and development."[54] Wise practices would find ways to promote "no failure" learning. As Banerjee maintained in an interview, "The right to education is a right which should be measured by whether the children are learning."[55]

Unfortunately, it would seem that we as literates have facilitated the failure of ALFE, that we are guilty of having the power to make literacy the norm, othering ALFE, and thereby oppressing, marginalizing, and stigmatizing them. The present and continued hegemony of literacy and the bias toward formal education with any accompanying lack of respect, tolerance, or provision for other ways of learning is intolerable. This exclusive emphasis can lead to shame, negative self-concept, and lack of respect for professions outside of academia. Kumashiro explained this kind of marginalization, "I use the term 'Other' to refer to those groups that are traditionally marginalized in society, i.e., that are *other than* the norm."[56] Pursuit of formal education and literacy has become the norm. Therefore, those lacking formal education and literacy feel acutely this sense of being outside the norm. As Kumashiro explained, "Oppression, however, is not always easy to recognize" but involves "marginalization of the Other."[57]

Certainly, great effort and billions of dollars have been spent to assist those lacking formal education. However, few have researched ALFE ways of learning and given them what they desire—opportunities to learn what they want the way they want, when they want, and in a way that does not lead to failure or bring them emotional harm.[58] Few have attempted to offer something like connected learning. Since ALFE number in the millions, this situation is worldwide, pervasive, and unacceptable.

Moreover, wisdom would conclude some ALFE need tender and immediate attention to any lurking and undiagnosed learning disabilities that might result in a sense of failure. As Groce and Bakhshi noted, "650 million people live with physical, sensory (blindness, deafness), intellectual or mental health disability—10 percent of the population of the world—and the majority of these have low levels of education and literacy."[59] Yet, very little research on shame and education exists, especially in the area of learning disabilities.

---

54. Merriam and Brockett, *Profession and Practice*, 23.
55. Damodaran, "Learning's Not about Enrolment."
56. Kumashiro, "Anti-Oppressive Education," 26.
57. Kumashiro, "Anti-Oppressive Education," 27, 29.
58. Kumashiro, "Anti-Oppressive Education."
59. Groce and Bakhshi, "Illiteracy among Adults," 1153.

Stygles[60] and Bohdanowicz[61] broached the topic, the latter adding that adults with dyslexia "can flourish with the right support."[62]

Tanner related a situation he called the "conundrum of failure" in the lives of adult dyslexics.[63] Just dealing with everyday education in most parts of the world can challenge teachers and school systems. Add to that mix the presence of learning disabilities, and these teachers could certainly find coping with all the needs in their classrooms difficult. Nevertheless, special education, teaching on dyslexia and learning disabilities, and training to dealing with these issues are necessary worldwide—not just for the western world.

How, then, can we reverse these kinds of negative experiences and promote "no failure" learning? I make some recommendations in the second half of this chapter.

Phronetic Conclusion 4: Connected Learning Can Be Redemptive

Like Allison and Broadus,[64] Battiste,[65] Merriam and Mohamed,[66] Tisdell,[67] Tisdell and Swartz,[68] Tisdell and Tolliver,[69] and others, I observed ALFE learning was highly connected to spirituality or faith. Neither the affective nor the spiritual dimension could seemingly be divorced from ALFE learning. For the Malaysian participants in Merriam and Mohamed's study, learning was "spiritual and/or philosophically driven."[70] Additionally, as a number of researchers also noted,[71] ALFE learning strategies are decidedly holistic, including spirituality. According to Tisdell, "Spirituality is currently a hot topic,"

60. Stygles, "Eliminating Shame."
61. Bohdanowicz, "How to End the Shame."
62. Bohdanowicz, "How to End the Shame," 46.
63. Tanner, "Adult Dyslexia."
64. Allison and Broadus, "Spirituality Then and Now."
65. Battiste, "Nourishing the Learning Spirit."
66. Merriam and Mohamed, "How Cultural Values Shape Learning."
67. Tisdell, "Spirituality and Emancipatory"; "Role of Spirituality"; "Spirituality and Adult Learning."
68. Tisdell and Swartz, "Adult Education."
69. Tisdell and Tolliver, "Role of Spirituality."
70. Merriam and Mohamed, "How Cultural Values Shape Learning."
71. See Fanta-Vagenshtein, "How Illiterate People Learn"; Fanta-Vagenshtein et al., "Technological Knowledge"; Madinger, "Coming to Terms with Orality"; Merriam and Kim, "Non-Western Perspectives"; Parker, *Cultural and Academic Stress*; Ventura et al., "Schooling in Western Culture."

"an important influence in the adult education field," and something she defines as "a journey or an experience leading toward wholeness."[72] Spirituality cannot be separated from learning, even though some have a penchant for teasing out individual concepts and isolating them from one another.

Allison and Broadus confided: "A belief in something or someone greater than oneself and a sense of connectedness are prominent definitive views of spirituality" and they found that faith or "an undeniable trust in things hope for and certainty of things yet to be seen" "brought clarity" to their purpose.[73] They also maintained in their study, "The cultural norms of Afrocentricity adhere to a worldview in which spirituality is the central core of life"[74] and "contend that spirituality, purpose, and cultural identity are critically intertwined."[75] I agree, as did Battiste, in a statement encompassing much of this theory of connected learning: "Learning then, as Aboriginal people have come to know it, is holistic, lifelong, purposeful, experiential, communal, spiritual, and learned within a language and a culture."[76]

As I conversed with adult after adult, I was assaulted by the participants' emotions of fear, shame, self-loathing, and lack of self-confidence. At the same time, I was pleasantly surprised by their undaunted tenacity, perseverance, determination, and hope in the face of poverty and so many other obstacles. Watching people in their sixties, seventies, and eighties learn and grow in a culture that generally believes those years too late for learning was awe-inspiring. Witnessing them ponder their faith and sacred scriptures as sources of purpose and hope inspired me. Additionally, Arrington observed in her research with the Christian Lisu in China that even though there were many non-readers, they had a form of "liturgical literacy," a respect for and connection to their faith and the Christian Bible that was manifest in their hymnody.[77] I depicted this type of connected learning in the second quadrant (upper left) of Figure 11.

Unfortunately, as Orenstein observed, "Adopting different learning techniques can be extremely painful," so that finding a solution strictly in the educational setting may be very difficult.[78] Like successful close non-formal and informal learning settings, schools could become places of "no failure learning"; but there is sometimes so much pain associated with the

---

72. Tisdell, "Spirituality and Adult Learning," 27–29.
73. Allison and Broadus, "Spirituality Then and Now," 77–80.
74. Allison and Broadus, "Spirituality Then and Now," 81.
75. Allison and Broadus, "Spirituality Then and Now," 84.
76. Battiste, "Nourishing the Learning Spirit," 15.
77. Arrington, "Hymns as Theological Mediator"; "Hymns of the Everlasting Hills."
78. Orenstein, "Picking Up the Clues," 45.

thought of formal schooling that perhaps the sacred could become a place for learning, for restoration, redemption, and showing grace. After this study, I feel that especially in post-war, poverty-stricken environments such as Cambodia, both educators and faith communities need to prepare to deal with negative self-concepts and emotions, with the shame associated with failure to live up to cultural norms and values. Unfortunately, this "poverty-shame nexus" is too common across the globe.[79]

In many global contexts, avoidance of shame and loss of face weaves intricately and delicately throughout life. Schoenhals observed,

> All Chinese adults are expected to have sensitivity to face, that is, to be able to feel the hurt that comes from public humiliation, and to desire to protect oneself from public dishonor. Having this sensitivity is so fundamental that any adult who does not seem to have . . . a "sense of honor and shame," is considered practically inhuman.[80]

Shame is "internally felt and externally imposed—it is co-constructed," according to Chase.[81] Unfortunately, the adults with whom I conversed felt this sensitivity to saving face quite painful, especially when one had the misfortune of experiencing the public dishonor of failing to complete formal education, whether due to extreme circumstances, learning disabilities, or poverty-related situations.

In examining the literature, I include at this juncture a study by Hinton exploring why Khmer people killed during the past genocide.[82] He concluded those who murdered did so because of the penchant for honor and power and the pervasive desire to save face in the Cambodian culture. "Because Cambodians want to be respected and obeyed, they vigilantly protect and try to enhance their honor," according to Hinton.[83] He added, "Given the strong cultural emphasis on avoiding shame, however, almost all Cambodians are extremely concerned with maintaining face."[84]

Given Cambodia is a group-oriented, face-saving culture,[85] this feeling of shame seemed not only personal but also collective, a public loss of face felt by ALFE and by those close to them. Schoenhals, in a study of a Chinese middle school mentioned earlier, avoided naming these *shame*

79. Chase and Bantebya-Kyomuhendo, "Poverty and Shame."
80. Schoenhals, *Paradox of Power*, 67.
81. Chase and Bantebya-Kyomuhendo, "Poverty and Shame," 284.
82. Hinton, "Dark Side of Honor"
83. Hinton, "Dark Side of Honor," 101.
84. Hinton, "Dark Side of Honor," 101.
85. Smith-Hefner, "Education, Gender, and Generational Conflict."

cultures, preferring to call cultures in which "their members are *expected* to feel sensitive to shame and to the opinions of others and society," where they "equate sensitivity to shame with virtue," *shame-socialized* versus *non-shame-socialized cultures*.[86] However, even in a non-shame-socialized culture such as the United States, illiteracy and shame walk hand in hand. Shame has also entered the western social scene through technological avenues.[87]

In this study, shame was so entwined with illiteracy, lack of formal schooling, and poverty that the knotted strands were nearly impossible to untie. As Jo reported regarding the "social construction of the poverty-shame nexus," poverty should not merely be viewed as the lack of material goods.[88] Among the poor, an ever-present gnawing lack of honor, dignity, and pride, unquantifiable necessities for well-being in one's own cultural milieu, flourishes. One, however, needs to be able "to go about without shame," as Reyles elaborated.[89] When that need goes unmet, "absolute deprivation"[90] moves in—something far worse, culturally and psychologically speaking, than missing a meal.[91] In *Voices of the Poor*, the researchers observed "shame and humiliation can result in increasing isolation as people are able to participate less and less in social ceremonies and traditions that once brought people together and helped to create and maintain the social bonds between people."[92] Similarly, Participate found in working with people living in poverty, "Empowerment, dignity, and hope are valued as much as livelihoods, education, and health."[93] These make up the so-called "missing dimensions of poverty data—dimensions that are of value to poor people, but for which we have scant or no data."[94]

The shame associated with poverty

> is one of the most harmful of emotions because it has the power to sap people of any agency and leave them feeling unable to change their circumstances. It is especially potent because, unlike guilt, the feeling of shame is not easily allayed since there is often nothing that the person experiencing it can do to make things better. . . . If poverty is everywhere associated with shame, then

86. Schoenhals, *Paradox of Power*, 191–92.
87. Crouch, "Return of Shame."
88. Jo, "Psycho-Social Dimensions."
89. Reyles, "Ability to Go."
90. Sen, "Poor, Relatively Speaking," 673.
91. Walker et al., "Poverty in Global Perspective."
92. Narayan, *Voices of the Poor*, 70.
93. Participate, *Experiences Living in Poverty*, 5.
94. Alkire, *Missing Dimensions*, 1.

shame, and its possible antonym dignity, might better facilitate a more comprehensive global discourse on poverty than one which is limited to relative and absolute measures of poverty.[95]

On a very important note, Chase and Bantebya-Kyomuhendo also added:

> Irrespective of the level of deprivation that people endure on a day-to-day basis, their standing and "face" in society, for most, appears to hold as much if not greater value than how much money is coming in to the household. . . . If . . . the maintenance of dignity and self-respect are as important as material security in enabling people fully to participate in society, governments and others responsible for alleviating poverty must accept additional responsibilities in this regard.[96]

In response, according to Bantebya-Kyomuhendo, people can withdraw, keep up appearances, deflect, and become defensive, angry, or resentful in trying to escape the "dreaded stigma."[97] When this emotion continues long enough, it becomes toxic and "can significantly interfere with an adult's ability to form an intimate relationship with another."[98]

Researchers may discuss the poverty-shame nexus, however, given this study, I would include lack of formal education as being crucial to the mix—a poverty-shame-limited education nexus or cycle of lack—with poverty or lack of resources resulting in lack of education, which ultimately feeds into lack of honor or dignity, a sense of shame. In this delicate mixture, adding a learning disability became a recipe for personal disaster. According to Scheff, "every social situation is rife with shame"[99]—how much more situations in which circumstances beyond one's control result in public loss of face. As is true with many Asian cultures, ALFE significant others actively shamed them, supposedly in order to motivate them to learn. A practice begun in childhood, shaming is seen as "opportunity education" in Asia, according to Fung,[100] or a form of social control.[101] In those instances, shaming did not cause learning, only increased shame.

"The opposite of Western shame is self-esteem—'I feel good about myself.' The opposite of Eastern shame is honor—others thinking highly of

---

95. Chase and Bantebya-Kyomuhendo, "Poverty and Shame," 299.
96. Chase and Bantebya-Kyomuhendo, "Poverty and Shame," 299.
97. Bantebya-Kyomuhendo, "Needy and Vulnerable," 117–24.
98. Adams, "Using Transactional Analysis," 2.
99. Scheff, "Shame in Self."
100. Fung, "Becoming a Moral Child."
101. Schoenhals, *Paradox of Power*.

me."[102] However, as Crouch observed, "large parts of our culture are starting to look something like a postmodern *fame*-shame culture. Like honor, fame is a public estimation of worth, a powerful currency of status."[103] In contrast to honor, "fame is bestowed by a broad audience, with only the loosest of bonds to those they acclaim."[104] Whether one desires fame or honor, Crouch explained, "The remedy for shame is not affirmation. It is incorporation into a community with new, different, and better standards for honor."[105] Those writing on shame, such as Hsieh, proposed a similar prescription.[106] Interestingly, the one word used repeatedly is the same one ALFE learners craved—*connection*. The solution for the disconnected feelings associated with shame is connection. Hsieh explained this kind of connection as "warmth, consistency, a sense of belonging, connectedness, support, and attachment" and defined "relational connection as a consistent, positive, emotional, and supportive bonding experience with significant others."[107] Hagerty et al. likewise maintained connectedness is manifested "when a person is actively involved with another person, object, or environment, and that involvement promotes a sense of comfort, well-being, and anxiety-reduction."[108] The ALFE in this study longed for that sort of positive connective experience in their learning.

Those who espouse a sacred book, such as Jews and Christians, have often been at the forefront of literacy efforts. Wisdom would conclude these communities should also forge ahead in addressing learning disabilities and the emotions connected to them. Churches, temples, synagogues, and the like could become places of learning and shelters for those who feel battered by failure in formal schooling. As Townsend and McWhirter observed, "Human beings have a powerful need for connectedness."[109] What better place to find solace and connection than in sacred learning and healing spaces?

"Many non-Western cultures insist . . . on the fundamental *connectedness* of human beings to each other. A normative imperative of these cultures is to maintain this interdependence among individuals."[110] Peoples with an "interdependent construal of self," such as in Cambodian

---

102. Georges, "Geography of Shame," para. 4.
103. Crouch, "Return of Shame," 37.
104. Crouch, "Return of Shame," 38.
105. Crouch, "Return of Shame," 37.
106. Hsieh, "Power of Shame."
107. Hsieh, "Power of Shame," 4.
108. Hagerty et al., "Emerging Theory," 293.
109. Townsend and McWhirter, "Connectedness," 191.
110. Markus and Kitayama, "Culture and Self," 227.

culture, see one's self "as part of an encompassing social relationship and recognizing that one's behavior is determined, contingent on, and, to a large extent organized by what the actor perceives to be the thoughts, feelings, and actions of *others* in the relationship."[111] This view is also "sociocentric, holistic, collective, allocentric, ensembled, constitutive, contextualist, connected, and relational."[112]

Cultures that have an independent view of self may not see the need for connected learning as portrayed in this study. Originally from Appalachia, I would love to conduct this study among people with an independent construal of self and compare the findings. However, a number of western researchers have already written about shame and the pervasiveness of that emotion in relation to illiteracy.[113] Their prescriptions also involved relationship and restored connection. What better places for dispensing this prescription than sacred places, such as synagogues, temples, and churches?

Phronetic Conclusion 5: Relevant Connected Learning Occurs Without Literacy

As mentioned when describing the Learning Quadrants, many "learning worlds" exist. Each lifeworld or learning world has value and one is not more important than any of the others. As each flows along its own continuum, there are differences in means of learning and funds of knowledge. Those who prefer warm connection and relationship, learning in a socially energized milieu, should not be compelled to enter the seemingly icy waters of lifeless print.[114] They should be allowed to learn without literacy. How is that possible? Thompson explained that her "study challenged the concept often seen in adult education that literacy is necessarily the first rung of adult education."[115] Likewise, Rogers declared nearly two decades ago: "Literacy comes second."[116]

A Freedom from Hunger article recounted the following story from a trainer in Haiti:

> He confesses to having driven hundreds of kilometers and having worked many hours on a training workshop before he

---

111. Markus and Kitayama, "Culture and Self," 227

112. Markus and Kitayama, "Culture and Self," 227.

113. See Brown, *Daring Greatly*; "On Empathy"; *Women Reclaiming Power*; Nelson, *Unashamed*; Welch, *Shame Interrupted*.

114. Botha, "Living Voice."

115. Thompson, "Perceptions of Teaching," para. 2.

116. Rogers, "Literacy Comes Second," 237.

realized that most of the farmers were illiterate and therefore wouldn't be able to do the exercises the way he had planned. Adapting the materials to make them work was hard, but it taught him a lesson: put learners first in all steps of a program.[117]

François and Olazabal continued with the following training tips all of which confirm the findings of this study: (1) Let learners make decisions, (2) apply what is learned, (3) promote learner-to-learner education, (4) reinforce as much as possible, and (5) train adult educators differently.[118] Their summary of the "confessions of two adult educators" was, "We had to change ourselves as educators before we could help others to change their lives."[119]

In the literature, adult learning has been shown to be experiential, hands on, and relevant.[120] Ong also noted, "For an oral culture learning or knowing means achieving close, empathetic, communal identification with the known."[121] This finding is not new. In working in a Senegalese village, Diouf et al. also noticed villagers preferred "demonstration followed by hands-on reflective practice with feedback."[122] Echoing the need for context in connected learning, Medhi et al. observed, "Non-literate participants did best when instructional material was specifically and exactly tailored to the skill."[123] Merriam and Mohamed also found learning needed to be "embedded in the concerns and activities of everyday life" for their older Malaysian participants.[124]

Many connected learners have not been socialized to find meaning in symbols written on paper or to value knowledge disconnected from a social context. Some educators, like myself, have not always reserved the time to promote this kind of learning. Guilty of majoring on providing information instead of connection, I have had the tragic tendency to merely hand people a book. Fingeret so eloquently described this dilemma:

> Educators believe that literacy is fundamental to competence and independence in modern society; it is difficult for us to conceptualize life without reading and writing as anything other

---

117. François and Olazabal, "Confessions of Two Adult Educators," 21.
118. François and Olazabal, "Confessions of Two Adult Educators," 23–24.
119. François and Olazabal, "Confessions of Two Adult Educators," 23.
120. See Aikman, *Intercultural Education*; MacKeracher, *Making Sense of Adult Learning*; Merriam and Bierema, *Adult Learning*; Merriam and Kim, "Non-Western Perspectives."
121. Ong, *Orality and Literacy* (1982), 45.
122. Diouf et al., "Adult Learning," 42.
123. Medhi et al., "Beyond Strict Illiteracy," 8.
124. Merriam and Mohamed, "How Cultural Values Shape Learning," 51.

than a limited, dull, dependent existence. As a result, adult basic educators continue to define their student populations in terms of incompetence, inability, and illiteracy, even though this kind of orientation has been labeled a "deficit" perspective and is under attack in a variety of social science disciplines. Perhaps part of the problem is that once we recognize the inadequacies inherent in our approach to illiterate adults, we have little to offer in its place.[125]

I propose we offer connected learning as a solution to this need. As it is, "the diploma disease developed and nurtured by the credential society has intensified the diminishing interest in the knowledge structures of non-credential societies."[126] How can we as a global learning community validate the needs of those who do not place value on formal education due to their beliefs, vocations, and life struggles?

As mentioned earlier, offering learning opportunities prior to literacy would do a great service to many adults worldwide who would like to continue learning. Wisdom would celebrate the connected learner, the ALFE, along with these ways of learning. Wisdom would adapt to their preferred learning paradigm. As Mazamisa affirmed, "Textuality is a form of resocialisation."[127] No one should be forced to change lifeworlds or become literate in order to learn.

Is this view, this emphasis on textuality, another form of paternalism? A number of scholars view literacy efforts as paternalistic and oppressive. For instance, in *The Bugbear of Literacy*, Coomaraswamy complained, "To impose our literacy (and our contemporary 'literature') upon a cultured but illiterate people is to destroy their culture in the name of our own."[128] He also called literacy a "curse." Draper similarly believed literacy to be "a form of control, not only of information, but also of people."[129] Finally, Street argued, "The Western concept of 'illiteracy' creates stigma" and "literacy campaigns have involved the construction of 'stigma' of illiteracy where many people had operated in the oral domain without feeling that it was a problem."[130]

---

125. Fingeret, "Social Network," 133.
126. Akinnaso, "Schooling, Language, and Knowledge," 70.
127. Mazamisa, "Reading from This Place," 72.
128. Coomaraswamy, *Bugbear of Literacy*, 54.
129. Draper, "Closed Text," 1.
130. Street, *Social Literacies*, 14.

Phronetic Conclusion 6: Technologies Promote Connection, But Must Be Accessible

Besides the socially constructed chasm previously described, some scholars report a third divide—the digital one.[131] Many advances in technology remain out of reach for the world's majority. It was sad to note the very people who could benefit most from these devices were excluded from using them because of the inaccessibility of some of their features.

ALFE would greatly benefit from access to video and audio resources and using them for increased connectivity, but barriers fill this path. First of all, the dominance of the English language presented a barrier for many ALFE in this study. They could learn to use basic phones with face panels providing numbers and colors but wanted access to the additional features of the latest smart phones.

Research by Phong and Sola determined 94.5 percent of Cambodians own phones, 60.5 percent of which are basic, with only 30 percent of the population reading Khmer script on their phones.[132] Twenty percent of their respondents revealed they were illiterate, and another 18 percent complained attempting to type in Khmer on their phones was too difficult.[133] Of the remaining population not owning a phone, most could access one. As expected, those with more formal education had increased internet access. Phong and Sola recommended increased availability of Khmer script in order to make the technology even more accessible. In addition, in their study they uncovered Cambodians gained information most from television (31.8 percent), secondly from the internet (24.9 percent), and next from radio (20.5 percent). Unsurprisingly, 17.8 percent of Cambodians gained information through "word of mouth."[134] Similar research conducted by the Broadcasting Board of Governors (BBG) and Gallup basically concurred with these findings; however, the BBG and Gallup report added, "Radio use rises with Cambodians' education levels."[135]

In fact, Chudgar noted in a study of mobile phone users in India, "Mobile phones are mainly perceived as a means to stay connected with friends and family."[136] Smith et al. concurred: "Research has illustrated that people in the developing world tend to use mobiles for more social than business

---

131. Bynner et al., *Three Divides*; Palaiologou, "Needs for Developing."
132. Phong and Sola, *Mobile Phones and Internet*, 14.
133. Phong and Sola, *Mobile Phones and Internet*, 14.
134. Phong and Sola, *Mobile Phones and Internet*.
135. Broadcasting Board of Governors (BBG) and Gallup, "Media Use in Cambodia," 1.
136. Chudgar, "Promise and Challenges," 27.

interactions."[137] In another study on mobile phone use by ALFE in India, Kenya, the Philippines, and South Africa, Medhi et al. discovered that the use of "a live operator" was much preferable to "text-based interfaces."[138] Bogale et al., in studying appropriate formats for delivering important messages in Ethiopia, observed, "Among these illiterate women, enjoying social-oriented presentation formats makes a message convincing and likeable. The mind follows what the heart tells them."[139]

In light of the inaccessibility of some technologies, it is refreshing to note a group of engineers and social scientists (mainly the Information and Communication Technologies for Development group and The Technology for Emerging Markets group at Microsoft Research India) work to develop technologies for the poor and the illiterate.[140] Wisdom would research, create, and promote more technologies that appeal to ALFE hearts in their search for knowledge and desire to learn, because as Smith et al. noted, mobile phones can provide "expanded possibilities for connectedness between people" and "the benefits of mobile phones might be proportionally greater in resource-constrained settings, e.g., the poor and rural populations."[141]

CHAPTER REFLECTIONS

In chapter 3, I proposed wisdom-based grounded theory on a quest for more than understanding, for wisdom to be applied to the learning of Cambodian ALFE. From the lives of the participants came wisdom to apply to my own teaching in Cambodia. One of the archived interviews from the NGO RDI included a young but experienced monk (Mr. Amit) who trained novices. His advice for teaching is apropos at this point. Mr. Amit proposed learners needed to embrace four dispositions or strategies in order to experience success. I could see these ways incorporated in the connected learning of many Cambodian ALFE:

- A strong love and will to learn (*chan-teyek*)
- Intense thought into making the process easier (*jen-tay-ack*)
- Perseverance and diligent effort (*vere-ree-yehek*)
- Practice or application with assistance from others (*vee-mahng-sah*)

---

137. Smith et al., "Mobile Phones," 79.
138. Medhi et al., "Designing Mobile Interfaces," 1.
139. Bogale et al., "Reaching the Hearts," 8.
140. See Donner et al., "Stages of Design"; Medhi et al., "Designing Mobile Interfaces"; Medhi et al., "Beyond Strict Illiteracy"; Medhi et al., "Text-Free User Interfaces."
141. Smith et al., "Mobile Phones," 78–79.

In summary, given the findings of this study and the theory of connected learning that emerged, wisdom would conclude orality is an area of study in need of renaming, ALFE prefer learning by means of persons and not texts, no failure learning is necessary for promoting lifelong learning of ALFE, faith and spirituality can provide redemption for hopeless ALFE caught in shame, people can learn without being literate first, and accessible technologies can provide connection for Cambodian AFLE. In light of these phronetic conclusions, I make a number of recommendations in the final chapter.

8

Recommendations: The Practical Wisdom Concluded

> "Above all and before all, do this: Get Wisdom! Write this at the top of your list:
>
> Get Understanding! Throw your arms around her—believe me, you won't regret it;
>
> never let her go—she'll make your life glorious. She'll garland your life with grace,
>
> she'll festoon your days with beauty."
>
> —Proverbs 4:7 (The Message)

In this final chapter I conclude by delineating recommendations for educators, faith communities, and policy makers, presenting ideas for further research, and providing a final reflection on connected learning. Given the conclusions that have been drawn, what would wisdom do? What actions would matter most to the participants?

WISDOM APPLIED: RECOMMENDATIONS

Given that ALFE preferred to learn through relational means, through connection, how would a theory of connected learning be exemplified in the areas just mentioned? This section provides recommendations for wise practices—for educators and faith communities, for policy makers and organizations, and for further research.

Recommendations for Practice

First, the current hegemony promoting literacy as the ultimate path needs to be replaced by a focus on learning by all means. The "us and them" mentality that considers those who have less formal education as other is inappropriate in an educational world that emphasizes being learner-centered. Second, we all learn from people. We are all relational and observational learners. Some of us have been resocialized to add print to our learning diets. Third, people from the world of books and technology can become sensitive to the possibility of learning disabilities and prepared to adapt materials when teaching to make resources more accessible. Additionally, technology has been inaccessible to the world's majority for too long. This trend should cease focus on the high-end user and address the inequity of the present situation. Finally, the affective and spiritual are necessary ingredients for ALFE learning. No program that facilitates learning can afford to neglect kindness and hope, honor and encouragement, and a remedy for the self-loathing that hound many ALFE.

RECOMMENDATIONS FOR EDUCATORS. If connection and connected learning in all areas of life were primary for ALFE, how can teaching, adult education, and literacy education adapt to this learning theory? According to Heschel, "What we need more than anything else is not *textbooks* but *textpeople*. It is the personality of the teacher which is the text that the pupil reads; the text that they will never forget."[1] Becoming connected teachers for the world's connected learners and for Cambodian ALFE in particular, therefore, involves some of the following major points listed below and taken together to form the acronym REMIT. One of the many possible meanings of the word *remit* is to restore. I hope this study and following these recommendations might further restoring connected learners to equal status with those who learn through print:

- Recognition and understanding of the issues related to connected learning
- Early intervention for learning disabilities
- Merging anthropology and education in order to understand and adapt
- Identifying with the connected learner
- Teaching to the Learning Quadrant

---

1. Dresner, *Heschel, Hasidism, and Halakha*, 31.

The next section begins a discussion of the five points of the REMIT strategy for becoming a connected teacher.

RECOGNITION AND UNDERSTANDING OF THE ISSUES SURROUNDING CONNECTED LEARNING. The first step in any restoration begins with an understanding of causes and issues. As seen in this research, adults who lack formal education, who cannot or prefer not to read, those who have traditionally been labeled as oral learners, have different learning needs from adults who learn through formal schooling or through print. They have been socialized to learn from people, a natural process of observing in order to learn. Connected learning, as depicted in Figures 9 and H1 in both of the Connected Learning Schematics, had a number of characteristics. The process of connected learning was found to be

- Relational, social, connected, holistic, encompassing, and integrated into all areas of life;
- Reflexive and closely related to self-efficacy and the avoidance of shame;
- Redemptive, closely connected to spirituality and faith, which provided hope, purpose, and assistance;
- Relevant, contextual, and highly linked to experience; and
- Repackaged in appropriate and accessible technologies.

EARLY INTERVENTION FOR LEARNING DISABILITIES. Many connected learners in traditional school settings experienced difficulty learning. Some ALFE learners in this study repeatedly explained their problem as *ree-un aht jole*, feeling the learning would not enter their minds. Because these adults worked and seemed successful in life, they appeared in my estimation to be suffering from undiagnosed learning disabilities or ULDs.[2] Having no label and no validation of or testing for their difficulties, these learners suffered in silence, attempted to learn with great difficulty, and ultimately discontinued formal education. Many expressed great relief when informed about learning disabilities such as dyslexia. Discovering issues like dyslexia made them feel their problems were not due to supposed mental deficiency but a result of a quantifiable problem many others face. I felt their shame seemed to be lessened by this news.

For the most part, the majority of teachers in Cambodia are not being trained to spot learning disabilities, even though research showed that

---

2. Orenstein, "Picking Up the Clues."

early identification is vital.³ Certainly, with the situation of the educational system in Cambodia, most teachers lack the opportunity to learn something other than pedagogy, classroom management, or the subjects of their instruction. For many of the participants, early intervention might have altered the course of their lives and their educational trajectory. It is beyond the scope of this paper to delineate all the ways of helping those with learning disabilities and dyslexia in particular; however, the participants' experiences drove me to read and research, to seek to educate myself and inform others in Cambodia about these obstacles in learning, to show more empathy to ALFE, and to seek to employ novel means of teaching and assisting these adult learners.⁴

MERGING ANTHROPOLOGY AND EDUCATION IN ORDER TO UNDERSTAND AND ADAPT. As Quillen wrote long ago, "Education is a cultural process."⁵ Schooling embraces a certain style of learning, certain information, and espouses a hidden curriculum. In addition, as most educators know, every classroom houses people with very different ways of learning and knowing. Very few educators work in mono-cultural environments with students exactly like themselves. Therefore, in order to cross cultures in education and teach outside our own learning quadrants, we must integrate anthropological concepts.

Crabtree and Sapp wrote an insightful research article with a provocative title: "Your Culture, My Classroom, Whose Pedagogy?"⁶ They observed "cultural asynchrony" in the school setting. All too often I observed Cambodians experiencing the imposition of foreign pedagogy in the classroom. Could we not be learner-centered in this area? Should we not provide these adult learners with the kind of educational experiences they desire? Diamond described the present schooling system as an "assembly line," a "factory system," which was "in startling contrast to the personal learning context in traditional and primitive societies."⁷

Leroy Little Bear encouraged respect for nonwestern worldviews, describing "Eurocentric" and indigenous knowledge as "jagged worldviews colliding."⁸ To follow the lead of connected learners, a number of shifts would need to occur. Merging ideas from anthropology with the world

---

3. Bohdanowicz, "How to End the Shame."
4. Gori and Facoetti, "Perceptual Learning."
5. Quillen, "Introduction to Anthropology," 1.
6. Crabtree and Sapp, "Your Culture."
7. Diamond, "Epilogue," 305.
8. Little Bear, "Jagged Worldviews Colliding."

of education could assist educators in understanding their situation more fully and to adapt more strategically. For instance, Hvitfeldt proposed giving learners what they need—relationship and immediate relevance.[9] Nguyen et al. advised "culturally appropriate pedagogy."[10] Watson urged implementing "a pedagogy of deep reciprocity."[11] Ladson-Billings also recommended "culturally relevant pedagogy," maintaining teachers should develop "fluid student-teacher relationships, demonstrate a connectedness with all of the students, develop a community of learners, encourage students to learn collaboratively and be responsible for one another."[12] Baldwin explored "culturally responsive pedagogy" for use in higher education and described six appropriate practices for teachers.[13] In addition, Moon advised considering the acronym CHIMES when "designing learning experiences" for these adult learners—communal, holistic, images, mnemonics, experiential, sensory.[14] Finally, DeCapua and Marshall promoted MALP—a Mutually Adaptive Learning Paradigm—a system of learning facilitation that gives "immediate relevance and strong interpersonal relationship," adds unfamiliar learning processes with those already ingrained, and teaches "decontextualization skills."[15]

Culturally sensitive pedagogy and a desire to be learner-centered could adapt to every quadrant of Figure 11. To accomplish this, Labatiuk[16] and Spindler[17] recommended "cultural therapy," which helped to "unravel the way in which cultural biases of a teacher (and students) affect the educational process, and what can be done to improve the teacher-student communication and help them understand oneself and others in the multicultural environment of a classroom."[18] That process was designed for the educator in order to bring "one's own culture in its manifold forms to a level of awareness that permits one to perceive it as a potential bias in social interaction and in the acquisition or transmission of skills and knowledge."[19] ALFE would welcome this sort of reflexivity in teaching.

9. Hvitfeldt, "Traditional Culture."
10. Nguyen et al., "Culturally Appropriate Pedagogy."
11. Watson, "Interpreting across the Abyss," 242.
12. Ladson-Billings, "Culturally Relevant Pedagogy," 480.
13. Baldwin, "Culturally Responsive Pedagogy."
14. Moon, "Fad or Renaissance," 10.
15. DeCapua and Marshall, "Students with Limited," 167–68.
16. Labatiuk, "George Spindler's Concept."
17. Spindler, "Three Categories of Cultural Knowledge."
18. Labatiuk, "George Spindler's Concept," 50.
19. Spindler, "Three Categories of Cultural Knowledge," 466.

IDENTIFYING WITH THE CONNECTED LEARNER. "Humans are adapted to be highly social, but the organizations through which we live our lives are not adapted to us. We are square (social) pegs being forced into round (nonsocial) holes," according to Lieberman.[20] Siegel, a physician, echoed by saying schooling's traditional "3Rs" needed three more—reflection, relationship, and resilience.[21]

Much like the attachment needed for successful learning in infancy, relationship plays a profound role in the learning process. Cozolino maintained, "Teacher-student attunement isn't a 'nice addition' to the learning experience, but a core requirement. . . . The social brain takes into account both what we are learning and from whom we are learning it."[22] Meek called the idea of caring for the learner as a social being and injecting warmth, "noticing regard."[23] According to Cohen, "the content of learning, especially in children, is often inseparable from the identity of their teachers."[24] This study on Cambodian ALFE seemed to show that these adult learners prefer relationship and also do not separate learning and the identity of the person from whom they learn.

Zhou observed learners' testing outcomes improved when teachers imitated students' behaviors, that mirror neurons activated even without the students' awareness.[25] This enterprise is non-verbal, affective, social, involving "intentional attunement" and empathic listening.[26] Caring is not optional if learners are to become engaged and successful. Studies show positive affect and a sense of belonging improve test results.[27] What does this mean practically? It means effective facilitation of learning includes the affective—culturally appropriate intentional listening, relationship building, exhibiting care and concern, for example.

TEACHING TO THE LEARNING QUADRANTS. Advice and research for teaching in the academic quadrant is abundant and beyond the scope of this study; however, given that little progress has been made in improving over-all literacy rates across the globe, Belzer surmised, we should "teach

20. Lieberman, *Social*, 12.
21. Siegel, "Daniel J. Siegel."
22. Cozolino, *Social Neuroscience of Education*, s.v. "Safe and Trusting Relationships," para. 2.
23. Meek, "Cultivating Connected Knowing."
24. Cohen, "Shaping of Men's Minds," 34.
25. Zhou, "Effects of Reciprocal Imitation."
26. Gallese, "Mirror Neurons."
27. Lieberman, *Social*.

low-skilled adults what they can do to help themselves improve in and out of programs and then provide them with the digital technologies to support that learning process, whenever and wherever they can work to improve skills."[28] For those working in the bottom right corner of Figure 11 of the Learning Quadrants, those involved in areas of contemporary orality, Papacharissi offered good advice:

> Different forms of orality open up different avenues to knowledge, in fact, *to situated knowledges*. No one form of orality leads to truer articulations of knowledge. What is important is to understand the texture of the path to (situated) knowledge each orality opens up. I suggest that online networked platforms, supportive of Big Data and a variety of similar analytical formulations, blend interpersonal and mass storytelling practice variables, offering a reconciliation of primary and secondary orality tendencies and tensions. Where secondary orality ensured distance, *digital orality* affirms voice, offering a digitally enabled path into the story. Where primary orality emphasized voice, *digital orality* propagates voice while preserving their atomized subjectivity. . . . It drives a digital form of storytelling, derivative of the blended conventions of both a primary and secondary orality.[29]

Connecting via stories is still an age-old, tried and true mode of learning.

Finally, when Dr. Rebekah Naylor discovered the Indian patients she treated and sent home well returned repeatedly with the same ailments, she developed a model village on the grounds of Bangalore Baptist Hospital to visually and experientially show mothers how to have healthy homes. Paige Patterson's description of her work is worth noting for teaching connected learners:

> She had discovered that children suffering from malnutrition went back home to their villages well, but because of nutritional misunderstandings, they soon returned suffering the same malady. Dr. Naylor hit upon the idea of requiring mothers to come and live in the hospital village, and while the children were treated, mothers were taught how to choose and prepare nutritiously significant meals in village circumstances—exactly like those in which they lived. . . . Dr. Naylor had demonstrated that the essential problem was lack of knowledge rather than poverty.[30]

28. Belzer, "Reflections on PIAAC Literacy," 2.
29. Papacharissi, "Unbearable Lightness," 5.
30. Morris, "Fellow Servants," para. 8.

ALFE need models like these in every area of life—to have an opportunity to observe good health practices, good parenting, and other helpful examples embodied. They are watching, but how do we make time for people without margin? We take the learning to them and allow observation. Operating in the top right quadrant involves models and taking time with learners. Tovar, in examining "functional illiteracy in the workplace," published some important information in this regard:

> Participants acknowledged the severity of functional illiteracy, the association between shame, fear and stigmatization which impacts health and safety training. . . . Worker specific training recommendations included incorporating small group activities, hands on training and the use of multiple methods of communication for a range of literacy and education levels. Management recommended use of shadowing experienced workers, use of pre-training materials, incorporating functional illiteracy techniques into the training and finding alternative ways to conduct training evaluations.[31]

In summary, the practical wisdom gained from this study would advise the use of a number of interventions—recognition and understanding of the issues related to connected learning, early intervention for learning disabilities, merging anthropology and education in order to understand and adapt, identifying with the connected learner, and finally, teaching to the quadrants in Figure 11. To promote this kind of person-connected learning, we as educators need a number of practices in our repertoire: respecting connected learning and connected learners; demonstrating relational connectedness;[32] learning to deal with shame, emotions, lack of self-efficacy and self-concept; promoting connected, cooperative, relational, or PIER learning—"People as Informal, Extended Resources for Learning";[33] distilling lessons to the most meaningful essentials; promoting more showing and less telling or experientially-based approaches;[34] respecting all professions, whether they require brain or brawn; embodying teaching and employing "noticing regard";[35] learning to recognize and deal with dyslexia and learning disabilities; being culturally sensitive/responsive and including culturally relative content;[36] working to teach and integrate appropriate and

31. Tovar, "Functional Illiteracy," iii.
32. Ladson-Billings, "Culturally Relevant Pedagogy."
33. Hill, "People as Informal."
34. Vautrot, "Why Don't They Come?"
35. Meek, "Cultivating Connected Knowing."
36. See Ladson-Billings, "Culturally Relevant Pedagogy"; DeCapua and Marshall,

accessible technologies; being unhurried;[37] taking advantage of proximate literacy[38] and literacy brokering,[39] to name a few.

RECOMMENDATIONS FOR FAITH COMMUNITIES. In his ancient text on teaching the Christian faith, Saint Augustine reminded the readers that when the Ethiopian eunuch read the Old Testament prophet Isaiah and did not understand what he was reading, God sent the apostle Philip in person (Acts 8:26–39), someone who "sat with him, and in human words and human language opened up to him what was hidden in that passage."[40] Moreover, the Creator God Himself came as a man to communicate with us. He personally connected with us on many levels. As Soukup elucidated, "Truth is not a statement at all, but is nothing less than a *person*."[41]

In light of this research and other studies, it would seem wise to make faith communities connected communities—connected with others as communities of participation in learning[42] and connected with God and others as communities of honor and grace in healing. In considering shame, Johnson advised: "If shame can interfere with a student's feeling of community . . . community may also be the best remedy."[43] Likewise, according to Vliet, "Recovering from shame can be seen as a process of rebuilding the self" and involves five processes—"connecting, refocusing, accepting, understanding, and resisting."[44]

CONNECTED AS COMMUNITIES OF PARTICIPATION IN LEARNING. If connection and connected learning in all areas of life are primary for ALFE, how can practices such as religious education, theological education, leader development, and discipleship be adapted? The faith community could be a sad, shaming place for those who cannot read. It was for some ALFE in this study. How can faith communities have non-reader friendly meetings? Study of sacred scriptures cannot subsist only in the bottom left quadrant of the Learning Quadrants in Figure 11. There needs to be a place for spiritual learning in all four quadrants.

"Students with Limited."
37. Osborne, "Practice into Theory."
38. See Basu et al., *Isolated and Proximate Illiteracy*; Maddox, "Worlds Apart?"
39. Perry, "Genres, Context, and Literacy Practices."
40. Augustine, *Teaching Christianity*, 103.
41. Soukup, "In Commemoration," 837.
42. Weber, *Communication of the Gospel*, 48.
43. Johnson, "Considering Shame," 13.
44. Vliet, "Shame and Resilience," 238.

The Creator God of the Christian Bible spoke, but He was also a writing God. He wrote on tablets for Moses (Exod 34:1). He arranged circumstances so that a Hebrew slave's son would be educated in a palace and learn to read and write, thus enabling him to record God's words. Yet, we learn of times when the Law was read and explained to the people orally (Neh 8:1–8) or read for the purpose of learning through hearing (Deut 31:11–14). Although Jesus did not write a book while on earth, others recorded his teachings by inspiration of God's Holy Spirit. How do people with a sacred text bridge the gap for those who cannot or do not read? The length of time it takes for a person to gain the highly literate skills for abstract Bible study is beyond nine grades of study.[45] While adults are learning to read on a part-time basis, what do they do in the meantime?

As Jordan noted, "People are relational beings and thrive on being connected with one another."[46] Buber held, "Man can become whole not in virtue of a relation to himself but only in virtue of a relation to another self."[47] When growing spirituality, we need this kind of learning in faith communities through connection. "New connections are established between persons who have heard and identified with the same stories. And the deeper the meaning of the story, the deeper are the relationships that are formed by the sharing, according to Boomershine."[48] Spaces with sacred stories can facilitate people connecting with God and others through holistic connections, traditioning,[49] fathering and mothering, re-socializing,[50] and through re-eventing education.[51]

The process of conversion and discipleship requires highly personal re-socialization, according to Berger and Luckmann.[52] Too often religious education, theological education, and leader development concentrates on the cognitive knowledge a person might need without a connected learning outlook. An emphasis solely on the cognitive can repel and discourage connected learners.[53] As for Christian cross-cultural work, Willis and Greeneish lamented:

---

45. Slack et al., *Memory and Recall*.
46. Jordan, "Relational Development," 7.
47. Buber, *Between Man and Man*, 199.
48. Boomershine, *Story Journey*, 8.
49. Keener, "Assumptions in Historical-Jesus Research."
50. Berger and Luckmann, *Social Construction of Reality*.
51. West, "Re-Eventing."
52. Berger and Luckmann, *Social Construction of Reality*.
53. Klem, "Dependence on Literacy Strategy."

> An estimated 90 percent of the world's Christian workers present the gospel and do discipleship using highly literate communication styles. 90 percent. Throw that up against the 67 percent who are oral learners and what do you have? A strategic problem.... The fact that we, as literate, print oriented, missionaries from the west, have missed this oral storying method for so long may be one of the single most serious tactical mistakes we have made in the last 200 years.[54]

Given the needs of connected learners, relying solely on print and making such "tactical mistakes" is unacceptable.

The apostle Paul in the New Testament tended to treat those he trained as if he were their parent (1 Thess 2:7, 11). Rabbis and their students were often closely connected; however, in the present-day, pastors "have focused on teaching/preaching without the responsibility of shepherding," according to Patz.[55] Patz proclaimed that congregants have a "great need of being fathered"[56]—a desired form of connected learning.

According to one biblical scholar,[57] Paul was also involved in "traditioning." Paul wrote in 1 Corinthians 15:3–5 (NASB): "For I delivered [*paradidomi*] to you as of first importance what I also received, that Christ died for our sins according to the Scriptures." The Greek word *paradidomi* meant to "hand down, pass on instruction from teacher to pupil."[58] Keener explained that this handing down or traditioning "tended toward 'net transmission' rather than 'chain transmission' (i.e., the sayings became the property of the rabbinic community, and not only of a single disciple of a teacher), transmission could be guarded more carefully in the first generation or two."[59] Learning occurred in group settings with mutual accountability and connectivity. People who ascribe to or follow a sacred book must consider how to facilitate literacy in faith communities. They may need to consult trained professionals to spark a movement to help people who struggle with dyslexia or other learning disabilities. This process might involve making communities of faith healthy learning places—even without reading.

The doctrine of perspicuity affirmed, "Scripture is clear enough for the simplest person to live by."[60] We must not make Bible learning more difficult

---

54. Willis and Greeneish, "What Do You Think."
55. Patz, "Fathers, Rabbis, and the Way of Jesus," para. 18.
56. Patz, "Fathers, Rabbis, and the Way of Jesus," para. 18.
57. Keener, "Assumptions in Historical-Jesus Research."
58. Thayer, "Paradidomi."
59. Keener, "Assumptions in Historical-Jesus Research," 44.
60. Pettegrew, "Perspicuity of Scripture," 214.

than its Author intended. In view of this research, it would be prudent for those promoting literacy efforts in faith communities to also connect learners with experienced professionals who can deal with learning disabilities. Above all these things, working with connected learners

> Requires as its primary concern that there shall be a full encounter with the living Christ at the earliest possible moment. . . . Millions of new literates relapse into semi-literacy and millions of literates do not use their ability to read because they lack "the burning heart" of faith within them. Where this encounter has taken place, those who have been gripped by Christ will want to read the Bible for themselves, whatever the cost.[61]

Indeed, nearly all the purposeful learners in this study who were Christians and learned to read found motivation, hope, and purpose in reading the Bible.

West related that theological education and leader development must be "re-evented" in the *verbomoteur* mode à la Jousse because "church leadership formation has morphed from oral, eventful, life-on-life leadership formation modes to the literacy-intensive, class-based, pen-to-paper theological professionalization mode."[62] West gave an extensive list of remedies, stating, "Jesus is unlike other rabbis in that He does not emphasize memory drills, but a changed disposition in life, in all its habits."[63] Similarly, Childs and Greenfield found the women they studied learned weaving in groups and that "the learning and the working were found to be 'a social event.'"[64]

Anderson, in studying Ethiopian preachers, found another kind of "eventing."[65] He witnessed how the preacher embodies the Word and "connects people with God in the sermon event."[66] Preaching in that situation did not necessarily involve study and analysis but creating an event, an experience, and an encounter with God. Anderson found,

> These rural Ethiopians thus generally approach life through participation in direct experience, and this reinforces an entirely different set of values than those found in the West. Most important, people share experiences together in community,

---

61. Weber, *Communication of the Gospel*, 70.
62. West, "Re-Eventing," 11.
63. West, "Re-Eventing," 12.
64. Childs and Greenfield, "Informal Modes of Learning," 304.
65. Anderson, "Implicit Rhetorical Theory."
66. Anderson, "Implicit Rhetorical Theory," 216.

rather than as individuals who learn through the solitude of reading a book.[67]

ALFE have much to teach literates in the area of facilitating a connection with God and with others in sacred spaces. Relating to God involves not merely cognitive study but also connection.

Saint Augustine, undoubtedly having much experience with ALFE in the early Christian church, reportedly told his congregants who could not read, "We are your books."[68] As one Augustinian scholar noted:

> The "uneducated" still engage in biblical exegesis, but not that of a lone grammarian sitting before a text in the study. The value of "exegesis" extends beyond the specialized work of a literary professional to the activity of one who intentionally participates in the prayer, worship, and reflection of the whole community and is challenged to live out one's life within that "school."[69]

Elaborating on the process of being God's Word for oral people, McCarthy elaborated on another recommended avenue of connection for faith communities:

> Augustine still stresses what each verse signifies, but he insists that its significance is crucially circumscribed by their singing together *consona voce* [with verbal explanation]. According to Augustine, "What [people] sing is all a piece with their minds and hearts."[70]

CONNECTED AS COMMUNITIES OF HONOR AND GRACE IN HEALING. Communities of faith could also become prime locations for dealing with shame and all the negative emotions that follow illiteracy and lack of formal education and make them communities of honor, grace, and healing. They could strive to become places known to welcome and embrace ALFE—emotionally encouraging places and sacred spaces that work to restore honor and give dignity to those who previously walked in shame.

In fact, Jesus came to bring relationship, to bestow grace, and to give honor by allowing His followers to become part of God's family. This is the mystery of God and His grace—His connection with us, His offer of

---

67. Anderson, "Implicit Rhetorical Theory," 237.
68. McCarthy, "'We are Your Books.'"
69. McCarthy, "'We are Your Books,'" 333.
70. McCarthy, "'We are Your Books,'" 340.

salvation and friendship, as well as His binding believers to Himself as a community connected as one. As Boomershine noted, then,

> The mark of authentic revelation is an appropriate connection to the sacred story. . . . Appropriate connections grow out of experiencing the meaning of the story in its original historical context. . . . When our/my story is connected appropriately with the story of God, there is revelation.[71]

Accordingly, Jesus experienced shame on earth, especially during His death on the cross; this "identification is a loving, empathetic communication with us."[72] Kraus added, "We must recall that the cross was designed above all to be an instrument of contempt and public ridicule. Crucifixion was the most shameful execution imaginable. . . . *The cross is the epitome of this identification with us in shame.*"[73] This kind of empathetic identification could become "the antidote to shame," dispensed exclusively by the faith community.[74] In "confronting shame in the culture, the church, and the clinic," Thomas advised restoring "the interpersonal bridge through face-to-face affirming relationships."[75] May faith communities embrace this mantle.

Shame is an anthropological phenomenon, varying according to one's culture, but it is also a "relational construct."[76] One cannot fully understand shame as a debilitating emotion until the stigma is felt or phenomenologically experienced. However, shame should not be an elusive anthropological concept analyzed under a microscope. It is a raw emotion, to be entered into and felt with another. Only through connection can it be healed. Thus, religious educators and leaders in faith communities cannot merely be dispensers of information for those bound in shame. They must become connectors and relators.

Pattison maintained, "Avoidance of shame/embarrassment/humiliation is the driving force behind . . . *impression management*: much of our life is spent anticipating, experiencing, and/or managing shame. That would mean that genuine pride, the signal of connection with the other, would be fairly rare."[77] In attempting to develop the trust so needed for connection in faith communities, Mayers's advice for walking through the

---

71. Boomershine, *Story Journey*, 10.
72. Kraus, *Jesus Christ our Lord*, 218.
73. Kraus, *Jesus Christ our Lord*, 216–17.
74. Brown, *Daring Greatly*.
75. Thomas, "Confronting Shame," 40.
76. Dotson, "Self-in-Relation," 8.
77. Pattison, "Shame and the Unwanted Self," 33.

stages of building trust—bonding, accepting self and others, and showing mutual respect—seems appropriate.[78] Pattinson lamented, "Sadly, Christian churches are among those groups who fail to understand how shame works and how it can be counteracted. . . . To deal with it, re-integration is required. . . . Loving personal relationships can help."[79] Kraus agreed, pronouncing: "Love banishes shame."[80]

According to participants in Lienhard's study, "Shame outweighs death."[81] Indeed, a Khmer proverb echoes the same thought: "Death is better than loss of face/reputation." In short, the remedy is *connection*, precisely the way ALFE prefer to learn. In fact, Walker and Rosen edited a work entitled *How Connections Heal*. In one chapter, Jordan proposed "relational learning" in counseling practice, often a place of healing.[82]

Lancaster evaluated "the relationship between internalized shame and connectedness"[83] via "relational-cultural theory" (RCT), which views "*disconnection* from others as the source of most psychological difficulties."[84] Miller and Stiver defined *disconnection* as "a psychological experience of rupture that occurs whenever a child or adult is prevented from participating in a mutually empathic and mutually empowering interaction."[85] An important development in this area, RCT "attempts to portray the true essence of shame by capturing its relational quality."[86] Hartling et al. recommended the following "relational practices" to "bridge the disconnections caused by shame": listening and responding, mutual empathy, authenticity, movement toward mutuality, and humor.[87] They offered a "relational-cultural theory" of counseling which moved beyond individualistic practices in order to become more "relationally conscious" of those who feel shame because "shame is an intense, enduring experience involving one's *whole being in relationship*."[88]

In connecting with God and others in community, there is place for bestowing what some view as the opposite of shame—for bestowing honor.

---

78. Mayers, *Christianity Confronts Culture*, 17–76.
79. Pattinson, "Shame and the Unwanted Self," 18.
80. Kraus, *Jesus Christ our Lord*, 152.
81. Lienhard, "Restoring Relationships," 97.
82. Jordan, "Relational Learning in Psychotherapy."
83. Lancaster, "Examining Shame," x.
84. Lancaster, "Examining Shame," 5.
85. Miller and Stiver, *Healing Connection*, 65.
86. Lancaster, "Examining Shame," 6.
87. Hartling et al., "Shame and Humiliation," 104–5.
88. Hartling et al., "Shame and Humiliation," 106.

As for the worth of this kind of honor, Neyrey maintained, "Honour is clearly the greatest of external goods. . . . It is honour above all else that great men claim and deserve."[89] A "dynamic and relational concept," according to DeSilva, "honor signifies respect for being the kind of person and doing the kinds of things the group values, shame signifies, in the first instance, being seen as less than valuable because one has behaved in ways that run contrary to the values of the group."[90] Malina viewed *honor* as "the value of a person in his or her own eyes (that is, one's claim to worth) plus that person's value in the eyes of his or her social group."[91] Notably, Georges explained shame in terms of exclusion and honor in terms of inclusion.[92]

Anthropologically, DeSilva portrayed western-like cultures as "face-to-space," individualistic and separated from others, as opposed to "face-to-face" cultures, with a "strong regard for the opinions of others,"[93] like the culture in Cambodia. Therefore, in "face-to-face" cultures,

> Honor and dishonor, then, are not only about the individual's sense of worth but also about the coordination and promotion of a group's defining and central values, about the strategies for the preservation of a group's culture in the midst of a complex web of competing cultures, and about the ways in which honor or dishonor are attained, displayed, and enacted.[94]

Faith communities exist as ideal places to visibly and tangibly restore this kind of cultural honor before others. As Lienhard noted, "Restoration of relationships is the central requirement. Also, reconciliation must be open and visible to all."[95] The findings of this study would serve to advise communities like these to begin to extend honor, to create rituals in which ALFE who have walked in shame learn, experience connection, and receive honor in group settings.

Another way of bestowing honor is to give grace. Peristiany and Pitt-Rivers, introducing the concept of *grace* to social anthropology, maintained *to grace* meant "to confer honour and dignity upon, do honour or credit."[96] Extending grace restores. Cloud also described grace as "unbroken,

---

89. Neyrey, *Honor and Shame*, 5.
90. DeSilva, *Honor, Patronage, Kinship, and Purity*, 25.
91. Malina, *New Testament World*, 27.
92. Georges, "Three Sources of Honor."
93. DeSilva, *Honor, Patronage, Kinship, and Purity*, 27.
94. DeSilva, *Honor, Patronage, Kinship, and Purity*, 42.
95. Lienhard, "Restoring Relationships," 240.
96. Peristiany and Pitt-Rivers, *Honour and Grace*, 240.

uninterrupted, unearned, accepting *relationship*."[97] ALFE—especially those living with toxic shame—yearn for this is the kind of connection. The remedy for disgrace is grace, according to Peristiany and Pitt-Rivers.[98] They add,

> If the anthropological study of friendship was so slow to be broached it was perhaps not unconnected with the failure to recognize the importance of grace. For grace is the essence of friendship. It is defined by theologians as "the friendship of God."[99]

Similarly, McNish and Dayringer advised: "Transformation of shame is the experience of grace."[100] In studying ancient biblical cultures, DeSilva also pointed to the necessity of grace and elaborated on the manner in which God, the Supreme Patron, extended grace to us and how we can extend the same to others.[101]

Recommendations for Policy Makers and Organizations

Reflecting on literacy and numeracy analyses by PIAAC (the Program for the International Assessment of Adult Competencies),[102] Belzer discovered literacy efforts are "making negative progress," showing "relatively unchanged skill levels, reflected by three major surveys conducted over a twenty-five-year span."[103] Belzer also warned,

> It simply cannot, on a large scale and given all the barriers adult learners face, produce the results we seek. . . . Given the poor turnout (estimates range from 4 percent to 8 percent) of adults in need of program services, the relatively few contact hours for those who do participate, and the under-resourcing of programs, we need to look beyond traditional means of improving adult literacy and numeracy skills.[104]

Wisdom in this area would promote a number of recommendations for policy makers and organizations. If connected learning is to be acknowledged and promoted, some shifts need to take place:

---

97. Cloud, *Changes That Heal*, s.v. "Grace and Truth Divided," para. 5.
98. Peristiany and Pitt-Rivers, *Honour and Grace*.
99. Peristiany and Pitt-Rivers, *Honour and Grace*, 239.
100. McNish and Dayringer, *Transforming Shame*, 20.
101. DeSilva, *Honor, Patronage, Kinship, and Purity*.
102. Murray et al., *Reconstructing the Evolution*.
103. Belzer, "Reflections on the PIAAC," 1.
104. Belzer, "Reflections on the PIAAC," 2.

- A shift from literacy to learning, such as the "learning webs" promoted by Illich;[105]
- A shift from institutionally-based learning to connected learning that is holistic in nature;
- A shift toward technology for all;
- A shift toward honoring every type of learning and learners, toward respectful I-Thou relationships with non-readers,[106] and a shift away from othering;[107]
- A shift toward promoting and honoring learning outside the classroom (intersecting with formal, non-formal, and informal learning);
- A shift toward "no failure learning," from shame to skill;[108] and
- A shift toward putting the best teachers in the early grades and equipping them to recognize learning disabilities in order to provide appropriate assistance at the most crucial junctures.

Such shifts would be of seismic proportions for both the world of education and for ALFE. For instance, Courtney and Gravelle trained teachers in rural Cambodian schools in a multi-strategy approach that improved reading ability.[109] They observed before this reading intervention that "most teachers in Cambodia use a one-strategy approach to teaching reading but that reading competence remains poor."[110] After their extensive research in India, Banerjee and Duflo ascertained that if interventions were not made in the area of education, scores of people would certainly express great disappointment.[111] Their private interventions made huge differences, while education in government schools was found to be lacking, with teachers often absent or teaching at a sub-par level[112]—also the case in Cambodia. If such a shift does not occur, more students will pass from grade to grade in these systems without learning to read, as was true for a number of ALFE in this study.

As Dornan and Portela noted:

105. Illich, *Deschooling Society*.
106. Buber, *Between Man*.
107. Borrero et al., "School as a Context."
108. Damodaran, "Learning's Not about Enrolment."
109. Courtney and Gravelle, "What Makes the Difference."
110. Courtney and Gravelle, "What Makes the Difference," 416.
111. See Banerjee and Duflo, "Mandated Empowerment"; Damodaran, "Learning's Not about Enrolment."
112. Banerjee and Duflo, "Mandated Empowerment."

> Children may somehow self-exclude themselves where they experience shame and this self-exclusion affects their learning. . . . How might policy affect these links? The implication of this analysis is two-fold. First, we find shame associated with corrosive effects on later child development outcomes and therefore policy which reduces shame is consistent with improving children's learning. Second, whilst not all shame is necessarily poverty induced, poverty is a consistent risk factor. . . . Factoring dignity into policy design is not only instinctually right, but consistent with improving policy effectiveness.[113]

These children become adult learners and face the same obstacles—shame and lack of dignity due to poverty and lack of formal education. The recommendations by Chase and Bantebya-Kyomuhendo ring true at this point:

> Irrespective of the level of deprivation that people endure on a day-to-day basis, their standing and "face" in society, for most, appears to hold as much if not greater value than how much money is coming in to the household. . . . If, as our work shows, the maintenance of dignity and self-respect are as important as material security in enabling people fully to participate in society, governments and others responsible for alleviating poverty must accept additional responsibilities in this regard. . . . Policymakers need simultaneously to have regard for the material, social, and psychological well-being of people facing economic and social hardship if they are to deliver effective and efficient anti-poverty programmes.[114]

If those involved in policy making or those involved in organizations addressing these issues immersed themselves as I did in the environment of ALFE, going so far as to phenomenologically experience life as non-readers, they would immediately begin some of the shifts mentioned earlier.

"Contrary to popular belief, adults who are illiterate or functionally illiterate have considerable experience as learners and have developed their own learning skills—skills that are unique to them."[115] We need to value these learners. Shirali, studying the life of "an illiterate, but wise and knowledgeable Himalayan woman named Ganga Devi" proclaimed vehemently about her situation and the treatment she received:

> People in India have not only bypassed, marginalized and devalued her, but have been living off the fat of her back and usurping

113. Dornan and Portela, "Feelings of Shame," 22.
114. Chase and Bantebya-Kyomuhendo, "Poverty and Shame," 300.
115. Parker, "Adult Perspectives," 108.

the meager resources of the third world. This development-literacy axis has deepened the gulf between peoples. This gulf is the root of all dehumanization and violence. What are the limits of the arrogance of the written word is the crucial question.[116]

Again, according to Egan, "Orality entails a set of powerful and effective mental strategies, some of which, to our cost, have become attenuated and undervalued in many aspects of our western cultures and educational systems."[117] Allowing this undervaluing to continue may cost greatly in the long run.

"The starting point—and undisputed assumption—for main policy discussions is that literacy (or schooling) is a 'good thing' and the terms are often used synonymously with 'education,'" as Robinson-Pant related.[118] Like others, she also noted the title for UNESCO's 2006 *Literacy for Life: Global Monitoring Report* seemed to insinuate a person could not have life without literacy and "that formal education is valued more, reinforcing the widespread belief that adult literacy is a second class education."[119] Adding to the evidence behind these thoughts, *The Hamburg Declaration on Adult Learning* concluded, "In every society literacy is a necessary skill in itself."[120] *The Second Global Report on Adult Learning and Education* proclaimed: "The abilities to read, write and operate with numbers have become an essential requirement for active participation in society,"[121] adding

> Literacy is therefore the unassailable foundation of all education and learning, and it is continuously relevant for all people, in all phases of life and in all regions of the world. For all of the above reasons, this report situates literacy at the centre of lifelong learning.[122]

For many of the ALFE in this study, this cannot be the case. They could learn without literacy and must be allowed to do so, with provisions for learning before they become literate. We have framed the whole argument as either-or, as two extremes, and judge them as being either good or bad. Should this continue to be the case?

116. Shirali, "*Ganga Devi*," 89.
117. Egan, "Literacy and Oral Foundations," 448.
118. Robinson-Pant, "'Why Literacy Matters,'" 781.
119. Robinson-Pant, "'Why Literacy Matters,'" 784.
120. UNESCO, *Hamburg Declaration on Adult Learning*, 2.
121. UNESCO Institute for Lifelong Learning, *Second Global Report on Adult Learning, Rethinking Literacy*, 17.
122. UNESCO Institute for Lifelong Learning, *Second Global Report on Adult Learning, Rethinking Literacy*, 2.

Recommendations for Further Research

As a result of this study, I see a number of possibilities for further research. I believe the number one need at present is for researching and developing appropriate and widely accessible media technologies for connected learners.[123] As a majority across the globe, these adults deserve this focus and concerted effort.

In Cambodia, specialists and special educators need to research the extent and types of learning disabilities and work to discover the best means for assisting those with learning disabilities. Moreover, courses need to be developed and conducted countrywide to inform educators about learning disabilities, as well as their treatment. I would imagine this kind of endeavor is a worldwide need.

Further work needs to be done with adults in the liminal state of being able to read somewhat, but not being able to write, as well as with those who are not illiterate but are not yet proficient as far as literacy standards go. I believe this group of people is more common than we realize and do not fare well learning in conjunction with proficient readers.

Finally, Bartlett et al. wrote the *Anthropology of Literacy*;[124] Lancy et al. compiled *An Anthropology of Learning in Childhood*;[125] and Rogers and Street wrote *Using Ethnographic Approaches to Understanding and Teaching Literacy*.[126] While this body of research attempted to examine learning related to illiteracy, functional illiteracy, and orality in ethnographic, anthropological, and educational terms, a full anthropology or ethnography of each of these worlds would be a helpful addition to the knowledge base in this area.

FINAL REFLECTIONS

It would seem those involved in promoting lifelong learning and non-formal education have difficulty separating literacy from learning. The UNESCO Institute for Lifelong Learning's *Global Report on Adult Learning and Education* maintained literacy was the "foundation for adult learning and education."[127] Can there be no learning apart from literacy? This research showed that learning can and does occur apart from literacy.

---

123. Palaiologou, "Needs for Developing."
124. Bartlett et al., "Anthropology of Literacy."
125. Lancy et al., *Anthropology of Learning*.
126. Rogers and Street, "Using Ethnographic Approaches."
127. UNESCO Institute for Lifelong Learning, *Second Global Report on Adult Learning, Rethinking Literacy*, 17.

In light of all I learned from these participants, I believe one productive action we could take as educators is to move from an emphasis on helping people learn to read to helping them learn in general.[128] For the persons who cannot learn to read, this shift would be monumental. It would mean a radical openness and acknowledgement of their preferred learning strategies. It would involve a deeply personal, relational, and connected approach; but it would promote worldwide learning, an open path for many who have felt the doors to education were tightly shut.

Organizations fight for literacy but not necessarily for the illiterate. Illiterates may not want to be changed or convert to a literate culture, but they do want to learn. As was shown in this study, adults learn when motivated to do so. Adults shut off from learning and growing can become depressed and lose hope. Examining the relationship between depression and illiteracy, Weiss et al.[129] and Francis et al. discovered,

> Depression severity was lower among participants assigned to receive literacy training plus standard depression treatment than it was among participants assigned to receive only stand depression treatment. . . . Depression . . . can be improved by identifying individuals with the disease who also have limited literacy, and providing them with literacy education.[130]

I would go further to advise providing these learners with the kinds of opportunities and connections they desire. After this study, I believe not only literacy learning but also any kind of learning opportunities would assist. This area merits further study as well.

I thought my literate ways might interfere with this study, but I was wrong. My learning was in such contrast to the ways of ALFE that their desire for connection and ways of learning came to the forefront during our interactions. Their strategies sat in direct and apparent contrast to my non-connecting ways. How could I have been so blind for so long?

In this study, lifelong learning was shown to be very difficult for some and absent for a few. Kapil argued in regard to UN learning-related goals:

> If lifelong learning is to be the education model for the LDCs in the post-2015 millennium decade, then the type of human capital these countries produce should match with the demand of their own society; not of the Global North.[131]

128. Thompson, "Perceptions of Teaching."
129. Weiss et al., "Literacy Education."
130. Francis et al., "Literacy Education Improve Depression," 826.
131. Kapil, "Lifelong Learning," 566.

Alfred advised focusing on social capital, the "significant benefits to poor and marginalized communities."[132] This kind of soft "commodity" akin to funds of knowledge discussed earlier "results from learning interactions that take place in a social, political, and cultural context." According to Alfred, "fundamental characteristics of these interactions are reciprocity, trust, and shared norms and values."[133] She urged, "The concept of learning should be broadened to include not only formal learning but also to include learning that takes place in networks and communities."[134]

Western standards of learning should not be imposed on people whose livelihoods require different skills than those required in academia. I concur with Egan's insight: "We need to see orality as an energetic and distinct set of ways of learning and communicating, not simply as an incomplete and imperfect use of the mind awaiting the invention of literacy."[135] Gee maintained, "What is at issue . . . is different ways of knowing, different ways of making sense of the world of human experience, that is different social epistemologies."[136] Will the social epistemology that prefers connected learning continue to be ignored? I hope not. As Watson urged: "To fail to engage the alterity of orality with sensitive attunement is an act of continued imperialism, which is morally unacceptable, epistemologically naïve."[137]

Do people prefer to study books or people? Ong presented orality as "the 'primary modeling system'—as an anachronistic deviant from the 'secondary modeling system' that followed it."[138] Connected learners have embraced this "primary modeling system" launched at birth and they continue to follow it during their lifelong learning journey. Why can we not promote and celebrate their chosen system and rally to provide learner-centered approaches connected to all areas of life?

The abyss between literates and nonliterates mentioned by Watson[139] has been socially constructed, a chasm that needs to be filled in because "they" are "us" and "we" are "them." We all learn in similar ways. We all begin by attaching to one trusted relationship, then continue to learn by observing and imitating others. We all listen and learn. We all connect. The only difference is that most of our friends who are ALFE do not prefer print.

132. Alfred, *Learning for Economic Self-Sufficiency*, x.
133. Alfred, *Learning for Economic Self-Sufficiency*, 223.
134. Alfred, *Learning for Economic Self-Sufficiency*, 223.
135. Egan, "Literacy and the Oral Foundations," 454.
136. Gee, "Orality and Literacy," 734.
137. Watson, "Interpreting across the Abyss," iv.
138. Ong, *Orality and Literacy* (1982), 12.
139. Watson, "Interpreting across the Abyss."

Whatever we do in promoting or facilitating learning, we must major on connecting because connection is a powerful force. As Ong noted, "Oral communication unites people in groups."[140] We need to give ALFE the space to learn the way they prefer—connecting by all means.

In conclusion, as mentioned in the significance statement, "oral learners or adults with limited formal education represent a majority of the world." These learners merit our study. In the process of exploring their ways of learning, I sought a positive term for them that reflected their ways of learning. As a result, I proposed the more descriptive term *connected learners* as a replacement term for those with limited formal education, those who cannot or do not read, for oral learners. The relational ways they learn were summarily depicted in Figure 9.

The findings and wisdom-focused ethnographic grounded theory elaborated here would be of benefit to educators and faith practitioners, to researchers and policy makers. Those who cross cultures to teach and those involved in relief and development efforts would do well to attend to the ways connected learners desire to be taught. This emerging theory is applicable to adult learning, literacy efforts, religious/theological education, and leadership development. Too often we hand people a book when they want a story, a model, honor, and a relationship.

The mean years of schooling in Cambodia has not increased significantly over the past decade. In fact, that statistic has decreased, as have the numbers of those involved in literacy efforts. The situation is dire and not improving. If we are to be ethical and wise educators and policy makers, we must attend to the learning needs of these millions, offering connected learning opportunities on a wider scale. In 1971 Pinker lamented, "We know much more about the sentiments of philosophers and social scientists than those of ordinary people in everyday life."[141] How might the lives of millions of adults—masses of ordinary people in everyday life—improve if we make connected learning a priority?

---

140. Ong, *Orality and Literacy* (1982), 67.
141. Pinker, *Social Theory*, 135.

Appendix A

Khmer Terms Used[1]

Table A1

Khmer Terms Used

Khmer Term	Phonetic Rendering	English Equivalent
វត្ត	wat	Buddhist monastery/temple
ពូកែ	poo-kie-ee	clever
មធ្យមសិក្សាបឋមភូមិ	mut-choom-suk-sah baht-tahm-ah-poom	diploma after 9th grade exam (lower secondary school)
ឌីប្លូម	dee-plome	diploma after 9th grade (colloquial)
មធ្យមសិក្សាទុតិយភូមិ	mut-choom-suk-sah too-tay-yah-poom	diploma after 12 grade (upper secondary school)
បាក់ឌុប	bahk-dope	diploma after 12th grade (colloquial)
បឋមសិក្សា	bah-tom-ah-suk-sah	elementary/primary school
ខ្មាសគេ	k'mah gay	embarrassed/ashamed
វិទ្យាសាស្ត្រពិត	vee-jee-ah-sah-put	exam after high school (means "true science")
ស្វ័យរិន	svay run	GED-like exam (colloquial)
វិទ្យាល័យ	vee-jee-ah-lie-ee	high school (grades 10-12)
ខ្ញុំរៀនអត់សូវពូកែទេ	k'nyom ree-un aht so poo-kie-ee tay	I am not so clever at studying.
ល្ងង់	l'ngong	ignorant/stupid
អនក្ខរកម្ម	ahn-kah-rah-kahm	illiteracy

1. These phonetic renderings are personal and simplified interpretations of the Khmer terms. This format was chosen so those unfamiliar with phonetic alphabets or other renderings would still be able to read the Khmer pronunciation. There is presently no completely standardized format for Khmer phonetic renderings.

Appendix A: Khmer Terms Used

Khmer Term	Phonetic Rendering	English Equivalent
មិនចេះអក្សរ	mun jeh ahk-saw	illiterate/to not know letters
រៀនហើយរៀនទៀត	ree-un howey ree-un tee-ut	Learn. Learn a bit more.
រៀនអស់មួយជីវិត	ree-un ah muy jee-vit	Learn all your life.
អនុវិទ្យាល័យ	ah-noot vee-jee-ah-lie-ee	middle school (grades 7-9)
វីរិយៈ	vere-ree-yehek	perseverance, effort
ថ្នាក់មត្តេយ្យ	tah-nahk may-tay	preschool level
ទូរស័ព្ទចុចពិល	tue-rah-sahp joe-it pul	phone, push button with flashlight
ទូរស័ព្ទធម្មតា	tue-rah-sahp tomada	phone, normal/regular/usual
វិមង្សា	vee-mahng-sah	practice, application, research
ការសិក្សា	gah suk-sah	study/studies (noun)
គ្រូ	kru	teacher
ចិត្ត	jen-tack	thought
ធ្វើខ្លួនឯង	twer clue-un iyng	to do on one's own
ចប់ថ្នាក់ទុប	jahp bahk-dope	to finish grade 12

Appendix A: Khmer Terms Used

Khmer Term	Phonetic Rendering	English Equivalent
បំពេញមុខវិជ្ជា	bomb-payn moke vee-jee-ah	to fulfill high school course requirements
រៀនពីគេ	ree-un pee gay	to learn from others
រៀន	ree-un	to learn/study
អត់ចេះ	aht jeh	to not know how to do something
សូត្រ	sote	to recite
រៀនសូត្រ	ree-un sote	to learn/recite/study
ទន្ទេញ	toon-ting	to memorize
មើលគេ	mull gay	to watch or observe others
គ្រូខ្មែរ	kru k'my	traditional Khmer healer
រៀនអត់ចូល	ree-un aht jole	when the learning will not go into one's head (colloquial)
អតុ៖	chan-tayek	will

Appendix B

Conversing with Orality: My Experience as a Non-Reader

WHEN I BEGAN MY dissertation research with problem statement and purpose in hand, I thought I had embarked on a cognitive expedition, a search for understanding. I imagined I was going fishing in a familiar stream, only using different lures. Qualitative research was new to me, but the participants were like old friends from a culture in which I had been immersed for over a decade and a half. I had just never asked these sorts of questions, so I was anxious to hear what they had to say, anxious to find some answers, and excited to arrive at some conclusions.

I never dreamed writing a dissertation and doing the research would be such an emotional journey. Gilbert wrote a book entitled *The Emotional Nature of Qualitative Research*.[1] Her thoughts comforted me, a thinking person entering a world of hurting people. Writing about "compassion stress," Rager's words proved painfully true as well: "Human subjects are carefully protected in the research process. However, the same consideration is not currently being given to the qualitative researcher, even those investigating topics that are likely to elicit powerful emotions."[2] I still feel the sting of the process.

I found the participants' stories "moving, at times frightening, and often inspirational," just as Rager did.[3] Nearly every time I interviewed tears flowed—from both me and the participants. Occasionally, joy visited our conversations when someone felt affirmed or heard; but all considered, I felt

1. Gilbert, *Emotional Nature*.
2. Rager, "Compassion Stress," 423.
3. Rager, "Compassion Stress," 425.

Appendix B: Conversing with Orality: My Experience as a Non-Reader

anguish hearing so many stories of difficult lives. In her research, Rager also shared about "compassion stress" and the "cost of caring."[4] During the study, I felt a tremendous weight of concern, compassion, and caring; and I still felt the weight when I returned to work with some of the same participants and delve into the world of learning disabilities and the world of connected learning. I resonated with Behar's work, *The Vulnerable Observer: Anthropology that Breaks Your Heart.*[5] What I saw, heard, and felt during the study broke my heart.

During the first days of my study—apart from the interviews, a gamut of emotions flooded my being as well. At the beginning of my grounded theory study and before the interviews, I had decided to include an identification stage, living in the shoes of the participants as a non-reader for five days. I surmised I might struggle that week and I was right. My emotions ranged from frustration to anger, from boredom to disbelief, from feelings of powerlessness to intense shame at having an education and being able to read while my friends could not. Privilege meeting inequity turned out to be a very uncomfortable thing.

MEETING ORALITY

During this study, I also met shame and orality. In her powerful study of orality in the lives of immigrant English language learners, Watson nearly shouted: "*We need to have this conversation with orality, the subaltern radical Other of literacy, putting our presumptions which are all based on literacy's constitutive relationship with academic excellence on the table for examination.*"[6] Her words make me want to stand on a desk and salute, "Yes, ma'am, I will!" To me, my whole dissertation journey involved this kind of conversation with orality.

The following autoethnography contains my reflections on meeting Orality, on living for a brief period as a non-reader. I took my notes transcribed from my digital recorder during those days, and refashioned the thoughts below as my side of the conversation with Orality. What would Orality have to say? I see the findings of my study as Orality's reply, helping me better understand the learning of adults with limited formal education, but my side of the conversation follows.

---

4. Rager, "Compassion Stress," 427.
5. Behar, *Vulnerable Observer*.
6. Watson, "Interpreting across the Abyss," 195.

WHY AUTOETHNOGRAPHY?

According to Wall, autoethnography "invites personal connection rather than analysis."[7] It "begins with a personal story"[8] and involves "highly personalized accounts that draw upon the experience of the author/researcher for the purposes of extending sociological understanding."[9] This form "should allow readers to feel the dilemmas, think with the story rather than about it,"[10] and move the reader to action.[11]

Hughes et al. defined *autoethnography* as "a form of critical self-study in which the researcher takes an active, scientific, and systematic view of personal experience in relation to cultural groups identified by the researcher as similar to the *self* (i.e., us) or as *others* who differ from the self (i.e., them)."[12] Jones et al. maintained autoethnography has four characteristics: "purposeful commenting on culture, making contributions to research, embracing vulnerability with purpose, and creating a reciprocal relationship with audiences in order to compel a response."[13] I include all these elements in the reflection that follows.

Ellis and Bochner delineated two forms of autoethnography—evocative and analytical.[14] Evocative is the more personal variety, while analytical adds "dialogue with informants."[15] In the section that follows, I chose to write an evocative form of autoethnography as if in conversation with Orality.

WHO IS CONVERSING WITH ORALITY?

Orality surrounded me during the sixteen years leading up to my dissertation research. She (Orality) met me as soon as I could finally converse in paragraphs in the Khmer language. My husband and I attempted to train local leaders. We used small booklets with short questions and spaces for their answers. Did it work? No! Fortunately, two researchers came to the rescue, finding the majority of people in the rural areas unable to read, most having a very limited education. Since the country just emerged from war

---

7. Wall, "Easier Said than Done," 39.
8. Wall, "Easier Said than Done," 39.
9. Sparkes, "Autoethnography and Narratives," 21.
10. Wall, "Easier Said than Done," 44.
11. Denshire, "On Auto-Ethnography."
12. Hughes et al., "Translating Autoethnography," 209.
13. Jones et al., *Handbook of Authoethnography*, 22.
14. Ellis and Bochner, "Analyzing Analytical Autoethnography."
15. Denshire, "On Auto-Ethnography," 835.

and genocide, it was a wonder they had any education at all. The researchers urged a more narrative approach and introduced us to Orality.

When I met her, I shook my head in disbelief. I had flown half way around the world to meet people just like the ones I left, only living in a tropical climate. Born in the Appalachian area of the United States, my own father had very little education—only seven grades. My maternal aunt and grandparents did not finish high school. My maternal grandfather could not read and write. Fortunately for me, my mother embraced learning and graduated as valedictorian of her high school class. When we were growing up, she read books to my sister and me. She enabled us to escaped the poverty of our ancestors and go on to attend college. Even though Orality surrounded my growing up, her presence eluded me.

Later, after my husband and I dutifully prepared to work in Cambodia, we arrived armed with more knowledge than the luggage we carried on the plane—graduate degrees in education, cross-cultural studies, training in our faith, and added backgrounds in healthcare. I was a clinical laboratory scientist and my husband was an optometrist. We came with a load of training and wanted to quickly dump it all on the Cambodian people. Of course, we immediately failed. Fortunately, we met Orality fairly early.

As we learned more about her, we heard people making her seem all about talk, but I found her intriguing, multi-faceted, and elusive. She definitely enjoyed telling stories, but that was not her total job description. Her repertoire was far more expansive. As I watched, I saw where she lived, and the people were not always talking. Sound was not the most predominant aspect of their lives. A lot of other things were going on—visual things, movements, smells, touch, experience. If I were ever going to fully figure out Orality, I would need to put on my wading boots and get involved in a fishing expedition. I might even have to swim with the fish. So, that is what I did.

REFLECTIONS: MY SIDE OF THE CONVERSATION

I invite you, the reader, to my side of a conversation with Orality. She shouted at me and presented her side of the conversation in the earlier portions of my dissertation. What follows are my reflections on living as a non-reader, my side of the conversation, an autoethnography of my comments on meeting this cultural and emotional side of Orality, sharing my vulnerable side, and inviting the reader to join in the stream of feelings.

Appendix B: Conversing with Orality: My Experience as a Non-Reader

An Introduction to Boredom and Uselessness

From my very first moments as a non-reader, I felt bored. I constantly thought, "What can I do?" None of my usual avenues could occupy my time. I could not do my usual computer work. I could not write. What, then, could I do? I felt envious watching other people read or use their computers. I wondered what they might be doing and jealously thought, "I can't do that." I stared at my husband in his normal blissful state, doing his computer work, answering emails. Anger lurked in the wings, ready to pounce at any moment.

Lowered into a pit of boredom, I became sad, hopeless, and a bit depressed. "Orality, what in the world do you have to offer? " I thought. What do people do when they can't read books or use a computer? Perhaps I just experienced the pain of print withdrawal, but I could not imagine living more than five days in that horrible state. Only my digital recording consoled me because I could not possibly remember all the things I needed to recall. How painful it was just to keep a few precious thoughts coursing through my mind so I wouldn't forget them. My mind coursed full of ideas, but I could not keep track of them all. I had to ruminate over and over again since I could not write down my thoughts. If I could somehow record those ideas, I would at least have some possibility of remembering them.

I allowed this bit of technology because I had to make notes for the week and because of the simplicity of the technology. I only had to press one button to begin recording and one button to stop. Still, my non-reading friends do not typically use this kind of device. Some have smart phones, but I did not yet know whether they used their phones this way. If not for the digital recorder, I would worry constantly that I would forget the precious few ideas I hold on to with all my brainpower. I could not afford to get distracted because I might forget something significant. I surely could not ask my husband to take all my notes for five whole days. What do people do to handle this problem?

Orality, how do you remember? How can some people remember long epics? I am sure their memories are better than mine, but how good are they? I had yet to meet a non-reader with a great memory, but I had met folks with just a few years of education who worked very hard to memorize long passages and stories. They told me they ruminated and read passages over and over again. I noticed they memorized verbatim with no variation. How in the world did monks memorize all their chants?

That was my memory dilemma. Research was just as bad. Normally when I had questions, I hunted down the answer on my own. I consulted the internet or a book or the library to find the information I needed.

Orality, what about the people living with you? They can't look up information the way I have in the past. What do they do? I had to bug my husband incessantly.

Yearning for the Rural Life and Dreading the Vulnerability

Living in the city with Orality seemed to make life worse. I could imagine living in the countryside might be easier. I could have a nice life walking with Orality there—a slower pace, with no reading necessary. If I were busy on a farm or a rice field, I imagine I would be exhausted in the evenings, then busy myself with housework and talking with family and friends. If life were happy and full of work and fellowship, I could vaguely imagine not missing books at all. In the evenings out in the countryside, I could spend time with people, watch television, and relax.

Unfortunately, as I pondered that life and the possibility of rural happiness, questions raced through my mind. What happens when you are a farmer and need to make purchases like seeds or fertilizer and you cannot read the packaging? You have to trust merchants are telling the truth, which I know might not be the case. Merchants sell plenty of banned chemicals in Cambodia, so I imagine oral friends must track down a very trusted source. Even then, could they really trust the other person? A merchant could sell you something that poisons you, your family, and your animals. I could consult my trusty husband, but I wouldn't trust just anyone. Orality, how do keep from being duped?

Shopping at the grocery store was nearly impossible—especially alone. Buying packaged goods required reading. How could I know whether I was buying shampoo or body wash? I already understand some of that confusion because of living in foreign countries. I often encountered products with script I couldn't read. I could not tell exactly what some of them were. I certainly could not decipher the ingredients. Now I understand why sellers often follow us around in stores and want to help when we shop. They know people need help.

What of these sellers? I usually do not know them or trust them. Do they honestly think I would take their advice and believe them? I suppose people who cannot read must take someone's advice when making purchases of things they can't decipher. When I need a recommendation—a book to purchase, a hotel to book—I would consult the internet and read all the feedback and reviews. Sometimes I might consult a friend, but when no one else is around, I could consult a great pool of other people's thoughts, written down or freely available on the internet. Oral people cannot. Once again, the sense of powerlessness and lack of agency overwhelmed me, threatening my very self and identity as a person. Orality, you do not make me feel very secure.

When you are oral, you have to trust other people to do your writing. When you want to send a message, you need to ask for help. You have to trust they will do it and you have to trust the timing of when they can do it and how they do it. That was excruciating for me. You might know exactly what you want to say, but they might not write it down the way you want. What a frustrating process. Another person acts for you, on your behalf. I felt powerless, mad, and frustrated. Not only did I have to get someone else to write for me, I had to wait for their timing. Patience did not come any easier during this waiting game. I felt totally at the mercy of another person who agreed to help me—for when, for how, for everything. That kind of powerlessness frightened me. Orality, how do your people cope?

The Pain of Proximate Literacy

I wondered whether the pain of illiteracy caused Dorothy Carey to lose her sanity, and created many arguments with her scholarly and literate husband. Think about it. The poor woman could not read. She left her home and everything she knew. Her husband busied himself translating and relating, with most likely little time for her needs. She couldn't keep a journal of her feelings or write home to family. Did she learn the language and thrive cross-culturally? I cannot imagine she did. On the other hand, Adoniram Judson's first wife Ann learned Burmese and Thai and translated materials. The difference is stark. Granted, there are probably many other factors surrounding the lives of both these women, but literacy is something to consider. If I were in the same situation as Dorothy Carey, I might have fallen prey to a pitiful existence, too.

I became the oral person to my literate husband, and we had a tendency to get angry at one another. I got upset at the speed at which something was done or the way an email was written or what was written on my behalf because I could not read and write the correspondence myself. Orality, you can be very frustrating.

To be honest, these issues were probably hardest on my husband, my literate helper. Just ask him. I suppose those who cannot read and write—especially in a village setting where it might not be needed very much—get accustomed to their situation and busy themselves with other work. But I knew what I was missing and that very knowledge made me depressed and angry. Meeting Orality certainly brought out the worst in me, and I did not expect that. Sometimes I just wanted to hibernate, to watch movies endlessly, or play games just to escape the sheer boredom I felt. Even the person

Appendix B: Conversing with Orality: My Experience as a Non-Reader

I felt I could trust the most seemed to be disappointing me. He did his best, but it was not good enough. Oral people must always feel disappointed. I wonder if they do, and how they deal with all these emotions.

The Inequity of Technology

I could not gather news unless someone told me what happened, I saw it on television, heard it on the radio or some other technology to which I had access, or someone talked about it. Because we did not have cable television, I had absolutely no access to news. I felt so limited and out of touch, left out. I found myself thinking, "I am so frustrated. I can't do anything I normally do. I can't sit and read. I can't use my phone. I can't use my computer. I don't know what is even going on in the world."

Thankfully, some aspects of the phone were easy to use, but some of them were not. I found that folks struggle to figure them out if they cannot read. The world seemed kinder to literates and not made for oral people. Why? Technology is definitely geared to the higher end of society, a select group of people who speak English or another majority language, and is not very friendly for the rest of us. Who decided that? I wanted to open my Bible in the mornings, but I had to wait. I tried technology during my morning quiet times, but it was frustrating to use. I knew I could open my morning devotions at the end of five days, but my friends with limited education have been waiting a lot longer. Who will consider the masses who don't read and write and don't speak English? What about everybody else? What about an "oral net"? What about fair access to all technology and knowledge? There's so much to which a minority of elites have access.

I once heard a story about a manufacturer who actually visited their customers in order to find how their product was used. They discovered they had mistaken notions and revised their commodity. I wish someone would enter the world of Orality, notice the products are not working, and make some revisions. No one actually develops technology for us. I experienced this and it needs to change. I wanted to shout for fairness along with my oral friends, "the billions at the bottom of the pyramid."[16] We need simple, affordable information technology, access to products that include talks on financial literacy, health, and education. Who is going to make these important global products? Out of my own need, I found myself wanting to create and improve technology. Orality, where are your technology proponents?

---

16. Prahalad, *Fortune at the Bottom*.

CONCLUSIONS

Like Schmid, "I had not anticipated how much harder it would be for me to deal with the interaction between 'their' poverty and 'my' privilege."[17] The difference felt stark to me when I immersed in the world of Orality. If someone who never learned read were to reflect on a conversation with Orality, they might paint a rosy picture of a leisurely, relational life in the village. I, on the other hand, spent five days going through text withdrawal.

The day after I completed this excruciating exercise, I listened to a recording of Bill Gates speaking at a 2007 Harvard graduation. He shared how he left Harvard without an awareness of the disparities in the world. After finding fame, he discovered what really mattered. More important than the great ideas to which he was exposed at that institution were the inequities he encountered in the real world. According to Gates, "Humanity's greatest advances are not in its discoveries, but in how those discoveries are applied to reduce inequity."[18] I shout in agreement with Gates. Orality felt like an inequity to me. How are we going to reduce it?

---

17. Schmid, "Reflections on and of Self," 174.
18. Gates, "Remarks of Bill Gates."

Appendix C

Participant Demographics

Table D1: Participant Demographics[1]

#	Date (2015)	Age	Sex	Grade Completed	Pseudonym & Religion	Province	Rural/ Urban
1	08/24	72	F	0	The Devout Three (B)	Takeo	R-U
		83	M	5		KCham	R-U
		77	F	0		Unknown	R-U
2	08/25	30+	F	0	Shu (U) &	Kratie	R-U
3	08/25	37	M	0	Vania (B) &	KThom	R-U
4	08/25	45	F	5	Yoshie (C)	Takeo	R-U
5	08/28	29	M	<6	Nestor (C)	Kandal	R
6	08/30	25	F	0	Tari (B)	Kandal	R-U
7	08/30	33	F	<6	Myong (C)	Kandal	R-U
8	08/30	70	F	0	Terina (C) &	Kandal	R
	08/30	35	F	5	Naida (U)	Kandal	R-U
9	08/30	38	F	2	Tova (U)	Kandal	R
10	08/30	29	M	3	Odis (U)	Kandal	R
	08/30	48	F	2	Anja (C)	Kandal	R
11	08/30	27	F	6	Veta (C)	Kandal	R-U
12	09/01	22	F	6	Sona (C)	Kandal	R-U

1. In the religion category, C = Christian, B = Buddhist, U = Unknown or Undecided. In the rural-urban category, R-U means the participant came from a rural area and now lives in an urban setting. Pseudonym names were generated at random from two websites: http://listofrandomnames.com; http://randomnames.com

Appendix C: Participant Demographics

#	Date (2015)	Age	Sex	Grade Completed	Pseudonym & Religion	Province	Rural/Urban
13	09/04	29	F	5	Kym (C)	Prey Veng	R-U
14	09/06	19	M	6	Kirby (C)	Kandal	R
15	11/03	V	F	V	The Bridge Group (C)	K. Cham	R
16	11/05	32	M	2	Morris (B)	Pursat	R
17	11/22	60	M	5	Eli (B)	S. Reap	R-U
18	12/14	55	F	3	Lidia (C)	Kandal	R
19	12/14	42	F	3	Pia (C)	Kandal	R
20	12/14	51	F	3	Alia (C)	Kandal	R
21	12/14	52	F	3	Lela (C)	Kandal	R
22	12/15	53	F	5	Amie (U)	Kandal	R
23	12/15	27	M	3	Benjamin (B)	Kandal	R-U
24	12/15	U	F	0	Saphira (B)	Unknown	R
25	12/15	40s	F	0	The Cemented Ladies (B) Prey Veng Pursat	Prey Veng	R-U
		40s	F	0			R-U
		50s	F	0			R-U
26	12/16	25	F	5	Lisha (B)	Takeo	R-U
27	12/16	25	F	0	Tera (B)	Kandal	R-U
28	12/19	58	M	1	The Cemented Men (B) Prey Veng Prey Veng Pursat	Prey Veng	R-U
		48	M	5			R-U
		35	M	0			R-U
		50	M	5			R-U
29	12/19	45	M	4	Cyril (B)	Prey Veng	R-U
30	02/22/16	30	M	6	Claude (C)	Kandal	R-U

Appendix D

Demographics of Additional Informants

Table E1: Demographics of Additional Informants[1]

#	Date (2015)	Age	Sex	Grade Completed	Pseudonym & Religion	Province	Rural/ Urban
1	09/03	31	F	0	Mei (B)	PPenh	U
2	09/03	V	M	<6	The Hardworking Group (B)	Various	R-U
3	11/20	V	M	<6	The KC Group	K. Cham	R-U
4	11/22	73	F	0	Lucky (B)	S. Reap	R-U
5	08/28	51	F	<6	Phung (C)	Kandal	R
6	2013				**RDI Archival Recordings**		R
	09/06	20s	F	<6	Talia (U)	Unknown	R
	09/06	20s	F	<6	Merissa (U)	Unknown	R
	09/06	20s	F	<6	Lee Lee (U)	Unknown	R
	09/06	NA	M	NA	Lenny (B)	Unknown	R
	09/06	NA	M	NA	Trey (B)	Unknown	R
	09/06	NA	M	NA	Amit (B)	Unknown	R
					Past Conversations:		
7	NA	20s	F	<6	Kelis (U)	Unknown	R-U
8	NA	20s	F	<6	Rue (B)	Siem Reap	R
9	NA	50s	F	<6	Ivy (C)	Prey Veng	R-U

1. In the religion category, C = Christian, B = Buddhist, U = Unknown or Undecided. In the rural-urban category, R-U means the participant came from a rural area and now lives in an urban setting. Pseudonym names were generated at random from two websites: http://listofrandomnames.com; http://randomnames.com

Appendix E

Interview Guide

FINDING PARTICIPANTS/ASKING DEMOGRAPHIC QUESTIONS:

- How do you feel about reading? (or) What do you think about reading?
- What is the last grade you completed?
- In what province were you born?
- How old are you?
- What is your religion?

INTERVIEW QUESTIONS:

- Would you please tell me about some recent experiences you have had with learning something:
    - a good experience?
    - a bad experience?
- What things help you learn?
- What things make it difficult to learn?
- What do you think about learning?
- What is something you would like to learn about/to do and how would you like to go about doing that?
- When you want to know or learn something, what do you do? Who do you ask?
- What else would you like to tell me about learning?

Appendix F

Intermediate Level Codes Visualized

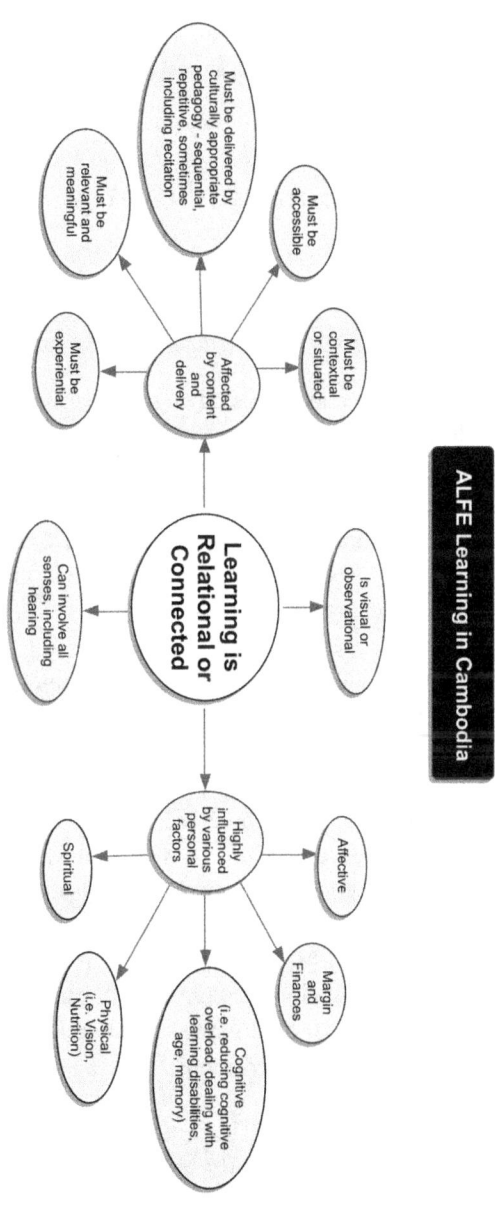

Appendix G

Verbal Informed Consent Form

What is your name? _____

My name is Lynn Thigpen and I am studying the learning experiences of Cambodian adults who do not prefer to read or cannot read, people who have not studied at all or studied up to the sixth grade. Even though I am old, I am a student at Biola University in California. I have lived in Cambodia a long time and have taught many people. But I have never stopped to ask them how they really would like to learn, so I would like to start now and learn from you and many others in Cambodia.

Would you allow me to talk with you about your learning experiences—good and bad—and how you learn best?

This conversation will take about one hour. If you would like to talk more, we can certainly talk longer than one hour because I would like to hear what you have to say. You are free to have this conversation with me or not have this conversation. I understand either way. You are also free to not answer any question you do not like.

Also, I will need to record our conversation so that I can better understand what you have told me and in order to translate it into English. May I have your permission to record our conversation?

This study will help people like me understand how people that do not read prefer to learn and learn best. I will use the information I learn to help people teach better and treat oral learners appropriately.

If after this conversation, you have questions or concerns, please feel free to call me.

I will protect your identity and no one reading my study will know who you are, so your answers will be completely confidential.

Verbal consent given and recorded: _____

Appendix H

Alternate Connected Learning Schematic

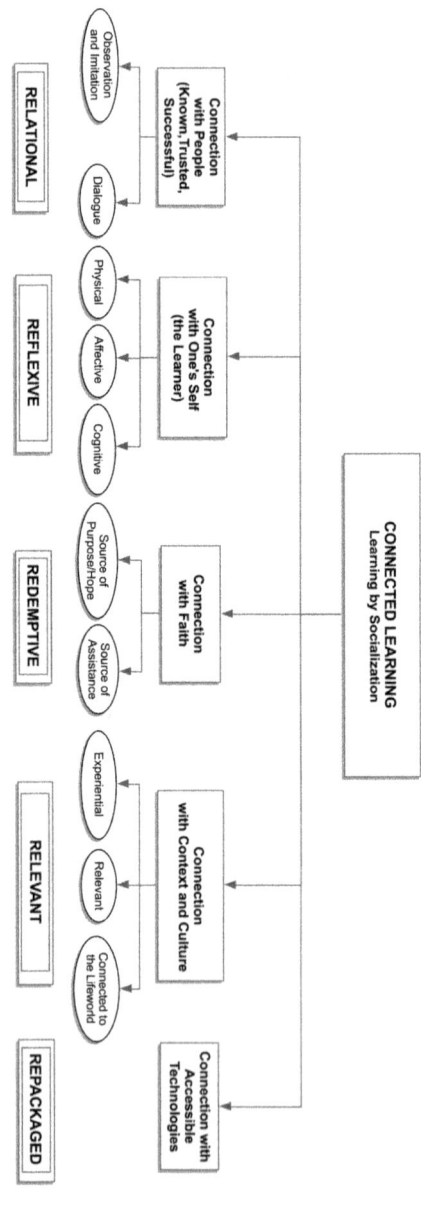

Bibliography

Abadzi, Helen. "Adult Illiteracy, Brain Architecture, and Empowerment of the Poor." *Adult Education and Development (AED)* 65 (2005) 19–34.
Abdulgaffar, Peang-Meth. "Understanding the Khmer: Sociological-Cultural Observations." *Asian Survey* 31 (1991) 442–55.
Abiy, Dessalegn S., et al. "Developing a Lifelong Learning System in Ethiopia: Contextual Considerations and Propositions." *International Review of Education* 60 (2014) 639–60.
Abney, Lynne. "Orality Assessment Tool." *International Orality Network*, 1992. Online. http://http://orality.net/media/420.
Abraham, Alex. "Contextualized Theological Education for Equipping the Unreached, Unengaged People Groups in North India." In *Beyond Literate Western Practices: Continuing Conversations in Orality and Theological Education*, edited by Samuel Chiang and Grant Lovejoy, 37–44. Hong Kong: International Orality Network, 2014.
Ackoff, Russell L. "From Data to Wisdom." *Journal of Applied Systems Analysis* 16 (1989) 3–9.
Adams, Susan A. "Using Transactional Analysis and Mental Imagery to Help Shame-Based Identity Adults Make Peace with Their Past." *Adultspan Journal* 7 (2008) 2–12.
Adeney, Miriam. "Feeding Giraffes, Counting Cows, and Missing True Learners: The Challenge of Buddhist Oral Communicators." In *Communicating Christ through Story and Song: Orality in Buddhist Contexts*, edited by Paul DeNeui and David Lim, 77–117. Pasadena, CA: William Carey, 2008.
Agger, Inger, et al. "Testimony Ceremonies in Asia: Integrating Spirituality in Testimonial Therapy for Torture Survivors in India, Sri Lanka, Cambodia, and the Philippines." *Transcultural Psychiatry* 49 (2012) 568–89.
Ai, Shoraku. "Educational Movement toward School-Based Management in East Asia: Cambodia, Indonesia, and Thailand." Paper prepared for the *Education for All Global Monitoring Report 2009: Overcoming Inequality: Why Governance Matters*. Paris: United Nations Educational, Scientific, and Cultural Organization (UNESCO), 2008.

———. "School Leadership and Management in Cambodia: National Culture and Its Impacts on Leading Educational Changes." *Journal of International Cooperation Studies* 13 (2006) 111–42.

Aikman, Sheila. *Intercultural Education and Literacy: An Ethnographic Study of Indigenous Knowledge and Learning in the Peruvian Amazon.* EBSCO: eBook Academic Collection, 1999.

Akesson, Ingrid. "Oral/Aural Culture in Late Modern Society? Traditional Singing as Professionalized Genre and Oral-Derived Expression." *Oral Tradition* 27 (2012) 67–84.

Akinnaso, F. Niyi. "Schooling, Language, and Knowledge in Literate and Nonliterate Societies." *Comparative Studies in Society and History* 34 (1992) 68–109.

Alberts, Tara. "Catholic Written and Oral Cultures in Seventeenth-Century Vietnam." *Journal of Early Modern History* 16 (2012) 383–402.

Alcala, Angelo L. *The Preliterate Student: A Framework for Developing an Effective Instructional Program.* College Park, MD: ERIC Digest, 2000.

Alfred, Mary V. *Learning for Economic Self-Sufficiency: Constructing Pedagogies of Hope among Low-Income, Low-Literate Adults.* Charlotte, NC: Information Age, 2010.

Alkire, Sabina. *The Missing Dimensions of Poverty Data: An Introduction.* Oxford: Oxford Poverty & Human Development Initiative (OPHI), University of Oxford, 2007. Online. http://www.ophi.org.uk/wp-content/uploads/OPHI-wp00.pdf.

Allison, Audrey M. W., and Patreece R. Boone Broadus. "Spirituality Then and Now: Our Journey through Higher Education as Women of Faith." *New Directions of Teaching and Learning* 120 (2009) 77–86.

Anderson, Victor D. "Implicit Rhetorical Theory of Preachers in Wolaitta Ethiopia with Implications for Homiletics Instruction in Theological Education." PhD diss., Biola University, 2008.

Andrews, Dee H., et al. "Storytelling as an Instructional Method: Descriptions and Research Questions." *The Interdisciplinary Journal of Problem-Based Learning* 3 (2009) 6–23.

———. *Storytelling as an Instructional Method: Research Perspectives.* Boston: Sense, 2010.

Andrews, Tom. "The Literature in a Grounded Theory: A Response to McCallin (2003)." *Grounded Theory Review* 5 (2006) 29–32.

Ang, Choulean. *Brah Ling.* Phnom Penh: Reyum, 2004.

———. *People and Earth.* Phnom Penh: Reyum, 2000.

———. "The Place of Animism within Popular Buddhism in Cambodia: The Example of the Monastery." *Asian Folklore Studies* 47 (1988) 35–41.

Angen, Maureen J. "Evaluating Interpretive Inquiry: Reviewing the Validity Debate and Opening the Dialogue." *Qualitative Health Research* 10 (2000) 378–95.

Ann, Sovatha. *Patron-Clientelism and Decentralization: An Emerging Local Political Culture in Rural Cambodia.* Dekalb: Northern Illinois University, 2008.

Annells, Merilyn. "Grounded Theory Method, Part I: Within the Five Moments of Qualitative Research." *Nursing Inquiry* 4 (1997) 120–29.

———. "Grounded Theory Method: Philosophical Perspectives, Paradigm of Inquiry, and Postmodernism." *Qualitative Health Research* 6 (1996) 379–93.

Ansre, Gilbert. "The Crucial Role of Oral Scripture: Focus Africa." *International Journal of Frontier Missions* 12 (1995) 65–68.

Aragon, Oriana R., et al. "Modulations of Mirroring Activity by Desire for Social Connection and Relevance of Movement." *SCAN* 9 (2014) 1762–69.

Ardelt, Monika. "Wisdom as Expert Knowledge System: A Critical Review of a Contemporary Operationalization of an Ancient Concept." *Human Development* 47 (2004) 257–85.

Ardila, Alfredo, et al. "Illiteracy: The Neuropsychology of Cognition without Reading." *Archives of Clinical Neuropsychology* 25 (2010) 689–712.

Arlund, Pam. "Church Planting Movements among Oral Learners." *Orality Journal* 2 (2013) 27–42.

Arnett, Jeffrey, J. "Socialization in Emerging Adulthood: From the Family to the Wider World, from Socialization to Self-Socialization." In *Handbook of Socialization: Theory and Research,* edited by J. Grusec and P. Hastings, 85–108. New York: Guilford, 2014.

Arrington, Aminta. "Hymns as Theological Mediator: The Lisu of South-West China and Their Music." *Studies in World Christianity* 21 (2015) 140–60.

———. "Hymns of the Everlasting Hills: The Written Word in an Oral Culture in Southwest China." PhD diss., Biola University, 2014.

Artinian, Barbara M. "An Overview of Glaserian Grounded Theory." In *Glaserian Grounded Theory in Nursing Research: Trusting Emergence,* edited by Barbara M. Artinian et al., 3–18. New York: Springer, 2009.

Artinian, Barbara M., et al., ed. *Glaserian Grounded Theory in Nursing Research: Trusting Emergence.* New York: Springer, 2009.

Aterianus-Owanga, Alice. "Orality Is My Reality: The Identity Stakes of the Oral Creation in Libreville Hop-Hop Practices." *Journal of African Cultural Studies* 27 (2015) 146–58.

Atkins, Jackson. "Multiplying Disciples in an Oral Context." In *Beyond Literate Western Practices: Continuing Conversations in Orality and Theological Education,* edited by Samuel Chiang and Grant Lovejoy, 77–84. Hong Kong: International Orality Network, 2014.

Augustine. *Teaching Christianity: De Doctrina Christiana.* 2nd ed. Translated by Edmund Hill. Hyde Park, NY: New City, 1997.

Avoseh, Majai B. "Proverbs as Theoretical Frameworks for Lifelong Learning in Indigenous African Education." *Adult Education Quarterly* 63 (2012) 236–50.

Ayres, David M. *Anatomy of a Crisis: Education, Development, and the State in Cambodia, 1953–1998.* Honolulu: University of Hawai'i Press, 2000.

———. "Tradition, Modernity, and the Development of Education in Cambodia." *Comparative Education Review* 44 (2000) 440–63.

Babchuk, Wayne A. "Grounded Theory as a Family of Methods: A Genealogical Analysis to Guide Research." *US-China Education Review* A (2011) 383–88.

Bacharach, Burt, and Hal David. "Alfie." Track 6 on Dionne Warwick, *Here Where There Is Love,* Scepter, 1966.

Baeq, Daniel S. "Spirit House: The Practice of *Rean Thevoda* in Cambodia." *International Journal of Frontier Missiology* 29 (2012) 33–46.

Bagdasar, Craig B. "Khmer Conflict Style: Cultural Foundations and Forms of Resolution." PhD diss., Union Institute, 1993.

Baiget, Joan. "Wisdom Management: The Last Frontier." In *ECKM2007—Proceedings of the 8th European Conference on Knowledge Management 2007,* edited by B. Martins and D. Remenyi, 96–100. Reading, UK: Academic Conferences Limited, 2007.

Baldwin, Timothy A. "Culturally Responsive Pedagogy: A Transformative Tool for CCCU Educators in Multicultural Classrooms." *Christian Education Journal* 12 (2015) 97–117.

Balingnasay, Gil P. "Training in the Philippines Context." In *Beyond Literate Western Practices: Continuing Conversations in Orality and Theological Education*, edited by Samuel Chiang and Grant Lovejoy, 45–54. Hong Kong: International Orality Network, 2014.

Ballantine, Jeanne H., et al. *Our Social World: Introduction to Sociology*. Thousand Oaks, CA: SAGE, 2016.

Bandura, Albert. *Social Learning Theory*. New York: General Learning, 1971.

Banerjee, Abhijit V., and Esther Duflo. "Mandated Empowerment: Handing Anti-Poverty Policy Back to the Poor?" *Annals of the New York Academy of Sciences* 1136 (2008) 333–41.

Bantebya-Kyomuhendo, Grace. "Needy and Vulnerable, but Poverty is Not My Identity." In *Poverty and Shame: Global Experiences*, edited by Elaine Chase and Grace Bantebya-Kyomuhendo, 113–24. Oxford: Oxford Scholarship Online, 2014.

Bar, Moshe, et al. "Very First Impressions." *Emotion* 6 (2006) 269–78.

Barrett, David, et al. "Christian World Communions: Five Overviews of Global Christianity." *International Bulletin of Missionary Research* 33 (2009) 25–31.

Bartlett, Lesley. "Literacy, Speech and Shame: The Cultural Politics of Literacy and Language in Brazil." *International Journal of Qualitative Studies in Education* 20 (2007) 547–63.

Bartlett, Lesley, et al. "The Anthropology of Literacy." In *A Companion to the Anthropology of Education*, edited by Bradley A. U. Levinson and Mica Pollock, 154–76. Malden, MA: Blackwell, 2011.

Baskin, Ken. "Complexity, Stories, and Knowing." *Emergence: Complexity and Organization* 7 (2005) 32–41.

Basu, Kaushik, et al. *Isolated and Proximate Illiteracy and Why These Concepts Matter in Measuring Literacy and Designing Education Programs*. Working Paper No. 00-W02. Nashville: Vanderbilt University, 2000.

Batchelor, Simon. "Christian and Secular Approaches to Development: Reflections on a Community Development Programme in Cambodia (Kampuchea)." *Transformation* 20 (2003) 125–33.

Battiste, Marie. "Nourishing the Learning Spirit: Living Our Way to New Thinking." *Education Canada* 50 (2009/2010) 14–18.

Battiste, Marie, and James Youngblood Henderson. *Protecting Indigenous Knowledge and Heritage: A Global Challenge*. Saskatoon: Purich, 2000.

Becker, Howard S., and Blanche Geer. "Participant Observation and Interviewing: A Comparison." *Human Organization* 16 (1957) 28–32.

Behar, Ruth. *The Vulnerable Observer: Anthropology That Breaks Your Heart*. Boston: Beacon, 1997.

Bekker, Nick. "Empowering Oral Learners/Leaders." In *Beyond Literate Western Practices: Continuing Conversations in Orality and Theological Education*, edited by Samuel Chiang and Grant Lovejoy, 73–80. Hong Kong: International Orality Network, 2014.

Belenky, Mary F., et al. *Women's Ways of Knowing: The Development of Self, Voice, and Mind*. New York: Basic, 1997.

Belzer, Alisa. "Reflections on the PIAAC Literacy and Numeracy Frameworks." *Adult Learning* 20 (2016) 1–3.
Benedict, Ruth. *The Chrysanthemum and the Sword*. New York: First Mariner, 1946.
Bentley, R. Alexander, and Michael J. O'Brien. "Tipping Points among Social Learners: Tools from Varied Disciplines." *Current Zoology* 58 (2012) 298–306.
Benveniste, Luis, et al. *Teaching in Cambodia*. Washington, DC: World Bank and the Cambodian Ministry of Education, Youth, and Sport, 2008.
Berger, Peter L., and Thomas Luckmann. *The Social Construction of Reality: A Treatise in the Sociology of Knowledge*. New York: Penguin, 1991.
Berkvens, Jan B. "Developing Effective Professional Learning in Cambodia." PhD diss., University of Twente, 2009.
———. "What International Aid Organizations Can Learn from International Adult Learning: Experiences from Cambodia." *The Journal of Agricultural Education and Extension* 18 (2012) 347–68.
Berkvens, Jan B., et al. "Improving Adult Learning and Professional Development in a Post-Conflict Area: The Case of Cambodia." *International Journal of Educational Development* 32 (2012) 241–51.
Bertrand, Didier. "The Therapeutic Role of Khmer Mediums (*Kru Boramei*) in Contemporary Cambodia." *Mental Health, Religion, and Culture* 8 (2005) 309–27.
Biakolo, Emevwo. "On the Theoretical Foundations of Orality and Literacy." *Research in African Literatures* 30 (1999) 42–65.
Bierly, Paul E., et al. "Organizational Learning, Knowledge, and Wisdom." *Journal of Organizational Change Management* 13 (2000) 595–618.
Bigelow, Martha H. "Orality and Literacy within the Somali Diaspora." *Language Learning: A Journal of Research in Language Studies* 60 (2010) 25–57.
Bigelow, Martha H., and Jill Watson. "The Role of Education Level, Literacy, and Orality in L2 Learning." In *The Routledge Handbook of Second Language Acquisition*, edited by S. Gass and A. Mackey, 461–75. New York: Routledge, 2012.
Birks, Melanie, and Jane Mills. *Grounded Theory: A Practical Guide*. Thousand Oaks, CA: SAGE, 2011.
Bit, Seanglim. *The Warrior Heritage: A Psychological Perspective of Cambodian Trauma*. Ann Arbor: University of Michigan, 1991.
Bjoraker, William. "The 'People of the Book' Are the People of the Story: Storytelling in Contemporary Jewish Ministry." *William Carey International Development Journal* 2 (2013) 23–35.
Bloomberg, Linda Dale, and Marie Volpe. *Completing Your Qualitative Dissertation: A Road Map from Beginning to End*. Thousand Oaks, CA: SAGE, 2012.
Bogale, Gebeyehu W., et al. "Reaching the Hearts and Minds of Illiterate Women in the Amhara Highland of Ethiopia: Development and Pre-Testing of Oral HIV/AIDS Prevention Messages." *Journal of Social Aspects of HIV/AIDS* 7 (2010) 2–9.
Bohdanowicz, Kate. "How to End the Shame of Dyslexia? Education." *The Times Educational Supplement* 5133 (2015) 46.
Boomershine, Thomas E. "Biblical Storytelling and Biblical Scholarship." Paper presented at the Network of Biblical Storytellers (NOBS) Scholars Conference, Asheville, NC, August 2010. Online. http://www.biblicalperformancecriticism.org/index.php/2011-08-26-20-28-44/articles-mainmenu-37/articles/54-biblical-storytelling-and-biblical-scholarship/file.
———. *Story Journey: An Invitation to the Gospel as Storytelling*. Nashville: Abingdon, 1988.

Booth, Isobel. "Radio Soap for Health Education: Lessons Learnt by Health Unlimited Rwanda." July 2003. Online. http://www.eldis.org/fulltext/soap.pdf.

Borrero, Noah E., et al. "School as a Context for 'Othering' Youth and Promoting Cultural Assets." *Teachers College Record* 114 (2012) 1–37.

Botha, J. E. "The Potential of Speech Act Theory for New Testament Exegesis: Some Basic Concepts." *HTS Theological Studies* 47 (1991) 277–93.

Botha, Pieter J. J. "Letter Writing and Oral Communication in Antiquity: Suggested Implications for the Interpretation of Paul's Letter to the Galatians." *Scriptura* 42 (1992) 14–34.

———. "Living Voice and Lifeless Letters: Reserve towards Writing in the Graeco-Roman World." *HTS Theological Studies* 49 (1993) 742–59.

———. "Mute Manuscripts: Analysing a Neglected Aspect of Ancient Communication." *Theologia Evangelica* 23 (1990) 35–47.

Bouhali, Florence, et al. "Anatomical Connections of the Visual Word Form Area." *The Journal of Neuroscience* 34 (2014) 15402–14.

Bowman, James. "Communicating Christ through Oral Tradition: A Training Model for Grass Roots Church Planters." *International Journal of Frontier Missions* 20 (2003) 25–27.

———. "Communicating Effectively to Non-Readers: Communicating God's Message in an Oral Culture." *International Journal of Frontier Missions* 21 (2004) 122–28.

Box, Harry. *Don't Throw the Book at Them: Communicating the Christian Message to People Who Don't Read.* Pasadena, CA: William Carey, 2014.

Boyden, Jo, and Michael Bourdillon. "Reflections: Inequality, School, and Social Change." In *Growing Up in Poverty: Findings from Young Lives*, edited by M. Bourdillon and J. Boyden, 269–80. New York: Palgrave Macmillan, 2014.

Bradley, Sarah M. *How People Use Pictures: An Annotated Bibliography and Review For Development Workers.* London: International Institute for Environment and Development (IIED) and the British Council, 1995.

Bradt, Kevin M. *Story as a Way of Knowing.* Kansas City: Sheed & Ward, 1997.

Breckenridge, Jenna P., et al. "Choosing a Methodological Path: Reflections on the Constructivist Turn." *Grounded Theory Review* 1 (2012) 64–71.

Brennan, Jonathan, et al. "Syntactic Structure Building in the Anterior Temporal Lobe during Natural Story Listening." *Brain Language* 120 (2012) 163–73.

Brickell, Katherine. "'We Don't Forget the Old Rice Pot When We Get the New One': Discourses on Ideals and Practices of Women in Contemporary Cambodia." *Signs* 36 (2011) 437–62.

Brinkley, Joel. *Cambodia's Curse: The Modern History of a Troubled Land.* New York: Public Affairs, 2011.

Broadcasting Board of Governors (BBG) and Gallup. "Media Use in Cambodia." Washington, DC: BBG, 2014. Online. https://www.bbg.gov/wp-content/media/2014/11/Cambodia-research-brief-FINAL.pdf.

Brod, Shirley. *What Non-Readers and Beginning Readers Need to Know: Performance-Based ESL Adult Literacy.* Denver: Spring Institute for International Learning, 1999.

Brown, Brené. "Brené Brown: On Empathy." December 10, 2013. RSA video. Online. https://www.youtube.com/watch?v=1Evwgu369Jw.

———. *Daring Greatly: How the Courage to be Vulnerable Transforms the Way We Live, Love, Parent, and Lead.* New York: AVERY, 2012.

———. *I Thought It Was Just Me: Women Reclaiming Power and Courage in a Culture of Shame*. New York: Gotham, 2007.
Brown, John S., and Richard P. Adler. "Minds on Fire: Open Education, the Long Tail, and Learning 2.0." *Educause Review* 43 (2008) 17–32.
Brown, John S., et al. "Situated Cognition and the Culture of Learning." *Educational Researcher* 18 (1989) 32–42.
Brown, Rick. "Communicating Effectively to Non-Readers: Communicating God's Message in an Oral Culture." *International Journal of Frontier Missions* 21 (2004) 122–28.
———. "Designing Programs for Oral Cultures." *Notes on Literature in Use and Language Programs* 46 (1995) 14–38.
———. "How to Make Oral Communication More Effective." *International Journal of Frontier Missions* 21 (2004) 173–78.
Brown, Sid. *A Buddhist in the Classroom*. New York: State University of New York Press, 2008.
Browning, David M., and Mildred Z. Solomon. "Relational Learning in Pediatric Palliative Care: Transformative Education and the Culture of Medicine." *Child and Adolescent Psychiatric Clinics of North America* 15 (2006) 795–815.
Bruner, Jerome. *Actual Minds, Possible Worlds*. Cambridge: Harvard University Press, 1986.
———. *Making Stories: Law, Literature, Life*. New York: Farrar, Straus, and Giroux, 2002.
Bruski, Daniel J. "Do They Get the Picture? Visual Literacy and Low-Literacy Adult ESL Learners." MA thesis, Hamline University, 2011.
Bryan, Christopher, and David Landon. *Listening to the Bible: The Art of Faithful Biblical Interpretation*. Oxford Scholarship Online, 2014.
Buber, Martin. *Between Man and Man*. Translated by Ronald Gregor-Smith. New York: Routledge, 1947.
———. *Pointing the Way: Collected Essays*. Translated by M. Friedman. New York: Harper & Brothers, 1957. Online. https://archive.org/details/Pointthewayco027171mbp.
Burt, Miriam, et al. "Working with Adult English Language Learners with Limited Literacy: Research, Practice, and Professional Development." *CAELA (Center for Applied Linguistics) Network Brief*, October 2008. Online. http://www.cal.org/adultesl/pdfs/working-with-adult-english-language-learners-with-limited-literacy.pdf.
Bush, Troy L. "Effective Church Planting: A Qualitative Analysis of Selected Church Planting Models." PhD diss., Southern Baptist Theological Seminary, 1999.
Bynner, John, et al. *The Three Divides: The Digital Divide and Its Relation to Basic Skills and Employment in Portland, USA, and London, England*. London: National Research and Development Centre for Adult Literacy and Numeracy, 2010.
Cambron-Goulet, Mathilde. "Orality in Philosophical Epistles." In *Between Orality and Literacy: Communication and Adaptation in Antiquity*, edited by R. Scodel, 148–74. Boston: Brill, 2014.
Carothers, John C. "Culture, Psychiatry, and the Written Word." *Psychiatry* 22 (1959) 307–20.
Carr, David. "Torah on the Heart: Literary Jewish Textuality within Its Near Eastern Context." *Oral Tradition* 25 (2010) 17–40.

Carruthers, Mary. *The Book of Memory: A Study of Memory in Medieval Culture.* New York: Cambridge University Press, 2008.
Carter, Kathy. "The Place of Story in the Study of Teaching and Teacher Education." *Educational Researcher* 22 (1993) 5–18.
Castro-Caldas, Alexandre, and Alexandra Reis. "Neurobiological Substrates of Illiteracy." *The Neuroscientist* 6 (2000) 475–82.
Castro-Caldas, Alexandre, et al. "The Illiterate Brain: Learning to Read and Write during Childhood Influences the Functional Organization of the Adult Brain." *Brain* 121 (1998) 1053–63.
———. "Neuropsychological Aspects of Illiteracy." *Neuropsychological Rehabilitation* 7 (1997) 327–38.
Cazden, Courtney, and Vera P. John. "Learning in American Indian Children." In *Anthropological Perspectives on Education,* edited by M. Wax et al., 252–72. New York: Basic, 1971.
Chan, Sam. "Storytelling Seeking Understanding." In *Beyond Literate Western Practices: Continuing Conversations in Orality and Theological Education,* edited by Samuel Chiang and Grant Lovejoy, 81–86. Hong Kong: International Orality Network, 2014.
Chandler, Daniel. "Biases of the Ear and Eye: Great Divide Theories, Phonocentrism, Graphocentrism, and Logocentrism." September 18, 1995. Online. http://visual-memory.co.uk/daniel/Documents/litoral.
Chandler, David. *A History of Cambodia.* 4th ed. Chiang Mai: Silkworm, 2008.
Charmaz, Kathy. *Constructing Grounded Theory: A Practical Guide through Qualitative Analysis.* Thousand Oaks, CA: SAGE, 2011.
Charmaz, Kathy, and R. G. Mitchell. "Grounded Theory in Ethnography." In *Handbook of Ethnography,* edited by P. Atkinson et al., 160–74. Thousand Oaks, CA: SAGE, 2007.
Chase, Elaine, and Grace Bantebya-Kyomuhendo. "Poverty and Shame." In *Poverty and Shame: Global Experiences,* edited by Elaine Chase and Grace Bantebya-Kyomuhendo, 285–301. Oxford: Oxford Scholarship Online, 2014.
Chavis, Annie M. "Social Learning Theory and Behavioral Therapy: Considering Human Behaviors within the Social and Cultural Context of Individuals and Families." *Social Work in Public Health* 26 (2011) 471–81.
Chemengich, Emmanuel. "The Case of Africa Theological Seminary." In *Beyond Literate Western Practices: Continuing Conversations in Orality and Theological Education,* edited by Samuel Chiang and Grant Lovejoy, 37–44. Hong Kong: International Orality Network, 2014.
Cheng, I-Hsuan. "Case Studies of Integrated Pedagogy in Vocational Education: A Three-Tier Approach to Empowering Vulnerable Youth in Urban Cambodia." *International Journal of Educational Development* 30 (2010) 438–46.
———. "Re-modelling and Reconceptualising Skills Development in Cambodia: How Are Social Enterprises Preparing Young People for Successful Transitions between Learning and Work?" *International Journal of Educational Development* 43 (2015) 134–41.
Chetrit, Joseph. "Textual Orality and Knowledge of Illiterate Women: The Textual Performance of Jewish Women in Morocco." In *Women and Knowledge in the Mediterranean,* edited by F. Sadiqui, 89–107. New York: Routledge, 2013.

Chhim, Sotheara. "*Baksbat* (Broken Courage): A Trauma-Based Cultural Syndrome in Cambodia." *Medical Anthropology: Cross-Cultural Studies in Health and Illness* 32 (2013) 160–73.

Chiang, Samuel. "The Oral Reality: Reaching and Discipling Oral Learners." Paper presented at the Global Mission Consultation and Celebration: From Edinburgh to Tokyo, Tokyo, Japan, May 2010. Online. http://www.tokyo2010.org/resources/Tokyo2010_T2_Samuel_Chiang.pdf.

Chiang, Samuel E., and Grant Lovejoy, eds. *Beyond Literate Western Models: Contextualizing Theological Education in Oral Contexts.* Hong Kong: International Orality Network, 2013.

———. *Beyond Literate Western Practices: Continuing Conversations in Orality and Theological Education.* Hong Kong: International Orality Network, 2014.

Chifungo, Davidson. "An Oral Hermeneutics within the Lay Preaching Context of the Nkhoma Synod of the Church of Central Africa Presbyterian (CCAP): A Critical Evaluation." PhD diss., University of Stellenbosch, 2013.

Chigas, George, and Dmitri Moxyakov. "Literacy and Education under the Khmer Rouge." *Yale University Genocide Studies Program.* Online. http://gsp.yale.edu/literacy-and-education-under-khmer-rouge.

Childs, Carla P., and Patricia M. Greenfield. "Informal Modes of Learning and Teaching: The Case of Zinacanteco Weaving." In vol. 2 of *Studies in Cross-Cultural Psychology,* edited by N. Warren, 269–304. London: Academic, 1980.

Chudgar, Amita. "The Promise and Challenges of Using Mobile Phones for Adult Literacy Training: Data from One Indian State." *International Journal of Educational Development* 34 (2014) 20–29.

Cibangu, Sylvain K. "Oral Communication and Technical Writing: A Reconsideration of Writing in a Multicultural Era." *Journal of Technical Writing and Communication* 39 (2009) 79–105.

Clanchy, M. T. *From Memory to Written Record: England 1066–1307.* 3rd ed. Malden, MA: Wiley-Blackwell, 2013.

Clark, M. Carolyn. "Narrative Learning: Its Contours and Its Possibilities." *New Directions for Adult and Continuing Education* 126 (2010) 3–11.

Clark, M. Carolyn, and Marsha Rossiter. "Narrative Learning in Adulthood." *New Directions for Adult and Continuing Education* 199 (2008) 61–70.

Clifford, James. *Person and Myth: Maurice Leenhardt in the Melanesian World.* Durham, NC: Duke University Press, 1992.

Cloud, Henry. *Changes That Heal: How to Understand Your Past to Ensure a Healthier Future.* Grand Rapids: Zondervan, 1992.

Codrington, Robert H. *The Melanesians: Studies in Their Anthropology and Folk-Lore.* Oxford: Oxford University Press, 1891.

Cohen, A. D., and K. Scott. "A Synthesis of Approaches to Assessing Language Learning Strategies." In *Language Learning Strategies around the World: Crosscultural Perspectives,* edited by R. Oxford, 89–106. Honolulu: Second Language Teaching and Curriculum Center, University of Hawai'i, 1996.

Cohen, Bruce B. "Alternative Instructional Strategies for Low-Literate Adults: The Effects of Static and Dynamic Visuals on Learning." PhD diss., Vanderbilt University, 2007.

Cohen, Yehudi A. "The Shaping of Men's Minds: Adaptations to the Imperatives of Culture." In *Anthropological Perspectives on Education*, edited by M. Wax et al., 19–50. New York: Basic, 1971.

Colgate, Jack. "Part I: Relational Bible Storying and Scripture Use in Oral Muslim Contexts." *International Journal of Frontier Missiology* 25 (2008) 135–42.

———. "Part II: Relational Bible Storying and Scripture Use in Oral Muslim Contexts." *International Journal of Frontier Missiology* 25 (2008) 199–207.

Collins, James, and Richard K. Blot. *Literacy and Literacies: Texts, Power, and Identity.* New York: Cambridge University Press, 2003.

Collins, Patricia H. "Learning from the Outsider Within: The Sociological Significance of Black Feminist Thought." *Social Problems* 33 (1986) s14–s32.

Colter, Angela. "The Audience You Didn't Know You Had." *Contents Magazine* 2 (2012). Online. http://contentsmagazine.com/articles/the-audience-you-didn't-know-you-had.

Compain, Alice. "Born across Borders, Raised in a Refugee Camp: The History of the Cambodian Hymnal." *EthnoDoxology* 1 (2002) 17–18.

Condelli, Larry, and Heide Spruck Wrigley. "Instruction, Language and Literacy: What Works Study for Adult ESL Literacy Students." In *Low-Educated Adult Second Language and Literacy Acquisition: Proceedings of the Inaugural Symposium, Tilburg University, August 2005*, edited by I. van de Craats et al., 111–33. Utrecht, Netherlands: LOT, 2006.

Constitution of Cambodia. 1993. Online. http://www.constitution.org/cons/cambodia.htm.

Coomaraswamy, Ananda K. *The Bugbear of Literacy.* London: Dennis Dobson, 1947. Online. http://www.worldwisdom.com/public/library/default.aspx.

Coomaraswamy, Ananda K., and Rama P. Coomaraswamy. *The Essential Ananda K. Coomaraswamy.* Bloomington, IN: World Wisdom, 2004.

Corbett, Michael. "'It Was Fine If You Wanted to Leave': Educational Ambivalence in a Nova Scotia Community 1963–1998." *Anthropology and Education Quarterly* 35 (2004) 451–71.

Corcoran, Henry A. "Biblical Narratives and Life Transformation: An Apology for the Narrative Teaching of Bible Stories." *Christian Education Journal* 4 (2007) 34–48.

Courtney, Jane. "What Are Effective Components of In-Service Teacher Training? A Study Examining Teacher Trainers' Perceptions of the Components of a Training Programme in Mathematics Education in Cambodia." *Journal of In-Service Education* 33 (2007) 321–39.

Courtney, Jane, and Maggie Gravelle. "Switching Sides: The Battle between Globalized Pedagogy and National Identity in the Development of an Early Literacy Programme in Cambodia." Paper presented at the Conference of Education and Citizenship in a Globalising World, Institute of Education, London, November 2010.

———. "What Makes the Difference? An Analysis of a Reading Intervention Program Implemented in Rural Schools in Cambodia." *Compare: A Journal of Comparative and International Education* 44 (2014) 416–34.

Cozolino, Louis. *The Social Neuroscience of Education: Optimizing Attachment and Learning in the Classroom.* New York: Norton, 2013.

Craats, Ineke van de, et al. "Research on Low-Educated Second Language and Literacy Acquisition." In *Low-Educated Adult Second Language and Literacy Acquisition: Proceedings of the Inaugural Symposium, Tilburg University, August 2005*, edited by I. van de Craats et al., 7–24. Utrecht, Netherlands: LOT, 2005.

Crabtree, Robbin D., and David Alan Sapp. "Your Culture, My Classroom, Whose Pedagogy? Negotiating Effective Teaching and Learning in Brazil." *Journal of Studies in International Education* 8 (2004) 105–32.
Cree, Anthony, et al. *The Economic and Social Cost of Illiteracy: A Snapshot of Illiteracy in a Global Context.* Melbourne: World Literacy Foundation, 2012.
Creswell, John W. *Qualitative Inquiry and Research Design: Choosing among Five Approaches.* Thousand Oaks, CA: SAGE, 2013.
———. *Research Design: Qualitative, Quantitative, and Mixed Methods Approaches.* Thousand Oaks, CA: SAGE, 2009.
Crouch, Andy. "The Return of Shame." *Christianity Today* 59 (2015) 32–41.
Cruikshank, Julie. "Orality and Literacy: Reflections across Disciplines." *Canadian Journal of History* 47 (2012) 712–13.
Cupchik, Gerald. "Constructivist Realism: An Ontology That Encompasses Positivist and Constructivist Approaches to the Social Sciences." *Forum: Qualitative Social Research Sozialforschung* 2 (2001). Online. http://nbn-resolving.de/urn:nbn:de:0114-fqs010177.
Currie, Gregory. *Narratives and Narrators: A Philosophy of Stories.* Oxford: Oxford University Press, 2010.
Cutz, German R. "Emic-Etic Conflicts as Explanation of Nonparticipation in Adult Education among the Maya of Western Guatemala." *Adult Education Quarterly* 51 (2000) 64–75.
———. "Reasons for the Nonparticipation of Adults in Rural Literacy Programs in Western Guatemala." EdD diss., Ball State University, 1997.
Damodaran, Harish. "Learning's Not about Enrolment, Latrines in School. We're Failing Children on a Massive Scale." *Indian Express*, February 1, 2015. Online. http://indianexpress.com/article/india/india-others/learnings-not-about-enrolment-latrines-in-school-were-failing-children-on-massive-scale.
Davis, Erik W. "Treasures of the Buddha: Imagining Death and Life in Contemporary Cambodia." PhD diss., University of Chicago, 2009.
Davis, Gene. "Is That Really God Speaking?" *International Journal of Frontier Missions* 12 (1995) 98.
Dawson, Walter. "Private Tutoring and Mass Schooling in East Asia: Reflections of Inequality in Japan, South Korea, and Cambodia." *Asia Pacific Education Review* 1 (2010) 43–61.
———. "Tricks of the Teacher: Teacher Corruption and Shadow Education in Cambodia." In *Buying Your Way into Heaven: Education and Corruption in International Perspective*, edited by Stephen P. Heyneman, 51–74. Rotterdam, Netherlands: Sense, 2009. Online. http://www.sensepublishers.com/media/131-buying-your-way-into-heaven.pdf.
DeCapua, Andrea, et al. *Meeting the Needs of Students with Limited or Interrupted Schooling: A Guide for Educators.* Ann Arbor: University of Michigan Press, 2009.
DeCapua, Andrea, and Helaine W. Marshall. "Serving ELLs with Limited or Interrupted Education: Intervention that Works." *TESOL Journal* 1 (2010) 49–70.
———. "Students with Limited or Interrupted Formal Education in US Classrooms." *The Urban Review* 42 (2010) 159–73.
DeCoker, Gary. "Seven Characteristics of a Traditional Japanese Approach to Learning." In *Learning in Likely Places: Varieties of Apprenticeship in Japan*, edited by J. Singleton, 68–84. New York: Cambridge University Press, 1998.

Dehaene, Stanislas. *Reading in the Brain: The New Science of How We Read.* New York: Penguin, 2010.

———. "Reading in the Brain. Revised and Extended: Response to Comments." *Mind and Language* 29 (2014) 320–35.

Dehaene, Stanislas, et al. "How Learning to Read Changes the Cortical Networks for Vision and Language." *Science* 330 (2010) 1359–64.

———. "Illiterate to Literate: Behavioural and Cerebral Changes Induced by Reading Acquisition." *Nature Reviews Neuroscience* 16 (2015) 234–44.

Dehaene, Stanislas, and Laurent Cohen. "The Unique Role of the Visual Word Form Area in Reading." *Trends in Cognitive Sciences* 15 (2011) 254–62.

DeNeui, Paul H., ed. *Communicating Christ through Story and Song: Orality in Buddhist Contexts.* Pasadena, CA: William Carey, 2008.

Denny, J. Peter. "Rational Thought in Oral Culture and Literate Decontextualization." In *Literacy and Orality,* edited by D. Olson and N. Torrance, 66–89. New York: Cambridge University Press, 1991.

Denshire, Sally. "On Auto-Ethnography." *Current Sociology Review* 62 (2014) 831–35.

DeSilva, David A. *Honor, Patronage, Kinship, and Purity: Unlocking New Testament Culture.* Downers Grove, IL: InterVarsity, 2000.

Dewey, Joanna. *Orality and Textuality in Early Christian Literature.* Atlanta: Society of Biblical Literature, 1994.

———. "Textuality in an Oral Culture: A Survey of the Pauline Traditions." *Semeia* 65 (1994) 37–65.

Deyo, Lisa A. "Perspectives on Learning in the Women's Economic and Empowerment Literacy Program in Nepal." EdD diss., University of Massachusetts Amherst, 2007.

DeYoung, Patricia A. *Understanding and Treating Chronic Shame: A Relational/Neurobiological Approach.* New York: Routledge, 2015.

Diamond, S. "Epilogue." In *Anthropological Perspectives on Education,* edited by M. Wax et al., 300–306. New York: Basic, 1971.

Dias, Maria, et al. "Reasoning from Unfamiliar Premises: A Study with Unschooled Adults." *Psychological Science* 16 (2005) 550–54.

Dijksterhuis, Ap. "Why We Are Social Animals." In *Perspectives on Imitation: From Neuroscience to Social Science,* edited by S. Hurley and N. Chater, 207–20. Cambridge: Massachusetts Institute of Technology Press, 2005.

Dinkins, Larry. "Objections and Benefits of an Oral Strategy for Bible Study and Teaching." *William Carey International Development Journal* 2 (2013) 13–20.

———. "Presenting Orality in Academic Contexts." In *Beyond Literate Western Practices: Continuing Conversations in Orality and Theological Education,* edited by Samuel Chiang and Grant Lovejoy, 103–8. Hong Kong: International Orality Network, 2014.

Diouf, Waly, et al. "Adult Learning in a Non-Western Context: The Influence of Culture in a Senegalese Farming Village." *Adult Education Quarterly* 51 (2000) 32–44.

Doak, Cecilia C., et al. *Teaching Patients with Low Literacy Skills.* Philadelphia: J. B. Lippincott, 1996.

Donner, Jonathan, et al. "Stages of Design in Technology for Global Development." *Computer: IEEE Computer Society* 41 (2008) 34–41.

Dornan, Paul, and M. Portela. "Do Feelings of Shame Undermine Children's Development?" Oxford Department of International Development working paper, 2014. http://rdw2015.org.

Dotson, Jennifer. "Self-in-Relation, Shame-in-Relation: Working with Shame as a Relational Construct." PsyD diss., Massachusetts School of Professional Psychology, 2009.

Draper, Jonathan A. "The Closed Text and the Heavenly Telephone: The Role of the *Bricoleur* in Oral Mediation of Sacred Text in the Case of George Khambule and the Gospel of John." In *Orality, Literacy, and Colonialism in Southern Africa*, edited by Jonathan Draper, 1–8. Leiden: Society of Biblical Literature, 2003.

———. "Confessional Western Text-Centered Biblical Interpretation and an Oral or Residual-Oral Context." *Semeia* 73 (1996) 59–78.

Dresner, Samuel H. *Heschel, Hasidism, and Halakha*. New York: Fordham University Press, 2002.

Duggan, Stephen J. "Education, Teacher Training and Prospects for Economic Recovery in Cambodia." *Comparative Education* 32 (1996) 361–75.

Duke, Chris, and Heribert Hinzen. "Adult Education and Lifelong Learning within UNESCO: CONFINTEA, Education for All, and Beyond." *Adult Learning* 22 (2011) 18–23.

Dunne, Ciaran. "The Place of the Literature Review in Grounded Theory Research." *International Journal of Social Research Methodology* 14 (2011) 111–24.

Dybicz, Phillip. "An Inquiry into Practice Wisdom." *Families in Society* 85 (2004) 197–203.

Dye, T. Wayne. "Scripture in an Accessible Form: The Most Common Avenue to Increased Scripture Engagement." *International Journal of Frontier Missiology* 26 (2009) 123–28.

Dyer, Paul D. "The Use of Oral Communication Methods (Storytelling, Song/Music, and Drama) in Health Education, Evangelism, and Christian Maturation." DMin diss., Bethel Theological Seminary, 1994.

Ebihara, May M. "Svay: A Khmer Village in Cambodia." PhD diss., Columbia University, 1968.

Egan, Kieran. "Literacy and the Oral Foundations of Education." *Harvard Educational Review* 57 (1987) 445–72.

Einstein, Albert, and Alice Calaprice. *The Ultimate Quotable Einstein*. Princeton: Princeton University Press, 2011.

Eisenbruch, Maurice. "The Ritual Space of Patients and Traditional Healers in Cambodia." *Bulletin de l'Ecole française d'Extreme-Orient* 79 (1992) 283–316.

Ellis, Carolyn, and Arthur P. Bochner. "Analyzing Analytical Autoethnography: An Autopsy." *Journal of Contemporary Ethnography* 35 (2006) 429–49.

Elmholdt, Claus. "Metaphors for Learning: Cognitive Acquisition versus Social Participation." *Scandinavian Journal of Educational Research* 47 (2003) 115–31.

Enbar, Adam, and Avi Flombaum. "Learn.co: A New Type of Learning Platform." *Flatiron School* (blog), August 30, 2016. Online. http://blog.flatironschool.com/introducing-learn-a-new-type-of-online-learning-platform.

Eng, Dorothy, et al. "Cambodian Parental Involvement: The Role of Parental Beliefs, Social Networks, and Trust." *The Elementary School Journal* 114 (2014) 573–94.

Eng, Netra, et al. *Social Accountability in Service Delivery in Cambodia*. Cambodia Development Resource Institute (CDRI) Working Paper Series 102. Phnom Penh: CDRI, 2015.

Evans, A. Steven. "Matters of the Heart: Orality, Story and Cultural Transformation—The Critical Role of Storytelling in Affecting Worldview." *Missiology: An International Review* 38 (2010) 185–99.

———. "'You Think in Lines, We Think in Circles': Oral Communication Implications in the Training of Indigenous Leaders." In *Developing Indigenous Leaders: Lessons in Mission from Buddhist Asia*, edited by P. DeNeui, 21–37. Pasadena, CA: William Carey, 2013.

Fanta-Vagenshtein, Yarden. "How Illiterate People Learn: Case Study of Ethiopian Adults in Israel." *Journal of Literacy and Technology* 9 (2008) 26–55.

Fanta-Vagenshtein, Yarden, et al. "Technological Knowledge among Non-Literate Ethiopian Adults in Israel." *Knowledge, Technology, and Policy* 22 (2009) 287–302.

Farrell, Thomas J. "Walter Ong's Thought as Framework and Orientation for Cultural Studies in the Humanities." *REN* 55 (2003) 339–54.

Fellows, Timothy S. "The Training of Semiliterate Rural Pastors in the Northwest Region Ethiopian Kale Keywet Church." PhD diss., Biola University, 2014.

Fforde, Adam, and Katrin Seidel. "Cambodia—Donor Playground? Defeat and Doctrinal Dysfunction in a Hoped-For Client State." *South East Asia Research* 23 (2015) 79–99.

Filmer, Deon, and Norbert Schady. "Getting Girls into School: Evidence from a Scholarship Program in Cambodia." *Economic Development and Cultural Change* 56 (2008) 581–617.

Fingeret, Arlene. "The Illiterate Underclass: Demythologizing and American Stigma." PhD diss., Syracuse University, 1982.

———. "Social Network: A New Perspective on Independence and Illiterate Adults." *Adult Education Quarterly* 33 (1983) 133–46.

Finkelstein, Sidney. *Sense and Nonsense of McLuhan*. New York: International, 1968.

Finnegan, Ruth H. *Literacy and Orality: Studies in the Technologies of Communication*. Derry, Northern Ireland: Callender, 2014.

———. "Literacy versus Non-Literacy: The Great Divide? Some Comments on the Significance of 'Literature' In Non-Literate Cultures." In *Modes of Thought: Essays on Thinking in Western and Non-Western Societies*, edited by R. Horton, 112–44. London: Faber, 1973.

———. "Orality and Literacy: Epic Heroes of Human Destiny?" *International Journal of Learning* 10 (2003) 1551–60.

———. "Response from an Africanist Scholar." *Oral Tradition* 25 (2010) 7–16.

———. "What Is Orality—If Anything?" *Byzantine and Modern Greek Studies* 14 (1990) 130–49.

Fisher, Walter R. "Clarifying the Narrative Paradigm." *Communication Monographs* 56 (1989) 55–58.

———. "Narration as a Human Communication Paradigm: The Case of Public Oral Argument." *Communication Monographs* 51 (1984) 1–22.

———. "The Narrative Paradigm: An Elaboration." *Communication Monographs* 52 (1985) 347–67.

Fishman, Talya. "Guarding Oral Transmission: Within and Between Cultures." *Oral Tradition* 25 (2010) 41–56.

Flanders, Christopher. *About Face: Rethinking Face for Twenty-First-Century Mission*. Eugene, OR: Pickwick, 2011.

Flyvbjerg, Bent, et al. *Real Social Science: Applied Phronesis.* New York: Cambridge University Press, 2012.

Foley, John Miles. "Word in Tradition, Words in Text: A Response." *Semeia* 65 (1995) 169–79.

Foster, Stuart J. "Oral Theology in Lomwe Songs." *International Bulletin of Missionary Research* 32 (2008) 130–34.

Francis, Laurie, et al. "Does Literacy Education Improve Symptoms of Depression and Self-Efficacy in Individuals with Low Literacy and Depressive Symptoms? A Preliminary Investigation." *Journal of the American Board of Family Medicine* 20 (2007) 23–27.

François, Edouine, and Maria Matilde Olazabal. "Confessions of Two Adult Educators." *Monday Developments Magazine* 29 (2011) 21–23.

Franklin, Karl. "Part I: Re-Thinking Stories." *International Journal of Frontier Missions* 22 (2005) 6–12.

———. "Part II: Proposing an Alternative Initial Strategy for Small Language Groups in the Pacific." *International Journal of Frontier Missions* 22 (2005) 45–52.

Freedom from Hunger. "Education Modules." 2016. Online. http://www.freedomfromhunger.org/education-modules.

Freeman, Yvonne S., et al. "Keys to Success for Bilingual Students with Limited Formal Schooling." *Bilingual Research Journal* 25 (2001) 203–13.

Fuller, C. J. "Orality, Literacy and Memorization: Priestly Education in Contemporary South India." *Modern Asian Studies* 35 (2001) 1–31.

Fung, Heidi. "Becoming a Moral Child: The Socialization of Shame among Young Chinese Children." *Ethos* 27 (1999) 180–209.

Furniss, Graham. *Orality: The Power of the Spoken Word.* New York: Palgrave Macmillan, 2004.

Gallese, Vittorio. "Mirror Neurons, Embodied Simulation, and the Neural Basis of Social Identification." *Psychoanalytic Dialogues* 19 (2009) 519–36.

Gartner, Anne, et al. "The Power of Narrative: Transcending Disciplines." *ultiBASE*, December 1996. Online. http://ultibase.mrmit.edu/au/Articles/dec96/gartn1.htm.

Gaskins, Suzanne. "Children's Daily Activities in a Mayan Village: A Culturally Grounded Description." *Cross-Cultural Research* 34 (2000) 375–89.

———. "Open Attention as a Cultural Tool for Observational Learning." Paper presented at the Kellogg Institute for International Studies Conference on Learning In and Out of School: Education across the Globe, University of Notre Dame, May 2012. Online. http://kellogg.nd.edu/learning.

Gaskins, Suzanne, and Ruth Paradise. "Learning through Observation in Daily Life." In *The Anthropology of Learning in Childhood,* edited by D. Lancy et al., 85–117. Lanham, MD: Alta-Mira, 2009.

Gates, William H. "Remarks of Bill Gates, Harvard Commencement 2007." *Harvard Gazette,* June 7, 2007. Online. http://news.harvard.edu/gazette/story/2007/06/remarks-of-bill-gates-harvard-commencement-2007.

Gee, James Paul. "Discourses In and Out of School: Looking Back." In *Framing Languages and Literacies: Socially Situated Views and Perspectives,* edited by Margaret Hawkins, 51–82. New York: Routledge, 2013.

———. "Orality and Literacy: From the Savage Mind to Ways with Words." *TESOL Quarterly* 20 (1986) 719–46.

Geeves, Richard, and Kurt Bredenberg. "Contract Teachers in Cambodia." Paris: UNESCO International Institute for Educational Planning, 2005.

Georges, Jason. "The Geography of Shame: East versus West." *HonorShame*, July 2, 2014. Online. http://honorshame.com/geography-shame-east-vrs-west.

———. "The Three Sources of Honor." *HonorShame*, August 24, 2016. Online. http://honorshame.com/sources-of-honor/2016a.

Gershon, Nahum, and Ward Page. "What Storytelling Can Do for Information Visualization." *Communication of the ACM* 44 (2001) 31–37.

Giddens, Anthony, and Jonathan Turner. *Social Theory Today*. Palo Alto, CA: Stanford University Press, 1987.

Gilbert, Kathleen R. *The Emotional Nature of Qualitative Research*. Boca Raton, FL: CRC, 2000.

Ginsburg, Mark B. "Improving Educational Quality through Active-Learning Pedagogies: A Comparison of Five Case Studies." *Educational Research* 1 (2010) 62–74.

Ginsburg, Mark B., and American Institutes for Research. *Active-Learning Pedagogies as a Reform Initiative: Synthesis of Case Studies*. Washington, DC: US Agency for International Development, 2009.

Glaser, Barney G. "The Constant Comparative Method of Qualitative Analysis." *Social Problems* 12 (1965) 436–45.

———. "The Future of Grounded Theory." *Qualitative Health Research* 9 (1999) 836–45.

———. "Staying Open: The Use of Theoretical Codes in Grounded Theory." *The Grounded Theory Review: An International Journal* 5 (2005) 1–20.

Glaser, Barney G., and Anselm L. Strauss. *The Discovery of Grounded Theory: Strategies for Qualitative Research*. Piscataway, NJ: Transaction, 1967.

———. *The Discovery of Grounded Theory: Strategies for Qualitative Research*. 7th ed. Piscataway, NJ: AldineTransaction, 2012.

———. "Discovery of Substantive Theory: A Basic Strategy Underlying Qualitative Research." *American Behavioral Scientist* 8 (1965) 5–12.

Glazer, Steven. *The Heart of Learning: Spirituality in Education*. New York: Jeremy P. Tarcher/Penguin, 1999.

Glezer, Laurie S., and Maximilian Risenhuber. "Individual Variability in Location Impacts Orthographic Selectivity in the 'Visual Word Form Area.'" *The Journal of Neuroscience* 33 (2013) 11221–26.

Goodman, Madeline, et al. *Literacy, Numeracy, and Problem Solving in Technology-Rich Environments Among US Adults: Results from the Program for the International Assessment of Adult Competencies 2012*. Washington, DC: US Department of Education, 2013.

Goody, Jack. *The Domestication of the Savage Mind*. New York: Cambridge University Press, 1995.

———. *The Interface between the Written and the Oral*. New York: Cambridge University Press, 1987.

———. *Myth, Ritual, and the Oral*. New York: Cambridge University Press, 2010.

Goody, Jack, and Ian Watt. "The Consequences of Literacy." *Comparative Studies in Society and History* 5 (1963) 304–45.

Goold, William C. "Envisioning a Model: Integrating Theological Education and Creative Arts in the Practice of Orality for Oral Preference Learners." In *Beyond Literate Western Practices: Continuing Conversations in Orality and Theological Education*, edited by Samuel Chiang and Grant Lovejoy, 87–102. Hong Kong: International Orality Network, 2014.

Gori, Simone, and Andrea Facoetti. "Perceptual Learning as a Possible New Approach for Remediation and Prevention of Developmental Dyslexia." *Vision Research* 99 (2014) 78–87.

Goulet, Jean-Guy A. *Ways of Knowing: Experience, Knowing, and Power among the Dene Tha*. Vancouver: University of British Columbia Press, 1998.

Gourley, Steve. *The Middle Way: Bridging the Gap between Cambodian Culture and Children's Rights*. Phnom Penh: NGO Committee on the Rights of the Child, 2009. Online. http://www.unicef.org/cambodia/The_Middle_Way_English_Proofed_Small.pdf.

Gravelle, Maggie. "Dilemmas in Development Raised by a Teacher Training Project in Cambodia." *Compass: The Journal of Learning and Teaching at the University of Greenwich* 2 (2010) 37–42.

Gray, Peter. "What If Medicine's First Principle Were Also Education's?" *Psychology Today*, September 10, 2016. Online. https://www.psychologytoday.com/blog/freedom-learn/201609/what-if-medicine-s-first-principle-were-also-education-s.

Greckhamer, Thomas, and Mirka Koro-Lungberg. "The Erosion of a Method: Examples from Grounded Theory." *International Journal of Qualitative Studies in Education* 18 (2006) 729–50.

Green, Melanie C., and Timothy C. Brock. "The Role of Transportation in the Persuasiveness of Public Narratives." *Journal of Personality and Social Psychology* 79 (2000) 701–21.

Green, Robin. "An Orality Strategy: Translating the Bible for Oral Communicators." MA thesis, Graduate Institute of Linguistics, 2007.

Groce, Nora E., and Parul Bakhshi. "Illiteracy among Adults with Disabilities in the Developing World: A Review of the Literature and a Call for Action." *International Journal of Inclusive Education* 15 (2011) 1153–68.

Gunn, Margaret. "Opportunity for Literacy? Preliterate Learners in the AMEP." *Prospect* 18 (2003) 37–53.

Hadisi, Mwana. "Exploring the Performance, Semantic, and Cognitive Dimensions of Orality." *Missiology* 40 (2012) 443–53.

Hagadorn, Susan L. "Khmer Rouge Survivors Retell Culture for the Children of Cambodia: A Critical Hermeneutic Orientation to Narrative Imagination and Ethical Action." EdD diss., University of San Francisco, 2004.

Hagerty, B. M., et al. "An Emerging Theory of Human Relatedness." *Image—Journal of Nursing Scholarship* 25 (1993) 291–96.

Hansen, Anne R. "The Image of an Orphan: Cambodian Narrative Sites for Buddhist Ethical Reflection." *The Journal of Asian Studies* 62 (2003) 811–34.

———. *Ways of the World: Moral Discernment and Narrative Ethics in a Cambodian Buddhist Text*. Cambridge, MA: Harvard University Press, 1999.

Harbin, James, and Patricia Humphrey. "Teaching Management by Telling Stories." *Academy of Educational Leadership Journal* 14 (2010) 99–102.

Hardaker, Glenn, and Aishah Admad Sabki. "Islamic Pedagogy and Embodiment: An Anthropological Study of a British Madrasah." *International Journal of Qualitative Studies in Education* 28 (2015) 873–86.

Hardman, Joel C. "A Community of Learners: Cambodians in an Adult ESL Classroom." *Language Teaching Research* 3 (1999) 145–66.

Harel, Guershon, and Boris Koichu. "An Operational Definition of Learning." *Journal of Mathematical Behavior* 29 (2010) 115–24.

Harris, Ian Charles. *Cambodian Buddhism: History and Practice*. Honolulu: University of Hawai'i Press, 2005.

Hartling, Linda M., et al. "Shame and Humiliation: From Isolation to Relational Transformation." In *The Complexity of Connection: Writings from the Stone Center's Jean Baker Miller Training Institute*, edited by J. Jordan et al., 103–28. New York: Guilford, 2004.

Hartnell, Malcolm R. "Oral Contextualization: Communicating Biblical Truth to the Digo of Kenya." PhD diss., Fuller Theological Seminary, 2009.

Harvey, John D. "Orality and Its Implications for Biblical Studies: Recapturing an Ancient Paradigm." *Journal of the Evangelical Theological Society* 45 (2002) 99–109.

Hasson, Uri. "I Can Make Your Brain Look Like Mine." *Harvard Business Review* 88 (2010) 32–33.

Hasson, Uri, et al. "Brain-to-Brain Coupling: A Mechanism for Creating and Sharing a Social World." *Trends in Cognitive Science* 16 (2012) 114–21.

Havelock, Eric A. "The Alphabetic Mind: A Gift of Greece to the Modern World." *Oral Tradition* 1 (1986) 134–50.

———. *The Muse Learns to Write: Reflections on Orality and Literacy from Antiquity to the Present*. New Haven, CT: Yale University Press, 1986.

———. *Preface to Plato*. Cambridge, MA: Harvard University Press, 1963.

Haven, Kendall. *Story Proof: The Science behind the Startling Power of Story*. Westport, CT: Libraries Unlimited, 2012.

Hayes, Elisabeth R. "A Typology of Low-Literate Adults Based on Perceptions of Deterrents to Participation in Adult Basic Education." *Adult Education Quarterly* 39 (1988) 1–10.

Hearon, Holly E., and Philip Ruge-Jones. *The Bible in Ancient and Modern Media: Story and Performance*. Eugene, OR: Cascade, 2009.

Heath, Helen, and Sarah Cowley. "Developing a Grounded Theory Approach: A Comparison of Glaser and Strauss." *International Journal of Nursing Studies* 41 (2004) 141–50.

Heath, Shirley B. "What No Bedtime Story Means: Narrative Skills at Home and School." *Language in Society* 11 (1982) 49–76.

Heekeren, Deborah van. "'Don't Tell the Crocodile': An Existentialist View of Melanesian Myth." *Critique of Anthropology* 24 (2004) 430–54.

Hegel, Georg Wilheim F. *Hegel's Philosophy of Mind*. Translated by William Wallace. Oxford: Oxford University Press, 2007.

Hernandez, Maria Y., and Kurt Organista. "Entertainment-Education? A Fotonovela? A New Strategy to Improve Depression Literacy and Help-Seeking Behaviors in At-Risk Immigrant Latinas." *American Journal of Community Psychology* 52 (2013) 224–35.

Heyneman, Stephen P. "Education and Corruption." *International Journal of Educational Development* 24 (2004) 637–48.

Heyneman, Stephen P., ed. *Buying Your Way into Heaven: Education and Corruption in International Perspective*. Rotterdam: Sense, 2009.

Hezser, Catherine. "Oral and Written Communication and Transmission of Knowledge in Ancient Judaism and Christianity." *Oral Tradition* 25 (2010) 75–92.

Hiebert, Paul G. *Anthropological Insights for Missionaries*. Grand Rapids: Baker, 1985.

———. *Transforming Worldviews: An Anthropological Understanding of How People Change*. Grand Rapids: Baker Academic, 2008.

———. "Western Images of Others and Otherness." In *This Side of Heaven: Race, Ethnicity, and Christian Faith*, edited by R. Priest and A. Nieves, 97–110. New York: Oxford University Press, 2007.

Hiebert, Paul G., et al. *Understanding Folk Religion: A Christian Response to Popular Beliefs and Practices*. Grand Rapids: Baker Academic, 1999.

Hill, Dianne. "People as Informal, Extended Resources for Learning." In *Proceedings of the Ninth International Symposium on Aviation Psychology*, edited by R. Jensen and L. Rakovan, 1219–22. Columbus: Ohio State University Aviation Psychology Laboratory, 1997.

Hill, Harriet. "Conversations about Orality." *Missiology: An International Review* 38 (2010) 215–17.

Hinton, Alexander L. "Why Did You Kill? The Cambodian Genocide and the Dark Side of Face and Honor." *The Journal of Asian Studies* 57 (1998) 93–122.

Holloway, Elizabeth L., and Laurien Alexandre. "Crossing Boundaries in Doctoral Education: Relational Learning, Cohort Communities, and Dissertation Committees." *New Directions for Teaching and Learning* 131 (2012) 85–97.

Holt, John C. "Caring for the Dead Ritually in Cambodia." *Southeast Asian Studies* 1 (2012) 3–75.

Holton, Judith A. "The Coding Process: Its Challenges." In *The SAGE Handbook of Grounded Theory*, edited by A. Bryant and K. Charmaz, 265–89. Thousand Oaks, CA: SAGE, 2007.

Howell, Alan. "Memorization and Maturation: An Experiment in Leadership Formation in Mozambique." *Evangelical Missions Quarterly Online* 50 (2013) 12–17. Online. http://www.emqonline.com/emq/Issue-326/2908.

Hsieh, Alexander L. "Power of Shame: The Moderating Effects of Parental and Peer Connection on the Relationship between Adolescent Shame and Depression, Self-Esteem, and Hope." PhD diss., Brigham Young University, 2013.

Hu, Munir. "How to Eradicate Illiteracy without Eradicating Illiterates?" In *Literacy as Freedom*, edited by N. Aksornkool, 48–73. Paris: UNESCO Literacy and Non-Formal Education Section, 2003.

Hudson, Matthew, et al. "Implicit Social Learning in Relation to Autistic-Like Traits." *Journal of Autism and Developmental Disorders* 42 (2012) 2534–45.

Hughes, John. *Horae Britannicae: Or, Studies in Ancient British History*. London: J. and T. Clarke, 1818.

Hughes, Sherick, et al. "Translating Autoethnography across the AERA Standards: Toward Understanding Autoethnographic Scholarship as Empirical Research." *Educational Researcher* 41 (2012) 209–19.

Hunt, Cheryl. "A Long and Winding Road: A Personal Journey from Community Education to Spirituality via Reflective Practice." *International Journal of Lifelong Education* 28 (2009) 71–89.

Hurteau, Robert. "Navigating the Limitations of Western Approaches to the Intercultural Encounter: The Works of Walter Ong and Harry Triandis." *Missiology: An International Review* 34 (2006) 201–17.

Husum, Hans, et al. "Training Pre-hospital Trauma Care in Low-Income Countries: The 'Village University' Experience." *Medical Teacher* 25 (2003) 142–48.

Hutchison, Andrew J., et al. "Using QSR-NVivo to Facilitate the Development of a Grounded Theory Project: An Account of a Worked Example." *International Journal of Social Research Methodology* 13 (2010) 283–302.

Hvitfeldt, Christina. "Picture Perception and Interpretation among Preliterate Adults." *Passage, A Journal of Refugee Education* 1 (1985) 27–30.

———. "Traditional Culture, Perceptual Style, and Learning: The Classroom Behavior of Hmong Adults." *Adult Education Quarterly* 36 (1986) 65–77.

Hyde, Steve. "A Missiological and Critical Study of Cambodia's Historical, Cultural, and Sociopolitical Characteristics to Identify Factors of Rapid Church Growth and Propose Its Future Prognosis." PhD diss., Bethany International University, 2015.

———. *Portrait of the Body of Christ in Cambodia: A Detailed Statistical Study of the Church in Cambodia and Its Characteristics.* Phnom Penh: Antioch Institute, 2012.

Illeris, Knud. "A Comprehensive Understanding of Human Learning." In *Contemporary Theories of Learning: Learning Theorists—In Their Own Words*, edited by K. Illeris, 7–21. New York: Routledge, 2009.

Illich, Ivan. *Deschooling Society.* New York: Harper & Row, 1971.

Innis, Harold A. *The Bias of Communication.* 2nd ed. Buffalo, NY: University of Toronto Press, 2008.

International Orality Network and Lausanne Committee for World Evangelization. *Making Disciples of Oral Learners.* Lima, NY: Elim, 2005.

Irele, F. Abiola. *The African Imagination: Literature in Africa and the Black Diaspora.* New York: Oxford University Press, 2001.

Irving, David. "Orality Applied in a Classroom Setting with Amazon Region Indian Students." In *Beyond Literate Western Models: Contextualizing Theological Education in Oral Contexts*, edited by Samuel Chiang and Grant Lovejoy, 85–92. Hong Kong: International Orality Network, 2013.

Ito, Mizuko, et al. *Connected Learning: An Agenda for Research and Design.* Irvine, CA: Digital Media and Learning Research Hub, 2013.

Jackson, Philip W. *Life in Classrooms.* New York: Holt, Rinehart, and Winston, 1968.

Jacob, Judith M. "The Short Stories of Cambodian Popular Tradition." In *Cambodian Linguistics, Literature, and History*, edited by D. A. Smyth, 243–62. London: School of Oriental and African Studies, University of London, 1993. Online. http://sealang.net/sala/soas93/htm/lang.htm.

Jacobsen, Trude, and Martin Stuart-Fox. *Power and Political Culture in Cambodia.* Asia Research Institute Working Paper Series 200. Singapore: National University of Singapore, 2013.

Jaffee, Martin S. "A Rabbinic Ontology of the Written and Spoken Word: On Discipleship, Transformative Knowledge, and the Living Texts of Oral Torah." *Journal of the American Academy of Religion* 65 (1997) 525–49.

Jagerson, Jennifer. "Hermeneutics and the Methods of Oral Bible Storytelling for the Evangelization and Discipleship of Oral Learners." *Great Commission Research Journal* 4 (2013) 251–61.

Jarvis, Peter. *Adult Learning in the Social Context.* Kent, England: Croom Helm, 1987.

———. "Learning to Be a Person in Society: Learning to Be Me." In *Contemporary Theories of Learning: Learning Theorists—in Their Own Words*, edited by K. Illeris, 21–34. New York: Routledge, 2009.

Jesson, Jill K., et al. *Doing Your Literature Review: Traditional and Systematic Techniques.* Los Angeles: SAGE, 2011.

Jimison, Holly B., et al. "The Use of Multimedia in the Informed Consent Process." *Journal of the American Medical Informatics Association* 5 (1998) 245–56.

Jo, Yongmie Nicola. "Psycho-Social Dimensions of Poverty: When Poverty Becomes Shameful." *Critical Social Policy* 33 (2012) 514–31.

Johnson, Diane E. "Considering Shame and Its Implications for Student Learning." *College Student Journal* 46 (2012) 3–17.
Johnson, Jean, and Diane Campbell. *Worldview Strategic Church Planting among Oral Cultures.* Springfield, MO: LIFE, 2007.
Jones, Dale. "Moving towards Oral Communication of the Gospel: Experiences from Cambodia." In *Communicating Christ through Story and Song: Orality in Buddhist Contexts,* edited by P. DeNeui, 174–202. Pasadena, CA: William Carey, 2008.
Jones, Rebecca J., et al. "Behavioral and Neural Properties of Social Reinforcement Learning." *The Journal of Neuroscience* 31 (2011) 13039–45.
Jones, Stacy Holman, et al. *Handbook of Autoethnography.* New York: Routledge, 2013.
Jonsson, Hjorleifur. "Healthy Houses—Perspective on Well-Being in Rural Cambodia." *World Health Forum* 17 (1996) 360–62.
Jordan, Brigitte, and Robbie Davis-Floyd. *Birth in Four Cultures: A Cross-Cultural Investigation of Childbirth in Yucatan, Holland, Sweden, and the United States.* Prospect Heights, IL: Waveland, 1993.
Jordan, Judith V. "Relational Development: Therapeutic Implications of Empathy and Shame." In *Women's Growth in Diversity,* edited by J. Jordan, 138–61. New York: Guilford, 1997.
———. "Relational Learning in Psychotherapy Consultation." In *How Connections Heal: Stories from Relational-Cultural Therapy,* edited by M. Walker and W. Rosen, 22–30. New York: Guilford, 2004.
Jordan, Judith V., et al. *The Complexity of Connection: Writings from the Stone Center's Jean Baker Miller Training Institute.* New York: Guilford, 2004.
Jousse, Marcel. *The Oral Style.* Translated by Edgard Sienaert and Richard Whitaker. New York: Routledge, 2015.
Kaartinen, Timo. "Handing Down and Writing Down: Metadiscourses of Tradition among the Bandanese of Eastern Indonesia." *Journal of American Folklore* 126 (2013) 385–406.
Kalab, Milada. "Study of a Cambodian Village." *The Geographical Journal* 134 (1968) 521–37.
Kapil, Dev Regmi. "Can Lifelong Learning Be the Post-2015 Agenda for the Least Developed Countries?" *International Journal of Lifelong Education* 34 (2015) 551–68.
Kaufman, Gershen. *The Psychology of Shame: Theory and Treatment.* 2nd ed. New York: Springer, 1996.
———. *Shame: The Power of Caring.* Rev. ed. Rochester, VT: Schenkman, 1992.
Keener, Craig S. "Assumptions in Historical-Jesus Research: Using Ancient Biographies and Disciples' Traditioning as a Control." *Journal for the Study of the Historical Jesus* 9 (2011) 26–58.
Kern, Richard, and Jean Marie Schultz. "Beyond Orality: Investigating Literacy and the Literacy in Second and Foreign Language Instruction." *The Modern Language Journal* 89 (2005) 381–92.
Keysser, Christian. *A People Reborn.* Pasadena, CA: William Carey, 1980.
Killingsworth, M. Jimmie. "Product and Process, Literacy and Orality: An Essay on Composition and Culture." *College Composition and Communication* 44 (1993) 26–39.
Kilpatrick, Sue, and Susan Johns. "How Farmers Learn: Different Approaches to Change." *The Journal of Agricultural Education and Extension* 9 (2003) 151–64.

Kim, Chae-Young, and Martyn Rouse. "Reviewing the Role of Teachers in Achieving Education for All in Cambodia." *Prospects* 41 (2011) 415–28.

Kimura, Rikio. *Developing Christian Relief and Development NGO's Cambodian Staff toward Becoming Servant Leaders*. Virginia Beach: School of Global Leadership & Entrepreneurship, Regent University, 2007. Online. http://www.regent.edu/acad/global/publications/sl_proceedings/2007/kimura.pdf.

Klem, Herbert V. "The Bible as Oral Literature in Oral Societies." *International Review of Mission* 67 (1978) 479–86.

———. "Dependence on Literacy Strategy: Taking a Hard Second Look." *International Journal of Frontier Missions* 12 (1995) 59–64.

———. *Oral Communication of the Scripture: Insights from African Oral Art*. Pasadena, CA: William Carey, 1982.

Knight, Karen, and Kurt MacLeod. *Integration of Teachers' Voices into Education for All in Cambodia: Teacher Status, Social Dialogue and the Education Sector*. Geneva: International Labour Organization, 2004.

Knight, Shirlee-ann. "User Perceptions of Information Quality in World Wide Web Information Retrieval Behaviour." PhD diss., Edith Cowan University, 2008.

Knight, Shirlee-ann, and Donna Cross. "Using Contextual Constructs Model to Frame Doctoral Research Methodology." *International Journal of Doctoral Studies* 7 (2012) 39–62.

Knighton, Ben. "Orality in the Service of Karamojong Autonomy: Polity and Performance." *Journal of African Cultural Studies* 18 (2006) 137–52.

Knodel, John, and Zachary Zimmer. "Gender and Well-Being of Older Persons in Cambodia." Paper prepared for the Workshop on Gender and Aging, Institute of Southeast Asia Studies, Singapore, February 2009. Online. http://www.psc.isr.umich.edu/pubs/pdf/rr09-665.pdf.

Knowland, Victoria C., and Michael S. C. Thomas. "Educating the Adult Brain: How the Neuroscience of Learning Can Inform Educational Policy." *International Review of Education* 60 (2014) 99–122.

Knowles, Malcolm S., et al. *The Adult Learner: The Definitive Classic in Adult Education and Human Resource Development*. 6th ed. Burlington, MA: Elsevier, 2005.

Knowlton, David C. "Informed Consent and Ethnography: Dissent, Consent, and Nonsense." In *Ethics in the Professions: Proceedings of the 8th Annual Utah Valley State College Conference by the Faculty*, edited by R. McDonald and D. Yells, 29–41. Orem, UT: Utah Valley State College Center for the Study of Ethics, 2006. Online. http://astro.berkeley.edu/~kalas/ethics/documents/ethics/2007facultyproceedings_g5small.pdf.

Koehler, Paul. F. *Telling God's Stories with Power: Biblical Storytelling in Oral Cultures*. Pasadena, CA: William Carey, 2010.

Kolb, David A., et al. "Conversation as Experiential Learning." In *Conversational Learning: An Experiential Approach to Knowledge Creation*, edited by A. Baker and P. Jensen, 51–66. Westport, CT: Quorum, 2002.

Kosmidis, Mary H., et al. "Semantic and Phonological Processing in Illiteracy." *Journal of the International Neuropsychological Society* 10 (2004) 818–27.

Krabill, James R. *Worship and Mission for the Global Church: An Ethnodoxology Handbook*. Pasadena, CA: William Carey, 2013.

Kraus, Norman. *Jesus Christ our Lord: Christology from a Disciple's Perspective*. Rev. ed. Eugene, OR: Wipf & Stock, 1990.

Kreng, Heng. "Factors Influencing College Students' Academic Achievement in Cambodia: A Case Study." *ASEAN Journal of Teaching and Learning in Higher Education (AJTLHE)* 5 (2013) 34–49.

Krzeszewski, Lori B. "Poverty, English, and Evangelism: A Qualitative Study of Young Adults in a Church-Based English Language Program in Cambodia." PhD diss., University of North Carolina Charlotte, 2011.

Kumashiro, Kevin K. "Toward a Theory of Anti-Oppressive Education." *Review of Educational Research* 70 (2000) 25–53.

Kutner, M., et al. *Literacy in Everyday Life: Results from the 2003 National Assessment of Adult Literacy*. NCES 2007–480. Washington, DC: National Center for Education Statistics, US Department of Education, 2007.

Kvernbekk, Tone, and Gudmundur Frimannsson. "Narrative: A Brief Introduction." *Scandinavian Journal of Educational Research* 57 (2013) 571–73.

Kwabena, Emmanuel. "Narrative Theology in Dialectic with Indigenous Cultural Stories as a Way of Shaping Reality: An Important Function of Educational." EdD diss., Presbyterian School of Christian Education, 1993.

Labatiuk, Iryna. "George Spindler's Concept of Cultural Therapy and Its Current Application in Education." *Forum Oswiatowe* 2 (2012) 49–60.

Lado, Ana. *Ways in Which Spanish-Speaking Illiterates Differ from Literates in ESL Classrooms*. Richmond, VA: Department of Education, 1990.

Ladson-Billings, Gloria. "Toward a Theory of Culturally Relevant Pedagogy." *American Educational Research Journal* 32 (1995) 465–91.

Lancaster, Jennifer M. "Examining Shame from a Relational-Cultural Perspective." PhD diss., University of Oklahoma, 2010.

Lancy, D., et al., eds. *The Anthropology of Learning in Childhood*. Lanham, MD: AltaMira, 2009.

Larkey, Linda K., and Michael L. Hecht. "A Model of Effects of Narrative as Culture-Centric Health Promotion." *Journal of Health Communication: International Perspectives* 15 (2010) 114–35.

Lave, Jean. *Cognition in Practice: Mind, Mathematics, and Culture in Everyday Life*. New York: Cambridge University Press, 1988.

Leathard, Helen L., and Michael J. Cook. "Learning for Holistic Care: Addressing Practical Wisdom (Phronesis) and the Spiritual Sphere." *Journal of Advanced Nursing* 65 (2009) 1318–27.

Leatherwood, Rick. "The Case and Call for Oral Bibles: A Key Component in Completing the Great Commission." *William Carey International Development Journal* 2 (2013) 5–12.

LeCompte, Margaret. "Learning to Work: The Hidden Curriculum of the Classroom." *Anthropology and Education Quarterly* 9 (1978) 22–37.

Ledgerwood, Judy, ed. *Cambodia Emerges from the Past: Eight Essays*. DeKalb, IL: Southeast Asia, 2002.

———. "Social Hierarchy, Patron-Client Relationships and Power." *Cambodian Recent History and Contemporary Society: An Introductory Course*. Online. http://www.seasite.niu.edu/khmer/ledgerwood/patrons.htm.

Ledgerwood, Judy, and John Vijghen. "Decision-Making in Rural Khmer Villages." In *Cambodia Emerges from the Past: Eight Essays*, edited by Judy Ledgerwood. DeKalb, IL: Southeast Asia, 2002.

Lee, Chih-Yuan Steven, et al. "Potentially Traumatic Experiences, Academic Performance, and Psychological Distress: The Role of Shame." *Journal of Counseling and Development* 94 (2014) 41–94.

Lee, Helen, et al. "Creating New Career Pathways to Reduce Poverty, Illiteracy, and Health Risks, While Transforming and Empowering Cambodian Women's Lives." *Journal of Health Psychology* 15 (2010) 982–92.

Lee, Kuem J. "Bible Storying: A Recommended Strategy for Training Church Leaders in Oral Societies." PhD diss., Southern Baptist Theological Seminary, 2005.

Leenhardt, Maurice. *Do Kamo: Person and Myth in the Melanesian World*. Translated by Basia Miller Gulati. Chicago: University of Chicago Press, 1947.

Levinson, Bradley, A., ed. *Schooling the Symbolic Animal: Social and Cultural Dimensions of Education*. Lanham, MD: Rowman & Littlefield, 2000.

Levi-Strauss, Claude. *The Savage Mind*. Chicago: University of Chicago Press, 1966.

Lewis, Helen B. *Shame and Guilt in Neurosis*. New York: International University Press, 1971.

Lewis, Michael. *Shame: The Exposed Self*. New York: Free Press, 1992.

Li, Guofang. *Culturally Contested Pedagogy: Battles of Literacy and Schooling between Mainstream Teachers and Asian Immigrant Parents*. Albany: State University of New York Press, 2006. EBSCO eBook Academic Collection.

Lieberman, Matthew D. *Social: Why Our Brains Are Wired to Connect*. New York: Crown, 2013.

Lienhard, Ruth. "Restoring Relationships: Theological Reflections on Shame and Honor among the Daba and Bana of Cameroon." PhD diss., Fuller Theological Seminary, 2010.

Linde, Charlotte. "Narrative and Social Tacit Knowledge." *Journal of Knowledge Management* 5 (2011) 160–71.

Lingenfelter, Judith E., and Sherwood Lingenfelter. *Teaching Cross-Culturally: An Incarnational Model for Learning and Teaching*. Grand Rapids: Baker Academic, 2003.

Lipsky, Sherry. "Khmer Women Healers in Transition: Cultural and Bureaucratic Barriers in Training and Employment." *Journal of Refugee Studies* 6 (1993) 372–88.

Little Bear, Leroy. "Jagged Worldviews Colliding." In *Walking Together: First Nations, Metis and Inuit Perspectives in Curriculum*. Alberta: Alberta Education, 2000.

Locard, Henri, and Tha Leang Ang. "Higher Education in Cambodia and the Atypical Example of the History Department at RUPP2." *Canadian and International Education* 39 (2010) art. 8.

Loder, James E. *The Logic of the Spirit: Human Development in the Theological Perspective*. San Francisco: Jossey-Bass, 1998.

———. *The Transforming Moment*. Colorado Springs: Helmers & Howard, 1989.

Loewen, Jacob A. "Bible Stories: Message and Matrix." *Practical Anthropology* 11 (1964) 49–54.

Lord, Albert B. "Perspectives on Recent Work on the Oral Traditional Formula." *Oral Tradition* 1 (1986) 467–503.

Loubser, J. A. *Oral and Manuscript Culture in the Bible: Studies on the Media Texture of the New Testament—Explorative Hermeneutics*. 2nd ed. Eugene, OR: Cascade, 2013.

Lovejoy, Grant. "Chronological Bible Storying: Description, Rationale, and Implications." Paper presented at the Non-Print Media Consultation, Nairobi, Kenya, June 2000.

———. "The Extent of Orality." *The Journal for Baptist Theology and Ministry* 5 (2008) 121–34.

———. "The Extent of Orality: 2012 Update." *Orality Journal* 1 (2012) 11–40.

———. *Making Disciples of Oral Learners*. Lima, NY: Lausanne Committee for World Evangelization and International Orality Network, 2004.

Lucien, Caleb E. "The Relationship of Illiteracy to Spiritual Maturity." MA thesis, Dallas Theological Seminary, 1989.

Luong, Gloria, et al. "The Multifaceted Nature of Late-Life Socialization: Older Adults as Agents and Targets of Socialization." In *Handbook of Socialization: Theory and Research*, edited by J. Grusec and P. Hastings, 109–32. New York: Guilford, 2014.

Luria, Aleksandr R. *Cognitive Development: Its Cultural and Social Foundations*. Cambridge: Harvard University Press, 1976.

Ly, Boreth J. "Storytelling on Stone: Patterns of Visual Narrative Intention on Ancient Khmer (Cambodian) Temples." PhD diss., University of California Berkeley, 2002.

Lyon, G. Reid, et al. "A Definition of Dyslexia." *Annals of Dyslexia* 53 (2003) 1–14.

Ma, Norith. "Leadership Traits and Villages' Involvement in Community Development Projects in Dangkor District, Cambodia." MA thesis, Universiti Pertanian, 1997.

MacKeracher, Dorothy. *Making Sense of Adult Learning*. Toronto: University of Toronto Press, 2004.

Maddox, Brian. "What Good Is Literacy? Insights and Implications of the Capabilities Approach." *Journal of Human Development* 9 (2008) 185–206.

———. "Worlds Apart? Ethnographic Reflections on 'Effective Literacy' and Intrahousehold Externalities." *World Development* 35 (2007) 532–41.

Madinger, Charles. "Applied Orality: More than Methods." *Mission Frontiers* 36 (2014) 6–8.

———. "Coming to Terms with Orality: A Holistic Model." *Missiology: An International Review* 38 (2010) 201–13.

Main, Shiho. "'The Other Half' of Education: Unconscious Education of Children." *Educational Philosophy and Theory* 44 (2012) 82–95.

Malicky, Grace V., and Tracey Derwing. "Literacy Learning of Adults in a Bilingual ESL Classroom." *Alberta Journal of Educational Research* 39 (1993) 393–406.

Malina, Bruce J. *The New Testament World: Insights from Cultural Anthropology*. Atlanta: John Knox, 1981.

Mam, Barnabas, and B. Hutchinson. "Communicating the Gospel through Story and Song in Cambodia." In *Communicating Christ through Story and Song: Orality in Buddhist Contexts*, edited by P. DeNeui, 203–36. Pasadena, CA: William Carey, 2008.

Markus, Hazel R., and Shinobu Kitayama. "Culture and Self: Implications for Cognition, Emotion, and Motivation." *Psychological Review* 98 (1991) 224–53.

Marmon, Ellen L. "Teaching through the Lenses of Orality and Literacy: One Professor's Journey." *Religious Education* 108 (2013) 312–27.

Marrs, Heath, and Stephen L. Benton. "Relationships between Separate and Connected Knowing and Approaches to Learning." *Sex Roles* 6 (2009) 57–66.

Matthews, Brett. "Internal Control of Community Finance Institutions in Cambodia." *CCA Working Paper* 1 (2004). Online. https://www.researchgate.net/publication/277719910_Internal_Control_of_Community_Finance_Institutions_in_Cambodia.

Maxey, James. "Bible Translation as Contextualization: The Role of Orality." *Missiology: An International Review* 38 (2010) 173–83.
Maxwell, Joseph A. *A Realist Approach for Qualitative Research*. Thousand Oaks, CA: SAGE, 2012.
Mayers, Marvin K. *Christianity Confronts Culture: A Strategy for Crosscultural Evangelism*. Grand Rapids: Zondervan, 1987.
Mazamisa, Welile. "Reading from This Place: From Orality to Literacy/Textuality and Back." *Scriptura* s9 (1991) 67–72.
McCarthy, Michael C. "'We are Your Books': Augustine, the Bible, and the Practice of Authority." *Journal of the American Academy of Religion* 75 (2007) 324–52.
McIlwain, Trevor. *Firm Foundations: Creation to Christ*. Sanford, FL: New Tribes Mission, 1991.
McIntyre, Roy C. "Using Ceremonies to Disciple Oral Learners among the Tribal People in Bangladesh." DMiss diss., Asbury Theological Seminary, 2005.
McIver, Lachlan J., et al. "Diarrheal Diseases and Climate Change in Cambodia: Environmental Epidemiology and Opportunities for Adaptation." *Asia Pacific Journal of Public Health* 28 (2016) 576–85.
McLuhan, Marshall. *Essential McLuhan*. New York: Basic, 1995.
———. *The Gutenberg Galaxy: The Making of Typographic Man*. 1962. Reprint. Toronto: University of Toronto Press, 2011.
McMenamin, Iain. "Process and Text: Teaching Students to Review the Literature." *PS: Political Science and Politics* 39 (2006) 133–35.
McNish, Jill, and Richard L. Dayringer. *Transforming Shame: A Pastoral Response*. New York: Routledge, 2004.
McPherson, Pamela. *Modes of Delivery for Preliterate Learners*. Sydney: AMEP Research Centre, Australian Government, Department of Immigration and Citizenship, 2008.
McQuiggan, Scott W., et al. "Story-Based Learning: The Impact of Narrative on Learning Experiences and Outcomes." *Intelligent Tutoring Systems* 5091 (2008) 530–39.
Medhi, Indrani, et al. "Beyond Strict Illiteracy: Abstracted Learning among Low-Literate Users." In *Proceedings of the 4th ACM/IEEE International Conference on Information Technologies and Development*, edited by P. T. H. Unwin, 1–9. New York: ACM, 2010.
———. "Designing Mobile Interfaces for Novice and Low-Literacy Users." *ACM Transactions on Computer-Human Interaction* 18 (2011) art. 2.
———. "It's Not Just Illiteracy." In *Proceedings of the 2010 International Conference on Interaction Design and International Development*, edited by A. Joshi and A. Dearden, 1–10. Swinton, England: British Computer Society, 2010.
———. "Text-Free User Interfaces for Illiterate and Semiliterate Users." *Information Technologies and International Development* 4 (2007) 37–50.
Meek, Esther L. "Cultivating Connected Knowing in the Classroom." *Tradition and Discovery: The Polanyi Society Periodical* 34 (2007) 40–48.
Meeks, Thomas W., and Dilip V. Jeste. "Neurobiology of Wisdom: A Literature Overview." *Archives of General Psychiatry* 66 (2009) 355–65.
Mello, Robin. "The Power of Storytelling: How Oral Narrative Influences Children's Relationships in Classrooms." *International Journal of Education and the Arts* 2 (2001). Online. http://www.ijea.org/v2n1/index.html.

Meltzoff, Andrew N. "Elements of a Developmental Theory of Imitation." In *The Imitative Mind: Development, Evolution, and Brain Bases*, edited by A. Meltzoff and W. Prinz, 19–41. New York: Cambridge University Press, 2003.

Merriam, Sharan B. *Non-Western Perspectives on Learning and Knowing*. Malabar, FL: Krieger, 2007.

———. *Qualitative Research in Practice: Examples for Discussion and Analysis*. San Francisco: Jossey-Bass, 2002.

Merriam, Sharan B., and Laura L. Bierema. *Adult Learning: Linking Theory and Practice*. San Francisco: Jossey-Bass., 2014

Merriam, Sharan B., and Ralph G. Brockett. *The Profession and Practice of Adult Education*. San Francisco: Jossey-Bass, 2007.

Merriam, Sharan B., and Young Sek Kim. "Non-Western Perspectives on Learning and Knowing." *New Directions for Adult and Continuing Education* 119 (2008) 71–81.

Merriam, Sharan B., and Mazanah Mohamad. "How Cultural Values Shape Learning in Older Adulthood: The Case of Malaysia." *Adult Education Quarterly* 51 (2000) 45–63.

Merriam, Sharan B., and Gabo Ntseane. "Transformational Learning in Botswana: How Culture Shapes the Process." *Adult Education Quarterly* 58 (2008) 183–97.

Merrifield, Juliet, and Mary Beth Bingman. "Living and Learning: Strategies for Survival in a Literate World." In *34th Annual Adult Education Research Conference (AERC) Proceedings*, edited by Daniele Flannery, 173–78. University Park: Pennsylvania State University, 1993.

Miller, J. B., and Irene Pierce Stiver. *The Healing Connection: How Women Form Relationships in Therapy and in Life*. Boston: Beacon, 1991.

Miller, Jane E., and Yana V. Rodgers. "Mother's Education and Children's Nutritional Status: New Evidence from Cambodia." *Asian Development Review* 26 (2009) 131–65.

Ministry of Education, Youth, and Sport of the Kingdom of Cambodia (MoEYS). "Education Strategic Plan 2009–2013." *MoEYS*. Online. http://www.moeys.gov.kh/en/policies-and-strategies/esp-2009-2013.html#.WCpuX8cediw.

———. "Non-Formal Education." *MoEYS*. Online. http://www.moeys.gov.kh/en/education/non-formal-education.html#.WCpupccediw.

Minz, Nijhar J. "Hope Amidst Hopelessness: Life Histories of Illiterate Oraon Tribal Women in Jharkhand, India." PhD diss., University of Minnesota, 2012.

Mobile Health without Borders. "Health Literacy to Improve Child Survival Rates and Quality of Life in Cambodia's Rural Population." *NovoEd*. Online. https://novoed.com/mhealth/reports/52141.

Moll, Luis C., et al. "Funds of Knowledge for Teaching: Using a Qualitative Approach to Connect Homes and Classrooms." *Theory into Practice* 31 (1992) 132–41.

Moll, Luis C., and James B. Greenberg. "Creating Zones of Possibilities: Combining Social Contexts for Instruction." In *Vygotsky and Education: Instructional Implications and Applications of Sociohistorical Psychology*, edited by Luis Moll, 319–48. New York: Cambridge University Press, 1990.

Montandon, Cleopatre. "Forme Sociales, Formes D'education Et Figures Theoriques" ["Social Forms, Forms of Education, and Theoretical Figures"]. In *Formel? Informel? Les formes de l'education [Formal? Informal? The Forms of Education]*, edited by C. Montandon and O. Maulini, 223–43. Brussels: De Boeck University, 2005.

Montgomery, Scott L., and Alok Kumar. "Telling Stories: Some Remarks on Orality in Science." *Science as Culture* 9 (2000) 391–404.

Moon, W. Jay. "Discipling through the Eyes of Oral Learners." *Missiology: An International Review* 38 (2010) 127–40.

———. "Encouraging Ducks to Swim: Suggestions for Seminary Professors of Oral Learners." *William Carey International Development Journal* 2 (2013) 5–12.

———. "Fad or Renaissance? Misconceptions of the Orality Movement." *International Bulletin of Mission Research* 40 (2016) 6–21.

———. "Rituals and Symbols in Community Development." *Missiology: An International Review* 40 (2012) 141–52.

———. "Teaching Oral Learners in Institutional Settings." In *Beyond Literate Western Models: Contextualizing Theological Education in Oral Contexts*, edited by Samuel Chiang and Grant Lovejoy, 143–52. Hong Kong: International Orality Network, 2013.

———. "Understanding Oral Learners." *Teaching Theology and Religion* 15 (2012) 29–39.

———. "Using Proverbs to Contextualize Christianity in the Bulisa Culture of Ghana, West Africa." PhD diss., Asbury Theological Seminary, 2005.

———. "Using Rituals to Disciple Oral Learners: Part 1." *Orality Journal* 2 (2013) 43–64.

Moore, Jennifer. "Classic Grounded Theory: A Framework for Contemporary Application." *Nurse Researcher* 17 (2010) 41–48.

Morain, Genelle. "Visual Literacy: Reading Signs and Designs in the Foreign Culture." *Foreign Language Annals* 9 (1976) 210–16.

Morales, Gilbert. "The Worldview and Learning Perspective in Oral Preference Learner Context." Paper presented at the International Orality Network Consultation, Hong Kong Baptist Theological Seminary, Hong Kong, June 2013. Online. http://legacy.orality.net/sites/default/files/Papers%20Presented/Gilbert%20Morales%20P3N5Web.pdf.

Morefield, John. "School Leadership Development in Cambodia: A Training Opportunity for Cambodian School Directors 2003–2004." New Horizons for Learning, Johns Hopkins School of Education, 2003. Online. http://education.jhu.edu/PD/newhorizons/Transforming%20Education/international/morefield_01.htm.

Morris, Mark. "Fellow Servants Honor Dr. Rebekah Naylor." *Mission Leader* (blog), February 13, 2009. Online. http://www.missionleader.com/?p=338.

Mortimore, Peter, ed. *Understanding Pedagogy and Its Impact on Learning*. Thousand Oaks, CA: SAGE, 1999.

Mossop, Liz, et al. "Analysing the Hidden Curriculum: Use of a Cultural Web." *Medical Education* 47 (2013) 134–43.

Mott, Bradford W., et al. "Towards Narrative-Centered Learning Environments." In *Proceedings of the 1999 AAAI Fall Symposium on Narrative Intelligence*, AAAI Technical Report FS-99-01 (1999) 78–82.

Motty, Bauta D. "Contextualizing Theological Education in Africa: A Case of ECWA Theological Seminary, Jos, Nigeria." In *Beyond Literate Western Models: Contextualizing Theological Education in Oral Contexts*, edited by Samuel Chiang and Grant Lovejoy, 153–62. Hong Kong: International Orality Network, 2013.

———. "Spreading the Word to Know the Truth." *Mission Frontiers* 36 (2014) 9.

Mueller, Chris. "Expert Has New Numbers on Deaths under KR." *Cambodia Daily*, April 20, 2015. Online. https://english.cambodiadaily.com/news/expert-has-new-numbers-on-deaths-under-kr-82130.

Murray, T. Scott, et al. *Reconstructing the Evolution of the American Supply of Cognitive Skills: A Synthetic Cohort Analysis*. Washington, DC: Data Angel, 2016.

Mushengyezi, Aaron. "Rethinking Indigenous Media: Rituals, 'Talking' Drums, and Orality as Forms of Public Communication in Uganda." *Journal of African Cultural Studies* 16 (2003) 107–17.

Narayan, Deepa. *Voices of the Poor: Can Anyone Hear Us?* Oxford: Oxford University Press, 2000.

Nash, John L. "Using Student Evaluations at a Cambodian University to Improve Teaching Effectiveness." EdD diss., Lehigh University, 2012.

Nasser, Latif. "The Great Divide, or How an Obscure Diagnosis from Colonial Africa Ended Up in Playboy Magazine." 2011. Online. http://isites.harvard.edu/fs/docs/icb.topic985058.files/Nasser%20The%20Great%20Divide.docx.

Nathanson, Donald L. "Dr. Donald L. Nathanson: The Role of Affect in Learning to Read—How Shame Exacerbates Reading Difficulties." Interview by David Boulton. *Children of the Code*, September 8, 2003. Online. http://www.childrenofthecode.org/interviews/nathanson.htm.

National Institute of Statistics, Directorate General for Health, and ICF Macro. *2010 Demographic and Health Survey: Key Findings*. Phnom Penh; Calverton, MD: National Institute of Statistics, Directorate General for Health, and ICF Macro, 2011. Online. http://dhsprogram.com/pubs/pdf/SR185/SR185.pdf.

Naude, Piet. "Theology with a New Voice? The Case for an Oral Theology in the South African Context." *Journal of Theology for Southern Africa* 94 (1996) 18–33.

Naylor, Mark. "Towards Contextualized Bible Storying: Cultural Factors Which Influence Impact in a Sindhi Context." MA thesis, University of South Africa Pretoria, 2004.

Needham, Susan. "'This Is Active Learning': Theories of Language, Learning, and Social Relations in the Transmission of Khmer Literacy." *Anthropology and Education* 34 (2003) 27–49.

Nelson, Heather D. *Unashamed: Healing Our Brokenness and Finding Freedom from Shame*. Wheaton, IL: Crossway, 2016.

Neyrey, Jerome H. *Honor and Shame in the Gospel of Matthew*. Louisville: Westminster John Knox, 1998.

Ngara, Constantine. "African Ways of Knowing and Pedagogy Revisited." *Journal of Contemporary Issues in Education* 2 (2007) 7–20.

Nguyen, David J., and Jay B. Larson. "Don't Forget about the Body: Exploring the Curricular Possibilities of Embodied Pedagogy." *Innovative Higher Education* 40 (2015) 331–44.

Nguyen, Manhanh. "Orality—A Tool to Bring the Gospel to Unreached People." Paper presented at the International Orality Network Consultation at Hong Kong Baptist Theological Seminary, Hong Kong, June 2013.

Nguyen, Phuong-Mai, et al. "Culturally Appropriate Pedagogy: The Case of Group Learning in a Confucian Heritage Culture Context." *Intercultural Education* 17 (2006) 1–19.

Nith, Bunlay, et al. "Active-Learning Pedagogies as a Reform Initiative: The Case of Cambodia." *EQUIP1*, January 22, 2010. Online. http://www.equip123.net/docs/E1-ActiveLearningPedagogy-Cambodia.pdf.

Nonoyama-Tarumi, Y., and Kurt Bredenberg. "Impact of School Readiness Program Interventions on Children's Learning in Cambodia." *International Journal of Educational Development* 29 (2009) 39–45.

Norwood, John V. "Developing a Course for Training Oral Learners in South Asia to Use Chronological Bible Storying for Evangelism and Church Planting." DMin diss., Southwestern Baptist Theological Seminary, 2003.

Noss, Philip A. "The Oral Story and Bible Translation." *Technical Papers for the Bible Translator* 32 (1981) 301–18.

Nowak, Anita T. "Introducing a Pedagogy of Empathic Action as Informed by Social Entrepreneurs." PhD diss., McGill University, 2011.

Ogisu, Takayo. "How Cambodian Pedagogical Reform Has Been Constructed: A Multi-Level Case Study." PhD diss., Michigan State University, 2014.

O'Leary, Moira P. "The Influence of Values on Development Practice: A Study of Cambodian Development Practitioners in Non-Governmental Organisations in Cambodia." PhD diss., La Trobe University, 2006.

O'Lemmon, Matthew. "Spirit Cults and Buddhist Practice in Kep Province, Cambodia." *Journal of Southeast Asian Studies* 45 (2014) 25–49.

Olson, Kirke. *The Invisible Classroom: Relationships, Neuroscience, and Mindfulness in School*. New York: Norton, 2014.

Om, Sokha. "Harnessing the Hope: Tapping into the Energy of Emerging Scholars in Cambodian Higher Education." *International Journal of Liberal Arts and Social Science* 1 (2013) 11–22.

Ong, Walter J. *Orality and Literacy: The Technologizing of the Word*. New York: Routledge, 1982.

———. *Orality and Literacy: The Technologizing of the Word*. 2nd ed. New York: Routledge, 2002.

———. *The Presence of the Word: Some Prolegomena for Cultural and Religious History*. 2nd ed. Albany: State University of New York Press, 2000.

———. *Rhetoric, Romance, and Technology: Studies in the Interaction of Expression and Culture*. Ithaca, NY: Cornell University, 1971.

Openjuru, George. "Adult Literacy and Development Link: A Perspective from a Non-Literate's Literacy Practices and Environment." *Adult Education and Development (AED)* 61 (2003) 7–18.

Orenstein, Myrna. "Picking Up the Clues: Understanding Undiagnosed Learning Disabilities, Shame, and Imprisoned Intelligence." *Journal of College Student Psychotherapy* 15 (2000) 35–46.

Organization for Economic Co-operation and Development (OECD). *Literacy in the Information Age: Final Report of the International Adult Literacy Survey*. Paris: OECD, 2000. Online. http://www.oecd.org/edu/skills-beyond-school/41529765.pdf.

Osborne, A. Barry. "Practice into Theory into Practice: Culturally Relevant Pedagogy for Students We Have Marginalized and Normalized." *Anthropology and Education Quarterly* 27 (1996) 285–314.

Oughton, Helen. "Funds of Knowledge: A Conceptual Critique." *Studies in the Education of Adults* 42 (2010) 63–78.

Overstreet, Mark M. "Fruitful Labor: Leadership Development and Global Implications for Theological Education in Oral Contexts." Paper presented at the International Orality Network Consultation, Hong Kong Baptist Theological Seminary, Hong Kong, June 2013. Online. http://legacy.orality.net/sites/default/files/Papers%20Presented/Mark%20Overstreet%20P2N4Web.pdf2013a.

———. "Theological Education as Incarnational Missiology: Empowering and Affirming Oral Learners in Oral Culture Pastor Training." In *Beyond Literate Western Models: Contextualizing Theological Education in Oral Contexts*, edited by Samuel Chiang and Grant Lovejoy, 29–38. Hong Kong: International Orality Network, 2013.

Pak, Kimchoeun, et al. *Accountability and Neo-Patrimonialism in Cambodia: A Critical Literature Review*. Cambodia Development Resource Institute (CDRI) Working Paper 34. Phnom Penh: CDRI, 2007. Online. http://www.utexas.edu/lbj/sites/default/files/file/WP34e.pdf.

Palaiologou, Nektaria. "Needs for Developing Culturally Oriented Supportive Learning with the Aid of Information and Communication Technologies." *Pedagogy, Culture, and Society* 17 (2009) 189–200.

Papa, Michael J., et al. "Entertainment-Education and Social Change: An Analysis of Parasocial Interaction, Social Learning, Collective Efficacy, and Paradoxical Communication." *Journal of Communication* 50 (2000) 31–55.

Papacharissi, Zizi. "The Unbearable Lightness of Information and the Impossible Gravitas of Knowledge: Big Data and the Makings of a Digital Orality." *Media, Culture, and Society* 37 (2015) 1–6.

Paradise, Ruth M. "Learning Through Social Interaction: The Experience and Development of the Mazahua Self in the Context of the Market." PhD diss., University of Pennsylvania, 1987.

———. "What's Different about Learning in Schools as Compared to Family and Community Settings?" *Human Development* 41 (1998) 270–78.

Paradise, Ruth M., and Barbara Rogoff. "Side by Side Learning: Learning by Observing and Pitching In." *Ethos* 37 (2009) 102–38.

Parker, Veronica A. "Adults' Perspectives on the Impact of Low-Level Literacy/Functional/Illiteracy on Their Lives: A Case Study of Literacy Program Participants." EdD diss., University of Houston, 1999.

Parker, William C. *Cultural and Academic Stress Imposed on Afro-Americans: Implications for Educational Change*. Princeton: Educational Testing Service, 1975.

Parry, Milman. *The Making of Homeric Verse: The Collected Papers of Milman Parry*. Oxford: Clarendon, 1971.

Participate. *People's Experiences of Living in Poverty: Early Findings for High Level Panel Deliberations*. Monrovia, Liberia: Institute of Development Studies, 2013.

Pattanayak, D. P. "Literacy: An Instrument of Oppression." In *Literacy and Orality*, edited by D. R. Olson and N. Torrance, 105–8. Cambridge: Cambridge University Press, 1991.

Pattison, Stephen. "Shame and the Unwanted Self." In *The Shame Factor: How Shame Shapes Society*, edited by R. Jewett et al., 9–29. Eugene, OR: Wipf & Stock, 2010.

Patz, Mike. "Fathers, Rabbis, and the Way of Jesus." *Mike Patz* (blog), July 27, 2015. Online. https://michaelpatz.com/2015/07/27/fathers-rabbis-and-the-way-of-jesus.

Pearson, Jenny. "No Visible Difference: A Women's Empowerment Process in a Cambodian NGO." *Development in Practice* 21 (2011) 392–404.

Pederson, Don. "Biblical Narrative as an Agent for Worldview Change." *International Journal of Frontier Missions* 14 (1997) 163–66.

Pellissery, Sony. "Persistence of Shaming in a Hierarchical Society." In *Poverty and Shame: Global Experiences*, edited by E. Chase and G. Bantebya-Kyomuhendo. Oxford Scholarship Online, 2014.

Peristiany, J. G. *Honor and Shame: The Values of Mediterranean Society*. Chicago: University of Chicago Press, 1966.

Peristiany, J. G., and Julian Alfred Pitt-Rivers. *Honor and Grace in Anthropology*. Cambridge: Cambridge University Press, 1992.

Perry, Kristen H. "Genres, Context, and Literacy Practices: Literacy Brokering among Sudanese Refugee Families." *Reading Research Quarterly* 44 (2009) 256–76.

Pettegrew, Larry D. "The Perspicuity of Scripture." *The Master's Seminary Journal* 15 (2004) 209–25.

Pettitt, Thomas. "The Gutenberg Parenthesis: Oral Tradition and Digital Technologies." *CommForum*, April 1, 2010. Online. http://web.mit.edu/comm-forum/forums/gutenberg_parenthesis.html.

Phong, Kimchhoy, and Javier Sola. *Mobile Phones and Internet in Cambodia 2015*. Phnom Penh: Open Institute, Development Innovations, 2015.

Pinker, Robert. *Social Theory and Social Policy*. London: Neinemann Educational, 1971.

Pobee, John S. "Oral Theology and Christian Oral Tradition: Challenge to Our Traditional Archival Concept." *Mission Studies* 6 (1989) 87–93.

Polanyi, Michael. *The Tacit Dimension*. Garden City, NY: Doubleday, 1966.

Ponraj, D. Devasahayam, and Chandon K. Sah. "Communication Bridges to Oral Cultures: A Method that Caused a Breakthrough in Starting Several Church Planting Movements in North India." *International Journal of Frontier Missions* 20 (2003) 28–31.

Porter, Doris. "Using the Vernacular Non-Print Media 'That They May Hear.'" *International Journal of Frontier Missions* 12 (1995) 105–6.

Prahalad, C. K. *The Fortune at the Bottom of the Pyramid*. Upper Saddle River, NJ: Pearson Education, 2009.

Preece, Julia. *Lifelong Learning and Development: A Southern Perspective*. New York: Continuum International, 2009.

Prior, Randall. "Orality: The Not-So-Silent Issue in Mission Theology." *International Bulletin of Missionary Research* 35 (2011) 143–47.

Prince, Raymond. "The 'Brain Fag' Syndrome in Nigerian Students." *Journal of Mental Science* 106 (1960) 559–70.

Quillen, I. James. "An Introduction to Anthropology and Education." In *Education and Anthropology*, edited by G. Spindler, 1–4. Stanford: Stanford University Press, 1995.

Rager, Kathleen B. "Compassion Stress and the Qualitative Researcher." *Qualitative Health Research* 15 (2005) 423–40.

Ramirez-Esparza, Nairan, et al. "Socio-Interactive Practices and Personality in Adult Learners of English with Little Formal Education." *Language Learning* 62 (2012) 541–70.

Rampey, Bobby, et al. *Skills of US Unemployed, Young, and Older Adults in Sharper Focus: Results from the Program for the International Assessment of Adult Competencies (PIAAC) 2012/2014*. Washington, DC: National Center for Education Statistics Institute of Education Sciences (IES), US Department of Education, 2016.

Rao, Nirmala, and Veronica Pearson. "Early Childhood Care and Education in Cambodia." *International Journal of Child Care and Education Policy* 3 (2009) 13–26.

Rao, Shakuntala. "Contemporary Orality: A New Theory for Understanding Speech." *The Florida Communication Journal* 20 (1992) 7–15.

Rasmussen, Susan J. "Revitalizing Shame: Some Reflections of 'Changing Idioms of Shame: Expressions of Disgrace and Dishonour in the Narratives of Turkish Women Living in Denmark.'" *Culture and Psychology* 13 (2007) 231–42.

Raun-Linde, Peggy A. "International Narratives in the Configuration of a Trans-National Model of Education and Development: An Emerging Pedagogy for Cambodia in Partnership with the United States." EdD diss., University of San Francisco, 2002.

Raven, Diederick. "How Not to Explain the Great Divide." *Social Science Information* 40 (2001) 373–409.

Reimer, Jill K. "Local Negotiation of Globalized Educational Discourses: The Case of Child Friendly Schools in Rural Cambodia." PhD diss., University of British Columbia, 2012.

Reimer, Julia. "Learning Strategies and Low-Literacy Hmong Adult Students." *MinneWITESOL Journal* 25 (2008). Online. http://www.minnewitesoljournal.org.

Reinsborough, Patrick, and Doyle Canning. *RE:Imagining Change: How to Use Story-Based Strategy to Win Campaigns, Build Movements, and Change the World.* Oakland: PM, 2010.

Rendell, Luke, et al. "Cognitive Culture: Theoretical and Empirical Insights into Social Learning Strategies." *Trends in Cognitive Sciences* 15 (2011) 68–76.

Reyles, Diego Z. "The Ability to Go About without Shame: A Proposal for Internationally Comparable Indicators of Shame and Humiliation." *Oxford Development Studies* 35 (2007) 405–30.

Rhoads, David. "Biblical Performance Criticism: Performance as Research." *Oral Tradition* 25 (2010) 157–98.

Richardson, Jayson. "Diffusion of Technology Adoption in Cambodia: The Test of a Theory." *International Journal of Education and Development Using Information and Communication Technology* 5 (2009) 151–71.

Rios-Aguilar, Cecilia, et al. "Funds of Knowledge for the Poor and Forms of Capital for the Rich? A Capital Approach to Examining Funds of Knowledge." *Theory and Research in Education* 9 (2011) 163–84.

Rizzolatti, Giacomo, and Laila Graighero. "The Mirror-Neuron System." *Annual Review of Neuroscience* 27 (2004) 169–92.

Robinson, George G. "The Gospel as Story and Evangelism as Story Telling." *Global Missiology* 4 (2012) 1–27.

Robinson-Pant, Anna. "PRA: A New Literacy?" *PLA Notes (IIED London)* 24 (1995) 78–82.

———. "'Why Literacy Matters': Exploring a Policy Perspective on Literacies, Identities, and Social Change." *Journal of Development Studies* 44 (2008) 779–96.

Rodriguez, Gloria M. "Power and Agency in Education: Exploring the Pedagogical Dimensions of Funds of Knowledge." *Review of Research in Education* 37 (2013) 87–120.

Rogers, Alan. "Literacy Comes Second: Working with Groups in Developing Societies." *Development in Practice* 10 (2000) 236–40.

Rogers, Alan, and Brian Street. "Using Ethnographic Approaches for Understanding and Teaching Literacy: Perspectives from Both Developing and Western Contexts." *Jorden Laeser* 10 (2011) 38–47.

Rogoff, Barbara. *Apprenticeship in Thinking: Cognitive Development in Social Context.* New York: Oxford University Press, 1990.

Rogoff, Barbara, et al. "Firsthand Learning through Intent Participation." *Annual Review of Psychology* 54 (2003) 175–203.

Roman, Sarah P. "Illiteracy and Older Adults: Individual and Societal Implications." *Educational Gerontology* 30 (2004) 79–93.

Rosenbloom, Jackie. "Adult Literacy in Cambodia: Research Report." *Pact*, February 2004. Online. http://www.pactcambodia.org/Publications/WORTH_Education/Adult_Literacy_in_Cambodia.pdf.

Rossiter, Marsha. *Narrative and Stories in Adult Teaching and Learning.* ERIC 241. Columbus, OH: ERIC Clearinghouse on Adult Career and Vocational Education, 2002.

———. "A Narrative Approach to Development: Implications for Adult Education." *Adult Education Quarterly* 50 (1999) 56–71.

Rowley, Jennifer. "Where Is the Wisdom That We Have Lost in Knowledge?" *Journal of Documentation* 62 (2006) 251–70.

———. "The Wisdom Hierarchy: Representations of the DIKW Hierarchy." *Journal of Information Science* 33 (2007) 163–80.

Rubin, David C. *Memory in Oral Traditions: The Cognitive Psychology of Epic, Ballads, and Counting-Out Rhymes.* New York: Oxford University Press, 1995.

Rudengren, Jan, and Joakim Ojendal. *Learning by Doing: An Analysis of the Seila Experiences in Cambodia.* Stockholm: Swedish International Development Cooperation Agency (SIDA), 2002.

Rutten, Kris, and Ronald Soetaert. "Narrative and Rhetorical Approaches to Problems of Education: Jerome Bruner and Kenneth Burke Revisited." *Study of the Philosophy of Education* 32 (2013) 327–43.

Ryan, Annette, et al. "Wise Women: Mentoring as Relational Learning in Perinatal Nursing Practice." *Journal of Clinical Nursing* 19 (2010) 183–91.

Rynkiewich, Michael A. "Mission, Hermeneutics, and the Local Church." *Journal of Theological Interpretation* 1 (2007) 47–60.

Salisbury, Thayer. "Testing Narrative Theory." *Evangelical Missions Quarterly* 12 (2004). Online. http://www.emisdirect.com/emq/issue-124/404.

Sample, Tex. *Ministry in an Oral Culture: Living with Will Rogers, Uncle Remus, and Minnie Pearl.* Louisville: Westminster John Knox, 1994.

Sauerberg, Lars Ole. "The Encyclopedia and the Gutenberg Parenthesis." Paper presented at the International Conference on Media in Transition 6: Stone and Papyrus, Storage and Transmission, Massachusetts Institute of Technology, Cambridge, MA, April 2009.

Sbaraini, Alexandra, et al. "How to Do a Grounded Theory Study: A Worked Example of a Study of Dental Practices." *BMC Medical Research Methodology* 11 (2011) 1–10.

Schechner, Richard. "What Is Performance Studies?" *Rupkatha Journal* 5 (2013) 2–11.

Scheff, Thomas J. "Shame in Self and Society." *Society for the Study of Symbolic Interaction* 26 (2003) 239–62.

Schmid, Jeanette. "Reflections on and of Self in South Africa." *Qualitative Social Work* 9 (2010) 169–84.

Schoenhals, Martin. *The Paradox of Power in a People's Republic of China Middle School*. Rev. ed. New York: Routledge, 2015.

Schore, Allan N. "Minds in the Making: Attachment, the Self-Organizing Brain, and Developmentally-Oriented Psychoanalytic Psychotherapy." *British Journal of Psychotherapy* 17 (2001) 299–328.

Schrader, Stuart M. "Performing Narrative: Telling the Story of Theory." *Teaching Education* 15 (2004) 203–14.

Schrage, Michael. "The Relationship Revolution." *Merrill Lynch Forum*, 1997. Online. http://web.archive.org/web/20030602035010/http://www.ml.com/woml/forum/relation3.htm.

Schunk, Dale H. *Learning Theories: An Educational Perspective*. Boston: Pearson, 2012.

Schwartz, Barry. "Practical Wisdom and Organizations." *Research in Organizational Behavior* 31 (2011) 3–23.

Scribner, Sylvia, and Michael Cole. "Cognitive Consequences of Formal and Informal Education." *Science* 182 (1973) 553–59.

Sells, Lisa. "Discipleship Revolution: Avery Willis's Last Dream." *Mission Frontiers*, January 1, 2011. Online. https://www.missionfrontiers.org/issue/article/avery-willis-last-dream.

Selvarajah, C., et al. "The Effect of Cultural Modeling on Leadership Profiling of the Cambodian Manager." *Asia Pacific Business Review* 18 (2012) 1–26.

Sen, Amartya. "Poor, Relatively Speaking." *Oxford Economic Papers, New Series* 35 (1983) 153–69.

Sfard, Anna. "Moving between Discourses: From Learning-as-Acquisition to Learning-as-Participation." *American Institute of Physics Conference Proceedings* 1179 (2009) 55.

———. "On Two Metaphors for Learning and the Dangers of Choosing Just One." *Educational Researcher* 27 (1998) 4–13.

Sheard, David. *An Orality Primer for Missionaries*. Self-published, 2007.

Shelton, Leslie H. "The Heart of Literacy: Transforming School-Induced Shame and Recovering the Competent Self." PhD diss., Union Institute, 2001.

Shinil, Kim. "Learning Perspective in the Asian Viewpoint." Paper presented at the International Adult and Continuing Education Conference, Seoul, Korea, May 1996. Online. http://files.eric.ed.gov/fulltext/ED401407.pdf.

Shirali, Kishwar A. "*Ganga Devi*: A Question of Literacy and Development." *Canadian Woman Studies* 9 (1988) 89–91.

Shuter, Robert. "The Hmong of Laos: Orality, Communication, and Acculturation." In *Intercultural Communication: A Reader*, edited by L. A. Samovar and R. E. Porter, 102–8. 4th ed. Belmont, CA: Wadsworth, 1985.

Siegel, Daniel J. "Daniel J. Siegel: The Power of Mindsight." Lecture delivered for TEDx Talks, October 18, 2009. YouTube Video. 24:20. http://www.youtube.com/watch?v=Nu7wEr8AnHw.

———. *Mindsight: The New Science of Personal Transformation*. New York: Bantam, 2010.

Sienaert, Edgard R. "Marcel Jousse: The Oral Style and the Anthropology of Gesture." *Oral Tradition* 5 (1990) 91–106.

Simmel, Georg. "The Sociological Significance of the 'Stranger.'" In *Introduction to the Science of Sociology*, edited by R. Park and E. Burgess, 322–27. Chicago: University of Chicago Press, 1921.

Simmons, Odis E., and Toni A. Gregory. "Grounded Action: Achieving Optimal and Sustainable Change." *Forum: Qualitative Social Research* 4 (2003) art. 27.

Singerman, Jeff. "Orality Observations among Francophone West African Adults: Storying to Orality." In *Beyond Literate Western Models: Contextualizing Theological Education in Oral Contexts*, edited by Samuel Chiang and Grant Lovejoy, 29–38. Hong Kong: International Orality Network, 2013.

Skilton-Sylvester, Ellen. "Should I Stay or Should I Go? Investigating Cambodian Women's Participation and Investment in Adult ESL Programs." *Adult Education Quarterly* 53 (2002) 9–26.

Slack, James B., et al. *Chronological Bible Storying: An Introduction to the Oral Communication of the Bible*. Johannesburg: International Publications Services, 1996. Online. https://orality.imb.org/files/1/426/Chronological%20Bible%20Storying.pdf.

———. *The Memory and Recall of Stories by Oral Communicators in the Context of Chronological Bible Storying*. Richmond, VA: International Mission Board, 2006.

———. "The Realities of Orality and Literacy in This Century." Paper presented at the Oral Bible Forum, Albuquerque, NM, July 2003.

Slack, James B., and Jim Maroney. *Church Planting Movement Assessment of the Cambodian Baptist Convention*. Richmond, VA: International Mission Board, 2001.

Slater, Michael D., and Donna Rouner. "Entertainment-Education and Elaboration Likelihood: Understanding the Processing of Narrative Persuasion." *Communication Theory* 12 (2002) 173–91.

Smith, Christian. *Moral, Believing Animals: Human Personhood and Culture*. New York: Oxford University Press, 2003.

Smith, Diane Pamela. "Visual Art and Orality." *Dharma Deepika: A South Asian Journal of Missiological Research* 25.11 (2007) 53–74. Online. https://orality.imb.org/files/1/290/Visual%20Art%20and%20Orality.pdf.

Smith, John D. "Worlds Apart: Orality, Literacy, and the Rajasthani Folk *Mahabharata*." *Oral Tradition* 5 (1990) 3–19.

Smith, Matthew L., et al. "Mobile Phones and Expanding Human Capabilities." *Mobile Telephony* 7 (2011) 77–88.

Smither, Edward. "A Celtic Approach to Reaching Oral Learners: A Survey of the Oral and Visual Strategies Used by the Iona Community circa 600–800." *Global Missiology* 1 (2014). Online. http://ojs.globalmissiology.org/index.php/english/article/viewFile/1715/3806.

Smith-Hefner, Nancy J. "Education, Gender, and Generational Conflict among Khmer Refugees." *Anthropology and Education Quarterly* 24 (1993) 135–58.

———. "Ethnicity and the Force of Faith: Christian Conversion among Khmer Refugees." *Anthropological Quarterly* 67 (1994) 24–38.

Snyder, Benson R. *The Hidden Curriculum*. New York: Alfred A. Knopf, 1971.

Snyder, Howard R. "A Case Study in Defining Literacy: David Olson's Journey from the Great Divide to the Great Beyond." *Interchange* 21 (1990) 1–12.

So, Damon. "How Should a Theological Institution Prepare Students/Leaders Who Will Go Out into the Field to Train Local People (Storytellers) to Tell Bible Stories

Effectively?" In *Beyond Literate Western Models: Contextualizing Theological Education in Oral Contexts,* edited by Samuel Chiang and Grant Lovejoy, 29–38. Hong Kong: International Orality Network, 2013.

Sogaard, Viggo. "The Emergence of Audio-Scriptures in Church and Mission." *Mission Frontiers* 12 (1995) 71–75.

Sopheak, Keng C., and Thomas Clayton. "Schooling in Cambodia." In *Going to School in East Asia,* edited by G. Postiglione et al., 41–60. Westport, CT: Greenwood, 2007.

Soukup, Paul A. "In Commemoration: Walter Ong and the State of Theology." *Theological Studies* 73 (2012) 824–40.

Sparkes, A. C. "Autoethnography and Narratives of Self: Reflections on Criteria in Action." *Sociology of Sport Journal* 17 (2000) 21–43.

Spindler, George D. "Three Categories of Cultural Knowledge Useful in Doing Cultural Therapy." *Anthropology and Education Quarterly* 30 (1999) 466–72.

Spindler, George, and Louise Spindler. *Fifty Years of Anthropology and Education: 1950–2000: A Spindler Anthology.* Mahwah, NJ: Taylor & Francis, 2009.

Springer, Simon. "Illegal Evictions? Overwriting Possession and Orality with Law's Violence in Cambodia." *Journal of Agrarian Change* 13 (2013) 520–46.

Stahl, Janet. "Telling Our Stories Well: Creating Memorable Images and Shaping Our Identity." *Missiology: An International Review* 38 (2010) 161–71.

Starcher, Richard L. "Qualitative Research in Missiological Study and Practice." *Dharma Deepika* (July–December 2011) 54–63.

Starling, Allan. "Audio-Communications and the Progress of the Gospel." *International Journal of Frontier Missions* 12 (1995) 77–79.

Steffen, Tom A. "Chronological Communication of the Gospel Goes from Country to City." Paper presented to the Evangelical Missiological Society, Southwest, March 18, 2011. Online. http://www.chiang-mai-orality.net/resources/Chronological.pdf.

———. "Chronological Practices and Possibilities in the Urban World." *Global Missiology* 4 (2013). Online. http://ojs.globalmissiology.org/index.php/english/article/view/1215/2797.

———. "Foundational Roles of Symbol and Narrative in the (Re)Construction of Reality and Relationships." *Missiology: An International Review* 26 (1998) 477–94.

———. "My Journey from Propositional to Narrative Evangelism." *Evangelical Missions Quarterly* 45 (2005) 458–64. Online. http://www.emqonline.com.

———. "Orality Comes of Age: The Maturation of a Movement." *International Journal of Frontier Missiology* 31 (2014) 139–47.

———. *Passing the Baton: Church Planting That Empowers.* La Habra, CA: Center for Organizational & Ministry Development, 1997.

———. "Pedagogical Conversions: From Propositions to Story and Symbol." *Missiology: An International Review* 38 (2010) 141–57.

———. *Reconnecting God's Story to Ministry: Cross-Cultural Storytelling at Home and Abroad.* La Mirada, CA: Center for Organizational and Ministry Development, 1996.

———. *Reconnecting God's Story to Ministry: Cross-Cultural Storytelling at Home and Abroad.* Pasadena, CA: William Carey, 2005.

———. "Socialization among the Ifugao: Guidelines for Curriculum Development." *International Journal of Frontier Missions* 14 (1997) 191–97.

———. "Storying the Storybook to Tribals: A Philippines Perspective of the Chronological Teaching Model." *International Journal of Frontier Missions* 12 (1995) 99–104.

———. "Tracking the Orality Movement: Some Implications for Twenty-First Century Missions." *Lausanne Global Analysis* 3 (2014) 21–24.

———. "What if? . . . Rethinking Theological Education." *Mission of God, Columbia Internationl University* (blog), April 22, 2014. Online. http://www.ciumissionofgod.org/blog/what-if-rethinking-theological-education.

Steffen, Tom A., and James O. Terry. "The Sweeping Story of Scripture Taught through Time." *Missiology: An International Review* 35 (2007) 315–35.

Stephens, Greg J., et al. "Speaker-Listener Neural Coupling Underlies Successful Communication." *Proceedings of the National Academy of Sciences of the United States of America (PNAS)* 107 (2010) 14425–30.

Sternberg, Robert J. "What Is Wisdom and How Can We Develop It?" *The Annals of the American Academy of Political and Social Science* 591 (2004) 164–74.

Sterne, Jonathan. "The Theology of Sound: A Critique of Orality." *Canadian Journal of Communication* 36 (2011) 207–26.

Stock, Brian. *Listening for the Text: On the Uses of the Past*. Philadelphia: University of Pennsylvania Press, 1996.

Street, Brian V. "Autonomous and Ideological Models of Literacy: Approaches from New Literacy Studies." *EASA Media Anthropology Network, E-Seminar* 9 (2006). Online. http://www.philbu.net/media-anthropology/street_newliteracy.pdf.

———. *Literacy in Theory and Practice*. New York: Cambridge University Press, 1995.

———. *Social Literacies: Critical Approaches to Literacy in Development, Ethnography, and Education*. New York: Routledge, 1995.

Strothmann, S. "Narrative Persuasion: How Emotional Appeal of Narratives and Source Characteristics Influence Belief Change." MA thesis, Maastricht University, 2009.

Stygles, Justin. "Eliminating Shame in Reading Instruction." *Literacy Today* 33 (2016) 10–11.

Suarez, David, and Jeffery H. Marshall. "Capacity in the NGO Sector: Results from a National Survey in Cambodia." *International Society for Third-Sector Research: Voluntas* 25 (2014) 176–200.

Sundersingh, Julian. "Toward a Media-Based Translation: Communicating Biblical Scriptures to Non-Literates in Rural Tamil Nadu, India." PhD diss., Fuller Theological Seminary, 1999.

Swap, Walter, et al. "Using Mentoring and Storytelling to Transfer Knowledge in the Workplace." *Journal of Management Information Systems* 18 (2001) 95–114.

Swearingen, C. Jan. "Oral Hermeneutics during the Transition to Literacy: The Contemporary Debate." *Cultural Anthropology* 1 (1986) 138–56.

Sweeney, Amin. *A Full Hearing: Orality and Literacy in the Malay World*. Berkeley: University of California Press, 1987.

Tan, Charlene. "Education Reforms in Cambodia: Issues and Concerns." *Educational Research for Policy and Practice* 6 (2007) 15–24.

———. "Educational Policy Trajectories in an Era of Globalization: Singapore and Cambodia." *Prospects* 40 (2010) 465–80.

Tangney, June Price, and Ronda L. Dearing. *Shame and Guilt*. New York: Guilford, 2002.

Tanner, Kathleen. "Adult Dyslexia and the 'Conundrum of Failure.'" *Disability and Society* 24 (2009) 785–97.

Tarone, Elaine. "Second Language Acquisition by Low-Literate Learners: An Under-Studied Population." *Language Teaching* 43 (2010) 75–83.

Taylor, Charles. *Sources of the Self: The Making of the Modern Identity.* New York: Cambridge University Press, 2006.
Taylor, Maurice, et al. "Collaborative Practices in Adult Literacy Programs." *Adult Basic Education* 13 (2003) 81–99.
Taylor, Stephen C. R. "A Study of the Relationship between Christian Education and the Belief System of Thai Christians." DMin thesis, International Theological Seminary, 1999.
Tek, V. "Barriers to Implementing Child-Friendly School Program in Svay Rieng Province." MA thesis, Royal University of Phnom Penh, 2008.
Terry, J. O. "In Defense of 'Storying.'" Richmond, VA: International Mission Board, 2004.
Than, Bunly. "The Status of Oral Folktale Narration in Contemporary Preah Theat Thmor Da Village." MA thesis, Royal University of Phnom Penh, 2004.
Thao, Yer Jeff. "The Voices of Mong Elders: Living, Knowing, Teaching, and Learning Within an Oral Tradition." PhD diss., Claremont Graduate University, 2002.
Thayer, Joseph. "Paradidomi." *NAS New Testament Greek Lexicon*, 1999. Online. http://www.biblestudytools.com/lexicons/greek/nas/paradidomi.html.
Thigpen, Lynn. "The Oral Bible School." Online. http://theoralbibleschool.com.
Thomas, Rebecca A. "Confronting Shame in the Culture, the Church, and the Clinic." PhD diss., Regent University, 2002.
Thompson, Ashley. *Calling the Souls: A Cambodian Ritual Text.* Phnom Penh: Reyum, 2005.
Thompson, LaNette W. "Discipleship at Arm's Length? Not Possible." *Lausanne World Pulse Archives* (blog), June 2011. Online. http://www.lausanneworldpulse.com/themedarticles.php/1417/06-2011?pg+all.
———. "Helping Adults Learn: Lessons from Andragogy and the Challenge of Context." In *Beyond Literate Western Models: Contextualizing Theological Education in Oral Contexts*, edited by Samuel Chiang and Grant Lovejoy, 104–12. Hong Kong: International Orality Network, 2013.
———. "The Nonliterate and the Transfer of Knowledge in West Africa." MA thesis, University of Texas at Arlington, 1998.
———. "Perceptions of Teaching Nonliterate Adults in Oral Cultures: A Modified Delphi Study." PhD diss., Baylor University, 2015.
Thornton, Phil. "Constructivism, Cross-Cultural Teaching, and Orality." *Orality Journal* 3 (2014) 31–40.
———. "Orality and Theological Education in Latin American Culture." In *Beyond Literate Western Practices: Continuing Conversations in Orality and Theological Education*, edited by Samuel Chiang and Grant Lovejoy, 55–62. Hong Kong: International Orality Network, 2014.
Timma, Hilary. "Experiencing the Workplace: Shaping Worker Identities through Assessment, Work and Learning." *Studies in Continuing Education* 29 (2007) 163–79.
Tisdell, Elizabeth J. "The Role of Spirituality in Culturally Relevant and Transformative Adult Education." *Adult Learning* 12 (2001) 13–14.
———. "Spirituality and Adult Learning." *New Directions for Adult and Continuing Education* 119 (2008) 27–36.
———. "Spirituality and Emancipatory Adult Education in Women Adult Educators for Social Change." *Adult Education Quarterly* 50 (2000) 308–35.

Tisdell, Elizabeth J., and Ann L. Swartz. "Adult Education and the Pursuit of Wisdom: New Directions for Adult and Continuing Education." *Jossey-Bass ACE Single Issue Adult and Continuing Education* 131 (2011).

Tisdell, Elizabeth J., and Derise E. Tolliver. "The Role of Spirituality in Cultural Relevant and Transformative Adult Education." *Adult Learning* 12 (2001) 13–14.

Tope, Daniel, et al. "The Benefits of Being There: Evidence from the Literature on Work." *Journal of Contemporary Ethnography* 34 (2005) 470–93.

Tovar, Dora A. "Functional Illiteracy in the Workplace: Impact on Worker Health and Safety." Doctor of Science diss., University of Massachusetts Lowell, 2013.

Townsend, Katharine C., and Benedict T. McWhirter. "Connectedness: A Review of the Literature with Implications for Counseling, Assessment, and Research." *Journal of Counseling and Development* 83 (2005) 191–201.

Tremblay, Gaetan. "From Marshall McLuhan to Harold Innis, or from the Global Village to the World Empire." *Canadian Journal of Communication* 37 (2012) 561–75.

Tsang, Nai Ming. "Orality and Literacy: Their Relevance to Social Work." *Journal of Social Work* 7 (2007) 51–70.

Turner, Victor. "Liminal to Liminoid, in Play, Flow, and Ritual: An Essay in Comparative Symbology." *The Rice University Studies* 60 (1974) 53–92.

Un, Leang. (2012). "A Comparative Study of Education and Development in Cambodia and Uganda from Their Civil Wars to the Present." PhD diss., University of Amsterdam, 2012.

United Nations (UN). "Transforming Our World: The 2030 Agenda for Sustainable Development." 2015. Online. http://www.un.org/ga/search/view_doc.asp?symbol=A/RES/70/1&Lang=E.

United Nations Development Program (UNDP). "About Cambodia." 2013. Online. https://web.archive.org/web/20130821021354/http://www.kh.undp.org/content/cambodia/en/home/countryinfo.

———. "About Cambodia." 2016. Online. http://www.kh.undp.org/content/Cambodia/en/home/countryinfo.

United Nations Educational, Scientific, and Cultural Organization (UNESCO). *Education and Fragility in Cambodia*. Paris: International Institute for Educational Planning (IIEP), 2011.

———. *Global Education Digest 2011: Comparing Education Statistics across the World*. Montreal: UNESCO Institute for Statistics, 2011.

———. *The Hamburg Declaration on Adult Learning*. Hamburg: UNESCO Institute For Education, 1997. Online. http://www.unesco.org/education/uie/confintea/declaeng.htm.

United Nations Educational, Scientific, and Cultural Organization (UNESCO) Institute for Lifelong Learning. *Harnessing the Potential of ICTs for Literacy Teaching and Learning*. Hamburg, Germany: UNESCO Institute for Lifelong Learning, 2014.

———. *Second Global Report on Adult Learning and Education*. Hamburg, Germany: UNESCO Institute for Lifelong Learning, 2013.

———. *Second Global Report on Adult Learning and Education, Rethinking Literacy: Summary and Recommendations*. Hamburg, Germany: UNESCO Institute for Lifelong Learning, 2013.

United Nations Educational, Scientific, and Cultural Organization (UNESCO) Institute for Statistics. *The Next Generation of Literacy Statistics: Implementing the Literacy Assessment and Monitoring Programme (LAMP)*. Montreal, Canada: UNESCO Institute for Statistics, 2009.

Urquhart, Cathy. "An Encounter with Grounded Theory: Tackling the Practical and Philosophical Issues." In *Qualitative Research in IS: Issues and Trends*, edited by E. Trauth, 104–40. Hershey, PA: Idea Group, 2001.

———. "The Evolving Nature of Grounded Theory Method: The Case of the Information Systems Discipline." In *The SAGE Handbook of Grounded Theory*, edited by A. Bryant and K. Charmaz, 339–59. Thousand Oaks, CA: SAGE, 2007.

Vautrot, Leaona, D. "Why Don't They Come? Perceptions of Illiterate Adults in an Appalachian Mountain Region Regarding Nonparticipation in Adult Literacy Programs." PhD diss., University of New Orleans, 2004.

Velez-Ibanez, Carlos G., and James B. Greenberg. "Formation and Transformation of Funds of Knowledge among US-Mexican Households." *Anthropology and Education Quarterly* 23 (1992) 313–35.

Venkatesan, Soumhya. "Learning to Weave; Weaving to Learn . . . What?" *Journal of the Royal Anthropological Institute* 16 (2010) Supplement 158–75.

Ventura, Paulo, et al. "Schooling in Western Culture Promotes Context-Free Processing." *Journal of Experimental Child Psychology* 100 (2008) 79–88.

Verghese, Mary. "Oral Bible Story Telling Training at New India Bible Seminary, Kerala, India." In *Beyond Literate Western Models: Contextualizing Theological Education in Oral Contexts*, edited by Samuel Chiang and Grant Lovejoy, 49–58. Hong Kong: International Orality Network, 2013.

Vinogradov, Patsy, and Martha Bigelow. "Using Oral Language Skills to Build on the Emerging Literacy of Adult English Learners." *CAELA (Center for Applied Linguistics) Network Brief.* Washington, DC: CAELA, 2010. Online. http://www.cal.org/caelanetwork.

Vitz, Paul C. "The Use of Stories in Moral Development: New Psychological Reasons for an Old Education Method." *American Psychologist* 45 (1990) 709–20.

Vliet, K. J. van. "Shame and Resilience in Adulthood: A Grounded Theory Study." *Journal of Counseling Psychology* 55 (2008) 233–45.

Vries, Lourens de. "New Guinea Communities without Writing and Views of Primary Orality." *Anthropos* 98 (2003) 397–405.

Vygotsky, L. S. *Educational Psychology.* Boca Raton, FL: St. Lucie, 1997.

Wafler, Stan. "The Interrelationship of Orality and Bible Translation." Unpublished paper, 2006. Online. https://reachingandteaching.org/downloads/Interrelationship.pdf.

Wagner, Julie, et al. "Training Cambodian Village Health Support Guides in Diabetes Prevention: Effects on Guides' Knowledge and Teaching Activities over 6 Months." *International Journal of Behavior Medicine* 23 (2016) 162–67.

Walker, Karen. "Cambodia's Postgraduate Students: Emerging Patterns and Trends." *ASEAN Journal of Teaching and Learning in Higher Education* 4 (2012) 1–13.

Walker, Maureen, and Wendy B. Rosen. *How Connections Heal: Stories from Relational-Cultural Therapy.* New York: Guilford, 2004.

Walker, Phil. "Africa Theological Seminary." In *Beyond Literate Western Models: Contextualizing Theological Education in Oral Contexts*, edited by Samuel Chiang and Grant Lovejoy, 39–48. Hong Kong: International Orality Network, 2013.

Walker, Robert, et al. "Poverty in Global Perspective: Is Shame a Common Denominator?" *Journal of Social Policy* 42 (2013) 215–33.

Wall, Sarah. "Easier Said than Done: Writing an Autoethnography." *International Journal of Qualitative Methods* 7 (2008) 38–53.

Wall, Theresa, and M. Leong. "The Tradition Continues: Sharing Knowledge to Serve LESLLA Learners." In *Low-Educated Second Language and Literacy Acquisition: Proceedings of the 5th Symposium Banff 2009*, edited by T. Wall and M. Leong, 1–2. Calgary, Canada: Bow Valley College, 2010. Online. http://www.leslla.org/files/resources/Conference_Proceedings_FINAL_Aug12.pdf.

Walter, Skip. "Knowledge versus Information." *Extreme Productivity by Design* (blog), January 2, 2008. Online. http://factor10x.blogspot.com/2008/01/knowledge-versus-information.html.

Walton, John H., and D. Brent Sandy. *The Lost World of Scripture: Ancient Literary Culture and Biblical Authority*. Downers Grove, IL: InterVarsity, 2013.

Waters, LaTonya M. "Exploration of the Lived Experiences of Illiterate African American Adults." EdD diss., Lamar University, 2009.

Waters, LaTonya M., and Sandra Harris. "Exploration of the Lived Experiences of Illiterate African American Adults." *The Western Journal of Black Studies* 33 (2009) 250–58.

Watkins, Chris, and Peter Mortimore. "Pedagogy: What Do We Know?" In *Understanding Pedagogy and Its Impact on Learning*, edited by P. Mortimore, 1–19. Thousand Oaks, CA: SAGE, 1999.

Watson, Jill A. "Interpreting across the Abyss: A Hermeneutic Exploration of Initial Literacy Development by High School English Language Learners with Limited Formal Schooling." PhD diss., University of Minnesota, 2010.

Weber, Hans R. *The Communication of the Gospel to Illiterates: Based on a Missionary Experience in Indonesia*. London: SCM, 1957.

Weerstra, Hans M. "Editorial: Reading the Non-Literate Peoples of the World." *International Journal of Frontier Missions* 12 (1995) 58.

Weinstein, Gail. "Literacy and Second Language Acquisition: Issues and Perspectives." *TESOL Quarterly* 18 (1984) 471–84.

Weiss, Barry D., et al. "Literacy Education as Treatment for Depression in Patients with Limited Literacy and Depression: A Randomized Controlled Trial." *Journal of General Internal Medicine* 21 (2006) 823–28.

Welch, Edward T. *Shame Interrupted: How God Lifts the Pain of Worthlessness and Rejection*. Greensboro, NC: New Growth, 2001.

Wendland, Ernst R. "Towards an 'Oratorical' Bible Translation in a Bantu Language: With Special Reference to Ezekiel's Oracle of the 'Dry Bones' In Chichewa." Paper presented at the World Congress on Religion (SBL International), Cape Town, South Africa, July 2000. Online. https://www.academia.edu/8951405/Towards_an_Oratorical_Bible_Translation_in_a_Bantu_Language_With_special_reference_to_Ezekiel_s_oracle_of_the_dry_bones_in_Chichewa.

Werner, David B., and Bill Bower. *Helping Health Workers Learn*. 13th ed. Berkeley: Hesperian Foundation, 2005.

West, Russell W. "The Re-Eventing of Theological Education: Toward a Pedagogy of Leadership Formation in the Verbomoteur Mode." Paper presented at the International Orality Network Forum, Asbury Theological Seminary, Wilmore, KY, April 2014.

Wiher, Hannes. "Worldview and Oral Preference Learners and Leaders." In *Beyond Literate Western Practices: Continuing Conversations in Orality and Theological Education*, edited by Samuel Chiang and Grant Lovejoy, 109–26. Hong Kong: International Orality Network, 2014.

Williams, Edward. *Poems, Lyric and Pastoral*. London: J. Nichols, 1794.
Willis, Avery, and James Greeneish. "What Do You Think, Mr. Guttenberg? The Challenges Print Evangelism Ministries Face in Meeting the Needs of Oral Cultures." *Lausanne World Pulse Archives* (blog), October 2006. Online. https://www.lausanneworldpulse.com/themedarticles-php/507/10-2006.
Willis, Peter. "Scheherazade's Secret: The Power of Stories and the Desire to Learn." *Australian Journal of Adult Learning* 51 (2011) 110–22.
Wilson, John D. "Let the Earth Hear His Voice." *International Journal of Frontier Missions* 14 (1997) 177–82.
———. "Scripture in an Oral Culture: The Yali of Irian Jaya." Adaptation of MTh diss., University of Edinburgh, 1999. Online. http://papuaweb.org/dlib/s123/wilson/mth.pdf.
———. "What It Takes to Reach People in Oral Cultures." *Evangelical Missions Quarterly* 27 (1991) 154–59.
Winger, Thomas M. "Orality as the Key to Understanding Apostolic Proclamation in the Epistles." ThD diss., Concordia Seminary, 1997.
———. "The Spoken Word: What's Up with Orality?" *Concordia Journal* 29 (2003) 133–51.
Wiseman, Theresa. "A Concept Analysis of Empathy." *Journal of Advance Nursing* 23 (1996) 1162–67.
Woerkum, C. M. J. van. "Orality and the Process of Writing." *Journal of Technical Writing and Communication* 37 (2007) 183–201.
Wolcott, Harry F. "On Ethnographic Intent." In *Interpretive Ethnography of Education at Home and Abroad*, edited by G. Spindler and L. Spindler, 37–57. Hillsdale, NJ: Lawrence Erlbaum, 1987.
Wolf, Michael S., et al. "Patients' Shame and Attitudes toward Discussing the Results of Literacy Screening." *Journal of Health Communication* 12 (2007) 721–32.
Wong, Ying, and Jeanne Tsai. "Cultural Models of Shame and Guilt." In *Handbook of Self-Conscious Emotions*, edited by J. Tracy et al., 210–20. New York: Guilford, 2007.
Wootton, Janet. "The Freedom of the Spirit: Praying in an Oral Tradition." *International Congregational Journal* 2 (2002) 104–21.
World Bank Group. "Cambodia: Projects and Programs." Online. https://www.worldbank.org/en/country/cambodia.
World Concern. "Khmer Leadership: Ancient Tradition, Current Practices." *Ratanak International*. Online. http://www.ratanak.org/resources/paper_KhmerLeadership.pdf.
Wray, David. "Teaching Literacy: The Foundations of Good Practice." *Education* 27 (1999) 53–59.
Wydick, Bruce, and Travis J. Lybbert. "Poverty, Aspirations, and the Economics of Hope." Paper presented at the Economics of Global Poverty Conference, Gordon College, Wenham, MA, 2015.
Yackley, Luke E. "Storytelling: A Key to Adult Learning." EdD diss., University of Delaware, 2006.
Yale University Genocide Studies Program. "Cambodian Genocide Program." *Genocide Studies Program*. Online. http://gsp.yale.edu/case-studies/cambodian-genocide-program.

Yoakum, Stuart T. "The Spoken Word: God, Scripture, and Orality in Missions." PhD diss., Southern Baptist Theological Seminary, 2014.

Young, H. Peyton. "Innovation Diffusion in Heterogeneous Populations: Contagion, Social Influence, and Social Learning." *The American Economic Review* 99 (2009) 1899–924. Online. http://www.jstor.org/stable/25592541.

Yuksel, Sedat. "The Role of Hidden Curricula on the Resistance Behavior of Undergraduate Students in Psychological Counseling Guidance at a Turkish University." *Asia Pacific Education Review* 7 (2006) 94–107.

Zahniser, A. H. Mathias. *Symbol and Ceremony: Making Disciples across Cultures.* Monrovia, CA: MARC, 1997.

Zepp, Raymond. "Perceptions of Leadership in Three Professions in Cambodia." *International Journal of Business and Social Science* 2 (2011) 233–37.

Zhou, Jiangyuan. "The Effects of Reciprocal Imitation on Teacher-Student Relationships and Student Learning Outcomes." *Mind, Brain, and Education* 6 (2012) 66–73.

Ziegahn, Linda. "The Formation of Literacy Perspective." In *Adult Learning in the Community,* edited by R. Fellenz and G. Conti, 1–29. Bozeman, MT: Kellogg Center for Adult Learning Research, 1990.

Author Index

Ackoff, Russell, 69–71
Alkire, Sabina, 166
Arrington, Aminta, 28, 33, 44, 46–47, 118, 139, 164
Ayres, David, 6, 8, 20–21, 27–28

Bantebya-Kyomuhendo, Grace, 165, 167, 193
Benedict, Ruth, 132
Berger, Peter, 123, 125, 184
Bigelow, Martha, 8, 30
Bit, Seanglim, 25
Botha, Pieter, 10, 32–33, 48, 115, 169
Buber, Martin, 99, 184, 192

Castro-Calda, Alexandre, 56
Cheng, I-Hsuan, 6, 23–24
Chiang, Samuel, 47, 51–53
Chifungo, Davidson, 53
Childs, Carla, 161, 186
Compain, Alice, 28
Condelli, Larry, 3–4, 33, 49
Coomaraswamy, Ananda and Rama, 108, 171
Courtney, Jane, 6–7, 13, 21–24, 192
Creswell, John, 15, 61–62, 66, 72, 75–76

Dehaene, Stanislas, 33, 112, 117–18
DeCapua, Andrea, 3, 49, 51, 142, 179
DeSilva, David, 190–91

Diamond, S., 125–26

Ebihara, May, 26

Fanta-Vagenshtein, Yarden, 6, 56, 114, 139, 143
Fasheh, Munir, 39, 57
Fingeret, Arlene, 6, 113, 171
Finnegan, Ruth, 39, 41, 156
Foley, John, 5, 30, 32
Furniss, Graham, 32, 115, 125, 155–56

Gaskins, Suzanne, 120–22
Gee, James, 4, 128, 197
Georges, Jason, 168, 190
Glaser, Barney, 15, 63, 69–71, 73, 76
Goody, Jack, 30, 32, 35, 115
Gravelle, Maggie, 6, 13, 21–22, 24, 192
Greenfield, Patricia, 161, 186
Greenberg, James, 103, 161

Hasson, Uri, 42, 146, 159
Havelock, Eric, 30, 32, 35–37, 44
Heath, Shirley, 34, 40, 54
Hiebert, Paul, 42, 109
Hvitfeldt, Christina, 45, 142, 179

Illeris, Knud, 11
Illich, Ivan, 127, 192
Innis, Harold, 32, 35–36, 144, 147, 155

Author Index

Jacob, Judith, 19, 27
Jarvis, Peter, 9, 50, 124
Johnson, Jean, 28–29
Jousse, Marcel, 44, 139, 156

Keysser, Christian, 44, 46, 53
Klem, Herbert, 7, 32–33, 48, 51–52, 56, 112, 184,
Knight, Shirlee-ann, 59, 61, 67, 71
Knowles, Malcolm, 9, 142

Ladson-Billings, Gloria, 179, 182
Lewis, Helen, 133–34
Li, Guofang, 33, 35
Lord, Albert, 30, 32
Lovejoy, Grant, 25, 40, 43, 47, 51–53, 57
Luckmann, Thomas, 101, 125, 127, 184
Luria, Aleksandr, 30
Lybbert, Travis, 100, 136, 141, 154

Maddox, Brian, 39, 183
Madinger, Charles, 11, 44, 47, 51, 146, 163
Malina, Bruce, 190
Marshall, Helaine, 3, 49, 51, 142, 179
Matthews, Brett, 19, 25, 31
Mayers, Marvin, 110, 188–89
Mazamisa, Welile, 125, 159, 171
McIlwain, Trevor, 43, 52–53
McLuhan, Marshall, 30, 38, 144
Medhi, Indrani, 91, 170, 173
Meek, Esther, 180, 182
Merriam, Sharan, 6, 56, 63, 77, 110, 142–43, 162–63, 170
Moll, Luis, 103–4, 110
Moon, Jay, 4, 7, 46, 147, 179
Motty, Bauta, 39, 117

Narayan, Deepa, 133, 166
Needham, Susan, 22, 23
Neyrey, Jerome, 133, 190

Ong, Walter, 4, 30–31, 35–37, 41, 51, 57, 123, 127, 139, 157–58, 170, 197
Orenstein, Myrna, 132, 163

Paradise, Ruth, 126, 139
Parker, Veronica, 2–3, 11–12, 35, 57, 110, 144, 193
Parker, William, 142, 163
Parry, Milman, 30
Peristiany, J. G., 133, 190–91

Reimer, Jill, 6, 11, 22, 24, 26
Rogers, Alan, 142, 170
Rogoff, Barbara, 114, 126, 139

Shuter, Robert, 38, 119, 144
Slack, James, 11, 14, 29, 41
Spindler, George, 161, 179
Steffen, Tom, 10, 33, 42–43, 48, 51–53
Strauss, 15, 63, 69, 76
Street, Brian, 5, 38, 172
Stock, Brian, 32–33, 112
Swearingen, Jan, 41, 53

Tan, Charlene, 23–24
Terry, James, 43, 53, 146
Thompson, LaNette, 5, 127

Ventura, Paulo, 126, 157
Vries, Lourens de, 32–33, 37–38

Watson, Jill, 7, 8, 30, 57, 179, 197, 203
Watt, Ian, 30, 32, 35, 115
Weber, Hans, 48 52, 56, 183, 186
West, Russell, 4, 156, 186
Wrigley, Heide, 3–4, 33, 49
Wydick, Bruce, 100, 136, 141, 154

Zahniser, Mathias, 33, 47

Subject Index

abyss, 35, 57, 63, 109, 197
Adults with Limited Formal Education (ALFE), 6, 28, 34, 79, 101–163, 174, 183, 187, 191
ALFE ways of learning, 61, 83, 86, 89, 91, 93, 100, 107, 130, 148, 158, 168
anthropology, 31, 34, 37, 103, 132, 137, 153, 156, 177–78, 182, 189–91, 203
applied orality, 7, 42, 47–48, 51, 57
aspirational hope, 141, 147, 154
Augustine, Saint, 183, 187
autoethnography, 103, 203–5
autonomous model of literacy, 38–39

biblical oral pedagogy, 53
biblical storytelling, 42
Buddhism, 18, 20, 22, 60, 64, 82, 96, 115, 122, 140–41, 147

Cambodia, 1–29, 58–67, 81
central understanding, 62–63, 68–80, 98–101, 108, 130, 146, 149, 153
ceremonies, 44, 46, 47
chasm, 2, 63, 172, 197
child-friendly pedagogies, 22
Chronological Bible Storying, 7, 11, 29, 42–43

communication, 10, 32, 38, 42, 46–48, 57, 109, 112, 115–16, 121–22, 139, 144, 159, 198
complex construct, 15, 29, 31, 58, 61
conceptual framework, 15, 29, 33–34, 54–55, 58–61, 77, 83, 87
connected learners, 151–57, 170, 176–86, 198
connected learning, 100–148, 152, 163, 177, 183, 215, 218
connected learning schematic, 101, 146, 148, 153, 177, 215, 218
connection, 100–124, 130–76, 189–98, 204
contemporary orality, 41, 116, 181
Contextual Constructs Model (CCM), 59, 67
conundrum of failure, 132, 163
culturally appropriate pedagogy, 179
culturally relevant pedagogy, 179
cultural therapy, 180

Data-information-knowledge-wisdom (DIKW) hierarchy, 69–74
default processing style/learning system, 101, 123, 126, 153, 157–58
depression, 196
digital orality, 116, 181
dignity, 71, 87, 94, 100, 133, 136–37, 151, 153, 167, 187, 190, 193

Subject Index

disconnection, 107, 114, 133, 138, 151, 189
donor playground, 21
dyslexia, 85, 163, 177–78, 182, 185

emic understanding, 35, 44, 62, 64, 65, 75
empathetic *Verstehen*, 149–52
epistemology, 34–35, 41, 61, 129, 197
ethnodoxology, 28, 33, 46
ethnography, 6, 55, 58, 60, 64–66, 77–78, 142, 195
ethnopoetics, 32, 47

faith/faith communities, 28, 44, 47, 60, 65, 81–82, 96, 100, 112, 115, 140–41, 147, 150, 154, 163–65, 173–74, 177, 183–88, 190, 198,
folktales, 27–28
functional illiteracy, 11, 38, 41, 182, 195
funds of knowledge, 101, 103–114, 141, 147, 169, 197

global inadequacy, 132
grace, 165, 175, 183, 187, 190–91
Great Divide, 30, 39, 41, 115, 157
grounded theory, 13, 15, 62–78, 149, 153, 173

hegemony, 5, 8, 22, 119, 162, 176
hidden curriculum, 50, 124, 127, 178
holistic, 4, 23, 44, 61, 76, 102, 105, 126, 128, 134, 142–43, 148–49, 153, 156–58, 163–64, 169, 177, 192
honor, 100, 133–37, 151, 153–54, 165–68, 176, 183, 187–90, 192, 198
Hmong, 38–39, 106–7, 112–13, 119, 142, 144
hymns, 28, 44, 118, 139, 141, 164

illiterate, 2–3, 6, 11, 24–26, 31, 35–40, 44, 47, 55–57, 72, 109, 113, 139, 170–73, 193–96
imitation, 101, 108, 117, 120–22
inequity, 8, 73, 176, 203, 209–210
incidental learners, 80, 85
International Orality Network (ION), 3, 7, 33, 51

Killing Fields, 17
Kru (teacher/healer), 18–19
Khmer, 12, 16, 60, 75, 81, 159, 172, 199–201
Khmer Rouge, 13, 17, 27–28, 83, 84

learner-centered, 22–23, 152, 176–79, 197
learner-directed, 119
learning, 9, 22, 29, 34–35, 54–61, 79, 81, 100, 194–95
learning disabilities, 85, 131–32, 151, 153–54, 157, 160–65, 168–69, 176–86, 192, 195
learning Quadrants, 108–119, 146–47, 157, 169, 178, 180–83
Least Developed Countries, 2
lifelong learning, 12–13, 19, 21, 82, 97, 128, 148, 174, 194–97
Lisu, 28, 44, 47, 118, 139, 164
literacy, 2–8, 10, 24–28, 30–45, 49, 51, 55, 57, 93–94, 112, 115, 117–19, 122, 139, 142, 154–58, 162, 169–71, 176, 180, 183, 186, 191–98
liturgical literacy, 111, 164
Low-Educated Second Language and Literacy Acquisition (LESLLA), 3, 49
low literacy, 10, 26, 31, 49, 134

maintenance learners, 81
marginalization, 137, 162, 193, 197
mastery learning, 144
Mull gay (watching to learn), 86, 88, 108, 119
Mutually Adaptive Learning Paradigm (MALP), 51, 179

narrative, 7, 9–11, 18, 27, 42–44, 47, 53, 91, 146, 205
no failure learning, 153, 160–61, 192
non-formal education, 10, 21, 25, 158
nonliterate, 5–6, 56, 197
non-readers, 5, 7, 25, 35, 41, 44, 49, 51, 110, 145, 152, 164, 193

Subject Index 267

non-western ways of learning and knowing, 13, 16, 56, 121, 143, 168
noticing regard, 180, 182

observation, 50, 102, 107, 117–28, 159, 182
oral learners, 4–5, 7–8, 10, 12, 13, 29, 35–36, 40, 43, 45, 48–49, 53, 61, 64, 73, 94, 145, 147, 156, 177, 185, 198
oral pedagogy, 10, 53
oral preference learner, 156
The Oral Style, 44, 139
oral theology, 46
oralist, 4, 156
orality, 2–8, 10–19, 22–49, 54, 57, 58, 61, 77, 106, 113–17, 122, 125, 146–47, 151–58, 174, 181, 194–95, 197, 202–210
Orality and Literacy, 4, 31–37, 48, 115
Orality Journal, 7, 51
Othering, 5, 39, 40, 154, 162, 192, 203

paradidomi, 186
pedagogy, 10, 22–24, 53, 158, 178–79
perspicuity, 185
persistent orality, 158
phronesis (wisdom), 27, 149, 150, 152
Pol Pot, 1, 17, 28, 84, 89, 96
poverty-shame nexus, 165–67
preliterate, 5, 45, 49
primary modeling system, 127, 157, 197
primary orality, 10, 32, 37, 41, 111, 113, 117, 147, 158, 181
Prior question of trust (PQT), xiv, 110
Program for the International Assessment of Adult Competencies (PIAAC), 3, 181, 191
Proverbs, 7, 42, 44, 46, 52, 56
proximate/proximal literacy, 111, 115, 183, 208
purposeful learners, 80–81, 86, 92, 93, 95, 140, 143, 158, 186

redemptive, 100, 140, 147, 154, 163, 177
Ree-un (study), 22, 81, 84, 95–97, 108

Ree-un aht jole (learning not absorbed), 85–86, 95, 132, 152, 177
re-eventing, 4, 34–35, 44, 139, 156, 184, 186
refugees, 22, 24, 28, 159
relational, 39, 55, 102–6, 109, 114–15, 130–31, 134, 142, 144, 147, 159, 168–69, 182, 184, 190, 196, 210
relational learning, 100–101, 106, 108, 116, 119, 128, 139, 147–49, 158, 175–77, 188–89, 198
rituals, 5, 18, 42, 44, 46, 79, 82–83, 95–97, 100, 102, 109, 124, 140–43, 147–48, 152, 154, 160–64, 174, 176–77, 183, 190
rote learning, 22, 142

school-induced shame, 160
scribal culture, 111, 115
secondary orality, 10, 41, 111, 116, 147, 158, 181
Second Language Acquisition (SLA), 12, 47–49
self-efficacy, 93, 100, 131, 135–36, 153, 161, 177, 182
semi-literacy, 38, 41, 186
shame, 81, 84, 87, 94, 98, 107, 125, 132–40, 144, 150–54, 160–67, 169, 174, 177–78, 182–83, 187–93
social capital, 197
social learning theory, 105, 107–8
socialization, 9, 32, 50, 53, 100–102, 107, 112–13, 117, 123–27, 129, 149, 153, 157–58, 184
spirituality, 60, 79, 82–83, 95, 97, 100, 140–41, 147, 160, 163–64, 177, 184
stigma, 136–37, 153–54, 157, 160, 167, 171–72, 182, 188
storying, 7, 11, 29, 42–43, 46, 52–53, 185
storytelling, 27, 29, 42–44, 53, 115–16, 146, 181
student-centered pedagogy, 22
Students with Limited of Interrupted Formal Education (SLIFE), 4, 49, 50, 54

Teaching English as a Foreign Language (TEFL), 3, 23, 31, 48–49
Teaching English to Speakers of Other Languages (TESOL), 3, 23, 31, 48–49, 51
textuality, 117, 171
traditional orality, 11

Undiagnosed learning disabilities (ULD), 131–32, 160, 162, 177

vehicles of connection, 100, 146–47, 154
Verbomoteur, 139, 156, 186

Verstehen, 149–52
Visual Word Form Area (VWFA), 117–18
vocational education, 23

ways of learning, 9, 54, 56, 58, 101, 121, 126, 142, 162, 196
wisdom, 69–71, 70–71, 74, 149–50, 153–54, 171, 174–75, 191–92
Wisdom-based grounded theory, 173

Yale University Cambodia Genocide Program, 17

Scripture Index

EXODUS

34:1 — 184

DEUTERONOMY

31:11–14 — 184

NEHEMIAH

8:2–6 — 115
8:1–8 — 184

PROVERBS

4:7 — 175

ISAIAH

29:12 — 15

JOHN

7:15 — 78

ACTS

8:26–39 — 183

1 CORINTHIANS

4:16 — 121
11:1 — 121
15:3–5 — 185

1 THESSALONIANS

2:7 — 185
2:11 — 185

www.ingramcontent.com/pod-product-compliance
Lightning Source LLC
Chambersburg PA
CBHW071241230426
43668CB00011B/1534